D1643313

the **wisden**
guide to

edited by
steven lynch

First published in the UK in 2011 by
John Wisden & Co
An imprint of Bloomsbury Publishing Plc
50 Bedford Square, London WC1B 3DP
www.wisden.com
www.bloomsbury.com

ISBN: 978 1 4081 5599 8

Cover by Greg Heinimann
Cover photographs © Getty Images
Inside photographs © Getty Images

A CIP catalogue record for this book is available from the British Library.

This book is produced using paper that is made from wood
grown in managed, sustainable forests. It is natural, renewable and
recyclable. The logging and manufacturing processes conform to the
environmental regulations of the country of origin.

Typeset in Mendoza Roman and Frutiger
by Saxon Graphics Ltd, Derby

Printed by MPG Books Ltd, Bodmin, Cornwall

INTRODUCTION

Welcome to the **Wisden Guide to International Cricket 2012**, which includes – in words and pictures, facts and figures – details of 200 leading players, telling you *how* they play as well as where they come from. This year there's a welcome comeback for Zimbabwe's players, after their return to Test cricket. You will also find a rundown on the players from other leading non-Test nations, and a handy guide to upcoming international fixtures. To help you identify everyone on the field or in the dressing-room, there are photographs and short descriptions of the international umpires, coaches and referees. Finally there is a section containing records for all international matches – Tests, one-dayers and Twenty20s – with a country-by-country breakdown too.

Many of the profiles in the book are edited versions from ESPN Cricinfo's player pages, used with their kind permission. We have tried to include every player likely to appear in Test cricket in 2012 – but, like all selectors, we will undoubtedly have left out someone who should have been included. Details of anyone who managed to escape our selectorial net can be found on www.cricinfo.com.

The statistics have been updated to **September 26, 2011**, the end of the international season in England. The abbreviation 'S/R' in the batting tables denotes runs per 100 balls; in the bowling it shows the balls required to take each wicket. A dash (–) in the records usually indicates that full statistics are not available (such as details of fours and sixes, or balls faced, in all domestic matches).

Thanks are due to Christopher Lane of Wisden, Charlotte Atyeo, Kate Turvey and Emily Sweet at A&C Black, Rob Brown and the typesetting team at Saxon, James Watson who designed the cover, and Cricinfo's technical wizards Robin Abrahams and Travis Basevi.

Finally, I couldn't have managed without the support of my wife Karina, who puts up with this annual intervention into our lives with amazing patience, and our sons Daniel and Mark.

Steven Lynch, September 2011

CONTENTS

4	Player Index	214	The Netherlands
6	**Player profiles A-Z**	216	Scotland
206	Afghanistan	218	Officials
208	Canada	226	Overall records
210	Ireland	232	Country-by-country records
212	Kenya	272	International schedule 2011–12

PLAYER INDEX

AUSTRALIA

Beer. Michael 19
Bollinger, Doug 24
Clarke, Michael 37
Copeland, Trent 39
Ferguson, Callum 51
Haddin, Brad 58
Harris, Ryan 60
Hauritz, Nathan 61
Hughes, Phillip 63
Hussey, David 64
Hussey, Michael 65
Johnson, Mitchell 73
Khawaja, Usman 79
Lee, Brett 87
Lyon, Nathan 88
Marsh, Shaun 96
Paine, Tim 122
Pattinson, James 128
Ponting, Ricky 132
Siddle, Peter 164
Smith, Steve 169
Warner, David 196
Watson, Shane 198
White, Cameron 200

BANGLADESH

Abdur Razzak 7
Imrul Kayes 67
Jahurul Islam 69
Junaid Siddique 75
Mahmudullah 94
Mashrafe Mortaza 99
Mohammad Ashraful 109
Mushfiqur Rahim 116
Nazmul Hossain v118
Raqibul Hasan 140
Robiul Islam 142
Rubel Hossain 144
Shafiul Islam 155
Shahadat Hossain 156
Shahriar Nafees 158
Shakib Al Hasan 160
Tamim Iqbal 177

ENGLAND

Anderson, James 13
Bairstow, Jonny 16
Bell, Ian 20
Bopara, Ravi 25
Bresnan, Tim 31
Broad, Stuart 32
Carberry, Michael 33
Cook, Alastair 38
Dernbach, Jade 41
Finn, Steven 53
Kieswetter, Craig 80

Morgan, Eoin 111
Onions, Graham 120
Panesar, Monty 123
Patel, Samit 127
Pietersen, Kevin 130
Prior, Matt 135
Shahzad, Ajmal 159
Stokes, Ben 173
Strauss, Andrew 174
Swann, Graeme 175
Tremlett, Chris 186
Trott, Jonathan 187
Woakes, Chris 202

INDIA

Dhoni, Mahendra Singh 42
Dravid, Rahul 44
Gambhir, Gautam 55
Harbhajan Singh 59
Khan, Zaheer 78
Kohli, Virat 81
Kumar, Praveen 83
Laxman, VVS 86
Mishra, Amit 107
Mithun, Abhimanyu 108
Mukund, Abhinav 115
Ojha, Pragyan 119
Patel, Munaf 126
Pujara, Cheteshwar 136
Raina, Suresh 137
Sehwag, Virender 154
Sharma, Ishant 161
Sharma, Rohit 162
Singh, RP 166
Sreesanth, S 171
Tendulkar, Sachin 182
Vijay, Murali 193
Yuvraj Singh 205

NEW ZEALAND

Bennett, Hamish 22
Boult, Trent 28
Elliott, Grant 48
Flynn, Daniel 54
Guptill, Martin 57
McCullum, Brendon 89
McCullum, Nathan 90
McIntosh, Tim 91
McKay, Andy 92
Martin, Chris 97
Mills, Kyle 105
Oram, Jacob 121
Ryder, Jesse 147
Southee, Tim 170
Taylor, Ross 181
Vettori, Daniel 192
Watling, B-J 197

4

PLAYER INDEX

Williamson, Kane 201
Young, Reece 203

PAKISTAN
Abdul Razzaq 6
Abdur Rehman 8
Adnan Akmal 9
Ahmed Shehzad 10
Aizaz Cheema 11
Asad Shafiq 14
Azhar Ali 15
Junaid Khan 74
Kamran Akmal 77
Misbah-ul-Haq 106
Mohammad Hafeez 110
Saeed Ajmal 148
Shahid Afridi 157
Tanvir Ahmed 178
Taufeeq Umar 179
Umar Akmal 189
Umar Gul 190
Wahab Riaz 195
Younis Khan 204

SOUTH AFRICA
Amla, Hashim 12
Botha, Johan 26
Boucher, Mark 27
de Villiers, AB 40
Duminy, J-P 45
Imran Tahir 66
Ingram, Colin 68
Kallis, Jacques 76
McLaren, Ryan 93
Miller, David 104
Morkel, Albie 112
Morkel, Morne 113
Parnell, Wayne 125
Prince, Ashwell 134
Rossouw, Rilee 143
Rudolph, Jacques 145
Smith, Graeme 168
Steyn, Dale 172
Theron, Rusty 184
Tsotsobe, Lonwabo 188

SRI LANKA
Chandimal, Dinesh 35
Dilshan, Tillekeratne 43
Eranga, Shaminda 49
Fernando, Dilhara 52
Herath, Rangana 62
Jayawardene, Mahela 71
Jayawardene, Prasanna 72
Kulasekara, Nuwan 82
Lakmal, Suranga 84
Malinga, Lasith 95

Mathews, Angelo 100
Mendis, Ajantha 102
Paranavitana, Tharanga 124
Perera, Thisara 129
Randiv, Suraj 139
Samaraweera, Thilan 149
Sangakkara, Kumar 152
Tharanga, Upul 183
Thirimanne, Lahiru 185
Welagedara, Chanaka 199

WEST INDIES
Barath, Adrian 17
Baugh, Carlton 18
Benn, Sulieman 21
Bishoo, Devendra 23
Bravo, Darren 29
Bravo, Dwayne 30
Chanderpaul, Shivnarine 34
Edwards, Fidel 46
Edwards, Kirk 47
Gayle, Chris 56
Nash, Brendan 117
Pollard, Kieron 131
Rampaul, Ravi 138
Roach, Kemar 141
Russell, Andre 146
Sammy, Darren 150
Samuels, Marlon 151
Sarwan, Ramnaresh 153
Simmons, Lendl 165
Smith, Devon 167

ZIMBABWE
Chigumbura, Elton 36
Ervine, Craig 50
Jarvis, Kyle 70
Lamb, Greg 85
Masakadza, Hamilton 98
Mawoyo, Tino 101
Meth, Keegan 103
Mpofu, Christopher 114
Price, Raymond 133
Sibanda, Vusi 163
Taibu, Tatenda 176
Taylor, Brendan 180
Utseya, Prosper 191
Vitori, Brian 194

OTHER COUNTRIES
Afghanistan 206
Canada 208
Ireland 210
Kenya 212
The Netherlands 214
Scotland 216

ABDUL RAZZAQ

PAKISTAN

Full name	**Abdul Razzaq**
Born	**December 2, 1979, Lahore, Punjab**
Teams	**Lahore, Zarai Taraqiati Bank, Leicestershire**
Style	**Right-hand bat, right-arm fast-medium bowler**
Test debut	**Pakistan v Australia at Brisbane 1999-2000**
ODI debut	**Pakistan v Zimbabwe at Lahore 1996-97**
T20I debut	**Pakistan v England at Bristol 2006**

THE PROFILE Abdul Razzaq was once rapid enough to open the bowling, and remains composed enough to bat anywhere, although the lower order suits him. His bowling is characterised by a galloping approach, accuracy, and reverse-swing, but it is his batting that is more likely to win matches. Particularly strong on the drive, he has two gears: block or blast. Cut off the big shots and he can get bogged down, although he is very patient, as demonstrated by a match-saving six-hour 71 against India in March 2005. Just before that he had batted bewilderingly slowly at Melbourne – 4 in 110 minutes – but when the occasion demands he can slog with the best of them: he spanked Tim Bresnan's last five balls at Lord's in September 2010 for fours. After a mid-career bowling slump he rediscovered some of his old guile, if not his nip, and if the pitch is helpful to seam – as Karachi was for his only Test five-for in 2004, or against India there in January 2006 – he can still be a danger. Razzaq's allround performance in that win over India was easily his most emphatic: 45 and 90, and seven wickets. He missed the 2007 World Cup with a knee injury, then joined the unauthorised Indian Cricket League, but after an amnesty he was among the first ICL players to reappear in official internationals, reinforcing the World Twenty20 squad in England in June 2009 and taking three wickets in the final victory over Sri Lanka. However, he was jettisoned after a lacklustre World Cup in 2011, when his only major contribution was 62 in vain against New Zealand, and faces a struggle to make yet another comeback.

THE FACTS Abdul Razzaq took a hat-trick against Sri Lanka at Galle in June 2000: he is one of only four players to have scored a hundred and taken a hat-trick in Tests (after England's Johnny Briggs, Wasim Akram of Pakistan and the New Zealander James Franklin) ... Razzaq took 7 for 51 – still his best figures – on his first-class debut, for Lahore City v Karachi Whites in the Quaid-e-Azam Trophy final in November 1996 ... He made 203 not out for Middlesex v Glamorgan in 2003 ... His record includes four ODIs for the Asia XI ...

THE FIGURES to 26.09.11

ᴇꜱᴘⁿcricinfo.com

Batting & Fielding	M	Inns	NO	Runs	HS	Avge	S/R	100	50	4s	6s	Ct	St
Tests	46	77	9	1946	134	28.61	41.04	3	7	230	23	15	0
ODIs	262	226	57	5063	112	29.95	81.47	3	23	382	124	33	0
T20Is	26	24	9	346	46*	23.06	126.27	0	0	17	20	2	0
First-class	117	183	27	5254	203*	33.67	–	8	28	–	–	32	0

Bowling	M	Balls	Runs	Wkts	BB	Avge	RpO	S/R	5i	10m
Tests	46	7008	3694	100	5–35	36.94	3.16	70.08	1	0
ODIs	262	10845	8503	267	6–35	31.84	4.70	40.61	3	0
T20Is	26	315	360	18	3–13	20.00	6.85	17.50	0	0
First-class	117	18564	10818	340	7–51	31.81	3.49	54.60	11	2

ABDUR RAZZAK

Full name	**Khan Abdur Razzak**
Born	**June 15, 1982, Khulna**
Teams	**Khulna**
Style	**Left-hand bat, slow left-arm orthodox spinner**
Test debut	**Bangladesh v Australia at Chittagong 2005-06**
ODI debut	**Bangladesh v Hong Kong at Colombo 2004**
T20I debut	**Bangladesh v Zimbabwe at Khulna 2006-07**

THE PROFILE Another of Bangladesh's seemingly never-ending supply of left-arm spinners, Abdur Razzak (no relation to the similarly named Pakistan allrounder) first made his mark when he helped unheralded Khulna to their first-ever National Cricket League title in 2001-02. Quite tall, with a high action, "Raj" played for the A team against Zimbabwe early in 2004, and made the most of his opportunity with 15 wickets, including 7 for 17 in the third encounter on the batting paradise of Dhaka's old Bangabandhu National Stadium. He has an uncanny ability to pin batsmen down, although his action has often been questioned, most recently late in 2008, when he was suspended by the ICC after tests showed he sometimes flexed his elbow by almost twice the permitted 15 degrees. After remedial work, he was cleared to resume playing in March 2009. He was immediately hurried back, playing in the World Twenty20 in England then taking seven wickets in Bangladesh's rare one-day clean sweep against a depleted West Indies side in the Caribbean in July. Razzak had played his first Test in April 2006, against Australia on a turning track at Chittagong (even the Aussies played three spinners), but failed to take a wicket, and has continued to struggle for penetration in Tests. But he has become an automatic one-day selection, maintaining a miserly economy-rate, and now tops his country's wicket-taking lists in ODIs. He was the only Bangladeshi signed up for the first year of the Indian Premier League in 2008, although he did not return for the second season.

THE FACTS Abdur Razzak took 5 for 29 in an ODI against Zimbabwe at Mirpur in December 2009 ... He took 7 for 11 (10 for 62 in the match) for Khulna at Sylhet in 2003-04 ... Razzak took a hat-trick – Bangladesh's second in ODIs, after one by Shahadat Hossain in 2006 – against Zimbabwe at Mirpur in December 2010 ...

THE FIGURES to 26.09.11   **ESPNcricinfo.com**

Batting & Fielding	M	Inns	NO	Runs	HS	Avge	S/R	100	50	4s	6s	Ct	St
Tests	9	17	5	214	43	17.83	65.64	0	0	30	4	3	0
ODIs	124	77	30	613	35	13.04	70.78	0	0	41	15	26	0
T20Is	13	9	5	11	5	2.75	32.35	0	0	0	0	2	0
First-class	50	83	14	1441	83	20.88	59.37	0	7	–	–	17	0

Bowling	M	Balls	Runs	Wkts	BB	Avge	RpO	S/R	5i	10m
Tests	9	2133	1185	18	3–93	65.83	3.33	118.50	0	0
ODIs	124	6489	4860	175	5–29	27.77	4.49	37.08	3	0
T20Is	13	294	328	20	4–16	16.40	6.69	14.70	0	0
First-class	50	11141	5093	159	7–11	32.03	2.74	70.06	5	1

ABDUR REHMAN

PAKISTAN

Full name	**Abdur Rehman**
Born	**March 1, 1980, Sialkot, Punjab**
Teams	**Sialkot, Habib Bank**
Style	**Left-hand bat, slow left-arm orthodox spinner**
Test debut	**Pakistan v South Africa at Karachi 2007-08**
ODI debut	**Pakistan v West Indies at Faisalabad 2006-07**
T20I debut	**Pakistan v South Africa at Johannesburg 2006-07**

THE PROFILE Abdur Rehman made his international debut late in 2006 at the ripe old age of 26 (elderly considering the usual subcontinental trait of ruthlessly exposing youth to the world's best), and immediately did well, with two wickets in each of his first three one-dayers against West Indies. He's not a huge turner of the ball, but is accurate and consistent, and can exploit the rough well. He first gave notice of his ability back in 1999, with five and six wickets in successive matches for Pakistan's Under-19s against South Africa, a home series for which he was chosen after only a couple of first-class matches. Senior opportunities were limited by Pakistan's several spinners, most of them better batsmen, but Rehman kept himself in contention with good domestic performances: in 2006-07 he was the leading bowler as Habib Bank won the Pentangular Cup, with 11 in an important victory over Sind. He missed the 2007 World Cup – a blessing in disguise, perhaps – but was recalled for the one-day series against Sri Lanka in Abu Dhabi. However, with Pakistan looking for variety and an ally for Danish Kaneria, Rehman got a Test chance against South Africa at home at the end of 2007, and took eight wickets on his debut – unusually, he took 4 for 105 in each innings – and finished the short series with 11 victims, one more than Kaneria managed. After three years out of the Test side he returned in 2010-11, and grabbed his chance with 29 wickets in six Tests, including six West Indian scalps on a Basseterre "bunsen" which he said he'd like to roll up and carry around with him.

THE FACTS Abdur Rehman had identical figures of 4 for 105 in each innings of his Test debut, the first instance of this since England's Willie Bates took 2 for 43 in both innings against Australia at Melbourne in 1881-82 ... Rehman took 8 for 53 for Habib Bank v Sui Gas in December 2005, a week after claiming 5 for 120 and 6 for 28 against Khan Research Labs in the same competition ... He made 96 for Habib Bank v National Bank at Multan in January 2006 ...

THE FIGURES to 26.09.11   ᴇꜱᴩ̃ᴨcricinfo.com

Batting & Fielding	M	Inns	NO	Runs	HS	Avge	S/R	100	50	4s	6s	Ct	St
Tests	8	10	2	177	60	22.12	36.19	0	1	22	3	1	0
ODIs	20	14	4	75	31	7.50	48.07	0	0	5	1	2	0
T20Is	7	4	2	15	7	7.50	88.23	0	0	0	0	6	0
First-class	110	149	17	2429	96	18.40	–	0	12	–	–	48	0

Bowling	M	Balls	Runs	Wkts	BB	Avge	RpO	S/R	5i	10m
Tests	8	2926	1275	40	4–65	31.87	2.61	73.15	0	0
ODIs	20	1050	755	15	2–20	50.33	4.31	70.00	0	0
T20Is	7	150	174	11	2–7	15.81	6.96	13.63	0	0
First-class	110	23764	10452	392	8–53	26.66	2.63	60.62	18	4

ADNAN AKMAL

Full name	**Adnan Akmal**
Born	**March 13, 1985, Lahore**
Teams	**Punjab, Sui Northern Gas**
Style	**Right-hand bat, wicketkeeper**
Test debut	**Pakistan v South Africa at Dubai 2010-11**
ODI debut	**Pakistan v Zimbabwe at Bulawayo 2011**
T20I debut	**No T20Is yet**

THE PROFILE One of three brothers to play – and keep wicket – for Pakistan, Adnan Akmal is usually considered the best pure keeper of the trio. He replaced his elder brother Kamran behind the stumps in October 2010, and took eight catches in his fourth Test, in New Zealand: it was a surprise when Faisalabad's Mohammad Salman was preferred, without any explanation, for the Tests and one-dayers in the West Indies and Ireland that followed the 2011 World Cup, in which Kamran had had a chequered time behind the stumps. Adnan, though, was back in favour by the time of the Zimbabwe tour in September, and gave a polished performance as Pakistan won the only Test. He then produced an important innings in what was his first one-day international, briefly batting alongside his other brother, Umar. But for a miscommunication back in 2004, Adnan might have played for Pakistan much earlier. By mistake, both he and Kamran were called up for a national camp before a one-day tournament and, after much confusion over who was actually wanted, Kamran was the one retained – even though Bob Woolmer, Pakistan's coach at the time, apparently thought Adnan was the country's best keeper. He kept plugging away on the domestic scene, improving his batting – he has now made two first-class hundreds in the Quaid-e-Azam Trophy – and the continuing errors of Kamran kept him in the frame. Eventually, with Kamran out of favour and his original replacement Zulqarnain Haider disappearing dramatically from Dubai claiming he had been threatened by match-fixers, Adnan received the summons to join the national squad. While he was travelling to the Gulf his brother Umar stepped in as Pakistan's wicketkeeper in a one-day international.

THE FACTS Adnan Akmal followed his brothers Kamran and Umar in keeping wicket in international matches for Pakistan ... Adnan took seven catches in an innings (11 in the match) for Lahore Blues v Karachi Blues at Karachi in December 2004 ... He scored 120 for Sui Northern Gas against Customs at Islamabad in November 2009...

THE FIGURES to 26.09.11   **ESPNcricinfo.com**

Batting & Fielding	M	Inns	NO	Runs	HS	Avge	S/R	100	50	4s	6s	Ct	St
Tests	5	6	1	131	44	26.20	58.48	0	0	20	0	19	2
ODIs	3	2	1	51	27	51.00	78.46	0	0	3	0	2	0
T20Is	0	0	–	–	–	–	–	–	–	–	–	–	–
First-class	81	125	11	2605	120	22.85	–	2	8	–	–	297	8

Bowling	M	Balls	Runs	Wkts	BB	Avge	RpO	S/R	5i	10m
Tests	5	0	–	–	–	–	–	–	–	–
ODIs	3	0	–	–	–	–	–	–	–	–
T20Is	0	0	–	–	–	–	–	–	–	–
First-class	81	0	–	–	–	–	–	–	–	–

PAKISTAN

AHMED SHEHZAD

Full name	**Ahmed Shehzad**
Born	**November 23, 1991, Lahore**
Teams	**Lahore, Habib Bank**
Style	**Right-hand bat, occasional legspinner**
Test debut	**No Tests yet**
ODI debut	**Australia v Pakistan at Dubai 2008-09**
T20I debut	**Australia v Pakistan at Dubai 2008-09**

THE PROFILE Ahmed Shehzad originally based his game on that of Ricky Ponting – not a bad role model – and had some success with this aggressive style in his early international outings. A solidly built right-hander with the ability to hit over the top, Shehzad was still only 19 when he hit 115 in a one-day international against New Zealand in February 2011, and added another hundred against West Indies in St Lucia a couple of months later – but in between he endured a disappointing World Cup, his top score from five innings being just 13. He had made his first-class debut in January 2007, just two months after his 15th birthday, and soon established himself as an opening batsman for Pakistan's Under-19 team. In August 2007 he made 167 as they chased down 342 to beat England in an Under-19 Test at Derby (the home attack included Steven Finn and Chris Woakes, who have both since played for England), and followed that with some impressive performances at home, scoring 315 runs – with a highest of 105 – as Australia's Under-19s were thrashed 5-0. Another century followed in a youth Test against Bangladesh, and he carried that form into a triangular tournament in Sri Lanka, which Pakistan won. Early in 2009 he made the Test squad for the home series against Sri Lanka, although he didn't actually play, then played his first one-day international in Dubai shortly afterwards. Since then he's been confined to the shorter formats, with some success, but a Test call might not be too far away, especially after a truncated 2010-11 domestic season in which he averaged 102.71 from six matches with three centuries, one of them a double.

THE FACTS Ahmed Shehzad was 19 when he scored 115 against New Zealand at Hamilton in February 2011: only Shahid Afridi, Imran Nazir and Salim Elahi have scored centuries at a younger age for Pakistan in ODIs ... Shehzad scored 254 for Habib Bank at Faisalabad in October 2010, and shortly afterwards made 123 and 109 not out for them at Sialkot ... He made 167 as Pakistan scored 342 to win an Under-19 Test against England at Derby in 2007 by three wickets ...

THE FIGURES to 26.09.11   **ESPNcricinfo.com**

Batting & Fielding	M	Inns	NO	Runs	HS	Avge	S/R	100	50	4s	6s	Ct	St
Tests	0	0	–	–	–	–	–	–	–	–	–	–	–
ODIs	19	19	1	477	115	26.50	67.56	2	0	52	6	7	0
T20Is	6	6	0	103	54	17.16	115.73	0	1	17	1	3	0
First-class	26	42	2	1835	254	45.87	57.92	5	8	245	18	22	0

Bowling	M	Balls	Runs	Wkts	BB	Avge	RpO	S/R	5i	10m
Tests	0	0	–	–	–	–	–	–	–	–
ODIs	19	15	20	0	–	–	8.00	–	0	0
T20Is	6	0	–	–	–	–	–	–	–	–
First-class	26	558	367	7	4–20	52.42	3.94	79.71	0	0

AIZAZ CHEEMA

Full name	**Aizaz Bin Ilyas Cheema**
Born	**September 5, 1979, Sargodha**
Teams	**Lahore, Pakistan International Airlines**
Style	**Right-hand bat, right-arm fast-medium bowler**
Test debut	**Pakistan v Zimbabwe at Bulawayo 2011**
ODI debut	**Pakistan v Zimbabwe at Bulawayo 2011**
T20I debut	**Pakistan v Zimbabwe at Harare 2011**

THE PROFILE Aizaz Cheema had to wait until he was 31 to get the call to play for Pakistan. Even then it looked as if he might not fulfil his dream, as after he was selected for the tour of the West Indies early in 2011 he was withdrawn from the squad, apparently after a doctor decided he was not fit enough. But he did make it onto the plane for the tour of Zimbabwe in September 2011, and shone in his first Test with four wickets in both innings: his match figures of 8 for 103 were Pakistan's second-best on debut. Cheema won his place on the back of a splendid 2010-11 domestic season – 58 wickets at 14.74, most of them for PIA. That included four six-fors in the space of three matches – two of them in the same game against Habib Bank – followed by seven in each innings against Karachi Blues. Cheema started as an out-and-out speedster, capable of breaking the 90mph barrier – Umar Akmal once called him the fastest bowler he had faced in domestic cricket, adding "he swings it at pace too" – but he has throttled back in recent years and now takes a lot of wickets with a cunning slower ball, although there were those who thought he overdid the slower stuff early on in his Test debut, as Zimbabwe got going. He also has a decent yorker and, like most Pakistani bowlers reared on unforgiving tracks, can reverse-swing the ball. Cheema celebrated his 32nd birthday during his Test debut in Harare, but says: "Honestly speaking I didn't feel this fit at the age of 21 or 22. I couldn't run then what I can run now."

THE FACTS Aizaz Cheema's match figures of 8 for 103 were the best by a Pakistan bowler on Test debut after Mohammad Zahid's 11 for 130 against New Zealand at Rawalpindi in 1996-97 ... Cheema was the 11th bowler to take four wickets in each innings of his first Test ... He took 7 for 65 and 7 for 45 for PIA against Karachi Blues at Karachi in January 2011 ... His best first-class figures are 7 for 24, for PIA at Islamabad in November 2007 ...

THE FIGURES *to 26.09.11* **ESPncricinfo.com**

Batting & Fielding	M	Inns	NO	Runs	HS	Avge	S/R	100	50	4s	6s	Ct	St
Tests	1	1	1	0	0*	–	0.00	0	0	0	0	0	0
ODIs	3	0	–	–	–	–	–	–	–	–	–	1	0
T20Is	1	0	–	–	–	–	–	–	–	–	–	0	0
First-class	63	64	25	344	33	8.82	–	0	0	–	–	13	0

Bowling	M	Balls	Runs	Wkts	BB	Avge	RpO	S/R	5i	10m
Tests	1	241	103	8	4–24	12.87	2.56	30.12	0	0
ODIs	3	180	136	8	4–43	17.00	4.53	22.50	0	0
T20Is	1	18	21	1	1–21	21.00	7.00	18.00	0	0
First-class	63	9036	4824	229	7–24	21.06	3.20	39.45	15	4

HASHIM **AMLA**

SOUTH AFRICA

Full name	**Hashim Mahomed Amla**
Born	**March 31, 1983, Durban, Natal**
Teams	**Dolphins**
Style	**Right-hand bat, occasional right-arm medium-pacer**
Test debut	**South Africa v India at Kolkata 2004-05**
ODI debut	**South Africa v Bangladesh at Chittagong 2007-08**
T20I debut	**South Africa v Australia at Brisbane 2008-09**

THE PROFILE An elegant, wristy right-hander with a fine temperament, Hashim Amla was the first South African of Indian descent to reach the Test team. His elevation was hardly a surprise after he reeled off four centuries in his first eight innings in 2004-05, after captaining the Dolphins (formerly Natal) at the tender age of 21. He captained South Africa at the 2002 Under-19 World Cup and, after starring for the A team, made his Test debut against India late in 2004. He was not an instant success, with serious questions emerging about his technique as he mustered only 36 runs in four innings against England shortly afterwards, struggling with an ungainly crouched stance and a bat coming down from somewhere in the region of gully. But he made his second chance count, with 149 against New Zealand at Cape Town in April 2006, followed by big hundreds against New Zealand (again) and India in 2007-08, before a fine undefeated 104 helped save the 2008 Lord's Test. He came into his own in India early in 2010 with a monumental 253 not out to set up victory at Nagpur, following by valiant twin centuries in defeat at Kolkata, and by late 2011 his average was over 50. Not originally seen as a one-day player, after slamming 140 against Bangladesh late in 2008 he made 80 not out and 97 in consecutive victories over Australia to make his place safe, then flourished to the extent that he was the only man worldwide to score 1000 ODI runs in 2010. Amla is a devout Muslim, whose beard rivals Mohammad Yousuf's as the most impressive in the game.

THE FACTS Amla scored 253 not out at Nagpur, and 114 and 123 not out at Kolkata in the two-Test series in India in February 2010: his series average of 490 has been exceeded only by England's Wally Hammond (563.00 v New Zealand in 1932-33) ... Amla averages 104.80 in Tests against New Zealand, but 17.25 v Sri Lanka ... His older brother Ahmed also plays for the Dolphins ...

THE FIGURES *to 26.09.11*   **ᴇＳＰＮcricinfo.com**

Batting & Fielding	M	Inns	NO	Runs	HS	Avge	S/R	100	50	4s	6s	Ct	St
Tests	51	90	7	3897	253*	46.95	50.24	12	19	483	5	46	0
ODIs	49	48	5	2462	140	57.25	92.76	8	14	243	12	17	0
T20Is	3	3	0	53	26	17.66	100.00	0	0	4	1	0	0
First-class	138	230	21	10202	253*	48.81	–	31	51	–	–	109	0

Bowling	M	Balls	Runs	Wkts	BB	Avge	RpO	S/R	5i	10m
Tests	51	42	28	0	–	–	4.00	–	0	0
ODIs	49	0	–	–	–	–	–	–	–	–
T20Is	3	0	–	–	–	–	–	–	–	–
First-class	138	315	224	1	1–10	224.00	4.26	315.00	0	0

JAMES **ANDERSON**

ENGLAND

Full name	**James Michael Anderson**
Born	**July 30, 1982, Burnley, Lancashire**
Teams	**Lancashire**
Style	**Left-hand bat, right-arm fast-medium bowler**
Test debut	**England v Zimbabwe at Lord's 2003**
ODI debut	**England v Australia at Melbourne 2002-03**
T20I debut	**England v Australia at Sydney 2006-07**

THE PROFILE When the force is with him, James Anderson is capable of irresistible spells, seemingly able to swing the ball round corners at an impressive speed. New Zealand were blown away in Nottingham in 2008 (Anderson 7 for 43); the following May the West Indians looked clueless in Durham, while back at Trent Bridge in 2010 Pakistan's inexperienced batsmen could hardly lay a bat on him (5 for 54 and 6 for 17). He followed that with 24 wickets in the 2010-11 Ashes triumph. And then there are the bad days, when the ball isn't coming out quite right and refuses to swing: he can then sometimes look downcast, and the purists start murmuring that he seems to be looking at the ground at the moment of delivery, rather than down the pitch at the target as the MCC coaching manual advocates. Anderson had played only occasionally for Lancashire when he was hurried into England's one-day squad in Australia in 2002-03 as cover for Andy Caddick. He didn't have a number – or even a name – on his shirt, but ten overs for 12 runs in century heat at Adelaide earned him a World Cup spot. There was a five-for in his debut Test, against Zimbabwe in 2003, and a one-day hat-trick against Pakistan ... but then a stress fracture sidelined him for most of 2006. But by the end of the following year Anderson looked the part of pack leader again. His batting also steadily improved: he went 54 Test innings before collecting a duck, an unlikely England record. At Cardiff in 2009 he survived for 69 nail-chewing minutes to help stave off defeat by Australia. He is also a superb fielder.

THE FACTS Anderson was the first man to take an ODI hat-trick for England, against Pakistan at The Oval in 2003 ... He took the first six wickets to fall on his way to career-best figures of 7 for 43 for England v New Zealand at Nottingham in 2008 ... Anderson went 54 Test innings before being out for a duck at The Oval in 2009, an English record (previously Geraint Jones's 51); only AB de Villiers (78), Aravinda de Silva (75) and Clive Lloyd (58) have started with more duckless innings in Tests ...

THE FIGURES *to 26.09.11*   **ESP**cricinfo.com

Batting & Fielding	M	Inns	NO	Runs	HS	Avge	S/R	100	50	4s	6s	Ct	St
Tests	63	81	33	572	34	11.91	35.99	0	0	71	1	30	0
ODIs	151	63	34	199	20*	6.86	42.16	0	0	14	0	42	0
T20Is	19	4	3	1	1*	1.00	50.00	0	0	0	0	3	0
First-class	126	146	58	894	37*	10.15	–	0	0	–	–	58	0

Bowling	M	Balls	Runs	Wkts	BB	Avge	RpO	S/R	5i	10m
Tests	63	13545	7338	240	7–43	30.57	3.25	56.43	11	1
ODIs	151	7502	6302	204	5–23	30.89	5.04	36.77	1	0
T20Is	19	422	552	18	3–23	30.66	7.84	23.44	0	0
First-class	126	24281	13045	472	7–43	27.63	3.22	51.44	23	3

ASAD SHAFIQ

PAKISTAN

Full name	**Asad Shafiq**
Born	**January 28, 1986, Karachi**
Teams	**Karachi, Pakistan International Airlines**
Style	**Right-hand bat, occasional legspinner**
Test debut	**Pakistan v South Africa at Abu Dhabi 2010-11**
ODI debut	**Pakistan v Bangladesh at Dambulla 2010**
T20I debut	**Pakistan v New Zealand at Hamilton 2010-11**

THE PROFILE A solid right-hander with a compact technique reminiscent of Javed Miandad, arguably Pakistan's finest batsman, Asad Shafiq is a product of the Karachi tape-ball circuit. He made a fine start in first-class cricket, scoring a double-century in only his seventh match and falling just short of 1000 runs in his debut summer of 2007-08, making 926 at 57.87. Second-season syndrome kicked in, and his average dipped to 21 the following year – although he performed better in one-day games – but he roared back in 2009-10 to put his name firmly in the selectors' sights: 1244 runs at a fraction under 50, with four more hundreds. He played his first one-day internationals during the Asia Cup in Sri Lanka in mid-2010, and although he missed the Tests in England that followed he played in the one-day internationals which rounded off that fractious tour, looking good in scoring 50 at Headingley and 40 at The Oval. A Test debut followed on a placid pitch in Abu Dhabi: Shafiq made an unhurried 61, and added 83 in his next Test, to help Pakistan to a ten-wicket victory over New Zealand at Hamilton. The five players who reached 50 in that match before him got out before making it to 60 but, as Cricinfo reported, "Shafiq moved into the sixties in style, using his feet to Martin Guptill and lofting the ball over midwicket for four". He looked a certainty for the 2011 World Cup, but sat out the first few matches before finally getting a game and hitting 78 not out against Zimbabwe: 46 followed against Australia, then 30 in the semi-final defeat by India to show that his earlier omission was a mistake.

THE FACTS Asad Shafiq scored 223 in only his seventh first-class match, for Karachi Whites at Faisalabad in December 2007 ... He scored 181, and put on 431 for the second wicket with Yasir Hameed – who scored 300 – for North West Frontier Province against Baluchistan at Peshawar in March 2008 ...

THE FIGURES to 26.09.11   **ESPNcricinfo.com**

Batting & Fielding	M	Inns	NO	Runs	HS	Avge	S/R	100	50	4s	6s	Ct	St
Tests	5	8	0	216	83	27.00	38.43	0	2	35	1	3	0
ODIs	22	21	2	630	78*	33.15	70.23	0	5	55	2	3	0
T20Is	5	5	0	86	38	17.20	113.15	0	0	10	2	2	0
First-class	41	73	5	2798	223	41.14	52.48	8	9	370	12	31	0

Bowling	M	Balls	Runs	Wkts	BB	Avge	RpO	S/R	5i	10m
Tests	5	0	–	–	–	–	–	–	–	–
ODIs	22	0	–	–	–	–	–	–	–	–
T20Is	5	0	–	–	–	–	–	–	–	–
First-class	41	68	66	0	–	–	5.82	–	0	0

AZHAR ALI

Full name	**Azhar Ali**
Born	**February 19, 1985, Lahore**
Teams	**Lahore, Khan Research Laboratories**
Style	**Right-hand bat, legspinner**
Test debut	**Pakistan v Australia at Lord's 2010**
ODI debut	**Pakistan v Ireland at Belfast 2011**
T20I debut	**No T20Is yet**

THE PROFILE Azhar Ali made steady progress in domestic cricket after a stuttering start in which he played only eight first-class matches in five seasons after his 2001-02 debut. Promotion to open paid off, though, and he made 409 runs at 68 in 2006-07 – with his first two hundreds – and improved on that in each of his next two seasons, good going in a country where opening has long been difficult. He toured Australia with the A team in 2009, and twice batted for more than five hours for seventies. Azhar has a compact and correct technique, and although he initially had a few problems against the shorter ball he seemed to have addressed them by the end of the 2010 England tour, during which he was unlucky to miss a maiden Test century at The Oval, stranded on 92 after more than four hours' batting. Azhar started that long trip batting at No. 3, after the selectors decided they could do without Younis Khan and Mohammad Yousuf (although Yousuf was eventually called up), and although his inexperience showed at first he played two important innings – 30 and 51 – as Pakistan beat Australia in the second Test at Headingley. Once the dust settled from a fractious tour, Azhar continued to do well in Tests, although he was still not seen as a one-day player. His 75 and 22 in the victory over Zimbabwe in September 2011 extended a sequence of 15 Test innings, starting at Lord's in 2010, in which he failed to reach double figures only once (a second-ball duck against West Indies). But despite this consistency the big innings he needed to cement his place in the side remained frustratingly elusive.

THE FACTS Azhar Ali scored 153 not out for Khan Research Labs against Sui Southern Gas in Rawalpindi in December 2009 ... After not making a century in his first nine first-class matches, spread over five seasons, he scored nine in his next 17 games ... Azhar took 14 for 128 for Lahore Greens against Azad Jammu & Kashmir in a Quaid-e-Azam Trophy Grade 2 (not first-class) match in October 2000 ...

THE FIGURES to 26.09.11   **ESPNcricinfo.com**

Batting & Fielding	M	Inns	NO	Runs	HS	Avge	S/R	100	50	4s	6s	Ct	St
Tests	13	25	2	880	92*	38.26	39.98	0	9	107	1	11	0
ODIs	1	1	0	39	39	39.00	60.00	0	0	4	0	0	0
T20Is	0	0	–	–	–	–	–	–	–	–	–	–	–
First-class	69	113	13	3825	153*	38.25	–	11	19	–	–	62	0

Bowling	M	Balls	Runs	Wkts	BB	Avge	RpO	S/R	5i	10m
Tests	13	42	32	0	–	–	4.57	–	0	0
ODIs	1	0	–	–	–	–	–	–	–	–
T20Is	0	0	–	–	–	–	–	–	–	–
First-class	69	1161	747	20	4–34	37.35	3.86	58.05	1	0

JONNY **BAIRSTOW**

Full name	**Jonathan Marc Bairstow**
Born	**September 26, 1989, Bradford**
Teams	**Yorkshire**
Style	**Right-hand bat, wicketkeeper**
Test debut	**No Tests yet**
ODI debut	**England v India at Cardiff 2011**
T20I debut	**England v West Indies at The Oval 2011**

THE PROFILE A star was born – or so it seemed – in the closing stages of the 2011 English season. England looked up against it, needing 75 from 50 balls to win the final ODI against India at Cardiff, when the debutant Jonny Bairstow strolled in. Seemingly unfazed, he clouted 41 from 21 balls, including three sixes. The second one, off the medium-pacer Vinay Kumar, disappeared into the River Taff, and third sailed out of the ground too. "I think we've just found a player," said England's one-day captain Alastair Cook. "I don't want to heap too much pressure on him, but to make your debut like that and go and play in such a controlled but positive way was incredible." The son of the former England player David Bairstow, Jonny is also a red-haired wicketkeeper, though good enough to play solely as a batsman. He was the inaugural Young Wisden Schools Cricketer of the Year in 2007, having already played for Yorkshire's second eleven and their academy. He signed a full-time contract for 2009, made an immediate impression with 82 on first-class debut against Somerset in June, and added five more fifties that season. He went close to 1000 first-class runs in 2010, but a century still eluded him – something he put right in fine style against Nottinghamshire in May 2011, converting his maiden ton into 205. Three more hundreds followed, including one in 81 balls in a one-dayer against Middlesex not long before he got the England call as cover for the injured Ben Stokes. That stirring debut followed: the only sadness was that his father wasn't there to see it. David Bairstow took his own life early in 1998, when Jonny was just eight.

THE FACTS Bairstow made 205 for Yorkshire against Nottinghamshire at Trent Bridge in May 2005 ... He scored 41 not out from 21 balls in his first Twenty20 international, against India at Cardiff in September 2011 ... Bairstow hit 50 and 109 not out for England Lions against Sri Lanka A at Scarborough in August 2011 ... His late father David played four Tests and 21 ODIs for England between 1979 and 1984 ...

THE FIGURES to 26.09.11   ᴇsᴘɴcricinfo.com

Batting & Fielding	M	Inns	NO	Runs	HS	Avge	S/R	100	50	4s	6s	Ct	St
Tests	0	0	–	–	–	–	–	–	–	–	–	–	–
ODIs	1	1	1	41	41*	–	195.23	0	0	1	3	0	0
T20Is	2	1	0	4	4	4.00	80.00	0	0	0	0	1	0
First-class	46	81	17	2889	205	45.14	–	3	22	–	–	98	5

Bowling	M	Balls	Runs	Wkts	BB	Avge	RpO	S/R	5i	10m
Tests	0	0	–	–	–	–	–	–	–	–
ODIs	1	0	–	–	–	–	–	–	–	–
T20Is	2	0	–	–	–	–	–	–	–	–
First-class	46	0	–	–	–	–	–	–	–	–

ADRIAN **BARATH**

Full name	**Adrian Boris Barath**
Born	**April 14, 1990, Chaguanas, Trinidad**
Teams	**Trinidad & Tobago**
Style	**Right-hand bat, occasional offspinner**
Test debut	**West Indies v Australia at Brisbane 2009-10**
ODI debut	**West Indies v Zimbabwe at Providence 2009-10**
T20I debut	**West Indies v Zimbabwe at Port-of-Spain 2009-10**

THE PROFILE Adrian Barath, a diminutive right-hander who usually opens, was long seen as one of the Caribbean's brightest batting talents, and fulfilled that promise with a superb Test-debut century at Brisbane in November 2009. He was only 19, and became West Indies' youngest centurion, breaking a record previously held by George Headley. Barath cut and carved like a veteran – but unfortunately his team-mates could muster only 73 runs between them, and West Indies still lost heavily. Barath's batting is based on orthodoxy: "As a youngster my dad saw me playing straight, which is unusual," he told Cricinfo. "Normally players begin by hitting across the line, but I was playing straight without anyone teaching me. Maybe it was because of television. I used to watch a lot and try and emulate what I saw." One of the best examples of those he was watching, Brian Lara, became an early mentor to his fellow Trinidadian. Barath was originally chosen for the series against Bangladesh in mid-2009, but joined the other senior players in boycotting the matches in a row over contracts. Earlier in 2009 he had showed his mettle by making 132 against England for West Indies A in St Kitts, sharing a partnership of 262 with Lendl Simmons. Not long after that Barath – who hit centuries in his second and third first-class matches when still a few months short of his 17th birthday – made a career-best 192 against the Leeward Islands in St Augustine. Barath has had injury problems since his stunning debut – he missed the 2011 World Cup after tweaking a hamstring – but remains a first choice when fit.

THE FACTS Barath was the 12th man to make a century in his first Test for West Indies, scoring 104 v Australia at Brisbane in November 2009 ... At 19 years 228 days he was West Indies' youngest Test century-maker, beating George Headley (20 years 230 days in 1929-30) ... After making 73 on his first-class debut in January 2007 when still only 16, Barath hit 131 in his second match and 101 in his third ...

THE FIGURES to 26.09.11   ᴇꜱᴘⁿcricinfo.com

Batting & Fielding	M	Inns	NO	Runs	HS	Avge	S/R	100	50	4s	6s	Ct	St
Tests	7	13	0	350	104	26.92	54.85	1	2	50	4	7	0
ODIs	9	9	0	273	113	30.33	62.18	1	1	23	3	2	0
T20Is	1	1	0	8	8	8.00	42.10	0	0	1	0	1	0
First-class	31	55	3	2174	192	41.80	–	6	12	–	–	22	0

Bowling	M	Balls	Runs	Wkts	BB	Avge	RpO	S/R	5i	10m
Tests	7	6	4	0	–	–	4.00	–	0	0
ODIs	9	0	–	–	–	–	–	–	–	–
T20Is	1	0	–	–	–	–	–	–	–	–
First-class	31	12	4	0	–	–	2.00	–	0	0

CARLTON **BAUGH**

WEST INDIES

Full name	**Carlton Seymour Baugh junior**
Born	**June 23, 1982, Kingston, Jamaica**
Teams	**Jamaica**
Style	**Right-hand bat, wicketkeeper**
Test debut	**West Indies v Australia at Port-of-Spain 2002-03**
ODI debut	**West Indies v Australia at Kingston 2002-03**
T20I debut	**West Indies v New Zealand at Auckland 2008-09**

THE PROFILE Jamaica's slender wicketkeeper/batsman Carlton Baugh has been a consistent scorer – he has 11 first-class hundreds to his name – at every level except the highest, where his attempts at aggression often cost him his wicket. He was tried as Ridley Jacobs's replacement as early as 2003, but did little with the bat beyond a neat 68 against England at Old Trafford the following year. The selectors turned to Trinidad's Denesh Ramdin, a better technical keeper than the rather manufactured Baugh, but on the face of it an inferior batsman: but Ramdin confounded the issue by producing several good innings, including 166 against England early in 2009. By then, though, Ramdin's keeping was going off the boil, and the following year he was dropped. After two run-heavy domestic seasons Baugh returned for the rain-soaked tour of Sri Lanka late in 2010, and did enough in his first Tests for more than six years to retain his place for the 2011 World Cup, even though he had played 24 ODIs in those intervening years without ever passing 30. However, Baugh injured a hamstring just before the tournament started and was replaced by Devon Thomas, who did well. But afterwards Thomas went down with chickenpox, and Baugh got the gloves back for the home series against Pakistan, and although he contributed little with the bat he retained his place for the matches against India that followed. He made an important 27 in the low-scoring first Test, which West Indies won, and 60 in another modest total in the third Test, to suggest that at last he was able to transfer that good first-class form to the Test arena.

THE FACTS Baugh has reached 150 three times in first-class cricket, two of them for West Indies on tour: 158 not out v Free State at Bloemfontein in December 2003, and 150 not out v Derbyshire in August 2004 – he also made 152 for Jamaica v Trinidad in February 2005 ... Baugh took five catches in an innings – and eight in the match – for Jamaica v Barbados at Bridgetown in March 2008 ... His father Carlton also played for Jamaica ...

THE FIGURES to 26.09.11   **ᴇsᴘᴨcricinfo.com**

Batting & Fielding	M	Inns	NO	Runs	HS	Avge	S/R	100	50	4s	6s	Ct	St
Tests	13	23	2	436	68	20.76	54.50	0	3	52	4	25	3
ODIs	42	30	9	418	49	19.90	68.52	0	0	30	6	33	9
T20Is	1	1	0	2	2	2.00	100.00	0	0	0	0	0	0
First-class	82	138	18	4176	158*	34.80	–	11	19	–	–	163	19

Bowling	M	Balls	Runs	Wkts	BB	Avge	RpO	S/R	5i	10m
Tests	13	0	–	–	–	–	–	–	–	–
ODIs	42	0	–	–	–	–	–	–	–	–
T20Is	1	0	–	–	–	–	–	–	–	–
First-class	82	0	–	–	–	–	–	–	–	–

MICHAEL **BEER**

Full name **Michael Anthony Beer**
Born **June 9, 1984, Malvern, Victoria**
Teams **Victoria**
Style **Right-hand bat, slow left-arm orthodox spinner**
Test debut **Australia v England at Sydney 2010-11**
ODI debut **No ODIs yet**
T20I debut **No T20Is yet**

THE PROFILE A tall left-arm spinner who toiled at club level in Melbourne for several years without getting past Victoria's second eleven, Michael Beer moved to Perth during the 2010 off-season, aged 26, as Western Australia searched for a front-line spinner. He was soon tried in the state team, settling in well without looking likely to run through sides: he has a nice high action, but doesn't spin the ball a huge amount. Beer claimed three wickets on first-class debut – ironically against Victoria – then in his third match took five against the England tourists, although he also leaked runs at more than five an over. One of his victims was Kevin Pietersen, who was perceived to have a problem with left-arm spinners – but it was still a major shock when Beer was named in the squad for the third Test at Perth in December 2010, after only five first-class matches. Journalists and headline-writers had a field day: "In times of stress the English make a cup of tea, the Aussies go for a Beer," joked Vic Marks in *The Observer*. Beer didn't play at the WACA, or at the MCG, but he made his debut in the final Test at Sydney, traditionally a good ground for the spinners. He looked steady, but no world-beater, finishing with the wicket of Paul Collingwood for 112: his figures would have been appreciably better if he hadn't overstepped in his third over before having the prolific Alastair Cook caught at mid-on. Cook, 46 at the time, sailed on to 189. Beer toured Sri Lanka later in the year, although he didn't play in the Tests: much will depend on how his second full season goes.

THE FACTS Beer played for Australia after only seven first-class matches, in which he'd taken 16 wickets with a best of 3 for 39 ... He took 6 for 109 in a two-day game for Australia A against a Zimbabwe XI at Kwekwe in July 2011 ... Beer played a few club games for St Kilda in Melbourne alongside Shane Warne ...

THE FIGURES to 26.09.11   **ESPNcricinfo.com**

Batting & Fielding	M	Inns	NO	Runs	HS	Avge	S/R	100	50	4s	6s	Ct	St
Tests	1	2	1	4	2*	4.00	15.38	0	0	0	0	1	0
ODIs	0	0	–	–	–	–	–	–	–	–	–	–	–
T20Is	0	0	–	–	–	–	–	–	–	–	–	–	–
First-class	14	22	11	99	24*	9.00	26.61	0	0	7	0	8	0

Bowling	M	Balls	Runs	Wkts	BB	Avge	RpO	S/R	5i	10m
Tests	1	228	112	1	1–112	112.00	2.94	228.00	0	0
ODIs	0	0	–	–	–	–	–	–	–	–
T20Is	0	0	–	–	–	–	–	–	–	–
First-class	14	2809	1506	33	3–39	45.63	3.21	85.12	0	0

IAN **BELL**

ENGLAND

Full name	**Ian Ronald Bell**
Born	**April 11, 1982, Walsgrave, Coventry**
Teams	**Warwickshire**
Style	**Right-hand bat, right-arm medium-pace bowler**
Test debut	**England v West Indies at The Oval 2004**
ODI debut	**England v Zimbabwe at Harare 2004-05**
T20I debut	**England v Pakistan at Bristol 2006**

THE PROFILE Ian Bell was earmarked for greatness long before he was drafted into the England squad in New Zealand in 2001-02, aged 19, as cover for the injured Mark Butcher. Tenacious and technically sound, with a cover-drive to die for, Bell is in the mould of Michael Atherton, who was burdened with similar expectations on his debut a generation earlier and was similarly adept at leaving the ball outside off. Bell had played only 13 first-class matches when called into that England squad, and his form dipped at first, but by 2004 he was on the up again. He finally made his Test debut against West Indies that August, stroking 70 at The Oval, before returning the following summer to lift his average to an obscene 297 against Bangladesh. Such rich pickings soon ceased: found out by McGrath and Warne, like so many before him, Bell mustered just 171 runs in the 2005 Ashes. But he bounced back better for the experience, collecting 313 runs in three Tests in Pakistan, including a classy century at Faisalabad. And when Pakistan toured in 2006, Bell repeated the dose, with elegant hundreds in each of the first three Tests. He improved his record against the Aussies in 2006-07 without going on to the big score, then in 2008 made 199 against South Africa at Lord's. He missed the start of the 2009 Ashes, returning only when Kevin Pietersen was injured, but has been very productive since: after 140 at Durban, plus two tons against Bangladesh, he hit top form with a cathartic century in the Ashes triumph at Sydney in January 2011, and four hundreds – one a double – in the home summer against Sri Lanka and India.

THE FACTS After three Tests, and innings of 70, 65 not out and 162 not out, Bell's average was 297.00; he raised that to 303.00 before Australia started getting him out – only Lawrence Rowe (336), David Lloyd (308) and "Tip" Foster (306) have ever had better averages in Test history ... Bell has made Test centuries on eight different English grounds (including Cardiff but, oddly, not yet his home ground of Edgbaston): no-one else has managed more than six ... Bell made 262 not out for Warwickshire v Sussex at Horsham in May 2004 ...

THE FIGURES to 26.09.11   **ESFM** cricinfo.com

Batting & Fielding	M	Inns	NO	Runs	HS	Avge	S/R	100	50	4s	6s	Ct	St
Tests	69	116	14	5027	235	49.28	52.72	16	28	585	21	57	0
ODIs	107	103	9	3232	126*	34.38	73.37	1	19	301	15	34	0
T20Is	7	7	1	175	60*	29.16	119.86	0	1	21	2	4	0
First-class	190	318	34	13368	262*	47.07	–	38	67	–	–	135	0

Bowling	M	Balls	Runs	Wkts	BB	Avge	RpO	S/R	5i	10m
Tests	69	108	76	1	1–33	76.00	4.22	108.00	0	0
ODIs	107	88	88	6	3–9	14.66	6.00	14.66	0	0
T20Is	7	–	–	–	–	–	–	–	–	–
First-class	190	2809	1564	47	4–4	33.27	3.34	59.76	0	0

SULIEMAN **BENN**

Full name	**Sulieman Jamaal Benn**
Born	**July 22, 1981, Haynesville, St James, Barbados**
Teams	**Barbados**
Style	**Left-hand bat, slow left-arm orthodox spinner**
Test debut	**West Indies v Sri Lanka at Providence 2007-08**
ODI debut	**West Indies v Sri Lanka at Port-of-Spain 2007-08**
T20I debut	**West Indies v Australia at Bridgetown 2008**

THE PROFILE Not many players can look down on Chris Gayle, but at 6ft 7ins (200cm) Sulieman Benn makes some of his team-mates look like schoolboys. Built like a fast bowler, and with the fiery attitude of one, Benn is also no stranger to controversy. In 2007, he was involved in an ugly incident in a club game, and two years later had a heated on-field argument with Brad Haddin and Mitchell Johnson in the Perth Test. There were more charges to come, as Benn was sent off the field in Dominica by Chris Gayle during South Africa's one-day whitewash in 2010, after apparently refusing to bowl over the wicket, and in the Tests that followed he was embroiled in several colourful exchanges. Then, after the 2011 World Cup, he was not selected for a while for reasons supposedly to do with his attitude, as the new coach Ottis Gibson sought to impose himself. But when he's not in trouble Benn can be a skilful, determined bowler, West Indies' most reliable spinner in years. His height gives him a curious aspect not unlike a windmill when he delivers, but it also makes facing him on a dry track a daunting prospect. He has been economical if unspectacular in one-day cricket, but did claim 4 for 6 in a Twenty20 international against Zimbabwe at Port-of-Spain early in 2010 (a match West Indies still managed to lose). He picked up eight wickets in the first Test against England at Kingston in February 2009 to help set up what was ultimately a series win, although his efforts were overshadowed as Jerome Taylor sent England crashing to 51 all out in the second innings.

THE FACTS Benn took 6 for 81 (from 46.4 overs) against South Africa at Bridgetown in June 2010 ... His eight wickets against England at Kingston in February 2009 were the most by any West Indian spinner in a Test since Lance Gibbs took nine in 1974-75 ... Benn took 3 for 16 as the Stanford Superstars beat England in a Twenty20 challenge in November 2008 ... Benn's highest score is 79 for Barbados v Windward Islands in Grenada in January 2009 ...

THE FIGURES *to 26.09.11*   ESPNcricinfo.com

Batting & Fielding	M	Inns	NO	Runs	HS	Avge	S/R	100	50	4s	6s	Ct	St
Tests	17	27	3	381	42	15.87	58.25	0	0	42	10	7	0
ODIs	25	16	2	109	31	7.78	72.18	0	0	10	1	1	0
T20Is	17	7	4	37	13*	12.33	88.09	0	0	5	1	7	0
First-class	64	97	14	1674	79	20.16	–	0	7	–	–	41	0

Bowling	M	Balls	Runs	Wkts	BB	Avge	RpO	S/R	5i	10m
Tests	17	4381	2112	51	6–81	41.41	2.89	85.90	3	0
ODIs	25	1247	924	29	4–18	31.86	4.44	43.00	0	0
T20Is	17	354	414	15	4–6	27.60	7.01	23.60	0	0
First-class	64	14638	6712	209	6–81	32.11	2.75	70.03	8	0

HAMISH **BENNETT**

Full name	**Hamish Kyle Bennett**
Born	**February 22, 1987, Timaru**
Teams	**Canterbury**
Style	**Left-hand bat, right-arm fast-medium bowler**
Test debut	**New Zealand v India at Ahmedabad 2010-11**
ODI debut	**New Zealand v Bangladesh at Dhaka 2010-11**
T20I debut	**No T20Is yet**

THE PROFILE Broad-shouldered fast bowler Hamish Bennett – a "country boy" from Timaru – has been playing representative cricket since he started the game aged six. He worked his way into the Canterbury side in December 2005, after a spell at New Zealand's Academy, and took 15 wickets in his first season, admittedly at more than 50 apiece. But he has undoubted pace, and after a sluggish start – that bowling average was still over 50 after his second season – increased accuracy led to better returns. In April 2008 Bennett took 7 for 50 as Canterbury mugged Wellington at home in the State Championship final, and the following season claimed 26 wickets. He was eventually rewarded with a call-up for the tour of Bangladesh late in 2010, to his evident surprise: "I was stunned." Bennett's international start had its ups and downs. He played in the last two matches of a sobering tour for New Zealand: expected to win easily, they were whitewashed 4-0 in the one-day internationals, terrible preparation for the impending World Cup. Bennett did enough to keep his place for the tour of India that followed, and won his first Test cap in the opening match at Ahmedabad ... but limped off with a groin strain on the first day before he'd taken a wicket, and played no further part on the tour. Then, after early success in the 2011 World Cup – he was too quick for the Kenyans, picking up 4 for 16, three lbw and the other bowled – he injured his ankle and had to be replaced in the squad. One odd fact about Bennett is that he has double-jointed thumbs. It's not known whether this will help him master reverse swing...

THE FACTS Bennett took 7 for 50 to help Canterbury beat Wellington in the final of the 2007-08 State Championship: the previous month he had taken 6 for 45 in a one-day match against Auckland ... He won the Man of the Match award on his World Cup debut, after taking 4 for 16 as Kenya were shot out for 69 at Chennai ...

THE FIGURES to 26.09.11   ≡sᴘⁿcricinfo.com

Batting & Fielding	M	Inns	NO	Runs	HS	Avge	S/R	100	50	4s	6s	Ct	St
Tests	1	1	0	4	4	4.00	13.33	0	0	0	0	0	0
ODIs	12	6	4	7	4*	3.50	25.00	0	0	0	0	0	0
T20Is	0	0	–	–	–	–	–	–	–	–	–	–	–
First-class	34	34	14	112	27	5.60	–	0	0	–	–	8	0

Bowling	M	Balls	Runs	Wkts	BB	Avge	RpO	S/R	5i	10m
Tests	1	90	47	0	–	–	3.13	–	0	0
ODIs	12	488	435	20	4–16	21.75	5.34	24.40	0	0
T20Is	0	0	–	–	–	–	–	–	–	–
First-class	34	5669	3442	91	7–50	37.82	3.64	62.29	1	0

DEVENDRA **BISHOO**

Full name	**Devendra Bishoo**
Born	**November 6, 1985, New Amsterdam, Berbice, Guyana**
Teams	**Guyana**
Style	**Left-hand bat, legspinner**
Test debut	**West Indies v Pakistan at Providence 2010-11**
ODI debut	**West Indies v England at Chennai 2010-11**
T20I debut	**West Indies v Pakistan at Gros Islet 2010-11**

THE PROFILE A slight, shy legspinner from Berbice, Devendra
Bishoo has risen rapidly since making his first-class bow in March
2008. A classical bowler who gives the ball a good wristy flick, he
took 5 for 29 on his debut, and the following year bamboozled
nine Leewards Islands batsmen on his way to 38 wickets in the season. In March 2010 he
took five in each innings against Barbados, by which time the regional selectors were already
looking in his direction, primarily because of his success in Twenty20 cricket. He was the
Man of the Series in the West Indian domestic 20-over tournament in July 2010 – he took
ten wickets, but almost more importantly went for little more than five an over, and took 2
for 24 from his four overs in the final against Barbados. Bishoo was called up as a late
replacement for the 2011 World Cup and was immediately thrust into the team, taking three
important wickets for 34 from his ten overs as England were restricted to 243 (which proved
to be just enough). West Indies' coach Ottis Gibson was among the impressed: "He showed
he has the ability to handle himself when he's put under pressure, and that's a very good sign.
He varied his pace and demonstrated he knows exactly what he's doing." When Pakistan
came to the Caribbean soon afterwards Bishoo took 11 wickets in the five ODIs, then made
his Test debut. It was another success: 4 for 68 in Pakistan's first innings, plus some
intelligent batting – he hung on for 94 minutes to help Shivnarine Chanderpaul stretch the
target to 219, which proved just beyond Pakistan.

THE FACTS Bishoo took 5 for 29 on his first-class debut, for Guyana v Combined
Campuses and Colleges at Providence in March 2008 ... He took 6 for 64 in his fifth match,
against Leeward Islands at Charlestown early in 2009 ... Bishoo took 4 for 68 on his Test
debut, 3 for 34 in his first ODI, and 4 for 17 in his first T20I ...

THE FIGURES to 26.09.11   ᴇ𝗌𝗽𝗻cricinfo.com

Batting & Fielding	M	Inns	NO	Runs	HS	Avge	S/R	100	50	4s	6s	Ct	St
Tests	5	9	2	87	26	12.42	48.60	0	0	7	1	6	0
ODIs	11	7	2	10	6*	2.00	38.46	0	0	2	0	1	0
T20Is	4	1	0	0	0	0.00	0.00	0	0	0	0	0	0
First-class	26	46	9	385	39	10.40	–	0	0	–	–	19	0

Bowling	M	Balls	Runs	Wkts	BB	Avge	RpO	S/R	5i	10m
Tests	5	1438	744	21	4–65	35.42	3.10	68.47	0	0
ODIs	11	588	410	19	3–34	21.57	4.18	30.94	0	0
T20Is	4	94	98	6	4–17	16.33	6.25	15.66	0	0
First-class	26	6212	3093	107	6–64	28.90	2.98	58.05	5	1

DOUG **BOLLINGER**

Full name **Douglas Erwin Bollinger**
Born **July 24, 1981, Baulkham Hills, Sydney**
Teams **New South Wales, Chennai Super Kings**
Style **Left-hand bat, left-arm fast-medium bowler**
Test debut **Australia v South Africa at Sydney 2008-09**
ODI debut **Australia v Pakistan at Dubai 2008-09**
T20I debut **No T20Is yet**

AUSTRALIA

THE PROFILE Until 2007-08 it looked as if Doug Bollinger's career would be an uneventful one. But after a fine domestic season he had his first national contract, a new wife ... and a fresh head of hair, courtesy of the same company that rethatched Shane Warne and Graham Gooch (it also led to a new nickname, "Doug the Rug", replacing "Bald Eagle"). Finally, just as he was preparing to depart on his honeymoon, Bollinger heard that he was a late addition for the West Indian tour in May 2008. He was unlucky not to have been named in the first place after topping the Shield wicket-takers with 45 at 15.44. A combative left-armer who mixes sharp pace with a consistent line and length, Bollinger finally won a Test cap at home at the SCG early in 2009, and ended up on the winning side. In England in 2009 Ben Hilfenhaus did so well that Bollinger was something of a back number, but injuries to others let him back in during the next home season, and he made the most of his reprieve, taking 37 wickets in seven Tests in 2009-10, and utterly dominating the dangerous Chris Gayle in one-dayers. He unwittingly caused controversy late in 2010 when, after being told by the Australian board to stay on to help Chennai win the Twenty20 Champions League, he arrived late for the tour of India then broke down at a vital stage of the first Test, which Australia narrowly lost. Then he looked short of a gallop in the second match of the Ashes series at Adelaide, and hasn't played a Test since – although he has continued to produce some whole-hearted one-day performances.

THE FACTS Bollinger has twice taken 5 for 35 in ODIs – against Pakistan in Abu Dhabi in May 2009, and against India at Guwahati the following November ... He took a one-day hat-trick for NSW v South Australia at Canberra in December 2004, dismissing Numbers 3, 4 and 5 in the order for ducks ... He claimed 6 for 47 for NSW v South Australia at Sydney in December 2008 ... For Worcestershire in 2007 Bollinger managed only 16 first-class wickets at 44.56 ...

THE FIGURES *to 26.09.11*   ESPNcricinfo.com

Batting & Fielding	M	Inns	NO	Runs	HS	Avge	S/R	100	50	4s	6s	Ct	St
Tests	12	14	7	54	21	7.71	33.96	0	0	7	0	2	0
ODIs	36	7	2	44	30	8.80	89.79	0	0	4	0	10	0
T20Is	0	0	–	–	–	–	–	–	–	–	–	–	–
First-class	69	77	34	326	31*	7.58	–	0	0	–	–	23	0

Bowling	M	Balls	Runs	Wkts	BB	Avge	RpO	S/R	5i	10m
Tests	12	2401	1296	50	5–28	25.92	3.23	48.02	2	0
ODIs	36	1798	1347	59	5–35	22.83	4.49	30.47	2	0
T20Is	0	0	–	–	–	–	–	–	–	–
First-class	69	12377	6752	240	6–47	28.13	3.27	51.57	12	2

RAVI **BOPARA**

Full name	**Ravinder Singh Bopara**
Born	**May 4, 1985, Forest Gate, London**
Teams	**Essex, Dolphins**
Style	**Right-hand bat, right-arm medium-pace bowler**
Test debut	**England v Sri Lanka at Kandy 2007-08**
ODI debut	**England v Australia at Sydney 2006-07**
T20I debut	**England v New Zealand at Manchester 2008**

THE PROFILE Ravi Bopara has had an up-and-down Test career. Uniquely he followed three successive ducks (against Sri Lanka late in 2007, including an embarrassing first-ball run-out) with three successive centuries against West Indies in 2009, despite being dropped after his maiden hundred in Barbados. Those hundreds meant he was inked in at No. 3 against Australia for the 2009 Ashes – helping usher Michael Vaughan into retirement – but his wristy technique proved too loose, and he made only 105 runs in seven innings before being dropped. His usually excellent fielding wavered too, as he dropped a couple of relative sitters, while his energetic medium-pacers proved toothless. He reacted to the chop by making 201 for Essex against Surrey, and was back for the chastening one-day series against Australia, making several starts without going on to a big score. Since then he's been on the fringes, although 60 against South Africa in the 2011 World Cup and 96 against India at The Oval in September helped secure that one-day place. Bopara has packed a lot in since he signed for Essex at 17 in 2002. A good county season in 2006 won him a place in the Academy squad which was based in Perth during that winter's Ashes whitewash. When Kevin Pietersen broke a rib in the first match of the one-day tournament, Bopara was summoned: not worried about having such big boots to fill, he made his debut in front of the Sydney Hill, and bowled Australia's "finisher", Michael Hussey, as England began the amazing turnaround that eventually won them that series. Then the 2007 World Cup Bopara made a gutsy 52 which almost conjured an unlikely victory against eventual finalists Sri Lanka.

THE FACTS Bopara hit 229 for Essex v Northamptonshire at Chelmsford in June 2007, putting on 320 for the third wicket with Grant Flower ... He made 104 (at Bridgetown), 143 (at Lord's) and 108 (at Chester-le-Street) in successive Test innings, all against West Indies, in 2009; his previous three Test innings had all been ducks ... Bopara scored 201 not out for Essex in the Friends Provident Trophy at Leicester in June 2008 ...

THE FIGURES *to 26.09.11*   **ESPN**cricinfo.com

Batting & Fielding	M	Inns	NO	Runs	HS	Avge	S/R	100	50	4s	6s	Ct	St
Tests	12	17	1	553	143	34.56	53.89	3	0	68	2	6	0
ODIs	64	60	12	1480	96	30.83	75.43	0	6	124	19	23	0
T20Is	15	13	1	244	55	20.33	94.94	0	1	22	1	4	0
First-class	121	203	24	7452	229	41.63	53.45	20	29	–	–	72	0

Bowling	M	Balls	Runs	Wkts	BB	Avge	RpO	S/R	5i	10m
Tests	12	326	212	1	1–39	212.00	3.90	326.00	0	0
ODIs	64	575	483	13	4–38	37.15	5.04	44.23	0	0
T20Is	15	64	62	6	4–10	10.33	5.81	10.66	0	0
First-class	121	8908	5715	134	5–75	42.64	3.84	66.47	1	0

JOHAN **BOTHA**

SOUTH AFRICA

Full name	**Johan Botha**
Born	**May 2, 1982, Johannesburg**
Teams	**Warriors, Northamptonshire, Rajasthan Royals**
Style	**Right-hand bat, offspinner**
Test debut	**South Africa v Australia at Sydney 2005-06**
ODI debut	**South Africa v India at Hyderabad 2005-06**
T20I debut	**South Africa v Australia at Brisbane 2005-06**

THE PROFILE Determined and fiercely competitive, Johan Botha started off as a rather ordinary medium-pacer, but one day Mickey Arthur – later South Africa's coach – spotted something else, and Botha dropped his ambitions for speed. He became an offspinner, and started studying the doosra. A year later he was touring Sri Lanka with South Africa A, scoring a few runs as well as taking key wickets. He made a promising Test debut in India late in 2005, gating Irfan Pathan during six tidy overs at Hyderabad, and when the selectors later suspected that the Sydney Test pitch would turn, Botha (who was already due to go to Australia for the one-dayers) was flown in early. He managed a couple of wickets, but delight turned to dismay when his jerky action was reported, and he was banned on suspicion of throwing. After remedial work he made a low-key international return in the Afro-Asia Cup in India in June 2007, but remains in the frame – especially in one-dayers and Twenty20 games, where he has the priceless ability to keep it tight. He also proved a canny stand-in captain when Graeme Smith was injured in Australia early in 2009, skippering his side to a 4-1 victory in the one-day series. But his doosra was reported again, and after tests showed his right elbow flexed by 26.7 degrees – nearly twice the permitted limit of 15 – Botha was told not to bowl his wrong'un again by the ICC. Even without it, he remains an important cog in South Africa's limited-overs attack, although his impact in Tests has been minimal. He also enjoyed successful stints in the IPL and in English Twenty20 cricket in 2011.

THE FACTS Botha's best bowling remains 6 for 42, for Eastern Province v Northerns at Port Elizabeth in March 2004, when still a medium-pacer ... He made 109 for Warriors v Dolphins at Port Elizabeth in October 2009 ... Botha made 101 for South Africa in an Under-19 Test v New Zealand (for whom Brendon McCullum made 186) in February 2001 ... He has captained South Africa in ten ODIs, winning eight ... Botha's record includes two ODIs for the Africa XI ...

THE FIGURES *to 26.09.11*   **ᴇѕᴘᴨ cricinfo.com**

Batting & Fielding	M	Inns	NO	Runs	HS	Avge	S/R	100	50	4s	6s	Ct	St
Tests	5	6	2	83	25	20.75	34.87	0	0	9	0	3	0
ODIs	74	46	15	575	46	18.54	85.31	0	0	52	2	33	0
T20Is	26	15	8	139	28*	19.85	120.86	0	0	10	6	15	0
First-class	67	111	18	3218	109	34.60	–	1	22	–	–	50	0

Bowling	M	Balls	Runs	Wkts	BB	Avge	RpO	S/R	5i	10m
Tests	5	1017	573	17	4-56	33.70	3.38	59.82	0	0
ODIs	74	3631	2790	69	4-19	40.43	4.61	52.62	0	0
T20Is	26	528	555	27	3-16	20.55	6.30	19.55	0	0
First-class	67	9760	4953	156	6-42	31.75	3.04	62.56	4	1

MARK **BOUCHER**

Full name	**Mark Verdon Boucher**
Born	**December 3, 1976, East London, Cape Province**
Teams	**Warriors, Kolkata Knight Riders**
Style	**Right-hand bat, wicketkeeper**
Test debut	**South Africa v Pakistan at Sheikhupura 1997-98**
ODI debut	**South Africa v New Zealand at Perth 1997-98**
T20I debut	**South Africa v New Zealand at Johannesburg 2005-06**

THE PROFILE A man to go to war with, but never against, Mark Boucher packs all the archetypical attributes of the South African cricketer into his short, stocky frame. He is relentlessly competitive, invariably aggressive, and as hard and uncompromising as the new ball. He likes to "walk onto the field as if you own the place". He has tucked most of international cricket's wicketkeeping records under his belt, passing 500 Test dismissals during 2010, with 1000 in sight in all formats. He is closing in on 150 Tests, although probably his most significant achievement came in only his second one, against Pakistan at Johannesburg in February 1998, when he helped Pat Symcox add 195, a Test ninth-wicket record, from a desperate 166 for 8. Boucher had made his debut a few months previously, still not 21, rushing to Pakistan to replace the injured Dave Richardson, who retired after the Australian tour that followed. Boucher was not everyone's first choice – Nic Pothas had also been waiting patiently – but once he got his hands into the gloves he refused to let them go, scrapping successfully to regain his spot when occasionally a form dip did cost him his place. He adapted his attacking batting to become something of a one-day "finisher" – qualities he has often transferred to the Test arena, notably helping Graeme Smith to anchor a tense series-clincher at Edgbaston in 2008. Boucher might now be in the autumn of his career, and no longer features in SA's one-day sides, but his commitment to his conditioning should earn him some extra time in Test cricket.

THE FACTS Boucher has more Test dismissals than anyone else, and only Adam Gilchrist (472) heads him in ODIs ... His 125 v Zimbabwe at Harare in 1999-2000 was a Test record for a nightwatchman until Jason Gillespie surpassed it in 2006 ... Boucher reached his century against Zimbabwe at Potchefstroom in September 2006 in only 44 balls, still the second-fastest in all ODIs ... His 75 consecutive Tests between 1997-98 and 2004-05 is a South African record ... His figures include one Test for the World XI and five ODIs for the Africa XI ...

THE FIGURES to 26.09.11   **ESPNcricinfo.com**

Batting & Fielding	M	Inns	NO	Runs	HS	Avge	S/R	100	50	4s	6s	Ct	St
Tests	139	196	23	5312	125	30.70	50.13	5	34	627	20	499	22
ODIs	292	218	56	4664	147*	28.79	84.72	1	26	354	83	400	22
T20Is	25	21	6	268	36*	17.86	97.45	0	0	22	2	18	1
First-class	201	292	41	8420	134	33.54	–	9	52	–	–	677	36

Bowling	M	Balls	Runs	Wkts	BB	Avge	RpO	S/R	5i	10m
Tests	139	8	6	1	1–6	6.00	4.50	8.00	0	0
ODIs	292	0	–	–	–	–	–	–	–	–
T20Is	25	0	–	–	–	–	–	–	–	–
First-class	201	26	26	1	1–6	26.00	6.00	26.00	0	0

TRENT **BOULT**

NEW ZEALAND

Full name	**Trent Alexander Boult**
Born	**July 22, 1989, Rotorua**
Teams	**Northern Districts**
Style	**Right-hand bat, left-arm fast-medium bowler**
Test debut	**No Tests yet**
ODI debut	**No ODIs yet**
T20I debut	**No T20Is yet**

THE PROFILE Fast bowler Trent Boult has been viewed as an international prospect ever since he was included, as a 17-year-old, in the New Zealand A winter training squad in 2007, which led to a place at the Under-19 World Cup in Malaysia early in 2008, where he derailed the hosts with 7 for 20. One reason the selectors like the look of him is that he's a left-armer, and New Zealand have always been fond of those, dating back to the likes of Richard Collinge, Graham Troup and Geoff Allott. Boult is also fairly quick, and has the potential to be a handy batsman too. He was chosen for the A-team tour of India late in 2008, making his first-class debut in Chennai before he'd played at home (his maiden wicket was that of Suresh Raina). Back in New Zealand some good one-day displays earned him a trip to Australia for the Chappell-Hadlee one-day series early in 2009, although he didn't actually play. A quiet home season with Northern Districts followed, but he came to the fore in 2010-11 with 32 wickets at 25.34, which helped earn him a national contract for the first time: "He receives his first contract after being in and around the team for some time and showing consistent domestic form and good development during the recent fast-bowling camps," explained Mark Greatbatch, New Zealand's acting chairman of selectors. Boult's favourite cricketer is Wasim Akram – a pretty good role model for an aspiring left-arm quick – and, cricket aside, he hopes to become a chef and open his own chain of restaurants across New Zealand.

THE FACTS Boult took 5 for 58 for Northern Districts v Otago in Dunedin in November 2008, in his first first-class match in New Zealand (his third overall) ... In 2010-11 he took 5 for 48 against Wellington and 5 for 35 v Auckland ... In the 2007-08 Under-19 World Cup he took 7 for 20 as Malaysia, the hosts, were shot out for 47 in Johor ... Boult's brother Jonothon has also played for ND ...

THE FIGURES *to 26.09.11*   **ᴇsᴘⁿcricinfo.com**

Batting & Fielding	M	Inns	NO	Runs	HS	Avge	S/R	100	50	4s	6s	Ct	St
Tests	0	0	–	–	–	–	–	–	–	–	–	–	–
ODIs	0	0	–	–	–	–	–	–	–	–	–	–	–
T20Is	0	0	–	–	–	–	–	–	–	–	–	–	–
First-class	18	22	5	252	46	14.82	43.75	0	0	28	9	11	0

Bowling	M	Balls	Runs	Wkts	BB	Avge	RpO	S/R	5i	10m
Tests	0	0	–	–	–	–	–	–	–	–
ODIs	0	0	–	–	–	–	–	–	–	–
T20Is	0	0	–	–	–	–	–	–	–	–
First-class	18	3141	1450	54	5–35	26.85	2.76	58.16	3	0

DARREN **BRAVO**

Full name	**Darren Michael Bravo**
Born	**February 6, 1989, Santa Cruz, Trinidad**
Teams	**Trinidad & Tobago**
Style	**Left-hand bat, occasional left-arm medium-pacer**
Test debut	**West Indies v Sri Lanka at Galle 2010-11**
ODI debut	**West Indies v India at Kingston 2009**
T20I debut	**West Indies v Zimbabwe at Port-of-Spain 2009-10**

THE PROFILE Darren Bravo is the younger half-brother of allrounder Dwayne, but although he can bowl a bit it is his batting – and quicksilver fielding, like Dwayne's – which aroused the interest of the selectors. A left-hander, Bravo junior has a style reminiscent of Brian Lara – not a bad role model – as Chris Gayle, his first international captain, spotted. "There are some similarities, like the batting technique, and they look alike a bit," said Gayle. "Brian is his idol, and he has the ability to go from strength to strength. He didn't show any form of nerves in the dressing-room." Bravo is actually a distant relative of Lara's, on his mother's side, and, like Lara, was born in Santa Cruz in Trinidad. "I go out there and play my game, the Darren Bravo game," he says, "and if in the eyes of the people it looks like Lara, then that is their judgment. At the end of the day it is just my game." Bravo scored 605 runs at 45 in 2008-09, his first full season for Trinidad & Tobago, including centuries against Barbados and the Windward Islands. This pushed him to the fringes of the West Indian side, and he made his debut alongside Dwayne in the short one-day series against India in June, scoring 19 and 21 in the only two innings the weather allowed him. Later in 2010 he made his Test debut in Sri Lanka, scoring half-centuries in all three matches, and continued that promising form into 2011, with three more fifties against Pakistan and India. With his flourishing backlift and a penchant for the flashing cover-drive, those Lara comparisons are likely to hang around for a while yet.

THE FACTS Darren Bravo made his debut for West Indies, alongside his half-brother Dwayne, in the one-day series against India at home in June 2009 ... He made 105 for Trinidad & Tobago v Windward Islands in January 2009, and 111 against Barbados the following month, when he and Kieron Pollard (174) put on 250 for the fourth wicket ... Bravo played in the Under-19 World Cup in Malaysia in 2008, scoring 59 against Papua New Guinea ...

THE FIGURES *to 26.09.11*　　　　　　　　　　　　　　　**ESPncricinfo.com**

Batting & Fielding	M	Inns	NO	Runs	HS	Avge	S/R	100	50	4s	6s	Ct	St
Tests	8	14	1	518	80	39.84	40.43	0	6	57	6	2	0
ODIs	28	25	3	736	86	33.45	73.08	0	5	51	21	4	0
T20Is	3	3	0	83	42	27.66	110.66	0	0	9	2	0	0
First-class	30	48	2	1684	111	36.60	–	0	3	10	–	–	24	0

Bowling	M	Balls	Runs	Wkts	BB	Avge	RpO	S/R	5i	10m
Tests	8	0	–	–	–	–	–	–	–	–
ODIs	28	0	–	–	–	–	–	–	–	–
T20Is	3	0	–	–	–	–	–	–	–	–
First-class	30	22	9	1	1–9	9.00	2.45	22.00	0	0

DWAYNE **BRAVO**

WEST INDIES

Full name	**Dwayne John Bravo**
Born	**October 7, 1983, Santa Cruz, Trinidad**
Teams	**Trinidad, Royal Challengers Bangalore, Victoria**
Style	**Right-hand bat, right-arm fast-medium bowler**
Test debut	**West Indies v England at Lord's 2004**
ODI debut	**West Indies v England at Georgetown 2003-04**
T20I debut	**West Indies v New Zealand at Auckland 2005-06**

THE PROFILE A genuine allrounder (a rare breed, especially in the Caribbean), Dwayne Bravo was born in Santa Cruz, like Brian Lara, and made his one-day debut in April 2004, on the tenth anniversary of Lara's 375. He won his first Test cap at Lord's three months later, aged 20, and took three wickets with his medium-paced swingers. He also displayed a cool, straight bat even though his team was facing a big total. West Indies lost the series, but at least they knew they had unearthed a special talent. Bravo hit his maiden century against South Africa in Antigua in April 2005, and played an even better innings the following November, 113 at Hobart against the rampant Australians. He continued to chip in with useful runs, while a selection of slower balls makes him a handful in one-dayers, if less so in Tests. He's also electric in the field. Bravo missed the 2009 home Tests against England with a niggling ankle injury, then was left out for the Tests in England that followed – despite being fit enough to play in the IPL – although he did lift the side visibly in both one-day series. Back in Australia at the end of 2009, he made another century, at Adelaide, then batted consistently at home against South Africa in June 2010. The previous year Bravo had been one of several players who boycotted the home series against Bangladesh as a contracts dispute festered, and he continues to flit between the international set-up and lucrative 20-over competitions: a decision to turn down a central contract cost him the West Indies vice-captaincy in 2011, not long before an injury in the first match ruled him out of the World Cup.

THE FACTS Dwayne Bravo's second Test century – 113 at Hobart late in 2005 – came during a stand of 182 with his fellow-Trinidadian Denesh Ramdin, the day after Trinidad & Tobago qualified for the football World Cup for the first time ... Bravo averages 30.72 with the ball in Tests against Australia – but 81.66 v Pakistan ... He played 27 Tests before finally finishing on the winning side, against Sri Lanka at Port-of-Spain in April 2008 ... Bravo's half-brother Darren has also played for West Indies ...

THE FIGURES *to 26.09.11*   **ESPN**cricinfo.com

Batting & Fielding	M	Inns	NO	Runs	HS	Avge	S/R	100	50	4s	6s	Ct	St
Tests	40	71	1	2200	113	31.42	48.59	3	13	269	21	41	0
ODIs	117	96	17	1910	112*	24.17	81.86	1	5	143	35	45	0
T20Is	22	20	5	344	66*	22.93	123.29	0	2	22	15	5	0
First-class	97	176	7	5218	197	30.87	–	8	29	–	–	83	0

Bowling	M	Balls	Runs	Wkts	BB	Avge	RpO	S/R	5i	10m
Tests	40	6466	3426	86	6–55	39.83	3.17	75.18	2	0
ODIs	117	4630	4055	136	4–19	29.81	5.25	34.04	0	0
T20Is	22	338	491	19	4–38	25.84	8.71	17.78	0	0
First-class	97	10763	5777	171	6–11	33.78	3.22	62.94	7	0

TIM **BRESNAN**

Full name	**Timothy Thomas Bresnan**
Born	**February 28, 1985, Pontefract, Yorkshire**
Teams	**Yorkshire**
Style	**Right-hand bat, right-arm fast-medium bowler**
Test debut	**England v West Indies at Lord's 2009**
ODI debut	**England v Sri Lanka at Lord's 2006**
T20I debut	**England v Sri Lanka at Southampton 2006**

THE PROFILE The stocky Tim Bresnan was tipped for higher honours in 2001 after becoming Yorkshire's youngest player for 20 years. He quickly progressed to England's youth team, and played in two Under-19 World Cups. The potential took a few years to ripen, but in 2005 he was given more responsibility in a transitional Yorkshire team, and responded with 47 wickets with swinging deliveries which, if a shade short of truly fast, travel at a fair rate. He can also bat, making three first-class centuries in 2007: he has reached 90 in Tests twice, too. A good start to the previous season had resulted in a place in a new-look one-day squad in June 2006, but Bresnan fell victim to the flashing blades of Sanath Jayasuriya and friends, and took only two wickets in four appearances in what became a clean sweep for Sri Lanka. He then suffered a back injury, and was not in serious consideration for a World Cup spot. He responded well with the bat in 2007, although his form with the ball dipped a little (34 wickets at 34), before a return to bowling form the following year led to a one-day recall. He finally made his Test debut in May 2009, but failed to shine at first and had to make way for Andrew Flintoff in the Ashes series. But he returned to Yorkshire, worked on his fitness, and came back a better player ... and a good luck charm too: England won the first ten Tests in which Bresnan played, including the victories at Melbourne and Sydney which sealed the 2010-11 Ashes triumph. He then had a quiet World Cup, save for a five-for in the tie against India.

THE FACTS Bresnan made all three of his first-class centuries during 2007, including 126 not out for England A v India at Chelmsford ... He was on the winning side in his first ten Tests, an England record ... Bresnan's 80 against Australia at Centurion in October 2009 is the highest score by an England No. 8 in ODIs ... His best bowling figures are 5 for 42 for Yorkshire at Worcester in July 2005 ... Bresnan made his Yorkshire debut in a one-day game in 2001, when only 16 ...

THE FIGURES *to 26.09.11*   **ESPNcricinfo.com**

Batting & Fielding	M	Inns	NO	Runs	HS	Avge	S/R	100	50	4s	6s	Ct	St
Tests	10	8	1	318	91	45.42	46.90	0	3	39	1	3	0
ODIs	52	40	12	608	80	21.71	92.54	0	1	64	2	14	0
T20Is	19	11	5	78	23*	13.00	111.42	0	0	6	0	5	0
First-class	106	139	24	3305	126*	28.73	48.07	3	17	–	–	42	0

Bowling	M	Balls	Runs	Wkts	BB	Avge	RpO	S/R	5i	10m
Tests	10	2031	968	41	5–48	23.60	2.85	49.53	1	0
ODIs	52	2601	2306	63	5–48	36.60	5.31	41.28	1	0
T20Is	19	364	460	12	3–10	38.33	7.58	30.33	0	0
First-class	106	17764	9072	297	5–42	30.54	3.06	59.81	5	0

STUART **BROAD**

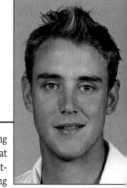

ENGLAND

Full name	**Stuart Christopher John Broad**
Born	**June 24, 1986, Nottingham**
Teams	**Nottinghamshire**
Style	**Left-hand bat, right-arm fast-medium bowler**
Test debut	**England v Sri Lanka at Colombo 2007-08**
ODI debut	**England v Pakistan at Cardiff 2006**
T20I debut	**England v Pakistan at Bristol 2006**

THE PROFILE Stuart Broad is an aggressive seamer with a strong high action and an ability to produce game-changing spells. He's at his best when pitching the ball up and nipping it away from the right-hander, but he is also adept at pulling his length back and peppering the ribs with a series of awkward short balls. Broad is also one of England's many bowling allrounders, with a classical batting technique and a penchant for the back-foot drive. With time on his side, and a willingness to learn, he has the scope to develop into one of England's finest fast bowlers. For the moment, the only slight issue in his development is a tendency towards petulance, a trait he seems to have inherited from his father Chris, the former England opening batsman who is now an ICC match referee. Stuart made an impressive start to his international career, keeping a cool head in the mayhem of a Twenty20 match, then claiming an early wicket on his one-day debut. In the 2009 Ashes he was unimpressive at first, but kept his place, and silenced the critics with a superb spell to set up England's series-winning victory at The Oval. Broad can bat, too, and made up for a disappointing spell with a superb 169 – a long-overdue maiden first-class century – against Pakistan at Lord's in August 2010. The following 12 months featured peaks and troughs: unrelated side injuries forced him home early from the Ashes tour and the World Cup, then a shoulder problem ended the home season prematurely. In between, though, he bowled magnificently at home against India, pitching the ball up more after struggling against Sri Lanka, and was named as England's new Twenty20 captain.

THE FACTS Broad scored 169 – the highest by an England No. 9 in Tests – and shared a record eighth-wicket partnership of 332 with Jonathan Trott, against Pakistan at Lord's in 2010 ... After being part of Peter Siddle's Test hat-trick at Brisbane in November 2010, Broad took one himself against India at Trent Bridge in July 2011 ... Broad took 6 for 91 (and scored 61) in the fourth Test against Australia at Leeds in 2009 ... Broad's father, Chris, played 25 Tests for England in the 1980s, scoring 1661 runs with six centuries – he's now a match referee (see page 221) ...

THE FIGURES to 26.09.11   **ESPNcricinfo.com**

Batting & Fielding	M	Inns	NO	Runs	HS	Avge	S/R	100	50	4s	6s	Ct	St
Tests	41	53	7	1335	169	29.02	63.54	1	8	173	9	13	0
ODIs	84	48	16	392	45*	12.25	71.66	0	0	24	5	18	0
T20Is	31	12	5	36	10*	5.14	112.50	0	0	3	1	15	0
First-class	87	109	20	2295	169	25.78	57.66	1	15	–	–	26	0

Bowling	M	Balls	Runs	Wkts	BB	Avge	RpO	S/R	5i	10m
Tests	41	8315	4225	132	6–46	32.00	3.04	62.99	4	0
ODIs	84	4256	3711	137	5–23	27.08	5.23	31.06	1	0
T20Is	31	655	821	37	3–17	22.18	7.52	17.70	0	0
First-class	87	16021	8750	305	8–52	28.68	3.27	52.52	14	1

MICHAEL **CARBERRY**

Full name	**Michael Alexander Carberry**
Born	**September 29, 1980, Croydon, Surrey**
Teams	**Hampshire**
Style	**Left-hand bat, occasional offspinner**
Test debut	**England v Bangladesh at Chittagong 2009-10**
ODI debut	**No ODIs yet**
T20I debut	**No T20Is yet**

ENGLAND

THE PROFILE Michael Carberry, a talented left-hand batsman and a superb fielder, moved to Hampshire after unfulfilling spells at Kent and Surrey. It seemed to provide just the spark he needed: in 2007 he passed 1000 runs in the Championship, which earned him an England Lions tour of India. He did well there, scoring two hundreds, and was also one of three centuries for the Lions against New Zealand at home at the Rose Bowl a few months later. In 2009 he scored 1251 runs at 69.50 in 12 Championship matches – the highlight a fluent 204 against Warwickshire – before breaking a finger. He spent the winter with the England Performance Programme in South Africa, and was drafted into the squad for the third Test as cover for Paul Collingwood, who had dislocated a finger. Collingwood played in the end, but Carberry's consolation was a trip to Bangladesh early in 2010. With Andrew Strauss giving the trip a miss Carberry made his Test debut at Chittagong, letting no-one down with 34 and 30, but the adaptable Jonathan Trott opened in the second match. Carberry kept his name in the frame by averaging over 50 again in 2010, but shortly after the season was found to have a blood clot on the lung: he made a slow recovery from the emergency operation to remove it. But he showed he was back to his best with a wonderful triple-century for Hampshire against Yorkshire in August, when he and Neil McKenzie put on 523, the ninth-biggest partnership in first-class cricket. Carberry averaged over 50 again in the season, just to remind Strauss and Cook – and the selectors – that there was another left-hand opener out there.

THE FACTS Carberry scored 300 not out for Hampshire v Yorkshire at Southampton in August 2011, sharing a record third-wicket stand of 523 with Neil McKenzie (237) ... Four weeks later, against Somerset at Taunton, Carberry made 182 and put on 373 for the second wicket with Jimmy Adams ... His maiden first-class century was for Surrey against Cambridge UCCE in 2002: his second was also at Fenner's, but for Kent in 2003 ...

THE FIGURES *to 26.09.11* **espncricinfo.com**

Batting & Fielding	M	Inns	NO	Runs	HS	Avge	S/R	100	50	4s	6s	Ct	St
Tests	1	2	0	64	34	32.00	45.71	0	0	9	0	1	0
ODIs	0	0	–	–	–	–	–	–	–	–	–	–	–
T20Is	0	0	–	–	–	–	–	–	–	–	–	–	–
First-class	121	213	19	8625	300*	44.45	52.56	26	37			57	0

Bowling	M	Balls	Runs	Wkts	BB	Avge	RpO	S/R	5i	10m
Tests	1	0	–	–	–	–	–	–	–	–
ODIs	0	0	–	–	–	–	–	–	–	–
T20Is	0	0	–	–	–	–	–	–	–	–
First-class	121	1252	891	13	2–85	68.53	4.26	96.30	0	0

WEST INDIES

SHIVNARINE **CHANDERPAUL**

Full name	**Shivnarine Chanderpaul**
Born	**August 16, 1974, Unity Village, Demerara, Guyana**
Teams	**Guyana**
Style	**Left-hand bat, occasional legspinner**
Test debut	**West Indies v England at Georgetown 1993-94**
ODI debut	**West Indies v India at Faridabad 1994-95**
T20I debut	**West Indies v New Zealand at Auckland 2005-06**

THE PROFILE Crouched and crabby, Shivnarine Chanderpaul proves there is life beyond the coaching handbook. He never seems to play in the V, or off the front foot, but uses soft hands, canny deflections and a whiplash pull to maintain a Test average nudging 50. Early on he struggled to convert fifties into hundreds, and also missed several matches through injury. That was rectified in 2000 when a large piece of floating bone was removed from his foot: suitably liberated, he set about rectifying his hundreds problem too, and now has 23 (20 against Australia, England, India and South Africa), including 104 as the Windies chased down a record 418 to beat the Aussies in Antigua in May 2003. The following year in England he ended his first bad trot by narrowly missing twin tons at Lord's. In 2005 he became captain during the first of several acrimonious disputes between the players and the board, and celebrated with 203 at home in Guyana, although he was too passive in the field to prevent South Africa taking the series. He stood down after struggling with bat and microphone in Australia, and was back to his limpet best in England in 2007, top-scoring in each of his five innings, and going more than 1000 minutes without being out in Tests for the third time in his career (he did it again in 2008). It's not all defence, though: he can blast with the best when he needs to. Chanderpaul became uncharacteristically vocal after high-level criticism of senior players in 2011, and was somewhat grudgingly restored to the Test side, becoming West Indies' most-capped player that July, a landmark he celebrated with another century.

THE FACTS Chanderpaul averages 67.48 in Tests against India, but only 28.77 v Zimbabwe ... He scored 303 not out for Guyana v Jamaica in January 1996 ... At Georgetown in April 2003 Chanderpaul reached his century against Australia in only 69 balls, the fourth-fastest in Test history by balls faced ... He marked becoming West Indies' most-capped player (133) with a century against India at Roseau in July 2011 ... ... Chanderpaul once managed to shoot a policeman in the hand in his native Guyana, mistaking him for a mugger ...

THE FIGURES *to 26.09.11*   **ESPN**cricinfo.com

Batting & Fielding	M	Inns	NO	Runs	HS	Avge	S/R	100	50	4s	6s	Ct	St
Tests	133	227	36	9367	203*	49.04	42.14	23	55	1032	27	54	0
ODIs	268	251	40	8778	150	41.60	70.74	11	59	722	85	73	0
T20Is	22	22	5	343	41	20.17	98.84	0	0	34	5	7	0
First-class	273	443	79	19944	303*	54.79	–	59	99	–	–	149	0

Bowling	M	Balls	Runs	Wkts	BB	Avge	RpO	S/R	5i	10m
Tests	133	1740	883	9	1–2	98.11	3.04	193.33	0	0
ODIs	268	740	636	14	3–18	45.42	5.15	52.85	0	0
T20Is	22	0	–	–	–	–	–	–	–	–
First-class	273	4694	2491	57	4–48	43.70	3.18	82.35	0	0

DINESH **CHANDIMAL**

Full name	**Lokuge Dinesh Chandimal**
Born	**November 18, 1989, Balapitiya**
Teams	**Nondescripts, Ruhuna**
Style	**Right-hand bat, wicketkeeper**
Test debut	**No Tests yet**
ODI debut	**Sri Lanka v Zimbabwe at Bulawayo 2010**
T20I debut	**Sri Lanka v New Zealand at Providence 2009-10**

THE PROFILE   Dinesh Chandimal is a batsman who can keep wicket, like one of his heroes Romesh Kaluwitharana. He's taller than the diminutive "Kalu", though, at 5ft 9ins (175cm), and duly collected a full national contract after a seamless run through Sri Lanka's age-group sides. First-class cricket also seemed to pose few terrors: he scored a century in his second match, against the New Zealand tourists in August 2009, and added two more in his next five games. He finished his first full home season with 895 runs at 52.64, and did well enough in limited-overs cricket to earn selection for the World Twenty20 in the West Indies early in 2010. He played in three of the matches there as a batsman, and was called up to keep wicket for the 50-overs team in a tri-series in Zimbabwe in June while Kumar Sangakkara took a rest. Still only 20, Chandimal did a passable impersonation of Sangakkara behind the stumps – and in front of them, too, spanking a superb 111 in only his second ODI, against India at Harare. Cricinfo observed: "He impressed with his shot-selection, his footwork and his aggressive bent of mind ... his sashays down the pitch were made possible because he used the crease well, often dropping well back to create his own length for his cut shots against the spinners." He sat out the 2011 World Cup, then came close to a Test debut in England when Tillekeratne Dilshan was injured, only for Lahiru Thirimanne – in better form – to get the nod instead. Chandimal showed the selectors might have got that wrong with a cool ODI century at Lord's, but then failed to fire in the home one-dayers against Australia.

THE FACTS   Chandimal scored 111 in an ODI against India at Harare in June 2010, and 105 not out against England at Lord's in July 2011 ... He hit 64 on his first-class debut, and 109 in his second match, both against the New Zealand tourists in August 2009 ... Chandimal made 244 for Sri Lanka A v South Africa A in Colombo in August 2010 ... He scored 143 in an Under-19 Test against India when he was 17 ...

THE FIGURES *to 26.09.11*   ᴇꜱᴘɴ cricinfo.com

Batting & Fielding	M	Inns	NO	Runs	HS	Avge	S/R	100	50	4s	6s	Ct	St
Tests	0	0	–	–	–	–	–	–	–	–	–	–	–
ODIs	12	12	3	348	111	38.66	83.05	2	1	29	9	8	1
T20Is	7	6	0	83	29	13.83	103.75	0	0	6	2	0	0
First-class	35	55	7	2809	244	58.52	74.31	9	14	317	57	63	12

Bowling	M	Balls	Runs	Wkts	BB	Avge	RpO	S/R	5i	10m
Tests	0	0	–	–	–	–	–	–	–	–
ODIs	12	0	–	–	–	–	–	–	–	–
T20Is	7	0	–	–	–	–	–	–	–	–
First-class	35	12	5	0	–	–	2.50	–	0	0

ELTON **CHIGUMBURA**

ZIMBABWE

Full name	**Elton Chigumbura**
Born	**March 14, 1986, Kwekwe**
Teams	**Southern Rocks**
Style	**Right-hand bat, right-arm fast-medium bowler**
Test debut	**Zimbabwe v Sri Lanka at Harare 2004**
ODI debut	**Zimbabwe v Sri Lanka at Bulawayo 2004**
T20I debut	**Zimbabwe v Bangladesh at Khulna 2006-07**

THE PROFILE Elton Chigumbura, who was fast-tracked into the national side not long after his 18th birthday when several leading players fell out with the board, made his first-class debut in the Logan Cup when only 15. A genuine allrounder, he is a big hitter fond of the lofted drive, bowls at a sharp pace, and is an athletic fielder. He looked out of his depth in his first Test, in May 2004, but was more at home by the time of the Champions Trophy in England that September. Three years later he played a vital role in the shock victory over Australia at the inaugural World Twenty20 in South Africa, removing both openers and rotating the strike well as Zimbabwe squeaked home in the final over. Then, after a poor run, he pounded the Kenyans in Nairobi in 2009, smashing 79, 68, 43 and 36 in successive innings at a strike-rate well above 100, and picking up seven wickets for good measure. He followed that with three cheap wickets and an unbeaten 60 in the first match of a one-day series in Bangladesh. Early in 2010 Chigumbura took over as captain when Prosper Utseya stood down, but after a promising start – and a county stint with Northamptonshire – the responsibility seemed to affect him and his form fell away: in 20 matches in charge he failed to reach 50 and took only two wickets. He was replaced in 2011 by Brendan Taylor, but kept his place in the side, and chipped in with three important wickets in the historic Test-comeback victory over Bangladesh at Harare in August. But soon after that he injured his knee, and missed the matches against Pakistan.

THE FACTS Chigumbura scored 186 for Northerns v Westerns at Harare in April 2008 ... In May 2009 he hit 103 not out from 56 balls in a Twenty20 match for Northerns v Centrals at Bulawayo ... Chigumbura has the highest strike-rate of anyone who has scored 1000 runs in ODIs for Zimbabwe ... Against West Indies at Port-of-Spain in May 2006 he took four catches, all near the long-on boundary ...

THE FIGURES to 26.09.11   **ESPncricinfo.com**

Batting & Fielding	M	Inns	NO	Runs	HS	Avge	S/R	100	50	4s	6s	Ct	St
Tests	7	13	0	192	71	14.76	40.16	0	1	29	3	2	0
ODIs	136	127	14	2673	79	23.65	83.01	0	13	211	78	45	0
T20Is	16	15	1	199	34	14.21	143.16	0	0	15	11	7	0
First-class	76	132	9	4145	186	33.69	–	4	28	–	–	32	0

Bowling	M	Balls	Runs	Wkts	BB	Avge	RpO	S/R	5i	10m
Tests	7	1033	595	12	5–54	49.58	3.45	86.08	1	0
ODIs	136	3457	3404	88	4–28	38.68	5.90	39.28	0	0
T20Is	16	192	271	13	4–31	20.84	8.46	14.76	0	0
First-class	76	9192	5094	174	5–33	29.27	3.32	52.82	4	0

MICHAEL **CLARKE**

Full name	**Michael John Clarke**
Born	**April 2, 1981, Liverpool, New South Wales**
Teams	**New South Wales**
Style	**Right-hand bat, left-arm orthodox spinner**
Test debut	**Australia v India at Bangalore 2003-04**
ODI debut	**Australia v England at Adelaide 2002-03**
T20I debut	**Australia v New Zealand at Auckland 2004-05**

THE PROFILE Michael Clarke was being touted as an Australian captain before he'd even played a Test. And when he marked his debut with 151 against India in October 2004, his future looked even brighter than the yellow motorbike he received as Man of the Match. Another thrilling century followed on his home debut, and his first Test season ended with the Allan Border Medal. Then came the fall. Barely a year later he was dropped after 15 centuryless Tests. He was told to tighten his technique, especially early on against swing. Clarke remained a one-day regular, but had to wait until the low-key Bangladesh series early in 2006 to reclaim that Test spot. He cemented his place with two tons in the 2006-07 Ashes whitewash, did well in the World Cup, and scored a century in each of Australia's three Test series in 2007-08: he has been a fixture ever since. In England in 2009 Clarke was the classiest batsman on show, finishing with two centuries and a near-miss (93). Soon afterwards he was entrusted with the Twenty20 captaincy, and took over as Test skipper too after the 2010-11 Ashes debacle. He started as a ravishing shotmaker who did not so much take guard as take off: he radiated a pointy-elbowed elegance reminiscent of the young Greg Chappell or Mark Waugh, who both also waited uncomplainingly for Test openings then started with hundreds. His bouncy fielding and searing run-outs, often from square on, add to his value, while his slow left-armers can surprise (they once shocked six Indians in a Test). A cricket nut since he was in nappies, "Pup" honed his technique against the bowling machine at his dad's indoor centre.

THE FACTS Clarke scored a century on his Test debut, 151 v India at Bangalore in 2004-05, and the following month added another in his first home Test, 141 v New Zealand at Brisbane: only two other batsmen (Harry Graham and Kepler Wessels) have done this for Australia ... Clarke averages 64.21 in ODIs against Sri Lanka, but only 15.50 v Scotland (and 0.00 v Ireland) ... He took 6 for 9 in a Test against India at Mumbai in November 2004...

THE FIGURES *to 26.09.11*   **ESPN**cricinfo.com

Batting & Fielding	M	Inns	NO	Runs	HS	Avge	S/R	100	50	4s	6s	Ct	St
Tests	72	119	12	4956	168	46.31	53.23	15	21	547	23	74	0
ODIs	203	185	42	6551	130	45.81	78.12	6	49	529	38	78	0
T20Is	34	28	5	488	67	21.21	103.17	0	1	29	10	13	0
First-class	133	227	21	9240	201*	44.85	–	31	36	–	–	132	0

Bowling	M	Balls	Runs	Wkts	BB	Avge	RpO	S/R	5i	10m
Tests	72	1758	854	21	6–9	40.66	2.91	83.71	1	0
ODIs	203	2307	1948	52	5–35	37.46	5.06	44.36	1	0
T20Is	34	156	225	6	1–2	37.50	8.65	26.00	0	0
First-class	133	2938	1542	32	6–9	48.18	3.14	91.81	1	0

ALASTAIR **COOK**

ENGLAND

Full name **Alastair Nathan Cook**
Born **December 25, 1984, Gloucester**
Teams **Essex**
Style **Left-hand bat, occasional offspinner**
Test debut **England v India at Nagpur 2005-06**
ODI debut **England v Sri Lanka at Manchester 2006**
T20I debut **England v West Indies at The Oval 2007**

THE PROFILE Wise judges were saying that the tall, dark and handsome Alastair Cook was destined for great things very early on. A left-hander strong on the pull, Cook was thrown in at the deep end by Essex the year after leaving Bedford School with a fistful of batting records, and has barely looked back since. He makes his runs with a languid ease reminiscent of David Gower, if slightly more stiff-legged. His early England career was full of successes, although a barren spell in 2010 – he looked vulnerable around off stump, with a tendency to play around the front pad – briefly threatened his place before a century against Pakistan at The Oval saved his skin. But the rest, as they say, is history: he piled up 766 runs in the 2010-11 Ashes triumph, and carried on like that at home, making a colossal 294 against India at Edgbaston. It's frightening to imagine what figures he could achieve if he stays fit: by the time he turned 27 he had 19 Test centuries (England's record is 22). Cook was in the Caribbean with the A team when the original England SOS came early in 2006, after a crop of injuries: he flew to India and, unfazed, stroked 60 and an unbeaten 104 in a memorable debut in Nagpur. Cook lost his one-day place for a while, not helped by some occasionally ponderous fielding, and missed the 2011 World Cup, but he returned to the side at home ... as captain, after Andrew Strauss stood down. Cook showed signs that he could up the tempo if required, with successive innings of 119 and 95 against Sri Lanka, and a rapid 80 not out from 63 balls to subdue India again.

THE FACTS Cook was the 16th England batsman to make a century on Test debut ... He made 766 runs against Australia in 2010-11, a number exceeded in an Ashes series only by Don Bradman (twice), Wally Hammond and Mark Taylor ... Cook's stand of 127 with Marcus Trescothick v Sri Lanka at Lord's in 2006 was the second-highest in Tests by unrelated players who share a birthday (they were both born on Christmas Day), behind 163 by Vic Stollmeyer and Kenneth Weekes (both born Jan 24) for West Indies at The Oval in 1939 ...

THE FIGURES to 26.09.11   ᴇsᴘᴨ cricinfo.com

Batting & Fielding	M	Inns	NO	Runs	HS	Avge	S/R	100	50	4s	6s	Ct	St
Tests	72	125	7	5868	294	49.72	49.06	19	26	677	5	64	0
ODIs	36	36	2	1325	119	38.97	78.44	2	8	147	2	14	0
T20Is	4	4	0	61	26	15.25	112.96	0	0	10	0	1	0
First-class	156	276	21	12094	294	47.42	53.52	35	60	–	–	147	0

Bowling	M	Balls	Runs	Wkts	BB	Avge	RpO	S/R	5i	10m
Tests	72	6	1	0	–	–	1.00	–	0	0
ODIs	36	0	–	–	–	–	–	–	–	–
T20Is	4	0	–	–	–	–	–	–	–	–
First-class	156	270	205	6	3–13	34.16	4.55	45.00	0	0

TRENT **COPELAND**

Full name **Trent Aaron Copeland**
Born **March 14, 1986, Gosford, New South Wales**
Teams **New South Wales**
Style **Right-hand bat, right-arm fast-medium bowler**
Test debut **Australia v Sri Lanka at Galle 2011**
ODI debut **No ODIs yet**
T20I debut **No T20Is yet**

THE PROFILE   Trent Copeland is a tall (6ft 5ins/195cm) fast bowler who has the happy knack of starting well. On his first-class debut for New South Wales in January 2010, he ran through Queensland's batting at the SCG, finishing with the eye-popping figures of 8 for 92. Only Clarrie Grimmett, with 8 for 12 for Victoria in 1923-24, had better figures in his first Sheffield Shield match. Copeland took two more in the second innings – oddly two of the batsmen who'd escaped his clutches in the first – to finish with ten for 149, although Queensland had the last laugh, winning by 168 runs. Copeland finished his maiden season with 35 wickets at 17.57, and took 45 more wickets in 2010-11, which earned him an Australia A place. He did well enough in Zimbabwe in July 2011 to be promoted to the full tour of Sri Lanka that followed, and 5 for 47 – four of them Test batsmen – against a Board XI in a warm-up game got him into the side for the first Test. And he started well again, dismissing Tillekeratne Dilshan with his second ball. That was his only wicket of the match, but he retained his place for the next Test, when his three wickets included Dilshan cheaply again. Copeland actually started in Sydney grade cricket as a wicketkeeper, with St George's third team. In 2005 he gave up the gloves to concentrate on his batting, but that allowed him the occasional trundle. In only his second spell he transformed what had looked like a dead game by taking four wickets for one run, all with reverse-swinging yorkers. A bowler was born, and he didn't stay in the thirds for long.

THE FACTS   Copeland took a wicket (Tillekeratne Dilshan) with his second ball in Test cricket, against Sri Lanka at Galle in August 2011 ... On his first-class debut in January 2010 Copeland took 8 for 92 for New South Wales against Queensland at Sydney, and finished with ten wickets in the match: he ended his first season second in the national averages with 35 wickets at 17.97 ...

THE FIGURES to 26.09.11   **ESPN**cricinfo.com

Batting & Fielding	M	Inns	NO	Runs	HS	Avge	S/R	100	50	4s	6s	Ct	St
Tests	3	4	1	39	23*	13.00	50.64	0	0	7	0	2	0
ODIs	0	0	–	–	–	–	–	–	–	–	–	–	–
T20Is	0	0	–	–	–	–	–	–	–	–	–	–	–
First-class	21	24	6	239	53	13.27	52.06	0	1	34	0	15	0

Bowling	M	Balls	Runs	Wkts	BB	Avge	RpO	S/R	5i	10m
Tests	3	648	227	6	2–24	37.83	2.10	108.00	0	0
ODIs	0	0	–	–	–	–	–	–	–	–
T20Is	0	0	–	–	–	–	–	–	–	–
First-class	21	5389	2175	99	8–92	21.96	2.42	54.43	5	1

AB de VILLIERS

SOUTH AFRICA

Full name	**Abraham Benjamin de Villiers**
Born	**February 17, 1984, Pretoria**
Teams	**Titans, Royal Challengers Bangalore**
Style	**Right-hand bat, occ. medium-pacer, wicketkeeper**
Test debut	**South Africa v England at Port Elizabeth 2004-05**
ODI debut	**South Africa v England at Bloemfontein 2004-05**
T20I debut	**South Africa v Australia at Johannesburg 2005-06**

THE PROFILE A batsman of breathtaking chutzpah and enterprise, as well as the skills and the temperament required to back up his creative intent. A fielder able to leap tall buildings and still come up with the catch. A wicketkeeper who is perfectly at ease donning pads and gloves. A fine rugby player, golfer, and tennis player. All AB de Villiers needs to show off his abundant gifts is a ball ... just about any ball. Cricket should be pleased to have him. Few drive the ball as sweetly and to the boundary as regularly, and – in South Africa, at any rate – even fewer possess the silkily snappy footwork required to put spinners in their place. He adjusts seamlessly to all formats, averaging in the mid-forties in both Tests and ODIs. His potential was recognised years before he made the leap to senior international level as an opening batsman against England in 2004-05. After a brief slump in form in 2006 and 2007, de Villiers returned to the straight and narrow early in 2008 with a blistering 103 not out off 109 balls against West Indies at Durban. Later that year came his career highlight to date, an undefeated 217 at Ahmedabad, South Africa's first double-century against India. South Africans do not take easily to the precociously talented, but it helps if they do not come across all precocious. Such is the case with de Villiers, whose lazy smile under an every-which-way thatch of blond hair has helped convince the nation that he's worth feeding despite all that talent. He obviously convinced the selectors, anyway, because he was appointed limited-overs captain in 2011.

THE FACTS de Villiers made 217 not out at Ahmedabad in April 2008, after India had been bowled out for 76 ... He averages 79.76 in Tests against West Indies, but 17.25 in four matches against Bangladesh ... de Villiers went a Test-record 78 innings before falling for a duck, against Bangladesh at Centurion in November 2008 ... His record includes five ODIs for the Africa XI ...

THE FIGURES *to 26.09.11*   **ESPN**cricinfo.com

Batting & Fielding	M	Inns	NO	Runs	HS	Avge	S/R	100	50	4s	6s	Ct	St
Tests	66	113	13	4741	278*	47.41	53.74	12	23	538	37	93	1
ODIs	119	115	16	4523	146	45.68	91.29	11	26	427	76	86	2
T20Is	33	32	6	604	79*	23.23	123.01	0	4	44	20	32	4
First-class	90	156	18	6590	278*	47.75	56.49	15	37	–	–	139	2

Bowling	M	Balls	Runs	Wkts	BB	Avge	RpO	S/R	5i	10m
Tests	66	198	99	2	2–49	49.50	3.00	99.00	0	0
ODIs	119	12	22	0	–	–	11.00	–	0	0
T20Is	33	0	–	–	–	–	–	–	–	–
First-class	90	228	133	2	2–49	66.50	3.50	114.00	0	0

JADE **DERNBACH**

Full name	**Jade Winston Dernbach**
Born	**April 3, 1986, Johannesburg, South Africa**
Teams	**Surrey**
Style	**Right-hand bat, right-arm fast-medium bowler**
Test debut	**No Tests yet**
ODI debut	**England v Sri Lanka at The Oval 2011**
T20I debut	**England v Sri Lanka at Bristol 2011**

THE PROFILE Jade Dernbach was born in South Africa, but his family came to England when he was 14, and he considers himself very English: "I don't owe anything to South Africa. I was just born there, did a bit of schooling there. My whole cricket career has been based in the UK." And his professional cricket has been for Surrey, as a fast-medium bowler of modest pace but a lot of variety. His speciality is the slower ball, which Surrey's manager Chris Adams describes as "an X-factor delivery – it has a very special variance, dynamite and unusual, an exceptional disguise". If that sounds a lot to live up to, the man they call "Dirtbag" has largely managed it so far. He made his first-team debut at 17, and matured quickly to be Surrey's leading first-class wicket-taker in 2006 with 46. A spell in Australia, playing grade cricket in Sydney, helped improve his allround game, and his first hint of international recognition came in 2009, when he was called up to the ECB Fast Bowling Programme in Florida and Chennai. He was part of the Performance squad which shadowed the successful main one during the 2010-11 Ashes tour, and was playing for the England Lions in the West Indies when he was called up for the World Cup as a replacement for the injured Ajmal Shahzad. England departed the competition almost immediately he arrived, but Dernbach stayed in the reckoning, and made his international debut at home in 2011. He took 4 for 22 in a Twenty20 game against India, but wickets were rarer in the 50-overs games. Still, Dernbach had established himself as a handy back-up performer, and earned an incremental England contract.

THE FACTS Dernbach took 6 for 47 for Surrey at Leicester in June 2009 ... He took a wicket (Sanath Jayasuriya of Sri Lanka) with his eighth delivery in Twenty20 internationals, and three days later took one with his ninth ball in ODIs (Angelo Mathews) ... Dernbach's bowling arm is covered in tattoos – "everything from Chinese script to a fish," according to *The Sun* ...

THE FIGURES *to 26.09.11*   ESPncricinfo.com

Batting & Fielding	M	Inns	NO	Runs	HS	Avge	S/R	100	50	4s	6s	Ct	St
Tests	0	0	–	–	–	–	–	–	–	–	–	–	–
ODIs	10	2	1	8	5	8.00	72.72	0	0	1	0	1	0
T20Is	4	1	0	3	3	3.00	75.00	0	0	0	0	1	0
First-class	65	78	29	478	56*	9.75	–	0	1	–	–	8	0

Bowling	M	Balls	Runs	Wkts	BB	Avge	RpO	S/R	5i	10m
Tests	0	0	–	–	–	–	–	–	–	–
ODIs	10	486	497	15	3–30	33.13	6.13	32.40	0	0
T20Is	4	82	79	7	4–22	11.28	5.78	11.71	0	0
First-class	65	10326	5927	182	6–47	32.56	3.44	56.73	9	0

MAHENDRA SINGH **DHONI**

Full name **Mahendra Singh Dhoni**
Born **July 7, 1981, Ranchi, Bihar**
Teams **Jharkhand, Chennai Super Kings**
Style **Right-hand bat, wicketkeeper**
Test debut **India v Sri Lanka at Chennai 2005-06**
ODI debut **India v Bangladesh at Chittagong 2004-05**
T20I debut **India v South Africa at Johannesburg 2006-07**

THE PROFILE The odds against a Virender Sehwag clone emerging from the backwaters of Jharkhand were highly remote – until MS Dhoni arrived (a one-time railway ticket collector, his first love was football). His batting is swashbuckling, and his wicketkeeping usually secure. It wasn't until 2004 that he became a serious contender: there was a rapid hundred as East Zone clinched the Deodhar Trophy, an audacious 60 in the Duleep Trophy final, and two tons against Pakistan A which established him as a clinical destroyer of bowling attacks. In just his fifth ODI – against Pakistan in April 2005 – Dhoni cracked a dazzling 148, putting even Sehwag in the shade, and followed that with 183 against Sri Lanka in November, beating Adam Gilchrist's highest ODI score by a wicketkeeper. He made an instant impact in Tests, too, pounding 148 at Faisalabad in his fifth match, when India were struggling to avoid the follow-on. His keeping improved, and he quickly became key in a revitalised side. He stepped up to captain India to the inaugural World Twenty20 title in September 2007, and was then the most expensive signing ($1.5million) for the inaugural IPL in 2008. He took over as full-time Test captain when Anil Kumble retired that November, rubber-stamping victory over Australia then defeating England and New Zealand in short series. He won eight of his first 11 Tests – an unprecedented start for an Indian skipper – then turned his attention to 50-over cricket, leading from the front with the bat to make sure the 2011 World Cup was won. After that, though, his reputation took a severe knock in England, as India subsided to 4-0 whitewash and surrendered their hard-won No. 1 Test ranking to their conquerors.

THE FACTS Dhoni's unbeaten 183 against Sri Lanka at Jaipur in November 2005 is the highest score in ODIs by a wicketkeeper, and included 120 in boundaries (10 sixes and 15 fours) ... Dhoni won eight of his first 11 Tests as captain, and didn't lose any ... The only other Indian to score a century in an ODI in which he kept wicket is Rahul Dravid ... Dhoni's record includes three ODIs for the Asia XI ...

THE FIGURES to 26.09.11   **ESPNcricinfo.com**

Batting & Fielding	M	Inns	NO	Runs	HS	Avge	S/R	100	50	4s	6s	Ct	St
Tests	61	95	10	3242	148	38.14	59.67	4	23	356	55	173	25
ODIs	191	171	44	6285	183*	49.48	87.88	7	41	484	127	181	60
T20Is	27	26	8	459	46	25.50	111.40	0	0	27	13	11	4
First-class	102	161	13	5404	148	36.51	–	7	37	–	–	281	44

Bowling	M	Balls	Runs	Wkts	BB	Avge	RpO	S/R	5i	10m
Tests	61	78	58	0	–	–	4.46	–	0	0
ODIs	191	12	14	1	1-14	14.00	7.00	12.00	0	0
T20Is	27	0	–	–	–	–	–	–	–	–
First-class	102	108	78	0	–	–	4.33	–	0	0

TILLEKERATNE **DILSHAN**

Full name	**Tillekeratne Mudiyanselage Dilshan**
Born	**October 14, 1976, Kalutara**
Teams	**Bloomfield, Basnahira, Royal Challengers Bangalore**
Style	**Right-hand bat, offspinner**
Test debut	**Sri Lanka v Zimbabwe at Bulawayo 1999-2000**
ODI debut	**Sri Lanka v Zimbabwe at Bulawayo 1999-2000**
T20I debut	**Sri Lanka v England at Southampton 2006**

THE PROFILE Tillekeratne Mudiyanselage Dilshan, who started life as Tuwan Mohamad Dilshan before converting to Buddhism, is a light-footed right-hander who made an unbeaten 163 against Zimbabwe in only his second Test in November 1999.

Technically sound, comfortable against pace, with quick feet and strong wrists, Dilshan has talent in abundance. But that bright start was followed by a frustrating time when he was shovelled up and down the order, and in and out of the side. After a lean series against England in 2001 he didn't play another Test until late 2003. He returned determined to play his own aggressive game, and was immediately successful. He continued to do well, and was one of four centurions in an innings victory over India in July 2008. He put a lean one-day trot behind him just in time for the 2007 World Cup, then against Bangladesh at Chittagong in January 2009 hit 162 and 143 then wrapped up the match with four wickets. Later that year Dilshan lit up the World Twenty20 in England with some spectacular batting, including his own trademark cheeky scoop over the shoulder. He made ten international centuries in 2009, although the following year was rather less spectacular. On the march to the 2011 World Cup final he was in fine form, scoring two centuries, and inherited the captaincy shortly afterwards when Kumar Sangakkara stepped down. Dilshan led from the front in England, making a superb 193 in the Lord's Test before a broken hand slowed him down – but he was back for the Australians' visit later in the year. Dilshan, who started out as a wicketkeeper, is an electric fielder, and once effected four run-outs in an ODI at Adelaide.

THE FACTS Dilshan's 193 in 2011 was Sri Lanka's highest score in a Test at Lord's ... He scored 168 against Bangladesh in Colombo in September 2005: he put on 280 with Thilan Samaraweera, a Sri Lankan fifth-wicket record in Tests ... Dilshan made his first ODI century in the record total of 443 for 9 against the Netherlands at Amstelveen in July 2006 ... He made 200 not out while captaining North Central Province v Central in Colombo in February 2005 ...

THE FIGURES to 26.09.11   ᴇsᴘɴcricinfo.com

Batting & Fielding	M	Inns	NO	Runs	HS	Avge	S/R	100	50	4s	6s	Ct	St
Tests	71	113	11	4382	193	42.96	65.68	12	18	539	20	75	0
ODIs	214	190	30	5616	160	35.10	87.44	10	23	579	35	89	1
T20Is	34	33	6	866	104*	32.07	125.32	1	5	104	17	14	2
First-class	208	336	22	12348	200*	39.32	–	33	51	–	–	339	23

Bowling	M	Balls	Runs	Wkts	BB	Avge	RpO	S/R	5i	10m
Tests	71	1820	899	24	4–10	37.45	2.96	75.83	0	0
ODIs	214	3385	2684	63	4–4	42.60	4.75	53.73	0	0
T20Is	34	138	177	4	2–4	44.25	7.69	34.50	0	0
First-class	208	4540	2214	68	5–49	32.55	2.92	66.76	1	0

RAHUL **DRAVID**

INDIA

Full name	**Rahul Sharad Dravid**
Born	**January 11, 1973, Indore, Madhya Pradesh**
Teams	**Karnataka, Rajasthan Royals**
Style	**Right-hand bat, occasional wicketkeeper**
Test debut	**India v England at Lord's 1996**
ODI debut	**India v Sri Lanka at Singapore 1995-96**
T20I debut	**India v England at Manchester 2011**

THE PROFILE Rahul Dravid has scored more than 10,000 runs in both Tests and ODIs at imposing averages – but impressive as his stats are, they don't show his importance, or the beauty of his batting. When he started, he was pigeonholed as a blocker (an early nickname was "The Wall"), but he grew in stature, reaching maturity under Sourav Ganguly's captaincy. As a New India emerged, so did a new Dravid: first, he became an astute one-day finisher, then produced several superb Test performances. His golden phase really began with a supporting act, at Kolkata early in 2001, when his 180 helped VVS Laxman create history against Australia. But after that Dravid became India's most valuable player: at one point he hit four double-centuries in eight months, finishing with an epic 270 to seal the 2004 Pakistan tour with a victory. In October 2005 he was appointed as one-day captain, began with a 6-1 hammering of Sri Lanka at home, and soon succeeded Ganguly as Test skipper too. He continued to score well, and bounced back from the crushing disappointment of early exit from the 2007 World Cup by leading India to a rare series victory in England, although his own batting lacked sparkle. He relinquished the captaincy after that, but the spark was missing: he lost his one-day place, but just as serious questions were being asked about his Test future, Dravid ground out 136 in nearly eight hours against England at Mohali, to ensure a series victory in December 2008. His touch returned: by 2011 he was 38, but three Test centuries in an almost singlehanded resistance against England showed that "The Wall" wasn't ready to be demolished just yet.

THE FACTS Dravid hit centuries in four successive Test innings in 2002, three in England and one against West Indies ... He kept wicket in 73 ODIs ... Unusually, Dravid averages more in away Tests (54.71) than at home in India (50.75) ... He averages 97.90 in Tests against Zimbabwe, but only 33.83 v South Africa ... Dravid's record includes one Test and three ODIs for the World XI, and one ODI for the Asia XI ...

THE FIGURES to 26.09.11   **ESPncricinfo.com**

Batting & Fielding	M	Inns	NO	Runs	HS	Avge	S/R	100	50	4s	6s	Ct	St
Tests	157	273	32	12775	270	53.00	42.45	35	60	1602	19	207	0
ODIs	344	318	40	10889	153	39.16	71.24	12	83	950	42	196	14
T20Is	1	1	0	31	31	31.00	147.61	0	0	0	3	0	0
First-class	291	484	67	23281	270	55.82	–	67	114	–	–	350	1

Bowling	M	Balls	Runs	Wkts	BB	Avge	RpO	S/R	5i	10m
Tests	157	120	39	1	1–18	39.00	1.95	120.00	0	0
ODIs	344	186	170	4	2–43	42.50	5.48	46.50	0	0
T20Is	1	0	–	–	–	–	–	–	–	–
First-class	291	617	273	5	2–16	54.60	2.65	123.40	0	0

J-P **DUMINY**

Full name **Jean-Paul Duminy**
Born **April 14, 1984, Strandfontein, Cape Town**
Teams **Cape Cobras, Deccan Chargers**
Style **Left-hand bat, occasional offspinner**
Test debut **South Africa v Australia at Perth 2008-09**
ODI debut **South Africa v Sri Lanka at Colombo 2004-05**
T20I debut **South Africa v Bangladesh at Cape Town 2007-08**

SOUTH AFRICA

THE PROFILE Slightly built but stylish, left-hander Jean-Paul Duminy had trouble finding a place in South Africa's strong middle order – but when an injury to Ashwell Prince finally let him into the Test side in Australia late in 2008, more than four years after his one-day debut, he certainly made it count. First Duminy stroked a nerveless 50 not out as his side made light of a target of 414 to start with victory at Perth, then he set up a series-winning victory at Melbourne with a superb 166, most of it coming during an eye-popping ninth-wicket stand of 180 with Dale Steyn. A four-hour 73 followed in the return series in a defeat at Durban: Duminy had arrived, a fact confirmed by a big-money IPL contract. He had first featured in a one-day series in Sri Lanka in 2004. He struggled there, scoring only 29 runs in five attempts, and dropped off the national radar for a couple of years. But he continued to make runs at home, and was given an extended one-day run after the 2007 World Cup, showing signs of developing into a late-innings "finisher": he batted into the final over in three successive victories against West Indies. He finished that series with 227 runs at 113.50, although he was less of a hit in England later in 2008. A horror run in Tests in 2009-10 – only one score above 11 in nine innings – cost him his place, but Duminy remained a one-day fixture, missing a century against Ireland during the 2011 World Cup by just one run. He is also a superb fielder, while his part-time offbreaks occasionally come in handy.

THE FACTS Duminy scored 169 as Cape Cobras followed on against the Eagles at Stellenbosch in February 2007 ... He scored 200 not out – with nine sixes – for the Cobras against the Dolphins at Paarl in December 2010 ... Both Duminy's ODI hundreds have come at Zimbabwe's expense ... Against Ireland in 2011 he became only the second man (after Adam Gilchrist) to be out for 99 in a World Cup match ...

THE FIGURES to 26.09.11   **ᴇsᴘɴcricinfo.com**

Batting & Fielding	M	Inns	NO	Runs	HS	Avge	S/R	100	50	4s	6s	Ct	St
Tests	12	20	2	518	166	28.77	40.91	1	3	61	3	12	0
ODIs	78	71	18	2194	129	41.39	85.07	2	13	137	27	31	0
T20Is	30	29	8	648	96*	30.85	126.31	0	3	54	21	15	0
First-class	63	105	18	4374	200*	50.27	50.09	13	22	–	–	48	0

Bowling	M	Balls	Runs	Wkts	BB	Avge	RpO	S/R	5i	10m
Tests	12	671	408	11	3–89	37.09	3.64	61.00	0	0
ODIs	78	943	789	20	3–31	39.45	5.02	47.15	0	0
T20Is	30	72	104	5	1–3	20.80	8.66	14.40	0	0
First-class	63	2402	1419	37	5–108	38.35	3.54	64.91	1	0

FIDEL **EDWARDS**

Full name	**Fidel Henderson Edwards**
Born	**February 6, 1982, Gays, St Peter, Barbados**
Teams	**Barbados**
Style	**Right-hand bat, right-arm fast bowler**
Test debut	**West Indies v Sri Lanka at Kingston 2002-03**
ODI debut	**West Indies v Zimbabwe at Harare 2003-04**
T20I debut	**West Indies v South Africa at Johannesburg 2007-08**

THE PROFILE Fidel Edwards had an extraordinary start in international cricket, the kind that can either haunt or add lustre to a career. He was spotted in the nets by Brian Lara early in 2003, and called up for his Test debut after only one match for Barbados: he promptly took five wickets against Sri Lanka. He added five in his first overseas Test, and six in his debut one-dayer. Edwards has a slingy round-arm action which leaves him vulnerable to back strains, and indeed he missed most of 2010 after back surgery to correct a slipped disc, which raised questions about his international future – but he roared back in mid-2011 with 19 wickets in three Tests against India. When he's fit, though, his unusual action and slippery pace has troubled many a distinguished batsman. Edwards bowls fast, can swing the ball and reverse it too, but insists that he doesn't go for out-and-out pace – which is just as well, because he has learned that pace without control leads straight to the boundary at international level. He showed his increased maturity with a testing spell in Antigua in June 2006 that had India's Virender Sehwag in all kinds of trouble before a hamstring twanged. And he hurried England's batsmen up in 2007, taking nine wickets in two Tests and ten – including 5 for 45 at Lord's – as West Indies won the one-day series 2-1. After that he grabbed eight more, including both openers in both innings, in the first Test against Australia at Kingston in May 2008. He's not much of a batsman, yet twice hung on tenaciously to deny England series-levelling victories in the Caribbean early in 2009.

THE FACTS Edwards had played only one first-class match – taking one wicket – before his Test debut against Sri Lanka at Kingston in June 2003, when he took 5 for 36 ... He later took 6 for 22 on his ODI debut, against Zimbabwe at Harare in November 2003 ... Edwards opened the bowling in Tests several times with his half-brother Pedro Collins ... Edwards averages 21.38 with the ball in Tests against India, but 90.36 in eight matches against South Africa ... Unoriginally, his nickname is "Castro" ...

THE FIGURES *to 26.09.11*   ESPNcricinfo.com

Batting & Fielding	M	Inns	NO	Runs	HS	Avge	S/R	100	50	4s	6s	Ct	St
Tests	46	74	22	303	30	5.82	25.61	0	0	36	2	8	0
ODIs	50	22	14	73	13	9.12	45.62	0	0	5	0	4	0
T20Is	13	3	2	10	7*	10.00	125.00	0	0	1	0	2	0
First-class	72	110	37	468	40	6.41	–	0	0	–	–	13	0

Bowling	M	Balls	Runs	Wkts	BB	Avge	RpO	S/R	5i	10m
Tests	46	7945	5191	141	7–87	36.81	3.92	56.34	10	0
ODIs	50	2138	1812	60	6–22	30.20	5.08	35.63	2	0
T20Is	13	231	333	10	3–24	33.30	8.64	23.10	0	0
First-class	72	11656	7537	228	7–87	33.05	3.87	51.12	13	1

KIRK **EDWARDS**

Full name	**Kirk Anton Edwards**
Born	**Nov 3, 1984, Mile and a Quarter, St Peter, Barbados**
Teams	**Barbados**
Style	**Right-hand bat**
Test debut	**West Indies v India at Roseau 2011**
ODI debut	**West Indies v India at Chennai 2010-11**
T20I debut	**No T20Is yet**

THE PROFILE Kirk Edwards announced himself on the world stage in style, becoming only the 13th West Indian to score a century on his Test debut, joining the likes of George Headley, Lawrence Rowe and Gordon Greenidge. Born into a cricket-loving family, Edwards started playing when he was very young, and piled up runs in age-group cricket. After impressive performances for the Barbados Under-19s, he was selected for the 2004 Under-19 World Cup. Two years later he made his first-class debut, but had to wait until 2009 for his maiden first-class hundred, against the Windward Islands. In 2010 he toured Bangladesh and England with West Indies A, scoring 147 in a 50-over match against the England Lions at Northampton. More runs for the A team won him selection for the one-day leg of the senior tour of Sri Lanka late in 2010, but that was rained off. In February 2011, a timely 171 against the England Lions led to a summons to the World Cup after Adrian Barath was injured, but Edwards only played one game. He did feature in the home one-dayers that followed, against Pakistan and India, but never got past 40, and it was something of a surprise when he was chosen for the third Test against India in Dominica. He showed wise judgment (and a certain amount of cheek) by asking two of the opposition's best batsmen, Rahul Dravid and VVS Laxman, for batting tips before the match – and made them rue their advice by batting for almost five hours in the second innings for 110, overcoming early problems against shorter deliveries, as West Indies built a match-saving total.

THE FACTS Edwards was the 13th West Indian to score a hundred on Test debut ... His century was the first in a Test at Roseau in Dominica ... Edwards scored 171 for Barbados against the England Lions at Bridgetown in February 2011 ... His first bowl in first-class cricket came during his Test debut ...

THE FIGURES *to 26.09.11*   **ESPncricinfo.com**

Batting & Fielding	M	Inns	NO	Runs	HS	Avge	S/R	100	50	4s	6s	Ct	St
Tests	1	2	0	116	110	58.00	51.78	1	0	9	1	0	0
ODIs	9	9	1	153	40*	19.12	59.30	0	0	8	3	0	0
T20Is	0	0	–	–	–	–	–	–	–	–	–	–	–
First-class	27	48	3	1885	171	41.88	–	3	13	–	–	13	0

Bowling	M	Balls	Runs	Wkts	BB	Avge	RpO	S/R	5i	10m
Tests	1	24	19	0	–	–	4.75	–	0	0
ODIs	9	0	–	–	–	–	–	–	–	–
T20Is	0	0	–	–	–	–	–	–	–	–
First-class	27	24	19	0	–	–	4.75	–	0	0

GRANT **ELLIOTT**

NEW ZEALAND

Full name	**Grant David Elliott**
Born	**March 21, 1979, Johannesburg, South Africa**
Teams	**Wellington**
Style	**Right-hand bat, right-arm medium-pacer**
Test debut	**New Zealand v England at Napier 2007-08**
ODI debut	**New Zealand v England at Edgbaston 2008**
T20I debut	**New Zealand v Australia at Sydney 2008-09**

THE PROFILE Grant Elliott left his native South Africa for New Zealand in 2001 looking for new horizons, and found them in March 2008 when he was named in NZ's Test squad less than a year after completing his residency qualification. He won his first cap in the final Test against England after Jacob Oram was injured, but was not an instant success, with two batting failures and a solitary wicket, although he made the squad for the one-dayers in England later in the year. A compact and correct batsman, and a swing bowler of modest pace, albeit from a nice high action, Elliott enjoyed a productive season for Wellington in 2006-07, with 361 runs at 45.12, and backed that up with 565 at 37.66 the following year. In England in 2008 he took three wickets in the second ODI, and made 56 in the third, but it was his controversial run-out in the fourth one at The Oval which made all the headlines – after he collided with the bowler while trying a quick single Elliott was lying on the ground clutching his thigh when the bails were removed, and England's captain Paul Collingwood declined to withdraw the appeal. Elliott stomped off, and later the dressing-room door was firmly shut in Collingwood's face. Elliott made more of a mark with the bat in Australia in 2008-09, following a matchwinning 61 not out at Melbourne with a superb rearguard 115 at Sydney. Wickets still proved hard to come by, but he looked to have cemented a one-day place. But a hand injury restricted him in 2009-10, and he lost his national contract. He bounced back the following season with some consistent scoring, although he missed the 2011 World Cup.

THE FACTS Elliott scored 196 not out for Wellington v Auckland in April 2008 ... He made 115 in an ODI against Australia at Sydney in February 2009 ... Elliott represented South Africa in the Under-19 World Cup in 1997-98 ... His maiden first-class century came for Griqualand West against Bangladesh at Kimberley in October 2000 ...

THE FIGURES *to 26.09.11*   **ESPncricinfo.com**

Batting & Fielding	M	Inns	NO	Runs	HS	Avge	S/R	100	50	4s	6s	Ct	St
Tests	5	9	1	86	25	10.75	26.70	0	0	3	0	2	0
ODIs	37	28	6	716	115	32.54	69.78	1	4	48	4	6	0
T20Is	1	1	1	23	23*	–	76.66	0	0	1	0	0	0
First-class	59	95	4	2814	196*	30.92	–	6	16	–	–	31	0

Bowling	M	Balls	Runs	Wkts	BB	Avge	RpO	S/R	5i	10m
Tests	5	282	140	4	2–8	35.00	2.97	70.50	0	0
ODIs	37	573	464	19	4–31	24.42	4.85	30.15	0	0
T20Is	1	6	11	1	1–11	11.00	11.00	6.00	0	0
First-class	59	5920	2695	74	4–56	36.41	2.73	80.00	0	0

SHAMINDA **ERANGA**

Full name	**Ranaweera Mudiyanselage Shaminda Eranga**
Born	**June 23, 1986, Chilaw**
Teams	**Chilaw Marians, Uva**
Style	**Right-hand bat, right-arm fast-medium bowler**
Test debut	**Sri Lanka v Australia at Colombo 2011**
ODI debut	**Sri Lanka v Australia at Hambantota 2011**
T20I debut	**No T20Is yet**

THE PROFILE A brisk fast-medium bowler who can nudge 90mph on the speed-gun, Shaminda Eranga made a spectacular start in international cricket, dismissing Brad Haddin with his second ball in ODIs (and adding Ricky Ponting a few overs later). A month later, called up for the third Test against Australia, he went one better, taking a wicket with his first ball, a widish delivery which Shane Watson obligingly sliced to backward point. Eranga will hope to last longer than the only other Sri Lankan to strike with his first ball in a Test – Chamila Gamage, who did it in 2002, won only one more cap and finished with just five wickets. Eranga has that many after his first Test, adding Michael Clarke, Mike Hussey and Haddin (again) to a distinguished bag to finish with 4 for 65 in the first innings. He was spotted in 2006 at an all-island pace-bowling competition by the former Test fast bowler Champaka Ramanayake. Eranga, who is also a handy tailend batsman, joined the Chilaw Marians, and while his early displays weren't exactly earth-shattering he did enough to earn a place in the national development squad. He made his debut for Sri Lanka A in 2010, and was named in the squad for a Test against West Indies late that year, although he didn't play in the end. "This young lad is fit and looks a willing horse," observed Aravinda de Silva, Sri Lanka's chief selector. In 2011, after some good displays for the A team on tour in England – he took seven wickets in the match against Durham – Eranga was flown back to Sri Lanka to join up with the main squad for the Australian series.

THE FACTS Eranga was the second Sri Lankan (after Chamila Gamage) to take a wicket with his first ball in a Test match, dismissing Australia's Shane Watson at Colombo in September 2011 ... The previous month Eranga had struck with his second wicket in ODIs, removing Brad Haddin at Hambantota ... Eranga took 5 for 86 for Chilaw Marians against Colts in Colombo in May 2011 ... He scored 78 not out for Chilaw v Ragama in May 2011 ...

THE FIGURES *to 26.09.11*   **ESPNcricinfo.com**

Batting & Fielding	M	Inns	NO	Runs	HS	Avge	S/R	100	50	4s	6s	Ct	St
Tests	1	1	0	12	12	12.00	30.76	0	0	2	0	1	0
ODIs	3	3	1	3	2	1.50	27.27	0	0	0	0	1	0
T20Is	0	0	–	–	–	–	–	–	–	–	–	–	–
First-class	35	48	19	694	78*	23.93	60.24	0	4	64	26	19	0

Bowling	M	Balls	Runs	Wkts	BB	Avge	RpO	S/R	5i	10m
Tests	1	254	127	5	4–65	25.40	3.00	50.80	0	0
ODIs	3	114	99	4	2–38	24.75	5.21	28.50	0	0
T20Is	0	0	–	–	–	–	–	–	–	–
First-class	35	3376	2237	66	5–86	33.89	3.97	51.15	1	0

CRAIG **ERVINE**

ZIMBABWE

Full name	**Craig Richard Ervine**
Born	**August 19, 1985, Harare**
Teams	**Southern Rocks**
Style	**Left-hand bat, occasional offspinner**
Test debut	**Zimbabwe v Bangladesh at Harare 2011**
ODI debut	**Zimbabwe v India at Bulawayo 2010**
T20I debut	**Zimbabwe v Sri Lanka at Providence 2010**

THE PROFILE Few in Zimbabwe were surprised when Craig Ervine reached the national side. A stylish left-hander, Ervine hails from a cricketing family: his grandfather, father, uncle and two brothers also played first-class cricket. Older brother Sean, an allrounder, made a promising international start before heading to England to play for Hampshire (a fraternal reunion at the 2011 World Cup was scuppered when Sean decided to stay put in Southampton after originally being selected). However, Craig is lucky to be playing cricket at all: as a teenager he slipped at home and fell on a broken glass, and needed a three-hour reconstructive operation on his right hand – amputation was initially considered an option. Recovery focused his ambitions, and he joined the national cricket academy. Ervine played for Midlands – scoring a century in only his third first-class match – and Zimbabwe A before heading to England (and later Ireland, too) to play club cricket. After four years away he returned to Zimbabwe in time to join the new Southern Rocks franchise for 2009-10, and was their leading Logan Cup runscorer with 575. His one-day form was less spectacular, although he usually scored quickly (at 154.54 per 100 balls in the domestic Twenty20). He made his international debut in the World Twenty20 in the Caribbean early in 2010, and then consolidated his place in ODIs, starting with 67 not out against India. He did well at the 2011 World Cup, making 85 against Canada and 66 against Kenya, although he was prouder of his 52 against Pakistan. Ervine continued to look the part, and made his Test debut in the comeback victory over Bangladesh at Harare in August 2011, making a timely undefeated 35 as the second-innings declaration loomed.

THE FACTS Ervine made his maiden first-class hundred (in a total of 185) in only his third match, for Midlands v Mashonaland at Kwekwe in April 2004 ... In successive matches in the Intercontinental Cup in 2010 Ervine hit 145 against the Netherlands at Amstelveen and 177 against Canada at King City ... His brother Sean, who now plays for Hampshire, played five Tests and 42 ODIs for Zimbabwe...

THE FIGURES to 26.09.11   **ESPncricinfo.com**

Batting & Fielding	M	Inns	NO	Runs	HS	Avge	S/R	100	50	4s	6s	Ct	St
Tests	2	4	1	96	49	32.00	47.05	0	0	14	0	3	0
ODIs	23	21	3	581	85	32.27	75.65	0	4	50	4	2	0
T20Is	3	2	0	31	30	15.50	65.95	0	0	2	0	1	0
First-class	31	55	3	2172	177	41.76	–	5	13	–	–	33	0

Bowling	M	Balls	Runs	Wkts	BB	Avge	RpO	S/R	5i	10m
Tests	2	0	–	–	–	–	–	–	–	–
ODIs	23	0	–	–	–	–	–	–	–	–
T20Is	3	0	–	–	–	–	–	–	–	–
First-class	31	210	143	3	2–44	47.66	4.08	70.00	0	0

CALLUM **FERGUSON**

Full name	**Callum James Ferguson**
Born	**November 21, 1984, North Adelaide, South Australia**
Teams	**South Australia, Pune Warriors**
Style	**Right-hand bat, right-arm medium-pacer**
Test debut	**No Tests yet**
ODI debut	**Australia v New Zealand at Melbourne 2008-09**
T20I debut	**Australia v New Zealand at Sydney 2008-09**

THE PROFILE After a few stutters, Callum Ferguson came of age in 2008-09. Easy to watch, more of an accumulator than a big hitter, he had suffered from getting out when set, but came back from a season of English club cricket more determined to cash in. His 644 first-class runs in the season that followed included two hundreds (his first for nearly four years) and, despite being lightly built, he showed some power too, with 401 one-day runs at almost a run a ball. He was called up for the Chappell-Hadlee one-dayers against New Zealand in February 2009, and made a rapid 55 not out in the last match: he continued this good start in South Africa, before kicking off the ODIs in England in September with 71 not out at The Oval and 55 at Lord's. All this was a welcome return to form: Ferguson had shone in 2004-05, his debut season, with 733 Shield runs – including 93 in his second match and a maiden century in his fourth – while the rest of South Australia's strokemakers struggled. But over the next three seasons he struggled to reproduce that form, before the retirements of Darren Lehmann and Matthew Elliott meant more responsibility. There was a setback in October 2009, when he badly injured his right knee while fielding in the Champions Trophy final victory over New Zealand. Ferguson needed reconstructive surgery and missed the whole of the next home season. He was back in 2010-11, and was soon recalled to the national side – but 46 against England at Sydney in February was not enough to earn him a World Cup place, and he missed the later tour of Sri Lanka too.

THE FACTS Ferguson made 132 for South Australia v Queensland at Brisbane in November 2008 ... In January 2002 he scored 258 not out for South Australia Under-19s v Queensland ... Ferguson scored 93 (v Queensland) in his second first-class match in 2004-05, and 103 (v New South Wales) in his fourth, in 2004-05 ...

THE FIGURES to 26.09.11   **ESPN**cricinfo.com

Batting & Fielding	M	Inns	NO	Runs	HS	Avge	S/R	100	50	4s	6s	Ct	St
Tests	0	0	–	–	–	–	–	–	–	–	–	–	–
ODIs	30	25	9	663	71*	41.43	85.32	0	5	64	0	7	0
T20Is	3	3	0	16	8	5.33	84.21	0	0	1	0	1	0
First-class	55	102	9	3346	132	35.97	56.82	6	20	–	–	25	0

Bowling	M	Balls	Runs	Wkts	BB	Avge	RpO	S/R	5i	10m
Tests	0	0	–	–	–	–	–	–	–	–
ODIs	30	0	–	–	–	–	–	–	–	–
T20Is	3	0	–	–	–	–	–	–	–	–
First-class	55	42	38	0	–	–	5.42	–	0	0

DILHARA **FERNANDO**

SRI LANKA

Full name	**Congenige Randhi Dilhara Fernando**
Born	**July 19, 1979, Colombo**
Teams	**Sinhalese SC, Uva**
Style	**Right-hand bat, right-arm fast-medium bowler**
Test debut	**Sri Lanka v Pakistan at Colombo 2000**
ODI debut	**Sri Lanka v South Africa at Paarl 2000-01**
T20I debut	**Sri Lanka v England at Southampton 2006**

THE PROFILE When Dilhara Fernando burst onto the international scene, young and raw, he was seen as the long-term replacement for Chaminda Vaas as the cutting edge of Sri Lanka's attack. He has natural pace – six months after his debut he was clocked at 91.9mph in Durban – hits the pitch hard, and moves the ball off the seam. He rattled India at Galle in 2001, taking five wickets and sending Javagal Srinath to hospital. At first he paid for an inconsistent line and length, but worked hard with the former Test opening bowler Rumesh Ratnayake and became more reliable. He also learnt the art of reverse swing, and developed a well-disguised slower one. But injuries intervened. Fernando was quick during the 2003 World Cup, but bowled a lot of no-balls, a problem he later blamed on a spinal stress fracture. He returned after six months, only for another fracture to be detected in January 2004. He reclaimed his place in the national squad later that year, and has been there or thereabouts ever since, although latterly he has found Test wickets elusive – in 11 matches between August 2007 and August 2011 he took only 17 at 67, almost double his career average – but the promise of pace ensures he is always in the mix. The no-ball problem does occasionally resurface: he was omitted after the first Test against Pakistan in March 2006 before returning later that year for the one-day series in England, which Sri Lanka swept 5–0. He was in the 2011 World Cup squad but didn't play, then toured England, where he appeared in two of the Tests before an injured knee ruled him out of the one-day series.

THE FACTS Fernando took 6 for 27 against England in Colombo in September 2007: overall he averages 20.05 with the ball against England in ODIs, but 70.42 in 14 matches against South Africa ... He averages 19.28 with the ball in Tests against Bangladesh – but 49.66 against India, even though his best figures of 5 for 42 came against them ... Fernando's record includes one ODI for the Asia XI ...

THE FIGURES *to 26.09.11*   **ESPN**cricinfo.com

Batting & Fielding	M	Inns	NO	Runs	HS	Avge	S/R	100	50	4s	6s	Ct	St
Tests	37	42	14	242	39*	8.64	35.43	0	0	29	1	10	0
ODIs	141	57	33	239	20	9.95	61.75	0	0	19	2	27	0
T20Is	16	5	2	24	21	8.00	120.00	0	0	4	0	3	0
First-class	105	102	30	554	42	7.69	–	0	0	–	–	39	0

Bowling	M	Balls	Runs	Wkts	BB	Avge	RpO	S/R	5i	10m
Tests	37	5689	3476	94	5–42	36.97	3.66	60.52	3	0
ODIs	141	6188	5362	180	6–27	29.78	5.19	34.37	1	0
T20Is	16	342	421	17	3–19	24.76	7.38	20.11	0	0
First-class	105	14070	8462	281	6–29	30.11	3.60	50.07	6	0

STEVEN **FINN**

Full name	**Steven Thomas Finn**
Born	**April 4, 1989, Watford, Hertfordshire**
Teams	**Middlesex**
Style	**Right-hand bat, right-arm fast-medium bowler**
Test debut	**England v Bangladesh at Chittagong 2009-10**
ODI debut	**England v Australia at Brisbane 2010-11**
T20I debut	**England v West Indies at The Oval 2011**

THE PROFILE Steven Finn, who measures up at 6ft 7ins (201cm), is the latest beanpole fast bowler to carry England's hopes, and his impressive arrival sounded the death knell for the international career of the previous one, Steve Harmison. Finn pings the ball down from the clouds with a heady blend of pace and bounce, and can rattle the best. He was earmarked as an England prospect early on, representing all the age-group teams from under-16 upwards, and became Middlesex's youngest-ever player in 2005, breaking Fred Titmus's record. After he took 53 Championship wickets in 2009, Finn went with the England Lions to the UAE, where he performed competently, although he still seemed to be well down the pecking order. But when Stuart Broad, Graham Onions and Ryan Sidebottom were all injured at the start of the Bangladesh tour early in 2010, Finn was parachuted in as cover. Barely 24 hours after arriving he did well in the warm-up game against Bangladesh A, and three days later made his Test debut, displaying good pace and bounce on a docile Chittagong surface. Back in England Finn took 14 wickets in a match for Middlesex, then claimed five-fors in both early-season Tests against Bangladesh, collecting the match award for his nine wickets at Lord's. He started the 2010-11 Ashes tour strongly – 6 for 125 at Brisbane – but looked a little tired after that and was eventually supplanted by Chris Tremlett and Tim Bresnan. Their successes meant that after taking 46 Test wickets in 2010 Finn played only once in 2011 – he took four wickets against Sri Lanka at Lord's to become the youngest Englishman to reach 50 – but, still only 22, he remains very much one to watch.

THE FACTS Finn took 9 for 37 (after 5 for 69 in the first innings) for Middlesex at Worcester in April 2010: his next two five-fors were for England in Tests against Bangladesh ... In 2011 Finn became the youngest bowler to reach 50 Test wickets for England, a record previously held by Ian Botham ... At 16 in 2005 Finn was the youngest player to appear in a first-class match for Middlesex, beating the record set by Fred Titmus in 1949 ...

THE FIGURES to 26.09.11   **ESPN**cricinfo.com

Batting & Fielding	M	Inns	NO	Runs	HS	Avge	S/R	100	50	4s	6s	Ct	St
Tests	12	13	9	35	19	8.75	27.34	0	0	6	0	3	0
ODIs	6	4	2	35	35	17.50	129.62	0	0	5	1	3	0
T20Is	1	0	–	–	–	–	–	–	–	–	–	1	0
First-class	61	76	24	381	32	7.32	32.01	0	0	48	1	14	0

Bowling	M	Balls	Runs	Wkts	BB	Avge	RpO	S/R	5i	10m
Tests	12	2074	1346	50	6–125	26.92	3.89	41.48	3	0
ODIs	6	328	283	7	2–16	40.42	5.17	46.85	0	0
T20Is	1	12	16	0	–	–	8.00	–	0	0
First-class	61	10487	6219	222	9–37	28.01	3.55	47.23	7	1

DANIEL **FLYNN**

NEW ZEALAND

Full name **Daniel Raymond Flynn**
Born **April 16, 1985, Rotorua**
Teams **Northern Districts**
Style **Left-hand bat, occasional left-arm spinner**
Test debut **England v New Zealand at Lord's 2008**
ODI debut **New Zealand v England at Christchurch 2007-08**
T20I debut **New Zealand v England at Christchurch 2007-08**

THE PROFILE The early days of Daniel Flynn's international career will be remembered for him walking off Old Trafford in May 2008 with fewer teeth than he started with, after being hit by James Anderson. Such an injury could have severely dented the confidence (as well as the gums) of a young batsman, but Flynn is made of sterner stuff. He made his first-class debut for Northern Districts soon after the 2003-04 Under-19 World Cup, in which he captained New Zealand. A stocky, powerful left-hander, he struck his maiden century in December 2005, but it wasn't until 2007-08 that he showed his true colours – particularly in one-dayers – and joined the national Twenty20 squad. He didn't get many opportunities at first, but made his Test debut at Lord's, defending coolly for 29 not out from 118 balls in the second innings, leading his captain Daniel Vettori to declare that "He's got the No. 6 spot basically for as long as he wants it." Flynn then suffered that sickening blow in the mouth in the next game. However, he was fit enough to play in the final Test at Trent Bridge, and generally looked a readymade replacement for the just-retired Stephen Fleming (an altogether different type of left-hander). In 2008-09 Flynn just missed a maiden Test century, making 95 against West Indies at Dunedin, and added 67 against India at Hamilton. However, he then lost his place after a run of low scores, and lost his central contract too for 2010-11. But he kept his name in the frame with 162 in an unofficial Test in Zimbabwe in October 2010, and was restored to that contract list after a good home season included a career-best 241 against Otago

THE FACTS Flynn made his maiden first-class hundred for Northern Districts v Otago at Gisborne in December 2005, then didn't make another one for almost two years ... He scored 241 for ND v Otago in March 2011, hitting nine sixes as well as 27 fours ... In one-day games in 2007-08 Flynn hit 143 (from 117 balls) v Wellington and 149 (from 141 balls, with six sixes) v Canterbury ...

THE FIGURES to 26.09.11   **ESPNcricinfo.com**

Batting & Fielding	M	Inns	NO	Runs	HS	Avge	S/R	100	50	4s	6s	Ct	St
Tests	16	29	5	689	95	28.70	40.57	0	4	89	3	7	0
ODIs	16	13	2	167	35	15.18	57.19	0	0	14	1	4	0
T20Is	4	4	0	37	23	9.25	115.62	0	0	1	2	2	0
First-class	64	107	12	3324	241	34.98	50.25	8	14	–	–	24	0

Bowling	M	Balls	Runs	Wkts	BB	Avge	RpO	S/R	5i	10m
Tests	16	0	–	–	–	–	–	–	–	–
ODIs	16	6	6	0	–	–	6.00	–	0	0
T20Is	4	6	7	0	–	–	7.00	–	0	0
First-class	64	271	156	1	1–37	156.00	3.45	271.00	0	0

GAUTAM **GAMBHIR**

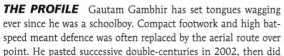

Full name	**Gautam Gambhir**
Born	**October 14, 1981, Delhi**
Teams	**Delhi, Kolkata Knight Riders**
Style	**Left-hand bat, occasional legspinner**
Test debut	**India v Australia at Mumbai 2004-05**
ODI debut	**India v Bangladesh at Dhaka 2002-03**
T20I debut	**India v Scotland at Durban 2006-07**

THE PROFILE Gautam Gambhir has set tongues wagging ever since he was a schoolboy. Compact footwork and high bat-speed meant defence was often replaced by the aerial route over point. He pasted successive double-centuries in 2002, then did well in the Caribbean with India A early in 2003, and joined the one-day squad when several seniors took a rest after the World Cup. He finally made the Test side late the following year, hitting 96 against South Africa in his second match and 139 against Bangladesh in his fifth. Leaner times followed, punctuated by cheap runs in Zimbabwe, and although he celebrated his one-day return after 30 months on the sidelines with 103 against Sri Lanka in April 2005, he struggled for big scores and soon found himself out again. After the disasters of the 2007 World Cup Gambhir was given another chance, and this time immediately looked the part. He made two one-day centuries in Australia early in 2008, and carried his good form into the inaugural IPL. He crashed 67, 104 and a superb 206 as Australia were beaten in October 2008, then – after a one-match ban for elbowing Shane Watson while running – helped ensure a series victory over England with 179 and 97 in the second Test. In ODIs he crashed 150 against Sri Lanka in Colombo in February 2009. Gambhir kept up this astonishing run of form with centuries in five successive Tests in 2009-10, although he had a quieter time after that. He was a star at the 2011 World Cup, never failing to reach double figures and taking India close to glory with 97 in the final, but then picked up various injuries in England which disrupted his game.

THE FACTS Gambhir made 206 against Australia at Delhi in October 2008: VVS Laxman also scored a double-century, the first time Australia had ever conceded two in the same innings ... Gambhir scored centuries in five successive Test matches in 2009 and 2010: only Don Bradman (six) has ever done better ... He made 214 (for Delhi v Railways) and 218 (for the Board President's XI v Zimbabwe) in successive innings early in 2002 ...

THE FIGURES to 26.09.11   **ESPN**cricinfo.com

Batting & Fielding	M	Inns	NO	Runs	HS	Avge	S/R	100	50	4s	6s	Ct	St
Tests	41	74	5	3336	206	48.34	52.23	9	16	411	7	30	0
ODIs	114	110	10	4073	150*	40.73	86.38	9	25	448	16	32	0
T20Is	23	22	0	621	75	28.22	124.20	0	6	74	8	5	0
First-class	126	215	21	10398	233*	53.59	–	32	45	–	–	79	0

Bowling	M	Balls	Runs	Wkts	BB	Avge	RpO	S/R	5i	10m
Tests	41	0	–	–	–	–	–	–	–	–
ODIs	114	6	13	0	–	–	13.00	–	0	0
T20Is	23	0	–	–	–	–	–	–	–	–
First-class	126	385	277	7	3–12	39.57	4.31	55.00	0	0

CHRIS **GAYLE**

Full name	**Christopher Henry Gayle**
Born	**September 21, 1979, Kingston, Jamaica**
Teams	**Jamaica, Royal Challengers Bangalore, West Australia**
Style	**Left-hand bat, offspinner**
Test debut	**West Indies v Zimbabwe at Port-of-Spain 1999-2000**
ODI debut	**West Indies v India at Toronto 1999-2000**
T20I debut	**West Indies v New Zealand at Auckland 2005-06**

THE PROFILE An attacking left-hander, Chris Gayle earned himself a black mark on his first tour when the new boys were felt to be insufficiently respectful of their elders. But a lack of respect, for opposition bowlers at least, has served him well since then. Tall and imposing, he loves to carve through the covers off either foot (without moving either of them much), and can take any opening bowler apart on his day. In a lean era for West Indian cricket in general – and fast bowling in particular – Gayle's pugnacious approach has become an attacking weapon in its own right, in Tests as well as one-dayers. His 79-ball century at Cape Town in January 2004, after South Africa had made 532, was typical. He came unstuck against England afterwards, when that lack of positive footwork was exposed – but men with little footwork often baffle experts, and in May 2005 he punched 317 against South Africa in Antigua. Gayle also bowls brisk non-turning offspin, which makes him a genuine one-day allrounder. He took over the captaincy after an injury to Ramnaresh Sarwan in 2007, and immediately showed unexpected flair for the job. But it ended in tears: after several acrimonious disputes with the board, Gayle declined a central contract, preferring to keep his options open for lucrative Twenty20 offers. He was stripped of the captaincy, responded by scoring 333 against Sri Lanka in his next Test in December 2010, then – after battling injury in the World Cup – was dropped altogether after a very public row with the board. Gayle stomped off to the IPL, and was the leading runscorer ... but was left out of the West Indian side as the standoff continued.

THE FACTS Gayle's 333 against South Africa in Antigua in May 2005 has been exceeded for West Indies only by Brian Lara (twice) and Garry Sobers ... The only others to have scored two Test triple-centuries are Lara, Don Bradman and Virender Sehwag ... Gayle hit the first century in Twenty20 internationals, 117 v South Africa at Johannesburg in September 2007 ... His record includes three ODIs for the World XI ...

THE FIGURES to 26.09.11   **ESPN**cricinfo.com

Batting & Fielding	M	Inns	NO	Runs	HS	Avge	S/R	100	50	4s	6s	Ct	St
Tests	91	159	6	6373	333	41.65	59.10	13	33	936	75	85	0
ODIs	228	223	16	8087	153*	39.06	83.95	19	43	946	169	99	0
T20Is	20	20	1	617	117	32.47	144.49	1	5	57	34	5	0
First-class	165	292	21	12127	333	44.74	–	29	59	–	–	143	0

Bowling	M	Balls	Runs	Wkts	BB	Avge	RpO	S/R	5i	10m
Tests	91	6857	2995	72	5–34	41.59	2.62	95.23	2	0
ODIs	228	6936	5473	156	5–46	35.08	4.73	44.46	1	0
T20Is	20	209	254	12	2–15	21.16	7.29	17.41	0	0
First-class	165	12133	5015	129	5–34	38.87	2.48	94.05	2	0

MARTIN **GUPTILL**

Full name	**Martin James Guptill**
Born	**September 30, 1986, Auckland**
Teams	**Auckland, Derbyshire**
Style	**Right-hand bat, occasional offspinner**
Test debut	**New Zealand v India at Hamilton 2008-09**
ODI debut	**New Zealand v West Indies at Auckland 2008-09**
ODI debut	**New Zealand v Australia at Sydney 2008-09**

THE PROFILE A tall right-hander, Martin Guptill made a bittersweet entry into first-class cricket in March 2006, not long after playing in the Under-19 World Cup, collecting a duck in his first innings then making 99 in the second before tickling a catch behind off his future Test team-mate Jesse Ryder. By 2007-08 Guptill was tickling the selectors, too: he topped the State Shield run-lists that season as Auckland reached the final. Guptill carried his purple patch into an Emerging Players tournament in Australia, finishing as NZ's highest run-scorer there too. His rise continued with an A-team tour of India and, after a maiden first-class century at home, he received the national call for the one-day series against the touring West Indians early in 2009. He lit up his debut in familiar surroundings in Auckland, reaching three figures with a huge six off Chris Gayle and finishing with a superb unbeaten 122 – the second-highest score by anyone in their first ODI. He was dropped three times before he reached 30, but his running (not one of New Zealand's strengths) was notable. Indeed, Guptill's general speed – between wickets or in the outfield, from a high-stepping run – is particularly remarkable as he has only two toes on his left foot after a forklift accident when he was 13. He consolidated his place in 2009-10, although his stats were boosted by 91 in a one-dayer against Bangladesh, and a massive 189 against them in the Hamilton Test, where he shared a big stand with Brendon McCullum. Now a regular in all three formats, he had a reasonable World Cup in 2011 before widening his experience with a county stint for Derbyshire.

THE FACTS Guptill was the fifth batsman to score a century in his first one-day international, following Dennis Amiss, Desmond Haynes, Andy Flower and Saleem Elahi (Colin Ingram joined the list in October 2010) ... Guptill made 189 v Bangladesh at Hamilton in February 2010, sharing a sixth-wicket partnership of 339 with Brendon McCullum ... On his first-class debut, against Wellington in Auckland in March 2006, Guptill made 0 and 99 ...

THE FIGURES to 26.09.11   ☰☰☰cricinfo.com

Batting & Fielding	M	Inns	NO	Runs	HS	Avge	S/R	100	50	4s	6s	Ct	St
Tests	15	28	1	944	189	34.96	44.73	1	6	110	11	11	0
ODIs	52	50	6	1572	122*	35.72	79.75	1	11	153	31	19	0
T20Is	23	21	2	439	54	23.10	116.13	0	1	38	18	9	0
First-class	47	84	5	2575	189	32.59	46.96	3	16	361	24	36	0

Bowling	M	Balls	Runs	Wkts	BB	Avge	RpO	S/R	5i	10m
Tests	15	194	136	3	3–37	45.33	4.20	64.66	0	0
ODIs	52	65	53	2	2–7	26.50	4.89	32.50	0	0
T20Is	23	6	11	0	–	–	11.00	–	0	0
First-class	47	314	216	4	3–37	54.00	4.12	78.50	0	0

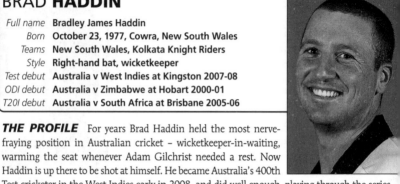

BRAD **HADDIN**

Full name	**Bradley James Haddin**
Born	**October 23, 1977, Cowra, New South Wales**
Teams	**New South Wales, Kolkata Knight Riders**
Style	**Right-hand bat, wicketkeeper**
Test debut	**Australia v West Indies at Kingston 2007-08**
ODI debut	**Australia v Zimbabwe at Hobart 2000-01**
T20I debut	**Australia v South Africa at Brisbane 2005-06**

THE PROFILE For years Brad Haddin held the most nerve-fraying position in Australian cricket – wicketkeeper-in-waiting, warming the seat whenever Adam Gilchrist needed a rest. Now Haddin is up there to be shot at himself. He became Australia's 400th Test cricketer in the West Indies early in 2008, and did well enough, playing through the series despite breaking a finger early on, which affected his batting. But he cemented his place with a blazing – almost Gilchristian – 169 against New Zealand at Adelaide in November, pulling and cutting strongly, and added another century in the first Ashes Test in 2009, before a valiant 80 in defeat at Lord's. After that, though, his fortunes waned: he broke another finger just before the start of the third Test, and after a brief return had to surrender the gloves to Tim Paine for the one-dayers that followed. Surgery meant he missed the Champions Trophy in South Africa too, then an elbow-tendon problem forced him out of the internationals in England in 2010: Paine again showed himself to be a capable deputy – and a potential rival, although Haddin consolidated his position with some feisty displays in the 2010-11 Ashes defeat, including another century at Brisbane. He had long been a consistent scorer at domestic level, making 916 runs at 57.25 in 2004-05, leading NSW to a one-wicket Shield final victory over Queensland. He passed 600 runs in each of the next two seasons, and although his output dipped to 489 in 2007-08, that still included three centuries. Haddin began his senior domestic career in 1997-98 with the Australian Capital Territory in their debut season in Australia's one-day competition.

THE FACTS Haddin took up a novel batting position behind the stumps for a free hit after a Shoaib Akhtar no-ball early in 2005: he reasoned that he had more time to sight the ball, and if it hit the stumps it would confuse the fielders (it did hit the stumps, and he managed a bye) … At Edgbaston in 2005 Haddin rolled a ball near Glenn McGrath, who stepped on it, badly sprained his ankle, and missed the match, which England eventually won by two runs: in 2009 Haddin himself missed the Edgbaston Test when he broke a finger minutes before the start …

THE FIGURES to 26.09.11   ≡ᴅᴘᵑcricinfo.com

Batting & Fielding	M	Inns	NO	Runs	HS	Avge	S/R	100	50	4s	6s	Ct	St
Tests	35	59	6	1995	169	37.64	58.36	3	8	226	33	128	3
ODIs	90	84	7	2466	110	32.02	81.81	2	15	233	54	124	8
T20Is	25	23	4	342	47	18.00	110.32	0	0	26	10	12	4
First-class	134	221	26	7819	169	40.09	–	13	42	–	–	424	29

Bowling	M	Balls	Runs	Wkts	BB	Avge	RpO	S/R	5i	10m
Tests	35	0	–	–	–	–	–	–	–	–
ODIs	90	0	–	–	–	–	–	–	–	–
T20Is	25	0	–	–	–	–	–	–	–	–
First-class	134	0	–	–	–	–	–	–	–	–

58

HARBHAJAN SINGH

INDIA

Full name	**Harbhajan Singh Plaha**
Born	**July 3, 1980, Jullundur, Punjab**
Teams	**Punjab, Mumbai Indians**
Style	**Right-hand bat, offspinner**
Test debut	**India v Australia at Bangalore 1997-98**
ODI debut	**India v New Zealand at Sharjah 1997-98**
T20I debut	**India v South Africa at Johannesburg 2006-07**

THE PROFILE Harbhajan Singh represents the spirit of the new Indian cricketer. Arrogance and cockiness translate into self-belief and passion on the field, and he has the talent to match. An offspinner with a windmilling, whiplash action, remodelled after questions about his action, he exercises great command over the ball, has the ability to vary his length and pace, and bowls a deadly doosra too – although his main wicket-taking ball is the one that climbs wickedly from a length. In March 2001 it proved too much for the previously all-conquering Australians, as Harbhajan collected 32 wickets in three Tests while none of his team-mates managed more than three. He has occasionally been bothered by injury, while in Pakistan early in 2006 he went for 0 for 355 in two Tests before bouncing back with five-fors in St Kitts and Jamaica. He still sailed past 400 Test wickets a week after turning 31: Muttiah Muralitharan has nominated him (somewhat optimistically, it has to be said) as the man most likely to pass his own stratospheric tally of 800. Harbhajan's rivalry with the Aussies – against whom he has taken 90 wickets in 16 Tests – boiled over in Sydney in January 2008 when he was charged with racially abusing Andrew Symonds. He was initially given a three-Test ban before the charge was reduced, on appeal. Then in April Harbhajan slapped his Indian team-mate Sreesanth after an IPL game, which cost him an 11-match ban. But when he can control his temper – as in New Zealand early in 2009, when he took 16 wickets in the three Tests – Harbhajan remains a world-beater, although he looked jaded in England in 2011, before a stomach-muscle injury sidelined him just short of a century of Test caps.

THE FACTS Harbhajan's match figures of 15 for 217 against Australia at Chennai in 2000-01 have been bettered for India only by Narendra Hirwani (16 for 136 in 1987-88, also at Chennai) ... Harbhajan took 32 wickets at 17.03 in that three-match series: his haul at Kolkata included India's first Test hat-trick ... He has taken 56 wickets at 22.60 in Tests against West Indies, but 25 at 52.04 v Pakistan ... His record includes two ODIs for the Asia XI ...

THE FIGURES *to 26.09.11*   **ESPГ**cricinfo.com

Batting & Fielding	M	Inns	NO	Runs	HS	Avge	S/R	100	50	4s	6s	Ct	St
Tests	98	138	22	2164	115	18.65	65.39	2	9	271	40	42	0
ODIs	229	123	33	1190	49	13.22	80.51	0	0	89	34	69	0
T20Is	23	10	3	99	21	14.14	120.73	0	0	10	4	6	0
First-class	162	219	39	3572	115	19.84	–	2	13	–	–	75	0

Bowling	M	Balls	Runs	Wkts	BB	Avge	RpO	S/R	5i	10m
Tests	98	27651	13084	406	8–84	32.22	2.83	68.10	25	5
ODIs	229	12059	8651	259	5–31	33.40	4.30	46.55	3	0
T20Is	23	504	541	18	3–30	30.05	6.44	28.00	0	0
First-class	162	41590	19605	683	8–84	28.70	2.82	60.89	39	7

RYAN **HARRIS**

AUSTRALIA

Full name	**Ryan James Harris**
Born	**October 11, 1979, Sydney**
Teams	**Queensland, Kings XI Punjab**
Style	**Right-hand bat, right-arm fast bowler**
Test debut	**Australia v New Zealand at Wellington 2009-10**
ODI debut	**Australia v South Africa at Hobart 2008-09**
T20I debut	**Australia v West Indies at Sydney 2009-10**

THE PROFILE   Ryan Harris leapt onto the international stage in 2009-10, a season he initially feared would be a write-off after knee surgery: he narrowly avoided a second operation before benefiting from injuries to others. A stocky, skiddy bowler who is faster than he looks, Harris quickly became too good to ignore. He made a dream start to his international career: in only his second ODI, against Pakistan in January 2010, he collected five wickets, and did the same in the next game. All this led to a Test debut in New Zealand, and he did well during both matches there, taking nine wickets in terribly windy conditions at Wellington. Then he looked the best of the home bowlers in the 2010-11 Ashes disaster, taking 6 for 47 as Australia bounced back to win the second Test at Perth, and there was widespread disappointment when he limped out of the series during the next Test with an ankle injury. That kept him out of the World Cup, but he was back in Sri Lanka later in 2011, taking 11 wickets in the first two Tests before a hamstring niggle kept him out of the third. In ODIs Harris sped to 41 wickets in his first 17 matches, an Australian record, and he is also a handy attacking batsman – an early limited-overs highlight was lofting a six over long-on when South Australia needed five to win against Queensland at Adelaide in December 2006. However, until his international debut at 29, he almost qualified as a journeyman. He was South Australia's top wicket-taker in 2007-08, and they might have tried harder to stop him moving to Queensland. He also played briefly for Sussex and Surrey.

THE FACTS   Harris took five-fors his second and third ODIs, a unique feat at the time (since bettered by Brian Vitori of Zimbabwe) ... Only Ajantha Mendis (48) had more wickets after 17 ODIs than Harris (Curtly Ambrose also had 41) ... Harris scored 94 for Surrey at Northampton in June 2009 ... He took 7 for 108 for South Australia v Tasmania at Adelaide in February 2008 ...

THE FIGURES *to 26.09.11*   **ESPN**cricinfo.com

Batting & Fielding	M	Inns	NO	Runs	HS	Avge	S/R	100	50	4s	6s	Ct	St
Tests	7	10	3	75	23	10.71	52.81	0	0	12	0	2	0
ODIs	17	11	6	43	21	8.60	122.85	0	0	3	1	4	0
T20Is	3	1	1	2	2*	–	200.00	0	0	0	0	0	0
First-class	48	77	10	1256	94	18.74	60.44	0	6	–	–	23	0

Bowling	M	Balls	Runs	Wkts	BB	Avge	RpO	S/R	5i	10m
Tests	7	1321	648	31	6–47	20.90	2.94	42.61	2	0
ODIs	17	845	661	41	5–19	16.12	4.69	20.60	3	0
T20Is	3	70	95	4	2–27	23.75	8.14	17.50	0	0
First-class	48	8892	4568	157	7–108	29.09	3.08	56.63	5	0

NATHAN **HAURITZ**

Full name	**Nathan Michael Hauritz**
Born	**October 18, 1981, Wondai, Queensland**
Teams	**New South Wales**
Style	**Right-hand bat, offspinner**
Test debut	**Australia v India at Mumbai 2004-05**
ODI debut	**Australia v South Africa at Johannesburg 2001-02**
T20I debut	**Australia v Pakistan at Dubai 2009**

THE PROFILE Nathan Hauritz leapfrogged several other spinners to finish the 2008-09 season as the only specialist slow bowler with an Australian contract. It was a stunning turnaround for a tidy, flighty offspinner who had been largely ignored – and indeed was not a regular choice for his state – since a promising Test debut in November 2004, when his five wickets included Sachin Tendulkar and VVS Laxman. But after Beau Casson, Jason Krejza, Cameron White and Bryce McGain took turns following Stuart MacGill's retirement early in 2008, Hauritz was suddenly picked for the second Test against New Zealand at Adelaide in November despite being left out by New South Wales the previous week. He took nine wickets in three home Tests, and also played his first ODI for nearly six years. He made the squad for the 2009 Ashes tour as the only specialist spinner and, despite being largely written off in the English media beforehand, did well enough in the three Tests he played, taking ten wickets at 32, which compared favourably with Graeme Swann's 14 at 40 in five matches for England. Back home, Hauritz took five-fors against Pakistan at both Melbourne and Sydney – surprisingly, his first such hauls in first-class cricket – before a foot problem sent him home early from England in 2010. But things went pear-shaped after that: he was strangely overlooked for the 2010-11 Ashes series – he sold off his gear in a garage sale, saying he no longer played for Australia – and then, after originally being selected, missed the World Cup with a shoulder injury. In September 2011, while the national team was in Sri Lanka without him, he was hit in the face in a nightclub.

THE FACTS Hauritz had never taken five wickets in a first-class innings until he took 5 for 101 v Pakistan in the Boxing Day Test at Melbourne in 2009: he promptly grabbed another five-for in the next Test ... Hauritz took a wicket (Anil Kumble) with his third ball in Test cricket, in November 2004 ... He scored 146- his maiden century – for NSW v South Australia in December 2010, and added an unbeaten 110 in the next match, against Queensland ...

THE FIGURES *to 26.09.11*

Batting & Fielding	M	Inns	NO	Runs	HS	Avge	S/R	100	50	4s	6s	Ct	St
Tests	17	24	7	426	75	25.05	49.88	0	2	50	3	3	0
ODIs	58	32	17	336	53*	22.40	96.27	0	1	21	8	24	0
T20Is	3	2	0	6	4	3.00	60.00	0	0	1	0	1	0
First-class	67	90	23	1472	146	21.97	–	2	4	–	–	37	0

Bowling	M	Balls	Runs	Wkts	BB	Avge	RpO	S/R	5i	10m
Tests	17	4200	2204	63	5–53	34.98	3.14	66.66	2	0
ODIs	58	2724	2152	63	4–29	34.15	4.74	43.23	0	0
T20Is	3	44	47	2	1–20	23.50	6.40	22.00	0	0
First-class	67	13057	6620	159	5–39	41.63	3.04	82.11	3	0

RANGANA **HERATH**

Full name	**Herath Mudiyanselage Rangana Keerthi Bandara Herath**
Born	**March 19, 1978, Kurunegala**
Teams	**Tamil Union, Basnahira**
Style	**Left-hand bat, left-arm orthodox spinner**
Test debut	**Sri Lanka v Australia at Galle 1999-2000**
ODI debut	**Zimbabwe v Sri Lanka at Harare 2003-04**
T20I debut	**Sri Lanka v Australia at Pallekele 2011**

THE PROFILE   Slow left-armer Rangana Herath first came to prominence late in 1999, when his so-called mystery ball – *Wisden* called it "a wonderful delivery, bowled out of the front of his hand, which turned back into right-handers" – befuddled the touring Australians. He took four wickets on Test debut at Galle, including Steve Waugh and Ricky Ponting, but was soon unceremoniously dumped as other spinners were tried as foils for Muttiah Muralitharan. Herath's unprepossessing body shape – he's rather short with a hint of excess padding around the midriff – may have counted against him, but he continued to be a regular wicket-taker in domestic cricket. He took 17 wickets in four Tests in 2004, including seven in a rare Murali-less Sri Lankan victory over Pakistan at Faisalabad, flighting the ball well and making it grip and turn. However, he was soon left out again, seemingly for good. But the wickets still kept coming at home: 45 in 2006-07 and 31 the following season, all at an average under 20, and he was eventually recalled in 2008, although he might have returned to anonymity but for an injury which forced Murali out of the home series against Pakistan in July 2009. Herath partnered Ajantha Mendis, and did so well – five wickets in each of the three Tests – that when Murali returned it was Mendis who made way. Herath took 11 wickets in three Tests in India that winter, but lost his place after an underwhelming bowling performance in Murali's final Test in July 2010, although he did manage a career-best with the bat. He looked unthreatening in England in 2011, but grabbed eight wickets in the defeat by Australia at Galle soon afterwards.

THE FACTS   Herath took 8 for 43 (11 for 72 in the match) for Moors v Police in Colombo in 2002–03 ... In January 2002 he took 8 for 47 (and caught one of the others) for Moors v Galle ... Herath took 72 wickets at 13.59 in Sri Lanka in 2000-01 ... He made 80 not out against India in Colombo in July 2010: he had never previously made more than 71 in first-class cricket, although he had reached 70 four times ...

THE FIGURES *to 26.09.11*   ᴇsᴘɴcricinfo.com

Batting & Fielding	M	Inns	NO	Runs	HS	Avge	S/R	100	50	4s	6s	Ct	St
Tests	29	37	6	428	80*	13.80	48.91	0	1	49	2	8	0
ODIs	16	5	2	17	9	5.66	54.83	0	0	0	0	4	0
T20Is	2	1	1	1	1*	–	100.00	0	0	0	0	0	0
First-class	193	273	62	3486	80*	16.52	–	0	12	–	–	88	0

Bowling	M	Balls	Runs	Wkts	BB	Avge	RpO	S/R	5i	10m
Tests	29	6996	3487	100	7–157	34.87	2.99	69.96	6	0
ODIs	16	674	483	14	3–28	34.50	4.29	48.14	0	0
T20Is	2	42	42	2	1–11	21.00	6.00	21.00	0	0
First-class	193	38454	17568	703	8–43	24.99	2.74	54.69	40	5

PHILLIP **HUGHES**

Full name	**Phillip Joel Hughes**
Born	**November 30, 1988, Macksville, New South Wales**
Teams	**New South Wales**
Style	**Left-hand bat**
Test debut	**Australia v South Africa at Johannesburg 2008-09**
ODI debut	**No ODIs yet**
T20I debut	**No T20Is yet**

THE PROFILE Phillip Hughes made an unconvincing start in Tests – a four-ball duck at the Wanderers after becoming Australia's youngest player since Craig McDermott 25 years previously – but he scored 75 in the second innings, and in the next Test showed that he was a highly accomplished if unconventional batsman. At Durban he became the youngest ever to make two centuries in the same Test, bringing up the first with two sixes. His 415 runs in the series were followed by centuries in each of his three Championship matches for Middlesex, which irritated England supporters angry he had been given the chance to fine-tune before the 2009 Ashes. As it happened it didn't do him much good, as he failed to shine in the first two Tests and was replaced by Shane Watson, a change made public by Hughes on Twitter before the official announcement, which provoked reactions ranging from rage to raucous laughter. His country-baked technique includes compulsive slicing through point and slashing to cover, as well as stepping away to provide room for tennis-style drives down the ground. The new opening pair of Watson and Simon Katich kept him out for much of 2009-10, although he did make 86 not out at Wellington when Watson was injured – but then a dislocated shoulder, suffered while boxing, knocked Hughes himself out, sparing him a return to English pitches to face Pakistan. In 2010-11 he continued to score heavily in domestic cricket … and continued to struggle in Tests. He was jettisoned after making only 97 runs in the first three Tests of the Ashes debacle, but restated his case in Sri Lanka later in 2011, with an important century in the third Test.

THE FACTS Hughes made 115 and 160 in only his second Test, against South Africa at Durban in March 2009: at 20 years 98 days he was the youngest to hit twin centuries in a Test, beating George Headley (20 years 271 days for West Indies v England in 1929-30) … Hughes hit 198 for NSW v South Australia at Adelaide in November 2008 … He played three Championship matches for Middlesex in 2009 – and scored centuries in each of them …

THE FIGURES *to 26.09.11*   ‎**ESPncricinfo.com**

Batting & Fielding	M	Inns	NO	Runs	HS	Avge	S/R	100	50	4s	6s	Ct	St
Tests	13	24	1	914	160	39.73	54.79	3	2	119	9	4	0
ODIs	0	0	–	–	–	–	–	–	–	–	–	–	–
T20Is	0	0	–	–	–	–	–	–	–	–	–	–	–
First-class	60	108	6	5210	198	51.07	59.31	17	26	704	30	38	0

Bowling	M	Balls	Runs	Wkts	BB	Avge	RpO	S/R	5i	10m
Tests	13	–	–	–	–	–	–	–	–	–
ODIs	0	0	–	–	–	–	–	–	–	–
T20Is	0	0	–	–	–	–	–	–	–	–
First-class	60	18	9	0	–	–	3.00	–	0	0

AUSTRALIA

DAVID **HUSSEY**

Full name	**David John Hussey**
Born	**July 15, 1977, Morley, Western Australia**
Teams	**Victoria, Nottinghamshire, Kings XI Punjab**
Style	**Right-hand bat, occasional offspinner**
Test debut	**No Tests yet**
ODI debut	**Australia v West Indies at Basseterre 2007-08**
T20I debut	**Australia v India at Melbourne 2007-08**

THE PROFILE David Hussey copied his older brother Michael's talent for ridiculous scoring in English county cricket. And, like Michael, David was forced to pile up mountains of runs in Australia before convincing the national selectors. It took his first 1000-run home season before he was finally chosen for a tour (a one-day series in the Caribbean early in 2008) and earned his first national contract. Earlier that year he made his Twenty20 debut against India at the MCG. He made his first ODI century in 2009 – but it was against Scotland, and couldn't get him into the side for the series against England that followed. He did make the squad for the 2011 World Cup, but had little chance to shine, playing only four matches, one a washout. Hussey was one of the big surprises in the inaugural IPL auction in 2008, when Kolkata paid $625,000 for him – far more than his brother fetched. Despite his crash-and-bash style, he is desperate not to be pigeonholed as a Twenty20 player. His first-class record suggests it's a reasonable request: he boasts an average in the mid-fifties, even higher than his brother's. But his one-day exploits include a 60-ball century – the second-fastest in Australia's domestic history – and in 2007-08 he was Victoria's Player of the Year in all three formats. Hussey was also a run-machine during his time with Nottinghamshire, with almost 6000 first-class runs at an average touching 65. An aggressive batsman with a strong bottom-hand technique, Hussey hit a breathtaking breakthrough 212 not out at nearly a run a ball in 2003-04, his first full season, as Victoria chased a record-breaking 455 for victory against NSW: Steve Waugh, the opposing captain, was impressed.

THE FACTS David Hussey hit 275 (27 fours, 14 sixes) for Nottinghamshire v Essex at Trent Bridge in May 2007 ... He reached 50 in only 19 balls – Australia's second-fastest ODI half-century – against West Indies in St Kitts in July 2008 ... Hussey fetched $625,000 at the inaugural IPL auction in February 2008, much more than his brother Michael ($350,000) and Australia's captain Ricky Ponting ($400,000) ...

THE FIGURES *to 26.09.11*   espncricinfo.com

Batting & Fielding	M	Inns	NO	Runs	HS	Avge	S/R	100	50	4s	6s	Ct	St
Tests	0	0	–	–	–	–	–	–	–	–	–	–	–
ODIs	39	32	2	940	111	31.33	89.35	1	6	66	19	17	0
T20Is	30	28	3	630	88*	25.20	126.00	0	3	36	28	17	0
First-class	155	242	25	11903	275	54.85	70.94	40	52	–	–	200	0

Bowling	M	Balls	Runs	Wkts	BB	Avge	RpO	S/R	5i	10m
Tests	0	0	–	–	–	–	–	–	–	–
ODIs	39	527	463	14	4–21	33.07	5.27	37.64	0	0
T20Is	30	288	306	16	3–25	19.12	6.37	18.00	0	0
First-class	155	2644	1639	25	4–105	65.56	3.71	105.76	0	0

MICHAEL **HUSSEY**

Full name	**Michael Edward Killeen Hussey**
Born	**May 27, 1975, Morley, Western Australia**
Teams	**Western Australia, Chennai Super Kings**
Style	**Left-hand bat, occasional right-arm medium-pacer**
Test debut	**Australia v West Indies at Brisbane 2005-06**
ODI debut	**Australia v India at Perth 2003-04**
T20I debut	**Australia v New Zealand at Auckland 2004-05**

THE PROFILE   English fans couldn't understand why Australia's selectors took so long to recognise Michael Hussey's claims. Bradmanesque in county cricket, he was less prolific at home, and seemed destined to remain unfulfilled. Finally he got a chance after 15,313 first-class runs, a record for an Australian before wearing baggy green – and made an attractive century in his second Test, then a memorable 122 against South Africa at the MCG, when he and Glenn McGrath added 107 for the last wicket. The fairytale continued in the 2006-07 Ashes, although his one-day form did finally drop off a little. Hussey has a tidy, compact style: skilled off front foot and back, he is attractive to watch once set. He reinvented himself in one-day cricket as an innovative batsman with cool head and loose wrists, and supplanted Michael Bevan as the Aussies' one-day "finisher". A patchy 2009 Ashes series was redeemed by a fighting century (his first for 16 Tests) at The Oval, although that was tinged with regret as he was last out as the urn was surrendered again. But a superb century turned the Sydney Test against Pakistan on its head in January 2010; and in the World Twenty20 semi-final in the Caribbean later that year Hussey's astonishing 60 off 24 balls dragged Australia past Pakistan and into the final. In the 2010-11 Ashes he was often a lone beacon of excellence for Australia, scoring two centuries before running out of steam. A hamstring tear made him a late arrival for the 2011 World Cup, but he showed no signs of slowing down afterwards, collecting another Test century in Sri Lanka in September. "Mr Cricket" intends to be around for a while yet.

THE FACTS   Hussey scored 229 runs in ODIs before he was dismissed, and had an average of 100.22 after 32 matches ... He took only 166 days to reach 1000 runs in Tests, beating the 228-day record established by England's Andrew Strauss in 2005 ... Hussey's 331 not out against Somerset at Taunton in 2003 is the highest individual score for Northamptonshire ... He has captained Australia in four ODIs, and lost the lot ... Hussey averages 62.78 in Tests in Australia, and 44.12 overseas ...

THE FIGURES *to 26.09.11*   **ESFN cricinfo.com**

Batting & Fielding	M	Inns	NO	Runs	HS	Avge	S/R	100	50	4s	6s	Ct	St
Tests	62	108	12	5113	195	53.26	49.33	15	26	579	28	59	0
ODIs	163	135	41	4750	109*	50.53	88.07	3	35	336	66	92	0
T20Is	27	20	7	457	60*	35.15	150.32	0	2	40	17	18	0
First-class	249	444	43	21217	331*	52.91	–	57	97	–	–	269	0

Bowling	M	Balls	Runs	Wkts	BB	Avge	RpO	S/R	5i	10m
Tests	62	228	112	4	1–0	28.00	2.94	57.00	0	0
ODIs	163	234	227	2	1–22	113.50	5.82	117.00	0	0
T20Is	27	6	5	0	–	–	5.00	–	0	0
First-class	249	1668	884	24	3–34	36.83	3.17	69.50	0	0

IMRAN TAHIR

SOUTH AFRICA

Full name **Mohammad Imran Tahir**
Born **March 27, 1979, Lahore, Pakistan**
Teams **Dolphins, Hampshire**
Style **Right-hand bat, legspinner**
Test debut **No Tests yet**
ODI debut **South Africa v West Indies at Delhi 2010-11**
T20I debut **No T20Is yet**

THE PROFILE Legspinner Imran Tahir is the ultimate journeyman cricketer. Since starting his first-class career in his native Pakistan in 1996-97 he has played for almost 20 first-class teams, ranging from Sui Gas to Yorkshire. He has helped out four English counties – in 2011 he had his second spell with Hampshire – but he finally settled in South Africa, after marrying a local girl. He has a fine record, with well over 500 first-class wickets at an average of 25. Early on he played for Pakistan Under-19s, but after his marriage threw in his lot with South Africa. Match-winning spinners have always been scarce there, and Tahir – who has all the variations, including a well-disguised googly – was soon being mentioned as a Test candidate. In fact he was selected for the Test squad – against England in January 2010 – before he was even eligible, which caused red faces all round. The situation was formalised after that, and he became a naturalised South Africa early in 2011. He had been picking up plenty of wickets on the domestic circuit for the Dolphins, his latest team, and was immediately chosen in the squad for the one-dayers against India. But the selectors kept him under wraps, and finally blooded him in the World Cup. Tahir made up for lost time, taking four West Indian wickets in his first game, three in his second (against the Netherlands) and four more against England. He was hindered after that by a cracked thumb, but finished with 14 wickets at 10.71, a fine start. Tahir is yet to play a Test – but might just prove to be the attacking spinner Graeme Smith has been craving throughout his tenure as Test captain.

THE FACTS Imran Tahir took 8 for 76 for Redco Pakistan v Lahore Blues at Lahore in December 1999 ... He took 8 for 114 for Warwickshire (his fourth English county) against Durham at Edgbaston in May 2010 ... Tahir's first ODI was during the 2011 World Cup: he took 4 for 41 against West Indies ...

THE FIGURES to 26.09.11   **ESPNcricinfo.com**

Batting & Fielding	M	Inns	NO	Runs	HS	Avge	S/R	100	50	4s	6s	Ct	St
Tests	0	0	–	–	–	–	–	–	–	–	–	–	–
ODIs	5	2	2	1	1*	–	50.00	0	0	0	0	2	0
T20Is	0	0	–	–	–	–	–	–	–	–	–	–	–
First-class	136	171	37	1919	77*	14.32	–	0	3	–	–	64	0

Bowling	M	Balls	Runs	Wkts	BB	Avge	RpO	S/R	5i	10m
Tests	0	0	–	–	–	–	–	–	–	–
ODIs	5	237	150	14	4–38	10.71	3.79	16.92	0	0
T20Is	0	0	–	–	–	–	–	–	–	–
First-class	136	26678	14327	575	8–76	24.91	3.22	46.39	43	9

IMRUL KAYES

Full name	**Imrul Kayes**
Born	**February 2, 1987, Meherpur, Kushtia**
Teams	**Khulna**
Style	**Left-hand bat, occasional offspinner**
Test debut	**Bangladesh v South Africa at Bloemfontein 2008-09**
ODI debut	**Bangladesh v New Zealand at Chittagong 2008-09**
T20I debut	**Bangladesh v Pakistan at Gros Islet 2010**

THE PROFILE The elevation of left-hand opener Imrul Kayes to Bangladesh colours was hastened by the mass defections to the unauthorised Indian Cricket League late in 2008. With more than a dozen leading players suddenly unavailable, "Sagar" was called up after a fine home season in 2007-08, when he was the leading scorer for Khulna less than a year after making his first-class debut. His haul included two centuries in separate matches against Sylhet, and he finished the season with 600 runs. Kayes has a solid, compact technique, and likes to hit through the covers off the back foot, but he had the misfortune to make his Test debut against South Africa: he rarely looked settled against their high-quality pacemen, and managed only 25 runs in four attempts in the Tests; on his debut he was out twice in the space of about three hours on the second day. He fared a little better against Sri Lanka, then made 33 – and added a two-hour 24 in the second innings, in an opening stand of 82 with Tamim Iqbal – in Bangladesh's victory over a depleted West Indian side in St Vincent in July 2009. He showed he was coming to terms with the international game with an ODI hundred in New Zealand early in 2010, followed by a patient 75 during a record opening stand with Tamim in the Lord's Test. He had two important innings during Bangladesh's up-and-down 2011 World Cup campaign, making 60 in the upset win over England then 73 not out in a more routine victory over the Netherlands, then added 93 against Australia shortly after the tournament to show he was maturing at the highest level.

THE FACTS Imrul Kayes made 101 v New Zealand in an ODI in Christchurch in February 2010 ... At Lord's in 2010 he and Tamim Iqbal put on 185 – a new national Test record – for the first wicket ... Both Kayes's first-class hundreds were scored for Khulna v Sylhet late in 2007 (121 at Fatullah and 138 at Khulna): in between he made 121 against them in a one-day game ...

THE FIGURES to 26.09.11   ESPNcricinfo.com

Batting & Fielding	M	Inns	NO	Runs	HS	Avge	S/R	100	50	4s	6s	Ct	St
Tests	14	28	0	488	75	17.42	45.10	0	1	73	0	13	0
ODIs	44	44	1	1256	101	29.20	65.34	1	9	128	11	12	0
T20Is	2	2	0	0	0	0.00	0.00	0	0	0	0	0	0
First-class	36	68	1	1702	138	25.40	–	2	6	–	–	23	0

Bowling	M	Balls	Runs	Wkts	BB	Avge	RpO	S/R	5i	10m
Tests	14	12	8	0	–	–	4.00	–	0	0
ODIs	44	0	–	–	–	–	–	–	–	–
T20Is	2	0	–	–	–	–	–	–	–	–
First-class	36	18	12	0	–	–	4.00	–	0	0

COLIN **INGRAM**

SOUTH AFRICA

Full name	**Colin Alexander Ingram**
Born	**July 3, 1985, Port Elizabeth**
Teams	**Warriors, Delhi Daredevils**
Style	**Left-hand batsman, occasional legspinner**
Test debut	**No Tests yet**
ODI debut	**South Africa v Zimbabwe at Bloemfontein 2010-11**
T20I debut	**South Africa v Zimbabwe at Bloemfontein 2010-11**

THE PROFILE A blond, bestubbled, bruising left-hander who answers to the nickname "Bozie", Colin Ingram is among the brightest talents produced by the Eastern Cape in recent years. Happily for a region of South Africa that has often seen its budding stars bloom fully elsewhere, Ingram has remained true to his roots and stayed with the Warriors. He brings a bracing brand of aggression to the batting, and made an immediate impact to being elevated to the senior one-day side after a successful stint in the A team. In his first ODI, against Zimbabwe at Bloemfontein in October 2010, Ingram hit 124 from 126 balls, and in his fifth game he repeated the dose, this time against Pakistan in Abu Dhabi a fortnight later, making a round 100. Things calmed down a little after that, and for a while he lost his place to David Miller, but it was Ingram who made the World Cup squad (he played only once, scoring 46 against Ireland) and Ingram who was preferred for a national contract afterwards. Some put his fluctuations in form down to being pushed up and down the order: he usually opens for the Warriors, and scored his two one-day hundreds for South Africa at No. 3. But Jacques Kallis is the man in possession there in the national side, and when Ingram moved down to No. 6 he looked less assured. Ingram, however, says: "I pride myself on being adaptable and flexible as a cricketer. When you are batting lower down the order, the situation dictates what you have to do, rather than when you are at No. 3 and you can just decide for yourself."

THE FACTS Ingram was the first South African – and only the sixth from any country – to score a century in his first one-day international, with 124 against Zimbabwe in October 2010 ... He scored 190 for Eastern Province v KwaZulu-Natal in Port Elizabeth in January 2009 ... Ingram made 127 in a 50-over match against Bangladesh A in March 2010, sharing a stand of 128 with David Miller ...

THE FIGURES to 26.09.11   **ESFn cricinfo.com**

Batting & Fielding	M	Inns	NO	Runs	HS	Avge	S/R	100	50	4s	6s	Ct	St
Tests	0	0	–	–	–	–	–	–	–	–	–	–	–
ODIs	12	11	2	374	124	41.55	89.26	2	0	33	6	3	0
T20Is	5	5	1	94	46*	23.50	123.68	0	0	11	3	1	0
First-class	47	82	3	2500	190	31.64	–	4	11	–	–	28	0

Bowling	M	Balls	Runs	Wkts	BB	Avge	RpO	S/R	5i	10m
Tests	0	0	–	–	–	–	–	–	–	–
ODIs	12	0	–	–	–	–	–	–	–	–
T20Is	5	0	–	–	–	–	–	–	–	–
First-class	47	1679	952	26	4–16	36.61	3.40	64.57	0	0

JAHURUL ISLAM

Full name	**Mohammad Jahurul Islam**
Born	**December 12, 1986, Rajshahi**
Teams	**Rajshahi**
Style	**Right-hand bat, occasional wicketkeeper**
Test debut	**Bangladesh v England at Mirpur 2009-10**
ODI debut	**Bangladesh v Pakistan at Dambulla 2010**
T20I debut	**Bangladesh v Australia at Bridgetown 2010**

THE PROFILE A superb domestic season in 2009-10, during which he was the only man to pass 1000 runs, with 1008 at 63 with four centuries, propelled the tall, aggressive Jahurul Islam into national contention, and when Raqibul Hasan fell out with the selectors and announced a short-lived retirement just before the home Test series against England, "Aumi" got the call. He made a duck in his first Test innings, courtesy of Graeme Swann, but took his revenge in the second, getting off the mark with a six off Swann over long-on, and adding another shortly afterwards to become only the second player (after his team-mate Shafiul Islam) to open his account in Tests with two sixes. Jahurul had long been earmarked for high honours: a product of the national academy, he made 78 on first-class debut in 2002-03, although he was into his fifth season before he finally cracked the three-figure barrier. In England in 2010 he hit 158 against Surrey, and did reasonably well in the first Test at Lord's (20 and 46) before two low scores in the second. He is also a handy stopgap wicketkeeper, and deputised in some of the one-dayers in Britain later in 2010 after Mushfiqur Rahim was injured. It didn't seem to affect his batting: at Bristol Jahurul made 40 during an important stand of 83 with Imrul Kayes, in a match Bangladesh ended up winning by five runs, their first-ever victory over England. He slipped out of the national side after that, although he remained in the selectors' minds – but a poor run in an A-team one-day series in South Africa in April 2011 (four innings, four single-figure scores) didn't help his cause.

THE FACTS Jahurul Islam's first two scoring shots in Test cricket were both sixes (against England in March 2010), equalling the feat of his team-mate Shafiul Islam earlier in the year ... Jahurul scored 158 against Surrey at The Oval in May 2010 ... He made 78 on first-class debut for Rajshahi v Sylhet at Fatullah in December 2002 ...

THE FIGURES to 26.09.11   **ᴇssɴ cricinfo.com**

Batting & Fielding	M	Inns	NO	Runs	HS	Avge	S/R	100	50	4s	6s	Ct	St
Tests	3	6	0	114	46	19.00	40.71	0	0	13	2	3	0
ODIs	6	6	1	156	41	31.20	73.58	0	0	13	1	6	0
T20Is	1	1	0	18	18	18.00	150.00	0	0	1	1	1	0
First-class	68	125	12	4109	158	36.36	48.43	8	26	–	–	72	2

Bowling	M	Balls	Runs	Wkts	BB	Avge	RpO	S/R	5i	10m
Tests	3	0	–	–	–	–	–	–	–	–
ODIs	6	0	–	–	–	–	–	–	–	–
T20Is	1	0	–	–	–	–	–	–	–	–
First-class	68	12	7	1	1–0	7.00	3.50	12.00	0	0

KYLE **JARVIS**

Full name	**Kyle Malcolm Jarvis**
Born	**February 16, 1989, Harare**
Teams	**Mashonaland Eagles**
Style	**Right-hand bat, right-arm fast-medium bowler**
Test debut	**Zimbabwe v Bangladesh at Harare 2011**
ODI debut	**Zimbabwe v Kenya at Harare 2009-10**
T20I debut	**Zimbabwe v Pakistan at Harare 2011**

THE PROFILE Tall and muscular, Kyle Jarvis has the basic attribute of a good fast bowler – raw pace – and is beginning to tighten his control with the aid of some expert coaching. The son of a former Test fast bowler, Malcolm Jarvis, Kyle was the chief strike bowler for Zimbabwe at the Under-19 World Cup in 2008 (he also played rugby for the national under-19 side). He was fast-tracked into the national side after the appointment as bowling coach of Heath Streak, who rated him highly. Jarvis was blooded in the home series against Kenya in October 2009 – less than a week after his first-class debut, also against the tourists – and made an impression with his pace, breaking the 90mph (144kph) barrier at times in those matches and subsequent ones against Bangladesh and South Africa. Control was occasionally a problem, though, and his ten overs went for 76 against South Africa at Centurion in November 2009, when J-P Duminy hurried to a century. Jarvis took 6 for 60 in his first Logan Cup match for the Mashonaland Eagles, and was included in the national squad for the short tour of the West Indies early in 2010, only to pull out with stress fractures in the back. His comeback to international cricket coincided with Zimbabwe's own: Jarvis made his debut in the match against Bangladesh at Harare in August 2011 which signalled his country's return after six years out of Test cricket. Jarvis looked the part, shaking up the opposition batsmen with his speed and taking 4 for 61 in the second innings, wrapping up the last two wickets to secure a famous victory as Zimbabwe marked their return in some style.

THE FACTS Jarvis took 6 for 60 for Mashonaland Eagles against Mountaineers at Mutare, in only his second first-class match ... He took 4 for 61 against Bangladesh in the second innings of his Test debut, which was only his seventh first-class game ... Jarvis's father, Malcolm, played five Tests and 12 ODIs, and took the last wicket in Zimbabwe's surprise victory over England at the 1992 World Cup ...

THE FIGURES *to 26.09.11*   **ESFN** cricinfo.com

Batting & Fielding	M	Inns	NO	Runs	HS	Avge	S/R	100	50	4s	6s	Ct	St
Tests	2	3	2	29	25*	29.00	26.36	0	0	4	0	0	0
ODIs	12	8	3	27	13	5.40	37.50	0	0	2	0	3	0
T20Is	2	1	0	0	0	0.00	0.00	0	0	0	0	0	0
First-class	8	11	6	87	25*	17.40	36.40	0	0	8	0	1	0

Bowling	M	Balls	Runs	Wkts	BB	Avge	RpO	S/R	5i	10m
Tests	2	369	224	7	4–61	32.00	3.64	52.71	0	0
ODIs	12	569	573	14	3–36	40.92	6.04	40.64	0	0
T20Is	2	48	45	4	3–15	11.25	5.62	12.00	0	0
First-class	8	1171	717	22	6–60	32.59	3.67	53.22	1	0

MAHELA **JAYAWARDENE**

Full name	**Denagamage Proboth Mahela de Silva Jayawardene**
Born	**May 27, 1977, Colombo**
Teams	**Sinhalese Sports Club, Wayamba, Kochi Tuskers Kerala**
Style	**Right-hand bat, right-arm medium-pacer**
Test debut	**Sri Lanka v India at Colombo 1997-98**
ODI debut	**Sri Lanka v Zimbabwe at Colombo 1997-98**
T20I debut	**Sri Lanka v England at Southampton 2006**

THE PROFILE A fine technician with an excellent temperament, Mahela Jayawardene's arrival heralded a new era for Sri Lanka's middle order. Perhaps mindful of his first Test, when he went in at 790 for 4, he soon developed an appetite for big scores. His 66 then, in the world-record 952 for 6 against India, was followed by a masterful 167 on a Galle minefield against New Zealand in only his fourth Test, and a marathon 242 against India in his seventh. However he lost form, hardly scored a run in the 2003 World Cup, and was briefly dropped. Jayawardene benefited from a settled spot at No. 4 after Aravinda de Silva retired: a good series against England was followed by more runs in 2004. He deputised as captain for the injured Marvan Atapattu in England in 2006, producing a stunning double of 61 and 119 to lead the rearguard that saved the Lord's Test. Later he put South Africa to the sword in Colombo, compiling a colossal 374 in a world-record stand of 624 with Kumar Sangakkara. In 2007 he inspired his side to the World Cup final with 548 runs at 60, including a century in the semi-final, then became Sri Lanka's leading Test runscorer during 2007-08, a period that included three successive centuries, one of them a double against England. He stepped down as captain early in 2009 to concentrate on his batting – not that leadership seemed to affect it much, as he averaged 66.93 in Tests when skipper. He made a classy century in the 2011 World Cup final – in vain – and although he misfired in England afterwards he is homing in on 10,000 runs in both Tests and ODIs.

THE FACTS Jayawardene made 374 against South Africa in July 2006, the highest by a right-hander in Tests ... He took 77 Test catches off Muttiah Muralitharan, a record for a fielder-bowler combination ... Jayawardene has scored 2646 runs and ten centuries in Tests at the SSC in Colombo, a record for a single ground ... Against New Zealand in August 2009 he was only the fifth batsman to be out twice in the nineties in the same Test ... His record includes five ODIs for the Asia XI ...

THE FIGURES *to 26.09.11*   **ᴇsℼⁿcricinfo.com**

Batting & Fielding	M	Inns	NO	Runs	HS	Avge	S/R	100	50	4s	6s	Ct	St
Tests	122	201	13	9852	374	52.40	52.14	29	40	1175	44	172	0
ODIs	352	330	34	9913	144	33.48	77.80	15	60	853	57	183	0
T20Is	35	35	5	953	100	31.76	139.32	1	6	105	23	11	0
First-class	205	326	22	15643	374	51.45	–	46	68	–	–	265	0

Bowling	M	Balls	Runs	Wkts	BB	Avge	RpO	S/R	5i	10m
Tests	122	553	297	6	2–32	49.50	3.22	92.16	0	0
ODIs	352	582	558	7	2–56	79.71	5.75	83.14	0	0
T20Is	35	6	8	0	–	–	8.00	–	0	0
First-class	205	2965	1616	52	5–72	31.07	3.27	57.01	1	0

PRASANNA **JAYAWARDENE**

SRI LANKA

Full name	**Hewasandatchige Asiri Prasanna Wishvanath Jayawardene**
Born	**October 9, 1979, Colombo**
Teams	**Bloomfield, Basnahira**
Style	**Right-hand bat, wicketkeeper**
Test debut	**Sri Lanka v Pakistan at Kandy 2000**
ODI debut	**Sri Lanka v Pakistan at Sharjah 2002–03**
T20I debut	**No T20Is yet**

THE PROFILE A neat, unflashy wicketkeeper rated by Kumar Sangakkara as the best in the world, Prasanna Jayawardene looked set for a long international career after touring England at 19, but became a back number after Sangakkara's own rocket-fuelled arrival in 2000. Waiting on the sidelines had already been a feature of Jayawardene's career: in his first Test, in June 2000, he was confined to the dressing-room throughout, as rain washed out play on the last two days before Sri Lanka fielded. With the selectors worried about overburdening Sangakkara in Tests, Jayawardene was recalled in April 2004. Sangakkara soon got the gloves back that time, but there was a sea-change two years later, after an England tour in which Jayawardene showed that his batting had improved. He was recalled for South Africa's visit in July 2006, and this time the decision to lighten Sangakkara's load paid off spectacularly: he hammered 287, and shared a world-record stand of 642 with Mahela Jayawardene (no relation) in the first Test. Prasanna contented himself with a couple of catches and a stumping as the South Africans went down by an innings, but finally seemed to have booked in for a long run behind the stumps – at least in Tests, with Sangakkara continuing in one-dayers – and cemented his place in June 2007 with a Test ton of his own, against Bangladesh. A finger injury kept him out briefly in 2009, but he was back for the New Zealand Tests in August, and later that year shared a Test-record stand of 351 with Mahela against India at Ahmedabad. He made another century at Cardiff in May 2011, but bagged a pair against Australia soon afterwards.

THE FACTS Prasanna Jayawardene made 154 not out against India at Ahmedabad in November 2009: he and Mahela Jayawardene (275) put on 351 for the sixth wicket, beating the old Test record of 346 by Don Bradman and Jack Fingleton in 1936-37 ... He took seven catches in an innings for Sebastianites v Sinhalese in Colombo in January 2000... All Jayawardene's ODIs have been in the United Arab Emirates (in Sharjah in 2003 and Abu Dhabi in 2007) ...

THE FIGURES to 26.09.11   **ESFN**cricinfo.com

Batting & Fielding	M	Inns	NO	Runs	HS	Avge	S/R	100	50	4s	6s	Ct	St
Tests	42	56	8	1474	154*	30.70	50.82	3	3	155	11	80	26
ODIs	6	5	0	27	20	5.40	61.36	0	0	3	0	4	1
T20Is	0	0	–	–	–	–	–	–	–	–	–	–	–
First-class	200	305	36	7733	229*	28.74	–	12	32	–	–	456	90

Bowling	M	Balls	Runs	Wkts	BB	Avge	RpO	S/R	5i	10m
Tests	42	0	–	–	–	–	–	–	–	–
ODIs	6	0	–	–	–	–	–	–	–	–
T20Is	0	0	–	–	–	–	–	–	–	–
First-class	200	18	9	0	–	–	3.00	–	0	0

MITCHELL **JOHNSON**

Full name	**Mitchell Guy Johnson**
Born	**November 2, 1981, Townsville, Queensland**
Teams	**Western Australia**
Style	**Left-hand bat, left-hand fast-medium bowler**
Test debut	**Australia v Sri Lanka at Brisbane 2007-08**
ODI debut	**Australia v New Zealand at Christchurch 2005-06**
T20I debut	**Australia v Zimbabwe at Cape Town 2007-08**

THE PROFILE   He's quick, he's tall, he's talented ... but most of all, Mitchell Johnson is a left-armer, and only two others before him (Alan Davidson and Bruce Reid) took 100 Test wickets for Australia. Dennis Lillee spotted him at 17, and called him a "once-in-a-generation bowler". Injuries kept intruding, but in December 2005 Johnson was supersubbed into the final one-dayer in New Zealand. However, the following season was a sobering one. Johnson, who runs up as if carrying a crate of milk bottles in his left hand, started by reducing India to 35 for 5 in a one-dayer in Kuala Lumpur, but narrowly missed out to the steadier Stuart Clark for the 2006-07 Ashes, then sat out the World Cup as Shaun Tait and Nathan Bracken bowled consistently well. Test rewards finally came in 2007-08, and he was composed in his first two matches against Sri Lanka, then grabbed 16 wickets against India and ten in the West Indies. Next season Johnson was superb against South Africa both home and away, adding a wicked in-ducker to his repertoire and claiming 33 wickets in six Tests (and also hammering a maiden century), but then he struggled in England, spraying the ball around from an arm seemingly lower than usual. He did take 5 for 69 in the innings victory at Headingley, but overall he was a disappointment given the advance hype. The start of 2010 was similarly up-and-down – ten wickets against New Zealand at Hamilton, but only 11 in five other matches, and it was the same story at the end of the year in the Ashes: dropped for the second Test, matchwinner in the third with nine wickets and a handy 62, then down to earth again.

THE FACTS   Johnson took 8 for 61 – the best bowling figures in Tests by any left-arm fast bowler – against South Africa at Perth in 2008-09 ... He was the world's leading Test wicket-taker in 2009, with 63 ... Johnson took 6 for 51 (and 10 for 106 in the match) for Queensland v Victoria in the Pura Cup final at Brisbane in March 2006 ... He reached his maiden Test (and first-class) century against South Africa at Cape Town in March 2009 with a six ...

THE FIGURES *to 26.09.11*   **ESPNcricinfo.com**

Batting & Fielding	M	Inns	NO	Runs	HS	Avge	S/R	100	50	4s	6s	Ct	St
Tests	45	65	8	1186	123*	20.80	58.80	1	6	144	23	12	0
ODIs	104	58	20	693	73*	18.23	99.00	0	2	55	18	24	0
T20Is	28	16	6	106	28*	10.60	117.77	0	0	8	3	4	0
First-class	76	107	20	1993	123*	22.90	–	2	10	–	–	19	0

Bowling	M	Balls	Runs	Wkts	BB	Avge	RpO	S/R	5i	10m
Tests	45	10299	5691	187	8–61	30.43	3.31	55.07	7	2
ODIs	104	5084	4124	163	6–31	25.30	4.86	31.19	3	0
T20Is	28	608	724	36	3–15	20.11	7.14	16.88	0	0
First-class	76	15602	8792	284	8–61	30.95	3.38	54.93	10	3

JUNAID KHAN

PAKISTAN

Full name	**Mohammad Junaid Khan**
Born	**December 24, 1989, Matra, NW Frontier Province**
Teams	**Abbottabad, Lancashire**
Style	**Right-hand bat, left-arm fast-medium bowler**
Test debut	**Pakistan v Zimbabwe at Bulawayo 2011**
ODI debut	**Pakistan v West Indies at Gros Islet 2010-11**
T20I debut	**Pakistan v West Indies at Gros Islet 2010-11**

THE PROFILE Junaid Khan had an unenviable task as the left-arm fast bowler called up in 2011 to replace the banned Mohammad Aamer. Junaid bowls at a good pace – the upper 80s mph according to the man himself – and moves the ball around when conditions are right. He was called up for Pakistan's 2011 World Cup squad as a late replacement for the unfit Sohail Tanvir, but didn't actually get a game, His debut had to wait until the West Indian tour that followed, and he made a slow start – only three wickets in six internationals, one of them a Twenty20 game. Junaid did grab six cheap scalps in the two matches that followed in Ireland, which was enough to keep him in the squad for the Zimbabwe tour that followed (in between he had a promising stint in limited-overs cricket for Lancashire). He made his Test debut at Bulawayo in September, but although he kept things quiet in the first innings – his 29 overs included 14 maidens, and he finished with 1 for 55 – he was generally overshadowed by fellow debutant Aizaz Cheema, who took eight wickets. Junaid is from the Khyber-Pakhtunkhwa (formerly North West Frontier) province, and plays at home for Abbottabad, who are among the weaker sides on Pakistan's domestic circuit. But he still managed to catch the selectors' eye, taking 75 wickets at a fraction under 24 apiece in first-class cricket in 2009-10 (Tanvir Ahmed, now a rival for a Test place, led the way with 97). That led to a summons to the Pakistan A team, and he did not disappoint, taking nine wickets in the match against Sri Lanka A at Hambantota in September 2010.

THE FACTS Junaid Khan took 7 for 46 (13 for 77 in the match) for Abbottabad at Peshawar in November 2007 ... He had figures of 4-0-4-5 as Khan Research Laboratories bowled Customs out for 79 – the last nine wickets went down for 13 – in a first-class match at Mirpur in February 2009 ... Junaid took 4 for 12 against Ireland in an ODI in Belfast in May 2011 ...

THE FIGURES to 26.09.11   ᴇꜱᴘɴcricinfo.com

Batting & Fielding	M	Inns	NO	Runs	HS	Avge	S/R	100	50	4s	6s	Ct	St
Tests	1	1	0	6	6	6.00	46.15	0	0	0	0	1	0
ODIs	9	2	1	2	1*	2.00	22.22	0	0	0	0	3	0
T20Is	2	1	1	3	3*	–	75.00	0	0	0	0	0	0
First-class	37	50	16	441	71	12.97	–	0	2	–	–	7	0

Bowling	M	Balls	Runs	Wkts	BB	Avge	RpO	S/R	5i	10m
Tests	1	186	64	1	1–55	64.00	2.06	186.00	0	0
ODIs	9	390	303	10	4–12	30.30	4.66	39.00	0	0
T20Is	2	36	38	2	2–23	19.00	6.33	18.00	0	0
First-class	37	7458	3716	169	7–46	21.98	2.98	44.13	13	3

JUNAID SIDDIQUE

Full name	**Mohammad Junaid Siddique**
Born	**October 30, 1987, Rajshahi**
Teams	**Rajshahi**
Style	**Left-hand bat, occasional offspinner**
Test debut	**Bangladesh v New Zealand at Dunedin 2007-08**
ODI debut	**Bangladesh v New Zealand at Auckland 2007-08**
T20I debut	**Bangladesh v Pakistan at Cape Town 2007-08**

THE PROFILE   Left-hander Junaid Siddique made a sensational start in Test cricket, when he and fellow debutant Tamim Iqbal flayed the New Zealand bowlers in an opening stand of 161 to light up the inaugural Test at Dunedin's University Oval at the start of 2008. Wisden said they began "with an entrancing display of classical strokes, their timing perfect as the ball was distributed around the short boundaries". Sadly, this fine start came to nothing: the other batsmen made only 83 between them, and Bangladesh lost yet again. "Imrose" also made a stylish 74 against South Africa at Mirpur – no-one else made more than 24 – and added 71 on his Twenty20 international debut. However, the faster bowlers noticed a compulsion to get onto the front foot – bred on slow, low pitches in Bangladesh – and Junaid began to cop a lot of short stuff. But he persevered, making 78 in victory over a depleted West Indian side in St Vincent in July 2009, while his ODI performances improved: after an anaemic start (62 runs in eight innings), he hit 85 against New Zealand in November 2008, then scored consistently against admittedly modest attacks in the West Indies and Zimbabwe. He settled in at No. 3, and made his first Test century against England at Chittagong in March 2010, before adding a maiden one-day international hundred against Ireland a few months later. Typically, though, Bangladesh lost both matches. An up-and-down 2011 saw Junaid struggle at the World Cup before doing well with the A team in South Africa ... then failing to make much impression as Bangladesh crashed to embarrassing defeats in the Test and one-day series in Zimbabwe later in the year.

THE FACTS   Junaid Siddique scored 74 on his Test debut at Dunedin in January 2008, putting on 161 for the first wicket with Tamim Iqbal, who was also winning his first cap: it was the highest opening stand between debutants in Tests since Billy Ibadulla and Abdul Kadir put on 249 for Pakistan v Australia at Karachi in 1964-65 ... Junaid hit 71 off 49 balls in his first Twenty20 international, against Pakistan at Cape Town in September 2007 ...

THE FIGURES *to 26.09.11*   **ESPN**cricinfo.com

Batting & Fielding	M	Inns	NO	Runs	HS	Avge	S/R	100	50	4s	6s	Ct	St
Tests	18	35	0	942	106	26.91	41.22	1	7	121	1	11	0
ODIs	54	53	1	1196	100	23.00	68.22	1	6	118	7	23	0
T20Is	5	5	0	134	71	26.80	159.52	0	1	13	6	0	0
First-class	45	82	1	2073	114*	25.59	–	2	12	–	–	31	0

Bowling	M	Balls	Runs	Wkts	BB	Avge	RpO	S/R	5i	10m
Tests	18	18	11	0	–	–	3.66	–	0	0
ODIs	54	12	13	0	–	–	6.50	–	0	0
T20Is	5	0	–	–	–	–	–	–	–	–
First-class	45	198	119	1	1–30	119.00	3.60	198.00	0	0

JACQUES **KALLIS**

SOUTH AFRICA

Full name	**Jacques Henry Kallis**
Born	**October 16, 1975, Pinelands, Cape Town**
Teams	**Warriors, Kolkata Knight Riders**
Style	**Right-hand bat, right-arm fast-medium bowler**
Test debut	**South Africa v England at Durban 1995-96**
ODI debut	**South Africa v England at Cape Town 1995-96**
T20I debut	**South Africa v New Zealand at Johannesburg 2005-06**

THE PROFILE In an era of fast scoring and high-octane entertainment, Jacques Kallis is a throwback – an astonishingly effective one – to a more sedate age, when your wicket was to be guarded with your life, and runs were an accidental by-product of crease-occupation. He blossomed after a quiet start into arguably the world's leading batsman, with the adhesive qualities of a Cape Point limpet. In 2005, he was the ICC's first Test Player of the Year, but his batting is not for the romantic: a Kallis century (of which there have now been 57 in international cricket) tends to be a soulless affair, with ruthless efficiency taking precedence over derring-do, and he has never quite dispelled the notion that he is a selfish batsman, something the Aussies played on during the 2007 World Cup. His team-mates, though, vouch for the fact that he bats the way he does precisely because he puts his team first and his personal ambitions some way behind. He had a purple patch at the turn of 2010-11, scoring five Test centuries – including a long-awaited maiden 200 – inside two months. Kallis has sailed to the top of South Africa's batting charts, and until Andrew Flintoff's emergence was comfortably the world's leading allrounder, capable of swinging the ball sharply at a surprising pace. Strong, with powerful shoulders and a deep chest, Kallis has the capacity to play a wide array of attacking strokes. He is approaching 150 Test caps, and has a batting average in the mid-fifties to go with nearly 550 international wickets all told. He's a fine slip fielder too.

THE FACTS Kallis and Shaun Pollock were the first South Africans to play 100 Tests, reaching the mark, appropriately enough, at Centurion in April 2006 ... Kallis averages 169.75 in Tests against Zimbabwe, and scored 388 runs against them in two Tests in 2001-02 without being dismissed ... Including his next innings he batted for a record 1241 minutes in Tests without getting out ... Kallis scored hundreds in five successive Tests in 2003-04 (only Don Bradman, with six, has done better) ... His record includes one Test and three ODIs for the World XI, and two ODIs for the Africa XI ...

THE FIGURES *to 26.09.11*   **ᴇsᴘᴨcricinfo.com**

Batting & Fielding	M	Inns	NO	Runs	HS	Avge	S/R	100	50	4s	6s	Ct	St
Tests	145	246	38	11947	201*	57.43	45.22	40	54	1315	86	166	0
ODIs	314	300	53	11227	139	45.45	72.77	17	82	880	130	122	0
T20Is	16	16	1	512	73	34.13	119.90	0	4	40	17	6	0
First-class	235	386	55	18299	201*	55.28	–	57	92	–	–	228	0

Bowling	M	Balls	Runs	Wkts	BB	Avge	RpO	S/R	5i	10m
Tests	145	18337	8643	270	6–54	32.01	2.82	67.91	5	0
ODIs	314	10450	8387	264	5–30	31.76	4.81	39.58	2	0
T20Is	16	186	229	5	2–20	45.80	7.38	37.20	0	0
First-class	235	27072	12607	405	6–54	31.12	2.79	66.84	8	0

KAMRAN AKMAL

Full name	**Kamran Akmal**
Born	**January 13, 1982, Lahore, Punjab**
Teams	**Lahore, National Bank**
Style	**Right-hand bat, wicketkeeper**
Test debut	**Pakistan v Zimbabwe at Harare 2002-03**
ODI debut	**Pakistan v Zimbabwe at Bulawayo 2002-03**
T20I debut	**Pakistan v England at Bristol 2006**

THE PROFILE Kamran Akmal made his first-class debut at the age of 15 as a useful wicketkeeper and a hard-hitting batsman. He has had good times since – and bad ones, as his keeping fell away, leading to several costly errors, none more so than in an iron-gloved performance that cost Pakistan victory at Sydney in January 2010: Akmal dropped four catches, most of them sitters, and failed with the bat too. After that he was briefly dropped, and although he returned his form since has been fitful, and he was replaced again after the 2011 World Cup by his brother Adnan (another brother, Umar, has also kept wicket for Pakistan). But Kamran seems to be a survivor, and no-one is writing him off just yet. It all started so promisingly: by October 2004 he was Pakistan's first-choice keeper, putting in a magnificent showing with the gloves in Australia, then, in 2005, hit five international centuries. Three of them came while opening in one-dayers, and two in Tests, one top save the match against India at Mohali, and a blistering 154 in the emphatic series-sealing win over England at Lahore. However, a nightmare series in England in 2006 set him back again. He retained his place without ever quite regaining his best touch with bat or gloves: he did make an important 119 against India in the Kolkata Test in November 2007, but continued fumbles behind the stumps eventually cost him an automatic place. There were still some highlights, though: Akmal started 2009 with an unbeaten 158 in a Test against Sri Lanka and a century against Australia, and also played his part as Pakistan won the World Twenty20 in England in June 2010.

THE FACTS Kamran Akmal scored five international hundreds in December 2005 and January 2006, including 154 in the Lahore Test against England, when he shared a sixth-wicket stand of 269 with Mohammad Yousuf ... Akmal has scored more Test hundreds than any other Pakistan wicketkeeper: Moin Khan made four and Imtiaz Ahmed three ... His brothers Umar and Adnan Akmal have both also played – and kept wicket for Pakistan ...

THE FIGURES to 26.09.11   **ESPncricinfo.com**

Batting & Fielding	M	Inns	NO	Runs	HS	Avge	S/R	100	50	4s	6s	Ct	St
Tests	53	92	6	2648	158*	30.79	63.10	6	12	372	14	184	22
ODIs	137	120	14	2924	124	27.58	84.31	5	9	341	31	136	25
T20Is	38	33	3	704	73	23.46	124.60	0	5	67	25	17	28
First-class	163	255	28	7480	268	32.95	–	14	36	–	–	551	45

Bowling	M	Balls	Runs	Wkts	BB	Avge	RpO	S/R	5i	10m
Tests	53	0	–	–	–	–	–	–	–	–
ODIs	137	0	–	–	–	–	–	–	–	–
T20Is	38	0	–	–	–	–	–	–	–	–
First-class	163	0	–	–	–	–	–	–	–	–

ZAHEER **KHAN**

INDIA

Full name	**Zaheer Khan**
Born	**October 7, 1978, Shrirampur, Maharashtra**
Teams	**Mumbai, Royal Challengers Bangalore**
Style	**Right-hand bat, left-arm fast-medium bowler**
Test debut	**India v Bangladesh at Dhaka 2000-01**
ODI debut	**India v Kenya at Nairobi 2000-01**
T20I debut	**India v South Africa at Johannesburg 2006-07**

THE PROFILE Like Waqar Younis before him, Zaheer Khan yorked his way into the cricket world's consciousness: his performances at the Champions Trophy in September 2000 announced the arrival of an all-too-rare star in the Indian fast-bowling firmament. Zaheer can move the ball both ways off the pitch and swing the old ball at a decent pace. After initial struggles, he came of age in the West Indies in 2002, when he led the attack with great heart. His subsequent displays in England and New Zealand – and some eye-catching moments at the 2003 World Cup – established him at the forefront of the new pace generation, but a hamstring injury relegated him to bit-part performer as India enjoyed some of their finest moments away in Australia and Pakistan. In a bid to jump the queue of left-arm hopefuls, Zaheer put in the hard yards for Worcestershire in 2006: against Essex, he took the first nine wickets to fall before Darren Gough's flailing bat spoilt his chances of a rare all-ten. It worked: Zaheer reclaimed his Test place, survived the fallout from the World Cup, and led the way in England in 2007, where his nine wickets at Trent Bridge clinched the match and the series: he was one of *Wisden*'s Cricketers of the Year. After an ankle injury he led the attack in the 2011 World Cup success – but his early exit from the England tour that followed, after a hamstring problem in the first Test, visibly deflated India, who subsided to a 4-0 whitewash. At 33, Zaheer faces yet another fight to regain full fitness, but the looming landmarks of 300 wickets in Tests and ODIs should help.

THE FACTS Zaheer Khan's 75 against Bangladesh at Dhaka in December 2004 is the highest score by a No. 11 in Tests: he dominated a last-wicket stand of 133 with Sachin Tendulkar ... He took 9 for 138 (including a spell of 9 for 28) for Worcestershire v Essex at Chelmsford in June 2006, but a last-wicket stand of 97 cost him the chance of taking all ten wickets ... Zaheer averages 17.46 with the ball in ODIs against Zimbabwe, but 46.42 against Australia ... His record includes six ODIs for the Asia XI ...

THE FIGURES to 26.09.11   ESPncricinfo.com

Batting & Fielding	M	Inns	NO	Runs	HS	Avge	S/R	100	50	4s	6s	Ct	St
Tests	79	105	23	1045	75	12.74	50.16	0	3	117	21	18	0
ODIs	191	99	35	781	34*	12.20	73.47	0	0	67	24	42	0
T20Is	12	4	2	13	9	6.50	130.00	0	0	0	1	2	0
First-class	144	188	38	2094	75	13.96	–	0	4	–	–	42	0

Bowling	M	Balls	Runs	Wkts	BB	Avge	RpO	S/R	5i	10m
Tests	79	15837	8676	273	7–87	31.78	3.28	58.01	10	1
ODIs	191	9617	7874	273	5–42	28.84	4.91	35.22	1	0
T20Is	12	250	327	13	4–19	25.15	7.84	19.23	0	0
First-class	144	29439	16270	592	9–138	27.48	3.31	49.72	32	8

USMAN **KHAWAJA**

Full name **Usman Tariq Khawaja**
Born **December 18, 1986, Islamabad, Pakistan**
Teams **New South Wales, Derbyshire**
Style **Left-hand bat, occ. right-arm medium-pacer**
Test debut **Australia v England at Sydney 2010-11**
ODI debut **No ODIs yet**
T20I debut **No T20Is yet**

THE PROFILE Born in Pakistan, Usman Khawaja moved to Australia when he was a young boy and achieved his dream of becoming the first Muslim to play for them when he was picked for the final Test of the 2010-11 Ashes at Sydney. In a series that had brought plenty of gloom for Australia, Khawaja was a ray of hope. He replaced the injured Ricky Ponting, and marked his arrival in style, pulling his second ball to the midwicket boundary, almost emulating the watching David Gower, another left-hander, who did something similar to the first ball he received in Tests in 1978. Khawaja made only 37 and 21, but his poise, temperament and charisma were enough for him to be hailed as Australia's top-order saviour, although he was left out again later in 2011 after modest performances in the first two Tests in Sri Lanka and the rise of Shaun Marsh. Khawaja had won rave reviews during his second and third seasons with New South Wales. After making 85 on his debut in 2007-08, he collected 554 runs at 42.61 the following season, then blossomed with three Sheffield Shield centuries in his haul of 698 runs in 2009-10. That earned him a trip to England, for the "neutral" Tests against his native Pakistan, although there was no great conflict of loyalty: "I will never forget where I come from, and no one should, but Australia has been my home ever since I can remember," he said. Khawaja didn't feature in those Tests, but laid the groundwork for his Ashes call-up with 214 in a Shield match at Adelaide in October 2010. While cricket is his first love, Khawaja is also a qualified pilot.

THE FACTS Khawaja scored 214 for New South Wales against South Australia at Adelaide in October 2010 ... He made 210 not out and 228 in successive matches for NSW's 2nd XI in October 2008 ... Khawaja was the first Muslim (and the first man born in Pakistan) to play Test cricket for Australia ...

THE FIGURES to 26.09.11   **ESPNcricinfo.com**

Batting & Fielding	M	Inns	NO	Runs	HS	Avge	S/R	100	50	4s	6s	Ct	St
Tests	3	5	1	118	37	29.50	36.19	0	0	9	2	0	0
ODIs	0	0	–	–	–	–	–	–	–	–	–	–	
T20Is	0	0	–	–	–	–	–	–	–	–	–	–	
First-class	38	63	5	2665	214	45.94	51.64	8	10	341	10	21	0

Bowling	M	Balls	Runs	Wkts	BB	Avge	RpO	S/R	5i	10m
Tests	3	0	–	–	–	–	–	–	–	–
ODIs	0	0	–	–	–	–	–	–	–	–
T20Is	0	0	–	–	–	–	–	–	–	–
First-class	38	72	47	1	1–21	47.00	3.91	72.00	0	0

CRAIG **KIESWETTER**

Full name	**Craig Kieswetter**
Born	**November 28, 1987, Johannesburg, South Africa**
Teams	**Somerset**
Style	**Right-hand bat, wicketkeeper**
Test debut	**No Tests yet**
ODI debut	**England v Bangladesh at Mirpur 2009-10**
T20I debut	**England v West Indies at Providence 2009-10**

THE PROFILE   Craig Kieswetter's attractive, uncomplicated front-foot technique pushed him to the brink of an England place before he'd even finished his qualification period, after choosing his adopted country ahead of his native South Africa (despite a late plea from Graeme Smith). The day after he was qualified, he hit 81 for the Lions against the full England side in Abu Dhabi. Fast-tracked into the limited-overs teams, he spanked a classy century in only his third match, in Bangladesh, then gave England a series of rapid starts in the World Twenty20 in the West Indies, crowning his campaign with 63 – and the match award – as the final was won. And then it all started to go wrong. Kieswetter, who had scored 1242 first-class runs in 2009, managed less than 500 in 2010. He did make more than 500 in one-dayers for the second year running – but at almost half his 2009 average, and duly lost his England place. The problem seemed to be twofold: bowlers had got wise to his strengths, and avoided them more; so, in a bid to combat the lack of drivable balls, Kieswetter moved his stance outside leg and was therefore exposing his stumps. By the end of 2010 he had moved back across, and looked better for it: the first-class average was back above 40 in 2011. After missing the World Cup Kieswetter was restored to the England side later in the year, making 61 and 72 against Sri Lanka and adding useful runs against India. He first came to prominence at Millfield School, and made his Somerset first-team debut in April 2007, scoring 69 not out off 58 balls and taking a catch his coach described as "world class".

THE FACTS   Kieswetter made 107 in only his third ODI, against Bangladesh at Chittagong in March 2010 ... All four of his first-class hundreds to date came in England during 2009 ... Kieswetter made 164 for Somerset v Nottinghamshire at Trent Bridge in July 2011 ... He scored 150 not out against Warwickshire at Taunton in April 2009, and next day hit 138 not out against them in a 50-over game ...

THE FIGURES to 26.09.11   **ESFN cricinfo.com**

Batting & Fielding	M	Inns	NO	Runs	HS	Avge	S/R	100	50	4s	6s	Ct	St
Tests	0	0	–	–	–	–	–	–	–	–	–	–	–
ODIs	23	23	1	674	107	30.63	92.83	1	4	69	22	22	6
T20Is	13	13	1	334	63	27.83	117.19	0	2	30	15	7	2
First-class	76	111	13	3765	164	38.41	–	8	20	–	–	220	3

Bowling	M	Balls	Runs	Wkts	BB	Avge	RpO	S/R	5i	10m
Tests	0	0	–	–	–	–	–	–	–	–
ODIs	23	0	–	–	–	–	–	–	–	–
T20Is	13	0	–	–	–	–	–	–	–	–
First-class	76	0	–	–	–	–	–	–	–	–

VIRAT **KOHLI**

Full name	**Virat Kohli**
Born	**November 5, 1988, Delhi**
Teams	**Delhi, Royal Challengers Bangalore**
Style	**Right-hand bat, occasional medium-pacer**
Test debut	**India v West Indies at Kingston 2011**
ODI debut	**India v Sri Lanka at Dambulla 2008**
T20I debut	**India v Zimbabwe at Harare 2010**

THE PROFILE An attacking player with a cool head and the hint of a swagger that suggests he knows he's pretty good, Virat Kohli has been making big scores from a young age. He made three double-centuries for Delhi's Under-17s, then captained India to victory in the Under-19 World Cup in Malaysia in 2008. By then he had already made his Ranji Trophy debut, making 90 (after Delhi had been 14 for 4) against Karnataka in his fourth match. The upward curve continued in 2007-08 with a maiden century against Rajasthan, and a superb 169 against Karnataka. He was consistent in one-day cricket without making big scores – that came later, with four hundreds in a fortnight in February 2009 – and was called up for a series in Sri Lanka in August 2008. He wasn't expected to play, but an injury to Virender Sehwag gave Kohli a chance: he reached double figures in all five innings, with 54 in the fourth game. Another good domestic season followed – 613 runs at 55, with a career-best 197 against Pakistan's national champions – then he improved his IPL form after a disappointing first campaign. Kohli enjoyed a dream run in ODIs in 2009-10: successive innings against Sri Lanka and Bangladesh produced 54, 107, 9, 91, 71 not out and 102 not out. He couldn't quite keep that up, but it did cement his place in the side. He kicked off the 2011 World Cup with a hundred against Bangladesh, and later contributed 35 as the final was won. He made his Test debut in the Caribbean shortly afterwards, but struggled and missed out on the Tests in England – although Suresh Raina's travails in that whitewash might soon offer Kohli another five-day chance.

THE FACTS Kohli scored 197 for Delhi against Pakistan's champions Sui Northern Gas in the Mohammad Nissar Trophy match at Delhi in September 2008... He made 105 for the Board President's XI against the Australian tourists at Hyderabad in October 2008 ... Kohli took a wicket with his first delivery in Twenty20 internationals (Kevin Pietersen stumped off a wide) at Old Trafford in August 2011 ...

THE FIGURES to 26.09.11   **ᴇsᴘɴcricinfo.com**

Batting & Fielding	M	Inns	NO	Runs	HS	Avge	S/R	100	50	4s	6s	Ct	St
Tests	3	5	0	76	30	15.20	33.62	0	0	6	1	5	0
ODIs	64	61	7	2347	118	43.46	82.14	6	16	217	15	30	0
T20Is	5	4	1	72	28	24.00	126.31	0	0	10	1	3	0
First-class	33	49	7	2207	197	52.54	56.45	7	8	304	14	32	0

Bowling	M	Balls	Runs	Wkts	BB	Avge	RpO	S/R	5i	10m
Tests	3	0	–	–	–	–	–	–	–	–
ODIs	64	166	174	1	1–44	174.00	6.28	166.00	0	0
T20Is	5	18	22	1	1–22	22.00	7.33	18.00	0	0
First-class	33	468	254	3	1–19	84.66	3.25	156.00	0	0

NUWAN **KULASEKARA**

Full name	**Kulasekara Mudiyanselage Dinesh Nuwan Kulasekara**
Born	**July 22, 1982, Nittambuwa**
Teams	**Colts, Basnahira, Chennai Super Kings**
Style	**Right-hand bat, right-arm fast-medium bowler**
Test debut	**Sri Lanka v New Zealand at Napier 2004-05**
ODI debut	**Sri Lanka v England at Dambulla 2003-04**
T20I debut	**Sri Lanka v Pakistan at King City 2008-09**

THE PROFILE Nuwan Kulasekara generates a lively pace from a bustling run-up and a whippy open-chested action, and moves the ball off the seam at around 80mph. He can also maintain a tight line and length, and, after adding a yard or two of pace, suddenly emerged as a formidable bowler, especially in one-day internationals. He did so well in 2008 (33 wickets at 20.87 in 21 matches) that by March 2009 he was proudly sitting on top of the ICC's world one-day rankings for bowlers. He maintained that form throughout 2009, and also began to look the part in Tests, too: he grabbed four wickets in each innings as Pakistan lost in Colombo in August, and ending that series with 17 victims. After that, though, the old worries about his supposed lack of pace returned, and he has been in and out of the side ever since, although he did play six matches in the 2011 World Cup, including the final. After that, though, nine ODIs against England and Australia produced only three wickets. Prior to this, Kulasekara's biggest mark on Test cricket had been with the bat: at Lord's in May 2006 he hung on for more than three hours for 64, helping Chaminda Vaas ensure that Sri Lanka managed a draw after following on 359 behind. Kulasekara also made an instant impression in his first one-dayer, taking 2 for 19 in nine overs as England subsided for 88 at Dambulla in November 2003. That came soon after a fine first season, in which he took 61 wickets at 21.06 for Colts. He started as a softball enthusiast before turning to cricket, first with Negegoda CC and then with Galle.

THE FACTS Playing for North Central Province at Dambulla in March 2005, Kulasekara dismissed all of Central Province's top six, finishing with 6 for 71 ... He took 7 for 27 for Colts v Bloomfield in January 2008 ... In March 2009 Kulasekara was top of the ICC world rankings for ODI bowlers ... He made 95 for Galle v Nondescripts in Colombo in October 2003: he and Primal Buddika doubled the score from 174 for 6 ...

THE FIGURES to 26.09.11   **ESPncricinfo**.com

Batting & Fielding	M	Inns	NO	Runs	HS	Avge	S/R	100	50	4s	6s	Ct	St
Tests	12	17	1	262	64	16.37	44.10	0	1	35	4	4	0
ODIs	98	63	24	645	57*	16.53	73.37	0	1	42	15	24	0
T20Is	15	10	2	56	19*	7.00	105.66	0	0	1	2	5	0
First-class	74	98	21	1434	95	18.62	–	0	4	–	–	26	0

Bowling	M	Balls	Runs	Wkts	BB	Avge	RpO	S/R	5i	10m
Tests	12	1678	879	26	4–21	33.80	3.14	64.53	0	0
ODIs	98	4488	3437	108	4–40	31.82	4.59	41.55	0	0
T20Is	15	329	453	14	3–4	32.35	8.26	23.50	0	0
First-class	74	10194	5502	243	7–27	22.64	3.23	41.95	9	1

PRAVEEN **KUMAR**

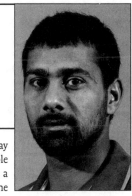

Full name	**Praveenkumar Sakat Singh**
Born	**October 2, 1986, Meerut, Uttar Pradesh**
Teams	**Uttar Pradesh, Royal Challengers Bangalore**
Style	**Right-hand bat, right-arm fast-medium bowler**
Test debut	**India v West Indies at Kingston 2011**
ODI debut	**India v Pakistan at Jaipur 2007-08**
T20I debut	**India v Australia at Melbourne 2007-08**

THE PROFILE A medium-pacer accustomed to plugging away on unresponsive Indian wickets, Praveen Kumar can also double up as a carefree hitter down the order and even, sometimes, as a surprise opener. He shone on debut in November 2005, with nine wickets against Haryana, and was a key performer – 41 wickets and 368 runs – as Uttar Pradesh won the Ranji Trophy in his first season. He followed that with 49 wickets the following term, and earned an A-team place for a one-day series in mid-2007 in Kenya, where he excelled with both bat and ball. Kumar was called up for the senior one-dayers against Pakistan, but went wicketless in his only match. However, another strong Ranji season – including 8 for 68 in vain in the final against Delhi – sent him to Australia for the one-day series early in 2008. He returned with reputation enhanced after ten wickets in his four games, including a matchwinning 4 for 46 in the second (and conclusive) final at Brisbane: he dismissed Adam Gilchrist and Ricky Ponting for single figures in both finals. After that Kumar did well in the inaugural IPL, then produced another matchwinning four-wicket effort against Pakistan in a one-dayer in Bangladesh. His progress stalled a little after that – only 18 first-class wickets at 37 in 2008-09 – and he missed the World Twenty20 in the Caribbean in 2010 with a side strain. He also missed the 2011 World Cup with an elbow injury but, not previously seen as a Test prospect, he was a lone star as India suffered a 4-0 whitewash in England later in the year, manfully undertaking long spells – and moving the ball around artfully – after Zaheer Khan limped out of the series.

THE FACTS Kumar took 8 for 68 for Uttar Pradesh v Delhi in the Ranji Trophy final at Mumbai in January 2008 ... He took 5 for 93 (and 4 for 55 in the second innings) on his first-class debut for UP v Haryana at Kanpur in November 2005 ... Kumar took an IPL hat-trick for Bangalore against Rajasthan in March 2010 ... He scored 78 and 57, and also took 5 for 73 and 5 for 87, for UP v Andhra at Anantapur in January 2006 ...

THE FIGURES to 26.09.11   ESPncricinfo.com

Batting & Fielding	M	Inns	NO	Runs	HS	Avge	S/R	100	50	4s	6s	Ct	St
Tests	6	10	0	149	40	14.90	93.71	0	0	21	5	2	0
ODIs	56	29	11	259	54*	14.38	87.20	0	1	22	6	11	0
T20Is	6	2	0	7	6	3.50	50.00	0	0	0	0	1	0
First-class	44	70	4	1579	98	23.92	75.94	0	8	169	55	8	0

Bowling	M	Balls	Runs	Wkts	BB	Avge	RpO	S/R	5i	10m
Tests	6	1611	697	27	5–106	25.81	2.59	59.66	1	0
ODIs	56	2630	2195	65	4–31	33.76	5.00	40.46	0	0
T20Is	6	102	103	6	2–14	17.16	6.05	17.00	0	0
First-class	44	10129	4665	199	8–68	23.44	2.76	50.89	14	1

SURANGA **LAKMAL**

Full name	**Ranasinghe Arachchige Suranga Lakmal**
Born	**March 10, 1987, Matara**
Teams	**Tamil Union, Ruhuna**
Style	**Right-hand bat, right-arm fast-medium bowler**
Test debut	**Sri Lanka v West Indies at Colombo 2010-11**
ODI debut	**Sri Lanka v India at Nagpur 2009-10**
T20I debut	**Sri Lanka v England at Bristol 2011**

THE PROFILE A fast-medium bowler who generates fair pace from a slingy action, Suranga Lakmal was first spotted by the Sri Lankan board's fast-bowling coaches while still at school. What impressed the coaches was Lakmal's height, which brought with it an ability to get bounce and swing at a tender age. But in his early days he had a major problem – he lacked the stamina to bowl long spells, and when he did manage one he often fell ill. This stemmed from a lack of nutrition, apparently quite a common problem in fast bowlers who come from outside Colombo – he hails from the southern city of Matara, Sanath Jayasuriya's home town – and as soon as Lakmal joined the academy the coaches started work on his stamina. It paid off: after some good performances with the A team he broke into the senior one-day side at the end of 2009. He got a bit of tap in his first match, before removing Virender Sehwag and Sachin Tendulkar early on in his second one. Lakmal's first Tests came late the following year, in the soggy home series against West Indies. In the third Test, he dismissed Chris Gayle with the first ball of the match, and impressed his coach, Trevor Bayliss: "He has bowled extremely well, even though he's only got one wicket – he is the least experienced in the team but he's been one of our better bowlers." Lakmal toiled away equally enthusiastically in England in 2011, taking three wickets in the first innings at Lord's, although he leaked runs at more than five an over. Soon after that his four scalps in the first Test against Australia at Galle included Ricky Ponting.

THE FACTS Lakmal took 5 for 78 – his only first-class five-for to date – for Tamil Union v Badureliya in Colombo in March 2008 ... He took a wicket (England's Michael Lumb) with his third ball in Twenty20 internationals, at Bristol in June 2011 ... Lakmal claimed 10 for 35 (5 for 21 and 5 for 14) for Tamil Union v Bloomfield in an under-23 tournament in July 2007 ...

THE FIGURES to 26.09.11   **ESPncricinfo.com**

Batting & Fielding	M	Inns	NO	Runs	HS	Avge	S/R	100	50	4s	6s	Ct	St
Tests	8	8	3	29	13	5.80	43.28	0	0	4	0	2	0
ODIs	11	4	4	1	1*	–	7.69	0	0	0	0	5	0
T20Is	2	0	–	–	–	–	–	–	–	–	–	0	0
First-class	42	45	10	294	31	8.40	54.44	0	0	30	6	12	0

Bowling	M	Balls	Runs	Wkts	BB	Avge	RpO	S/R	5i	10m
Tests	8	1289	821	18	3–55	45.61	3.82	71.61	0	0
ODIs	11	461	506	11	3–43	46.00	6.58	41.90	0	0
T20Is	2	42	49	3	2–26	16.33	7.00	14.00	0	0
First-class	42	5565	3828	115	5–78	33.28	4.12	48.39	1	0

GREG **LAMB**

Full name	**Gregory Arthur Lamb**
Born	**March 4, 1981, Harare**
Teams	**Mashonaland Eagles**
Style	**Right-hand bat, offspinner**
Test debut	**Zimbabwe v Pakistan at Bulawayo 2011**
ODI debut	**Zimbabwe v West Indies at Providence 2009-10**
T20I debut	**Zimbabwe v West Indies at Port-of-Spain 2009-10**

THE PROFILE   An allrounder who bowls handy offspin and bats in the middle order, Greg Lamb joined Hampshire in 2001 after a spell at the Zimbabwe Cricket Academy as a youngster. In 2005 he and fellow Zimbabwean Sean Ervine were on the winning side in the C&G Trophy final against Warwickshire at Lord's, and Lamb was also a valuable member of the squad that finished second in the Championship that season. In 2006 he struggled to nail down a regular four-day place, but topped the county's averages in the Twenty20 Cup with 183 runs at the healthy strike-rate of 115.82. But form and opportunities fell away after that: after a forgettable 2007, he had a few more opportunities the following year, but only made an impact in one-day games. The writing was on the wall, and he left the Rose Bowl after making no first-team appearances during 2009. Lamb returned to Zimbabwe, and the move paid off immediately. He averaged 55.68 for Mashonaland Eagles in the Logan Cup, with two hundreds, and 64 in one-dayers, and produced some handy bowling spells too: before the end of the season he had been called up for the tour of Zimbabwe early in 2010. Lamb made his international debut in the Caribbean, and although he did little of note at first beyond taking three wickets in a rare one-day victory over India at Harare in June, he retained his place for the 2011 World Cup, where he was again anonymous. It was something of a surprise when he was called up for Zimbabwe's second Test back, against Pakistan in September 2011, but he enjoyed a good allround debut, scoring 39 then taking three top-six wickets.

THE FACTS   Lamb scored 171 for Mashonaland Eagles against Mid West Rhinos at Kwekwe in January 2010, and added 159 in the return match at Harare two months later ... He took 7 for 73 (9 for 92 in the match) for the CFX Academy against Midlands art Kwekwe in March 2000: in the next match, against Manicaland at Mutare, he added his maiden century ... Lamb was part of the Hampshire side which won the C&G Trophy final at Lord's in 2005 ...

THE FIGURES *to 26.09.11*   **ESP∩cricinfo.com**

Batting & Fielding	M	Inns	NO	Runs	HS	Avge	S/R	100	50	4s	6s	Ct	St
Tests	1	2	0	46	39	23.00	38.33	0	0	4	0	2	0
ODIs	15	14	3	197	37	17.90	51.70	0	0	6	1	0	0
T20Is	5	4	2	32	14*	16.00	59.25	0	0	1	0	0	0
First-class	55	86	9	2482	171	32.23	–	5	11	–	–	42	0

Bowling	M	Balls	Runs	Wkts	BB	Avge	RpO	S/R	5i	10m
Tests	1	192	141	3	3–120	47.00	4.40	64.00	0	0
ODIs	15	642	467	12	3–45	38.91	4.36	53.50	0	0
T20Is	5	73	80	4	2–14	20.00	6.57	18.25	0	0
First-class	55	4210	2429	55	7–73	44.16	3.46	76.54	1	0

VVS **LAXMAN**

INDIA

Full name	**Vangipurappu Venkata Sai Laxman**
Born	**November 1, 1974, Hyderabad, Andhra Pradesh**
Teams	**Hyderabad, Kochi Tuskers Kerala**
Style	**Right-hand bat, occasional offspinner**
Test debut	**India v South Africa at Ahmedabad 1996-97**
ODI debut	**India v Zimbabwe at Cuttack 1997-98**
T20I debut	**No T20Is yet**

THE PROFILE   At his best, VVS Laxman (his admirers swear the initials stand for "Very Very Special") is a sight for the gods. Wristy and willowy, he can match – sometimes even better – Tendulkar for strokeplay. His on-side game is comparable to his idol Azharuddin's, yet he is decidedly more assured on the off, and has the rare gift of being able to hit the same ball to either side. The Australians, who have suffered more than most, paid him the highest compliment after India's 2003-04 tour by admitting they did not know where to bowl to him. Laxman, a one-time medical student, graduated after a five-year international apprenticeship in March 2001, when he tormented Steve Waugh's thought-to-be-invincible Aussies with a majestic 281 to stand the Kolkata Test on its head. His form dipped after that, until an uncharacteristic grinding century in Antigua in May 2002 marked his second coming: he has been a picture of consistency since, often dazzling, but less prone to collaborating in his own dismissal. Laxman was left out of the 2003 World Cup, but made an emphatic one-day return with a string of hundreds in Australia, followed by a matchwinning 107 in the deciding one-dayer of India's ice-breaking tour of Pakistan in March 2004. Eventually he was confined to Tests, gliding past 8000 runs in the West Indies in June 2011 before having a modest time with the bat in the whitewash by England. Early in 2008 Laxman had scored his third Test century at Sydney, and the Australians conceded another double-century at Delhi in 2008-09, followed by 64 in the next Test – Laxman's 100th – as the series was won.

THE FACTS   Laxman's 281 against Australia at Kolkata in March 2001 was India's highest Test score at the time (since passed by Virender Sehwag), and included a national-record fifth-wicket stand of 376 with Rahul Dravid … He averages 55.58 against Australia, and his highest four scores (281, 200 not out, 178, 167) have all come against them … Laxman has scored two triple-centuries for Hyderabad – 353 against Karnataka at Bangalore in April 2000, and 301 not out against Bihar at Jamshedpur in February 1998 …

THE FIGURES *to 26.09.11*   **ESF**cricinfo.com

Batting & Fielding	M	Inns	NO	Runs	HS	Avge	S/R	100	50	4s	6s	Ct	St
Tests	127	212	32	8328	281	46.26	49.28	16	54	1096	5	127	0
ODIs	86	83	7	2338	131	30.76	71.23	6	10	222	4	39	0
T20Is	0	0	–	–	–	–	–	–	–	–	–	–	–
First-class	258	420	52	19067	353	51.81	–	53	95	–	–	269	1

Bowling	M	Balls	Runs	Wkts	BB	Avge	RpO	S/R	5i	10m
Tests	127	324	126	2	1–2	63.00	2.33	162.00	0	0
ODIs	86	42	40	0	–	–	5.71	–	0	0
T20Is	0	0	–	–	–	–	–	–	–	–
First-class	258	1835	754	22	3–11	34.27	2.46	83.40	0	0

BRETT **LEE**

Full name	**Brett Lee**
Born	**November 8, 1976, Wollongong, New South Wales**
Teams	**New South Wales, Kolkata Knight Riders**
Style	**Right-hand bat, right-arm fast bowler**
Test debut	**Australia v India at Melbourne 1999-2000**
ODI debut	**Australia v Pakistan at Brisbane 1999-2000**
T20I debut	**Australia v New Zealand at Auckland 2004-2005**

THE PROFILE   Brett Lee excelled as an exponent of extreme speed over a decade without quite achieving the all-conquering success required to earn the tag of a true Test great. For most of his career he operated as brutal support for Glenn McGrath and Jason Gillespie, then was a highly dependable attack leader until his body held him back. But at his fastest and best he gained outswing with the new ball and reversed the older one, a daunting prospect for batsmen who knew he could nudge 100mph. The flashing smile, charging run-up and leaping celebrations added to the theatre for a bowler who made an instant impact: 42 victims came in his opening seven Tests to establish an A-list reputation, but he was soon in rehab after an elbow operation. His ankles were a popular site for surgery, and there were also side strains and stress fractures in a familiar cycle of breathtaking pace, painful injury and long-term layoff. He became a smarter operator under Ricky Ponting, learning when to deliver a burst of speed or a containing spell. In nine Tests following McGrath's retirement, Lee took 58 wickets at 21.55, but life became harder again and after returning from more ankle surgery – his last act in a Test was limping off the MCG with a broken foot – he missed the 2009 Ashes with a side strain. After that he concentrated on the shorter formats, where he could still try to operate at optimum speed while reducing the load on that aching body. He did well in the 2011 World Cup – four-fors against Canada and Pakistan – and continued to show the youngsters the way in Sri Lanka later in the year.

THE FACTS   Lee took a World Cup hat-trick against Kenya in 2002-03 ... His older brother Shane played 45 ODIs for Australia between 1995 and 2001 ... Lee averages 21.09 with the ball in Tests against New Zealand, but 40.61 v England ... He was on the winning side in each of his first ten Tests, a sequence ended by England's win at Leeds in 2001 ... Lee took 5 for 47 in his first Test innings, but did not improve on that until his 44th match ...

THE FIGURES to 26.09.11   **ESPMcricinfo.com**

Batting & Fielding	M	Inns	NO	Runs	HS	Avge	S/R	100	50	4s	6s	Ct	St
Tests	76	90	18	1451	64	20.15	52.97	0	5	182	18	23	0
ODIs	205	98	40	957	57	16.50	81.72	0	2	53	26	52	0
T20Is	21	10	5	95	43*	19.00	143.93	0	0	8	4	6	0
First-class	116	139	25	2120	97	18.59	–	0	8	–	–	35	0

Bowling	M	Balls	Runs	Wkts	BB	Avge	RpO	S/R	5i	10m
Tests	76	16531	9554	310	5–30	30.81	3.46	53.32	10	0
ODIs	205	10415	8173	357	5–22	22.89	4.70	29.17	9	0
T20Is	21	451	601	22	3–27	27.31	7.99	20.50	0	0
First-class	116	24193	13746	487	7–114	28.22	3.40	49.67	20	2

NATHAN **LYON**

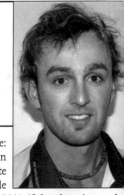

Full name **Nathan Michael Lyon**
Born **November 20, 1987, Young, New South Wales**
Teams **South Australia**
Style **Right-hand bat, offspinner**
Test debut **Australia v Sri Lanka at Galle 2011**
ODI debut **No ODIs yet**
T20I debut **No T20Is yet**

THE PROFILE   As rags-to-riches stories go, it's right up there: Nathan Lyon is a groundsman at Adelaide Oval, bowls a bit in the nets when he can, gets noticed by the coach, plays for the state and does reasonably well, then, in a time of an Australia-wide drought of quality spin, is called up for the tour of Sri Lanka in 2011. If that doesn't sound implausible enough, Lyon then goes even further – a first-ball wicket, and figures of 5 for 34. The dream debut of the lanky Lyon started when he replaced his fellow newcomer, Trent Copeland, who had earlier taken a wicket with his second ball. Lyon went one better, sending down a venomous offbreak which Kumar Sangakkara – a veteran of almost 100 Tests and more than 8000 runs – could only edge low to Michael Clarke at slip. Unlike some, Lyon built on that early success, polishing off the tail to finish with 5 for 34. Things got harder after that – just one tailender in the second innings, and two wickets in the next Test – but Lyon looked level-headed enough to know that he was, as Australia's wicketkeeper Brad Haddin put it, still "work in progress" as a bowler. The first Test was, after all, just the sixth match of a first-class career which had only begun in February 2011. "He's got similar drift to what Graeme Swann has," observed Haddin. "He's got quite a nice little shape on it – I think he's got something there that's going to be pretty good for Australian cricket." Lyon's early cricket was for the Australian Capital Territory in Canberra, where he worked as a groundsman before he got the job in Adelaide.

THE FACTS   Lyon was the third Australian (after Tom Horan in 1882-83 and Arthur Coningham in 1894-95) to take a wicket with his first ball in a Test, dismissing Kumar Sangakkara of Sri Lanka at Galle in September 2011 … Lyon finished with 5 for 34, his best figures in first-class cricket (this was only his sixth match) …

THE FIGURES to 26.09.11   **ESPN**cricinfo.com

Batting & Fielding	M	Inns	NO	Runs	HS	Avge	S/R	100	50	4s	6s	Ct	St
Tests	3	4	3	17	13	17.00	40.47	0	0	2	0	2	0
ODIs	0	0	–	–	–	–	–	–	–	–	–	–	–
T20Is	0	0	–	–	–	–	–	–	–	–	–	–	–
First-class	8	13	3	106	37	10.60	32.02	0	0	12	0	2	0

Bowling	M	Balls	Runs	Wkts	BB	Avge	RpO	S/R	5i	10m
Tests	3	569	295	8	5–34	36.87	3.11	71.12	1	0
ODIs	0	0	–	–	–	–	–	–	–	–
T20Is	0	0	–	–	–	–	–	–	–	–
First-class	8	1800	933	22	5–34	42.40	3.11	81.81	1	0

BRENDON **McCULLUM**

Full name	**Brendon Barrie McCullum**
Born	**September 27, 1981, Dunedin, Otago**
Teams	**Otago, Kochi Tuskers Kerala**
Style	**Right-hand bat, wicketkeeper**
Test debut	**New Zealand v South Africa at Hamilton 2003-04**
ODI debut	**New Zealand v Australia at Sydney 2001-02**
T20I debut	**New Zealand v Australia at Auckland 2004-05**

THE PROFILE Brendon McCullum stepped up to the national side as a wicketkeeper-batsman after an outstanding career in international youth cricket, where he often dominated opposition attacks. Not surprisingly he found it hard to replicate that at the highest level at first – he started as a batsman in ODIs in Australia in 2001-02 – although there were occasional fireworks in domestic cricket. But he finally made his mark in England in 2004, with an entertaining 96 at Lord's. He collected his maiden century in Bangladesh in October, and added another hundred in the two-day victory over Zimbabwe in August 2005. With some onlookers murmuring the name "Gilchrist", McCullum hammered 86 from 91 balls as New Zealand overhauled Australia's 346 at Hamilton in February 2007 with one wicket to spare. But he really made his mark in April 2008, when he enlivened the opening night of the much-hyped Indian Premier League by smacking 158 not out from 73 balls for Kolkata Knight Riders. There were signs he was having trouble tempering his attacking instincts in the longer game, but still in the summer of 2008 he lit up Lord's again with 97. Then he walloped ten sixes in 166 in a one-day mismatch against Ireland. Although he was by now considered a limited-overs specialist, McCullum showed he could still hack it in Tests with 84 and 115 against India in March 2009 and 185 against Bangladesh a year later. Shortly after that, after regular back niggles, he announced that he would no longer keep wicket in Tests, and in only his second match unencumbered by the gloves applied himself for 543 minutes to score 225 against India at Hyderabad in November 2010.

THE FACTS McCullum made 185, the highest score by a New Zealand wicketkeeper in Tests, against Bangladesh at Hamilton in February 2010 ... He was the first man to score 1000 runs in Twenty20 internationals ... McCullum hit 166, and shared an opening stand of 274 with James Marshall, in an ODI against Ireland at Aberdeen in July 2008 ... His brother Nathan has also played for New Zealand ...

THE FIGURES to 26.09.11   **ESPNcricinfo.com**

Batting & Fielding	M	Inns	NO	Runs	HS	Avge	S/R	100	50	4s	6s	Ct	St
Tests	57	97	6	3389	225	37.24	62.21	6	19	413	41	167	11
ODIs	192	164	24	4037	166	28.83	88.74	3	19	366	115	214	14
T20Is	40	40	7	1100	116*	33.33	128.35	1	6	112	39	25	4
First-class	100	173	10	5866	225	35.98	–	10	33	–	–	272	19

Bowling	M	Balls	Runs	Wkts	BB	Avge	RpO	S/R	5i	10m
Tests	57	36	18	0	–	–	3.00	–	0	0
ODIs	192	–	–	–	–	–	–	–	–	–
T20Is	40	–	–	–	–	–	–	–	–	–
First-class	100	36	18	0	–	–	3.00	–	0	0

NATHAN **McCULLUM**

Full name	**Nathan Leslie McCullum**
Born	**September 1, 1980, Dunedin, Otago**
Teams	**Otago, Pune Warriors**
Style	**Right-hand bat, offspinner**
Test debut	**No Tests yet**
ODI debut	**New Zealand v Sri Lanka at Colombo 2009**
T20I debut	**New Zealand v South Africa at Durban 2007-08**

THE PROFILE The older brother of Brendon McCullum, Nathan is an offspinning allrounder from Otago who played a few matches in the IPL in 2011. Less lavishly gifted than his brother, this McCullum had to work patiently at his game to earn his national colours. He was in the 30-man preliminary squad for the Champions Trophy in 2006 but didn't make the cut, and had to wait until the inaugural World Twenty20 in South Africa in September 2007 for the chance to appear alongside Brendon in New Zealand colours. He scored a single in his only match and didn't bowl – and promptly disappeared back into domestic cricket for nearly 18 months. He was back for the World Twenty20 in England in 2009, and this time added more to the cause, particularly with some tight bowling and taut fielding. Three 50-overs outings produced fewer runs and even fewer wickets, but McCullum was back for the third edition of the World Twenty20 in the West Indies in 2010, where he turned the match against Sri Lanka with a four and a six in the last over, after earlier taking a wicket and three catches: for once he overshadowed his brother, who failed to score. He then took 3 for 16 in his four overs against Zimbabwe to ensure New Zealand reached the second phase. McCullum took eight wickets on helpful pitches at the 2011 World Cup, and made a half-century against Australia. Limited-overs cricket is his forte: he has only one century and a couple of five-fors in a first-class career spanning more than a decade. In his younger days, he was also a useful footballer.

THE FACTS McCullum's best bowling figures of 6 for 90 came for New Zealand A against India A at Chennai in September 2008 ... He scored 106 not out for Otago v Northern Districts at Hamilton in March 2008 ... McCullum's brother Brendon has also played for New Zealand, while their father Stu represented Otago ...

THE FIGURES to 26.09.11   ≡ᴱ≡ᴾ cricinfo.com

Batting & Fielding	M	Inns	NO	Runs	HS	Avge	S/R	100	50	4s	6s	Ct	St
Tests	0	0	–	–	–	–	–	–	–	–	–	–	–
ODIs	27	23	2	449	65	21.38	82.68	0	3	31	9	9	0
T20Is	25	16	8	169	36*	21.12	106.96	0	0	10	5	11	0
First-class	50	76	6	1850	106*	26.42	–	1	11	–	–	53	0

Bowling	M	Balls	Runs	Wkts	BB	Avge	RpO	S/R	5i	10m
Tests	0	0	–	–	–	–	–	–	–	–
ODIs	27	1101	853	20	3–24	42.65	4.64	55.05	0	0
T20Is	25	404	426	26	4–16	16.38	6.32	15.53	0	0
First-class	50	9210	4337	103	6–90	42.10	2.82	89.41	2	0

TIM **McINTOSH**

Full name	**Timothy Gavin McIntosh**
Born	**December 4, 1979, Auckland**
Teams	**Auckland**
Style	**Left-hand bat**
Test debut	**New Zealand v West Indies at Dunedin 2008-09**
ODI debut	**No ODIs yet**
T20I debut	**No T20Is yet**

THE PROFILE A stylish, steady left-hand opener, Tim McIntosh made his debut for Auckland in March 1999. In December 2000 he hit 182 against Canterbury, and has been a consistent scorer at domestic level ever since, apart from a loss of form in 2004-05 when he moved to Canterbury but managed only 49 runs in six matches. Two years before that he had made 820 at 58 for Auckland, and soon returned there. Apart from his early days with New Zealand's Under-19s McIntosh had never aroused much interest from the selectors, but he hit 268 against Canterbury in March 2008, then later that year made 191 against Wellington and 78 against the touring West Indians, at a time when the Test openers were going through a bad trot. McIntosh made a nervous debut in Dunedin – it took him 38 balls to get off the mark – but he finished with 34 and 24 not out, then produced a classy 136 in the second Test at Napier. He batted for 455 minutes, and many of his 21 fours came square through point. It earned him comparisons with another dogged left-handed Kiwi opener, Mark Richardson, who was also in his 30th year when he started what became a successful Test career in 2000. Slimmer pickings followed for McIntosh: 69 in almost five hours in the first Test in Colombo in August 2009 was followed by three single-figure scores. But he made another century in India late in 2010, and although he did not get a national contract – he is unlikely to feature in one-dayers, although he did score two centuries for Auckland in 2011 – McIntosh remains the opener in residence in Tests.

THE FACTS McIntosh scored 268 for Auckland v Canterbury in March 2008: the next-highest score was 42 … He made 205 v Otago at Lincoln in November 2006 … McIntosh's hundred against West Indies at Napier in December 2008 was only the second by a New Zealand opener in a Test since 2004 …

THE FIGURES to 26.09.11   **ESPN cricinfo.com**

Batting & Fielding	M	Inns	NO	Runs	HS	Avge	S/R	100	50	4s	6s	Ct	St
Tests	17	33	2	854	136	27.54	36.20	2	4	98	7	10	0
ODIs	0	0	–	–	–	–	–	–	–	–	–	–	–
T20Is	0	0	–	–	–	–	–	–	–	–	–	–	–
First-class	109	188	14	6033	268	34.67	–	16	27	–	–	94	0

Bowling	M	Balls	Runs	Wkts	BB	Avge	RpO	S/R	5i	10m
Tests	17	0	–	–	–	–	–	–	–	–
ODIs	0	0	–	–	–	–	–	–	–	–
T20Is	0	0	–	–	–	–	–	–	–	–
First-class	109	196	98	0	–	–	3.00	–	0	0

ANDY **McKAY**

NEW ZEALAND

Full name	**Andrew John McKay**
Born	**April 17, 1980, Auckland**
Teams	**Wellington**
Style	**Right-hand bat, left-arm fast-medium bowler**
Test debut	**New Zealand v India at Nagpur 2010-11**
ODI debut	**New Zealand v Bangladesh at Napier 2009-10**
T20I debut	**New Zealand v Sri Lanka at Lauderhill 2010**

THE PROFILE A brisk left-arm seamer who played for Auckland for five years before shifting to Wellington in 2009, Andy McKay was, somewhat ironically for a qualified physiotherapist, held back by injuries – he once missed a whole season with a side strain – and did not make the full New Zealand team until he was almost 30. He showed promise in 2007-08 with 24 wickets, and followed that up with 23 next term. In 2009-10, when Shane Bond's brief comeback fizzled out, New Zealand were in the market for a pace spearhead, and the selectors had a close look at McKay, who was having a decent debut season for Wellington. In his first three one-dayers he hurried the Bangladeshis with his pace: his five wickets were all top-five batsmen, and three of them fell for single figures. Hopes of a Test debut soon afterwards were scuppered by a stress fracture in the foot, but he was back for the brief Twenty20 series in America and the one-day triangular later in the year in Sri Lanka, where he struggled to make much impact after dismissing Yuvraj Singh cheaply in the first match. Shortly after that he did make his Test debut, proving expensive as India ran up a matchwinning total at Nagpur, although he did dismiss Sachin Tendulkar. McKay went into the 2010-11 domestic season without a five-for to his name, but put that right with two, against Auckland and Canterbury, on the way to 30 wickets at 20 apiece. He was a late replacement for the World Cup, and was hurried into the side for the semi-final, where he bowled with good pace and economy – in vain, though, as New Zealand lost to Sri Lanka.

THE FACTS McKay took 5 for 92 for Wellington against Auckland in February 2011, and 5 for 54 v Canterbury the following month (he took nine wickets in both matches) ... His first 16 international matches were all against Bangladesh, India or Sri Lanka ... McKay's first two Twenty20 internationals were both in Florida in the United States ...

THE FIGURES to 26.09.11   **ESPncricinfo.com**

Batting & Fielding	M	Inns	NO	Runs	HS	Avge	S/R	100	50	4s	6s	Ct	St
Tests	1	2	1	25	20*	25.00	45.45	0	0	3	0	0	0
ODIs	14	8	5	10	4*	3.33	27.77	0	0	0	0	3	0
T20Is	2	1	0	0	0	0.00	0.00	0	0	0	0	0	0
First-class	30	36	16	236	36*	11.80	–	0	0	–	–	2	0

Bowling	M	Balls	Runs	Wkts	BB	Avge	RpO	S/R	5i	10m
Tests	1	186	120	1	1–120	120.00	3.87	186.00	0	0
ODIs	14	650	549	20	4–62	27.45	5.06	32.50	0	0
T20Is	2	34	31	2	2–20	15.50	5.47	17.00	0	0
First-class	30	5498	2968	100	5–54	29.68	3.23	54.98	2	0

RYAN McLAREN

Full name	**Ryan McLaren**
Born	**February 9, 1983, Kimberley**
Teams	**Knights, Middlesex, Kings XI Punjab**
Style	**Left-hand bat, right-arm fast-medium bowler**
Test debut	**South Africa v England at Johannesburg 2009-10**
ODI debut	**South Africa v Zimbabwe at Benoni 2009-2010**
T20I debut	**South Africa v England at Johannesburg 2009-2010**

THE PROFILE Ryan McLaren made an eye-catching start to his first-class career: his first four seasons produced more than 1000 forthright runs, and over 100 wickets with some aggressive seam bowling. But an international call-up seemed far off, with Shaun Pollock and Jacques Kallis entrenched in the South African side and the likes of Andrew Hall and Johan van der Wath in the queue. Like several of his compatriots McLaren opted for county cricket as a Kolpak player, and soon became a key performer for Rob Key's Kent, taking a hat-trick as they won the Twenty20 Cup final in 2007. After signing a three-year contract before another impressive county season in 2008 McLaren was named in South Africa's one-day squad that October – but Kent refused to release him, and he was forced to return to Canterbury. At the end of the 2009 season, though, they did let him go – and South Africa lost no time in blooding him. McLaren kept things tight in five one-dayers against Zimbabwe and England, then injuries to others led to a first Test cap on a fast-bowler-friendly pitch at Johannesburg, where the England series was emphatically squared: his contribution was a handy 33 not out and the wicket of England's first-innings top-scorer Paul Collingwood. McLaren is accurate and bowls at a nagging pace, factors which helped him pick up 5 for 19 in a Twenty20 international in the West Indies in May 2010. He has done little with the bat on the international stage, though, which may be why he was dropped and missed the 2011 World Cup, but he remains marketable in the Twenty20 game, as contracts with Punjab and Middlesex showed.

THE FACTS McLaren took a hat-trick for Kent against Gloucestershire in the English Twenty20 Cup final at Edgbaston in August 2007 ... He made 140 for Eagles v Warriors at Bloemfontein in March 2006 ... McLaren took 5 for 19 against West Indies in May 2010, the second-best figures in Twenty20 internationals at the time ... He took 8 for 38 for Eagles v Cape Cobras at Stellenbosch in February 2007 ... His father, uncle and cousin all played for Griqualand West ...

THE FIGURES to 26.09.11   ESPNcricinfo.com

Batting & Fielding	M	Inns	NO	Runs	HS	Avge	S/R	100	50	4s	6s	Ct	St
Tests	1	1	1	33	33*	–	58.92	0	0	5	0	0	0
ODIs	10	8	2	37	12	6.16	61.66	0	0	4	0	5	0
T20Is	5	3	3	8	6*	–	88.88	0	0	0	0	1	0
First-class	87	126	21	3021	140	28.77	–	2	16	–	–	43	0

Bowling	M	Balls	Runs	Wkts	BB	Avge	RpO	S/R	5i	10m
Tests	1	78	43	1	1–30	43.00	3.30	78.00	0	0
ODIs	10	432	366	8	3–51	45.75	5.08	54.00	0	0
T20Is	5	119	144	9	5–19	16.00	7.26	13.22	1	0
First-class	87	13946	6938	277	8–38	25.04	2.98	50.34	11	1

SHAUN **MARSH**

AUSTRALIA

Full name	**Shaun Edward Marsh**
Born	**July 9, 1983, Narrogin, Western Australia**
Teams	**Western Australia, Kings XI Punjab**
Style	**Left-hand bat, occasional left-arm spinner**
Test debut	**Australia v Sri Lanka at Galle 2011**
ODI debut	**Australia v West Indies at Kingstown 2007-08**
T20I debut	**Australia v West Indies at Bridgetown 2008**

THE PROFILE   As a child Shaun Marsh spent a lot of time in the Australian set-up travelling with his father Geoff, the former Test opener. That grounding and a backyard net helped him develop into one of Australia's finest young batsmen. It also gave him a taste of what to expect when he joined the one-day side in the Caribbean in 2008. That came after a fine domestic season: he was also the surprise hit of the inaugural IPL, finishing as the leading runscorer. More gifted than his father – "He's got a few more shots than me," Geoff once admitted – Shaun is a left-hander who reached his maiden first-class hundred in 2003 with successive sixes over midwicket off Mark Waugh, while Steve looked on approvingly. The second century had to wait until 2004-05 as Marsh struggled with concentration, the finest trait of his father's batting. Once he was in the one-day mix for Australia, he also had an up-and-down time. In 2008-09 he had successive scores of 79 and 78 against South Africa, but tore a hamstring while fielding against New Zealand, and when he returned to the squad in Dubai he hurt his leg again. That kept him out of the World Twenty20 in England in June 2009. He returned with a century in India then, after a back injury, made a classy 59 (and took two superb boundary-riding catches) as Australia ended the one-day series against England in July 2010 with a victory at Lord's. He finally got a Test chance in Sri Lanka in 2011, with Ricky Ponting on paternity leave. Watched by his dad, Marsh grabbed the opportunity greedily, making a superb 141, and adding 81 in the next Test.

THE FACTs   Marsh was the 19th Australian to score a century on Test debut, five years after he hit 81 in his first ODI ... Marsh made 166 not out for Western Australia v Queensland at Perth in November 2007 ... His father Geoff won 50 Test caps (they are only the second father-son combination to play Tests for Australia), and his younger brother Mitchell captained Australia to victory in the 2010 Under-19 World Cup ...

THE FIGURES to 26.09.11   **ESPNcricinfo.com**

Batting & Fielding	M	Inns	NO	Runs	HS	Avge	S/R	100	50	4s	6s	Ct	St
Tests	2	3	0	240	141	80.00	41.52	1	1	26	0	0	0
ODIs	35	35	1	1244	112	36.58	76.36	2	8	115	13	7	0
T20Is	5	5	0	57	29	11.40	98.27	0	0	3	3	0	0
First-class	63	115	15	3898	166*	38.98	45.89	7	21	–	–	51	0

Bowling	M	Balls	Runs	Wkts	BB	Avge	RpO	S/R	5i	10m
Tests	2	0	–	–	–	–	–	–	–	–
ODIs	35	0	–	–	–	–	–	–	–	–
T20Is	5	0	–	–	–	–	–	–	–	–
First-class	63	174	131	2	2–20	65.50	4.51	87.00	0	0

CHRIS **MARTIN**

Full name	**Christopher Stewart Martin**
Born	**December 10, 1974, Christchurch, Canterbury**
Teams	**Canterbury**
Style	**Right-hand bat, right-arm fast-medium bowler**
Test debut	**New Zealand v South Africa at Bloemfontein 2000-01**
ODI debut	**New Zealand v Zimbabwe at Taupo 2000-01**
T20I debut	**New Zealand v Kenya at Durban 2007-08**

THE PROFILE Chris Martin is an angular fast-medium bowler who receives almost as much attention for his inept batting as for his nagging bowling, which has produced almost 200 Test wickets, including 11 as New Zealand whipped South Africa at Auckland in March 2004. Seven more scalps followed in the next game. It was all the more remarkable as they were his first Tests in almost two years: he had been overlooked since Pakistan piled up 643 at Lahore in May 2002 (Martin 1 for 108). He got his original chance after a crop of injuries, but did not disgrace himself in the first portion of his Test career, taking 34 wickets at 34 in 11 Tests, including six as Pakistan were crushed by an innings at Hamilton in 2000-01. Since his return he has largely maintained that average, happy to bowl long spells à la Ewen Chatfield – he took 5 for 152 at Brisbane in November 2004, after a surprisingly unproductive England tour. Back in England in 2008, he again failed to make much impression in the Tests (four wickets at 58.75), but returned to form at home with 14 wickets against India, including seven in a high-scoring draw at Wellington. But whatever Martin does with the ball he is likely to be remembered more for his clueless batting: 29 of his 43 Test dismissals have been for ducks, he finally reached double figures against Bangladesh in his 36th match (a Test record) in January 2008, and has bagged six pairs (no-one else has more than four). Mind you, he did once manage 25 for Canterbury, helping Chris Harris put on 75.

THE FACTS Very few players approach Martin's negative ratio of Test runs to wickets: two that do are England's Bill Bowes (28 runs, 68 wickets) and David Larter (15, 37) ... Martin is the only man to have bagged six pairs in Tests ... He finally reached 100 Test runs in his 87th innings: the previous record was 40, by India's Bhagwat Chandrasekhar ... In Tests Martin averages 24.59 with the ball against South Africa, but 86.53 v Australia ...

THE FIGURES *to 26.09.11*

Batting & Fielding	M	Inns	NO	Runs	HS	Avge	S/R	100	50	4s	6s	Ct	St
Tests	61	89	46	109	12*	2.53	20.45	0	0	15	0	13	0
ODIs	20	7	2	8	3	1.60	29.62	0	0	0	0	7	0
T20Is	6	1	1	5	5*	–	83.33	0	0	0	0	1	0
First-class	170	213	104	441	25	4.04	–	0	0	–	–	31	0

Bowling	M	Balls	Runs	Wkts	BB	Avge	RpO	S/R	5i	10m
Tests	61	12216	6899	199	6–54	34.66	3.38	61.38	9	1
ODIs	20	948	804	18	3–62	44.66	5.08	52.66	0	0
T20Is	6	138	193	7	2–14	27.57	8.39	19.71	0	0
First-class	170	32898	16970	537	6–54	31.60	3.09	61.26	22	1

HAMILTON **MASAKADZA**

Full name	**Hamilton Masakadza**
Born	**August 9, 1983, Harare**
Teams	**Mountaineers**
Style	**Right-hand bat, right-arm medium-pacer**
Test debut	**Zimbabwe v West Indies at Harare 2001**
ODI debut	**Zimbabwe v South Africa at Bulawayo 2001-02**
T20I debut	**Zimbabwe v Bangladesh at Khulna 2006-07**

THE PROFILE Hamilton Masakadza was still a schoolboy when he set the record – since beaten by Bangladesh's Mohammad Ashraful – as the youngest man to score a century on Test debut. That was against West Indies in July 2001, when he made a composed 119 from No. 3 – driving well, and showing few signs of nerves in the nineties – which was largely responsible for Zimbabwe saving the match after trailing by 216 on first innings. A year later, though, he put his cricket career on hold while at university in South Africa. He was called back to face England in December 2004: not surprisingly, he struggled at first, before registering his maiden ODI fifty in the final match. Masakadza's return to the Test team brought mixed results, but he was the best batsman, technically, on the tour of South Africa early in 2005, showing an application lacking in his team-mates. After being criticised for not being able to score quickly enough early on in his career, Masakadza's ability in one-day cricket – admittedly largely against lesser teams like Bangladesh and Kenya – has steadily increased: 2009 was a bumper year, bringing him more than 1000 runs in ODIs at an average of 43.48 and a strike-rate of 88. It included two towering scores of more than 150, both against Kenya in October. Late the following year, though, he went through a lean patch, and was rather surprisingly left out for the 2011 World Cup squad. But Masakadza was soon back, and helped set up Zimbabwe's victory in their comeback Test, against Bangladesh at Harare in August, with a five-hour 104, a second Test century more than ten years after his first.

THE FACTS Masakadza was only the second Zimbabwean, after Dave Houghton in 1992-93, to make a century on Test debut: he made 119 against West Indies in July 2001, when 11 days short of his 18th birthday ... His second Test hundred came more than ten years later, against Bangladesh in August 2011 ... Masakadza is the only man ever to make two scores above 150 in the same ODI series – 156 and 178 not out at home to Kenya in October 2009 ... His brother Shingirai, a fast bowler, has also played for Zimbabwe ...

THE FIGURES to 26.09.11   **ESPricricinfo.com**

Batting & Fielding	M	Inns	NO	Runs	HS	Avge	S/R	100	50	4s	6s	Ct	St
Tests	17	34	1	913	119	27.66	42.94	2	3	118	5	8	0
ODIs	110	110	4	2938	178*	27.71	73.94	3	18	291	38	49	0
T20Is	16	16	0	426	79	26.62	114.51	0	3	39	12	7	0
First-class	92	160	9	6374	208*	42.21	–	16	30	–	–	66	0

Bowling	M	Balls	Runs	Wkts	BB	Avge	RpO	S/R	5i	10m
Tests	17	168	52	3	1–9	17.33	1.85	56.00	0	0
ODIs	110	1076	967	27	3–39	35.81	5.39	39.85	0	0
T20Is	16	36	61	1	1–9	61.00	10.16	36.00	0	0
First-class	92	2834	1276	45	4–11	28.35	2.70	62.97	0	0

MASHRAFE MORTAZA

Full name **Mashrafe bin Mortaza**
Born **October 5, 1983, Norail, Jessore, Khulna**
Teams **Khulna**
Style **Right-hand bat, right-arm fast-medium bowler**
Test debut **Bangladesh v Zimbabwe at Dhaka 2001-02**
ODI debut **Bangladesh v Zimbabwe at Chittagong 2001-02**
T20I debut **Bangladesh v Zimbabwe at Khulna 2006-07**

THE PROFILE Mashrafe Mortaza has long been the standard-bearer for Bangladesh's pacemen, although injuries have bedevilled him: he hurt his right knee after only 6.3 overs in the first Test in West Indies in July 2009, and had to undergo an operation (on both knees, in fact). This was doubly disappointing as it was his first match as captain, and it ended in only Bangladesh's second Test victory – their first overseas, against an admittedly under-strength West Indies. He returned as captain for the mid-season one-dayers in Britain in 2010, guiding Bangladesh to their first win over England, but injured the knee again in a domestic game at the end of the year. He was not thought ready for the 2011 World Cup, and although he played two ODIs against Australia shortly afterwards – and took five wickets – his long-suffering right knee then went under the knife again. Mashrafe won his first Test cap in 2001-02, in what was also his first-class debut. Though banging it in is his preferred style, "Koushik" has proved adept at reining in his attacking instincts to concentrate on line and length. He did well in the second Test against England in 2003-04, taking 4 for 60 in the first innings to keep Bangladesh in touch, but then twisted his knee, which kept him out of Tests for over a year. Mashrafe's 4 for 38 in the 2007 World Cup set up the famous defeat of India, and he remains the only fast bowler to take 100 ODI wickets for Bangladesh. He is not a complete mug with the bat: he has a first-class century to his name, and over 20% of his ODI runs have come in sixes.

THE FACTS Mashrafe Mortaza was the first Bangladeshi to make his first-class debut in a Test match: only three others have done this since 1899 ... Mashrafe started the famous ODI victory over Australia at Cardiff in 2005 by dismissing Adam Gilchrist for 0 ... His 6 for 26 v Kenya in Nairobi in August 2006 remain Bangladesh's best bowling figures in ODIs ... Only Mike Hendrick of England has claimed more Test wickets (87) without ever taking a five-for ... Mashrafe's record includes two ODIs for the Asia XI ...

THE FIGURES *to 26.09.11*   **ESPNcricinfo.com**

Batting & Fielding	M	Inns	NO	Runs	HS	Avge	S/R	100	50	4s	6s	Ct	St
Tests	36	67	5	797	79	12.85	67.20	0	3	95	22	9	0
ODIs	120	92	16	1177	51*	15.48	86.22	0	1	95	40	37	0
T20Is	13	12	3	141	36	15.66	120.51	0	0	6	8	1	0
First-class	51	91	7	1341	132*	15.96	–	1	5	–	–	21	0

Bowling	M	Balls	Runs	Wkts	BB	Avge	RpO	S/R	5i	10m
Tests	36	5990	3239	78	4–60	41.52	3.24	76.79	0	0
ODIs	120	5986	4660	151	6–26	30.86	4.67	39.64	1	0
T20Is	13	297	435	10	2–28	43.50	8.78	29.70	0	0
First-class	51	8391	4371	123	4–27	35.53	3.12	68.21	0	0

ANGELO **MATHEWS**

SRI LANKA

Full name	**Angelo Davis Mathews**
Born	**June 2, 1987, Colombo**
Teams	**Colts, Basnahira**
Style	**Right-hand bat, right-arm fast-medium bowler**
Test debut	**Sri Lanka v Pakistan at Galle 2009**
ODI debut	**Sri Lanka v Zimbabwe at Harare 2008-09**
T20I debut	**Sri Lanka v Australia at Nottingham 2009**

THE PROFILE Angelo Mathews is capable of batting anywhere in the top order, and also bowls at a lively medium-pace. He made a quiet start in first-class cricket in 2006-07, but made big strides the following season, scoring 696 runs at 58 and also making two hundreds for the A team in South Africa. He scored 52 not out in his third ODI, in Bangladesh in January 2009, and shortly after that hammered 270 in a domestic match. Later that year he helped Sri Lanka to the World Twenty20 final in England, notably with three West Indian wickets at The Oval, which effectively settled the semi in the first over. There was also handy batting (35 not out in the final) and frenetic fielding, especially a gymnastic juggling effort – leaping around on and behind the boundary – the legality of which MCC had to confirm. Mathews is aiming to sharpen up his pace, but it seems inevitable that it will be batting with which he makes his name in the long run, an impression sharpened by his 99 – he cried when he was narrowly run out – in a Test against India in Mumbai in December 2009. After a consistent time the following year more heartache followed in 2011: a late six in the semi helped ensure Sri Lanka reached the World Cup final, but Mathews already knew he wouldn't be playing in that, as he had injured his leg. That kept him out of the IPL and the England tour, but he was back for the home series against Australia, reaching that elusive century in the third Test, after another near-miss (trying for a six when 95) in the first one at Galle.

THE FACTS Mathews was run out for 99 against India in Mumbai in December 2009 ... He made 270 for Basnahira North v Kandurata in Colombo in February 2009 ... Mathews took 6 for 20 in an ODI against India in Colombo in September 2009 ... In the World Twenty20 in England in 2009 his shirt had "Mathew" on the back before he added the final "s" with a marker pen ...

THE FIGURES to 26.09.11   **ESPNcricinfo.com**

Batting & Fielding	M	Inns	NO	Runs	HS	Avge	S/R	100	50	4s	6s	Ct	St
Tests	16	22	4	801	105*	44.50	51.97	1	4	94	8	6	0
ODIs	53	42	11	1065	77*	34.35	83.39	0	7	78	12	15	0
T20Is	24	19	8	298	58	27.09	126.27	0	1	20	10	9	0
First-class	47	70	10	3137	270	52.28	52.49	9	13	343	31	29	0

Bowling	M	Balls	Runs	Wkts	BB	Avge	RpO	S/R	5i	10m
Tests	16	786	421	6	1–13	70.16	3.21	131.00	0	0
ODIs	53	1392	1087	34	6–20	31.97	4.68	40.94	1	0
T20Is	24	283	346	15	3–16	23.06	7.33	18.86	0	0
First-class	47	3249	1548	36	5–47	43.00	2.85	90.25	1	0

TINO **MAWOYO**

Full name	**Tinotenda Mbiri Kanayi Mawoyo**
Born	**January 8, 1986, Umtali (now Mutare)**
Teams	**Mountaineers**
Style	**Right-hand bat, occasional medium-pacer**
Test debut	**Zimbabwe v Bangladesh at Harare 2011**
ODI debut	**Zimbabwe v Bangladesh at Dhaka 2006-07**
T20I debut	**No T20Is yet**

THE PROFILE A top-order batsman, Tino Mawoyo had already played first-class cricket when he captained Zimbabwe at the Under-19 World Cup in 2004. To start with his appearances were limited by educational commitments, but he turned out enough to emphasise his class, and played for the A team against Bangladesh in 2006. He made his full ODI debut later that year, also in Bangladesh, but missed the World Cup that followed. Mawoyo appeared to be set for a more permanent place in the national side when he was appointed captain of Zimbabwe A, but he was subsequently reduced to the ranks, reportedly after some inappropriate behaviour while the team was in a training camp. Nevertheless, he remained one of Zimbabwe's most talented young batsmen, and was a key player as Easterns completed the domestic double in 2006-07: Mawoyo was their leading runscorer in the first-class Logan Cup. By 2009-10 he was heading the run-charts in the national one-day competition too, but then experienced wildly varied emotions as the 2011 World Cup approached. Initially left out of the final squad, he was called up when Sean Ervine withdrew – then had to pull out himself shortly before the tournament after injuring a stomach muscle. The disappointment forced a rethink: Mawoyo lost weight, and elbowed his way into the side for Zimbabwe's comeback Tests later in the year. He shared opening stands of 102 and 69 with Vusi Sibanda in the first Test, against Bangladesh at Harare, and carried his bat for 163 in the second, resisting the Pakistan attack for well over ten hours. "I perform well under pressure," said Mawoyo afterwards, "it gives me a little extra drive to do well."

THE FACTS Mawoyo carried his bat for 163 in only his second Test, against Pakistan at Bulawayo in September 2011: he was only the third opener to do this for Zimbabwe, after Mark Dekker and Grant Flower, also against Pakistan ... Mawoyo scored 208 not out for Mountaineers against New Zealand A in a non-first-class game in October 2010 ... He was an injury replacement for the 2011 World Cup, but got injured himself and couldn't go ...

THE FIGURES to 26.09.11   ESPncricinfo.com

Batting & Fielding	M	Inns	NO	Runs	HS	Avge	S/R	100	50	4s	6s	Ct	St
Tests	2	4	1	253	163*	84.33	38.68	1	0	34	0	2	0
ODIs	2	2	0	24	14	12.00	42.85	0	0	1	0	0	0
T20Is	0	0	–	–	–	–	–	–	–	–	–	–	–
First-class	72	126	9	3485	163*	29.78	43.94	3	18	–	–	47	0

Bowling	M	Balls	Runs	Wkts	BB	Avge	RpO	S/R	5i	10m
Tests	2	0	–	–	–	–	–	–	–	–
ODIs	2	0	–	–	–	–	–	–	–	–
T20Is	0	0	–	–	–	–	–	–	–	–
First-class	72	72	44	2	1–0	22.00	3.66	36.00	0	0

AJANTHA **MENDIS**

SRI LANKA

Full name	**Balapuwaduge Ajantha Winslo Mendis**
Born	**March 11, 1985, Moratuwa**
Teams	**Army, Wayamba, Somerset**
Style	**Right-hand bat, right-arm off- and legspinner**
Test debut	**Sri Lanka v India at Colombo 2008**
ODI debut	**Sri Lanka v West Indies at Port-of-Spain 2007-08**
T20I debut	**Sri Lanka v Zimbabwe at King City 2008-09**

THE PROFILE Those batsmen who thought one Sri Lankan mystery spinner was enough found more on their plate during 2008, when Ajantha Mendis stepped up to join Muttiah Muralitharan in the national side. Mendis sends down a mesmerising mixture of offbreaks, legbreaks, top-spinners, googlies and flippers, plus his very own "carrom ball" – one flicked out using a finger under the ball, in the style of the old Australians Jack Iverson and John Gleeson. He is also very accurate. Mendis was a prolific wicket-taker in 2007-08 for the Army (he received not one but two promotions following his meteoric rise) and was called up for the West Indian tour early in 2008 after taking 46 wickets in six matches. After doing well there he ran rings round the Indians – the supposed masters of spin – in the Asia Cup, rather ruining the final with 6 for 13. In his first Test series – against India again – he took 26 wickets at 18.38 in three home Tests, and even achieved the rare feat of outperforming Murali (21 wickets at 22.23). There were signs in 2009, though, that batsmen were beginning to work out Mendis's variations. Some tight spells were instrumental in Sri Lanka reaching the World Twenty20 final in England, but shortly after that he was dropped for two home Tests against Pakistan and New Zealand. He remained effective in one-dayers, and it was a surprise when, after keeping things tight in the 2011 World Cup, he was left out of the side for the final. Test success continued to be elusive, but it was a different story in the shorter stuff: he took 6 for 16 in a Twenty20 game against Australia in August 2011.

THE FACTS Mendis claimed 26 wickets in his first Test series, against India in 2008, the most by anyone in a debut series of three Tests, beating Alec Bedser's 24 for England v India in 1946 ... Mendis took 6 for 16, the best figures in Twenty20 internationals, against Australia at Pallekele in August 2011 ... He took 6 for 13 in the Asia Cup final against India at Karachi in July 2008, and 7 for 37 for Army v Lankan CC at Panagoda in February 2008 ...

THE FIGURES to 26.09.11   **ESPIncricinfo.com**

Batting & Fielding	M	Inns	NO	Runs	HS	Avge	S/R	100	50	4s	6s	Ct	St
Tests	16	17	6	164	78	14.90	43.50	0	1	19	1	2	0
ODIs	58	26	12	106	15*	7.57	66.25	0	0	8	0	7	0
T20Is	20	5	3	7	4*	3.50	46.66	0	0	1	0	2	0
First-class	44	58	6	688	78	13.23	58.05	0	1	74	6	12	0

Bowling	M	Balls	Runs	Wkts	BB	Avge	RpO	S/R	5i	10m
Tests	16	3993	2014	62	6–117	32.48	3.02	64.40	3	1
ODIs	58	2708	1938	95	6–13	20.40	4.29	28.50	3	0
T20Is	20	456	425	39	6–16	10.89	5.59	11.69	1	0
First-class	44	9214	4542	211	7–37	21.52	2.95	43.66	12	2

KEEGAN **METH**

Full name	**Keegan Orry Meth**
Born	**February 8, 1988, Bulawayo**
Teams	**Matabeleland Tuskers**
Style	**Right-hand bat, right-arm fast-medium bowler**
Test debut	**No Tests yet**
ODI debut	**Zimbabwe v Kenya at Bulawayo 2005-06**
T20I debut	**No T20Is yet**

THE PROFILE An allrounder who takes the new ball for Matabeleland Tuskers and bats in the lower middle order, Keegan Meth's bowling is his stronger suit and, although he is not truly fast, he does have the invaluable ability to move the ball both ways through the air. His made his international debut when just 18, in the wake of the messy dispute that cost Zimbabwe several senior players in 2004-05: when he played his first ODI he had never appeared in a senior first-class or one-day game at home. It was obvious that his elevation had come too early, and he was discarded after the Caribbean tour early in 2006: he remained on the fringes for a while, and broadened his experience by playing club cricket in Ireland. Meth blossomed in the revamped franchise system, leading the Tuskers' attack with increasing proficiency. In 2010-11 he was a key factor in their Logan Cup triumph, collecting 54 wickets at 13.31, and almost singlehandedly securing victory over the Mountaineers in the final with 13 for 109. That led to a call for the pre-World Cup tour of Bangladesh, but he struggled in the unfamiliar conditions and slipped out of contention again, missing the Cup itself. He was back later in 2011, in the squad for Zimbabwe's comeback Test against Bangladesh (although he didn't play in the end), and featured in the last one-dayer, which ended painfully when he was smashed in the mouth by a straight drive after earlier dismissing Imrul Kayes and Shakib Al Hasan. Meth was confident the accident wouldn't affect him long-term ... and was quite proud that the video of it was viewed around 200,000 times on YouTube.

THE FACTS Meth took 6 for 40 and 7 for 69 as Matabeleland Tuskers beat Mountaineers in the 2010-11 Logan Cup final at Mutare ... He lost four teeth (and subsequently more than a stone in weight, as he was unable to eat) after being hit in the mouth by a ball during an ODI against Bangladesh at Bulawayo in August 2011 ... Meth's mother Yvonne confirms that his first name is spelt like the former England football captain's (not "Keagan" as sometimes shown) ...

THE FIGURES *to 26.09.11*   ESPNcricinfo.com

Batting & Fielding	M	Inns	NO	Runs	HS	Avge	S/R	100	50	4s	6s	Ct	St
Tests	0	0	–	–	–	–	–	–	–	–	–	–	–
ODIs	8	5	0	76	53	15.20	55.07	0	1	6	1	1	0
T20Is	0	0	–	–	–	–	–	–	–	–	–	–	–
First-class	22	30	1	757	94	26.10	61.39	0	5	84	11	10	0

Bowling	M	Balls	Runs	Wkts	BB	Avge	RpO	S/R	5i	10m
Tests	0	0	–	–	–	–	–	–	–	–
ODIs	8	244	234	3	2–56	78.00	5.75	81.33	0	0
T20Is	0	0	–	–	–	–	–	–	–	–
First-class	22	3494	1505	87	7–42	17.29	2.58	40.16	6	1

DAVID **MILLER**

SOUTH AFRICA

Full name	**David Andrew Miller**
Born	**June 10, 1989, Pietermaritzburg**
Teams	**Dolphins, Durham**
Style	**Left-hand bat, occasional offspinner**
Test debut	**No Tests yet**
ODI debut	**South Africa v West Indies at North Sound 2010**
T20I debut	**South Africa v West Indies at North Sound 2010**

THE PROFILE An explosive left-hander, David Miller was called up to the full South African limited-overs sides at 20 in the wake of the national team's disappointing performance at the World Twenty20 in the Caribbean in 2010. His first assignment was back in the West Indies – and he did as well as could have been expected, smashing his sixth ball in international cricket (from Sulieman Benn) into the stands on the way to 33 in the first Twenty20 match. He made a similarly brisk start in one-day internationals, calmly swinging the pacy Ravi Rampaul over square leg for six more during another cameo knock. Although he had not appeared for the national age-group sides, Miller had a stint at the South African Academy in mid-2009, and then caught the eye during a successful domestic season, in which he was the Dolphins' leading scorer in both 50- and 20-overs cricket. A rapid unbeaten 90 from 52 balls against the Lions in a Pro20 match at Potchefstroom in February 2010 ensured his selection for a triangular A-team tournament in Bangladesh, and it was while he was there that Miller received the call from the national selectors: "We are looking to strengthen our power-hitting in the middle order," explained chairman Andrew Hudson, the former Test opener. But Miller's form fell away in 2010-11, with four successive single-figure scores in ODIs against Pakistan and India: others moved ahead in the queue and Miller missed the 2011 World Cup. But he's young enough to bounce back, and started the rehabilitation process with a Twenty20 stint for Durham.

THE FACTS Miller hit four sixes en route to his maiden first-class century, 108 not out for Dolphins v Eagles at Kimberley in December 2009 ... He raised his highest score to 149 against the Lions at Durban in April 2011 ... Miller also made a century in 55 balls in a 50-over match for South Africa A v Bangladesh A at Mirpur in April 2010 ...

THE FIGURES to 26.09.11   **cricinfo**.com

Batting & Fielding	M	Inns	NO	Runs	HS	Avge	S/R	100	50	4s	6s	Ct	St
Tests	0	0	–	–	–	–	–	–	–	–	–	–	–
ODIs	13	10	3	186	51	26.57	120.77	0	1	12	7	4	0
T20Is	6	6	3	123	36*	41.00	133.69	0	0	10	5	1	0
First-class	27	42	4	1142	149	30.05	56.28	2	5	161	22	22	0

Bowling	M	Balls	Runs	Wkts	BB	Avge	RpO	S/R	5i	10m
Tests	0	0	–	–	–	–	–	–	–	–
ODIs	13	0	–	–	–	–	–	–	–	–
T20Is	6	0	–	–	–	–	–	–	–	–
First-class	27	26	23	0	–	–	5.30	–	0	0

KYLE **MILLS**

Full name	**Kyle David Mills**
Born	**March 15, 1979, Auckland**
Teams	**Auckland**
Style	**Right-hand bat, right-arm fast-medium bowler**
Test debut	**New Zealand v England at Nottingham 2004**
ODI debut	**New Zealand v Pakistan at Sharjah 2000-01**
T20I debut	**New Zealand v Australia at Auckland 2004-05**

THE PROFILE Injuries at inopportune times have hampered Kyle Mills. They delayed his arrival as an international player, and impinged again in 2009-10, when knee and shoulder problems shortened his season and kept him out of the IPL: he did, however, make it to the World Twenty in the West Indies, although he proved expensive in his two matches there in May. A genuine swing bowler of lively pace, Mills yo-yoed in and out of the team after the 2003 World Cup, but he did enough to tour England in 2004, and made his Test debut in the third match at Trent Bridge. But he suffered a side strain there, and missed the one-day series. That was a shame, as one-day cricket is really his forte: he played throughout 2005-06, chipping in with wickets in almost every game, even if his once-promising batting had diminished to the point that he managed double figures only once in 16 matches. A feisty temper remains, though: he was fined after an on-field incident in the 2011 World Cup ... and he was only the 12th man at the time. Ankle surgery, then knee trouble – which necessitated another op – sidelined him early in 2007, but after missing that year's World Cup, Mills bounced back, following up 5 for 25 in a one-dayer in South Africa with a Test-best 4 for 16 against England at Hamilton in March 2008. He lost his Test spot after some anaemic performances the following season, but remained a one-day force, starting the Chappell-Hadlee Series in Australia in February 2009 by taking the match award after claiming four prime scalps.

THE FACTS Mills spanked his only first-class century from No. 9 at Wellington in 2000-01, helping Auckland recover from 109 for 7 to reach 347 ... His 5 for 25 at Durban in November 2007 are NZ's best one-day figures against South Africa ... Mills achieved the only ten-wicket haul of his career, and in the process reached 100 first-class wickets, for Auckland v Canterbury in December 2004 ...

THE FIGURES to 26.09.11   **ESFN cricinfo.com**

Batting & Fielding	M	Inns	NO	Runs	HS	Avge	S/R	100	50	4s	6s	Ct	St
Tests	19	30	5	289	57	11.56	38.58	0	1	37	3	4	0
ODIs	129	78	27	843	54	16.52	80.74	0	2	63	31	34	0
T20Is	22	15	4	126	33*	11.45	115.59	0	0	9	5	5	0
First-class	68	98	25	2014	117*	27.58	–	1	13	–	–	22	0

Bowling	M	Balls	Runs	Wkts	BB	Avge	RpO	S/R	5i	10m
Tests	19	2902	1453	44	4–16	33.02	3.00	65.95	0	0
ODIs	129	6338	4998	192	5–25	26.03	4.73	33.01	1	0
T20Is	22	490	701	25	3–37	28.04	8.58	19.60	0	0
First-class	68	10852	5250	181	5–33	29.00	2.90	59.95	3	1

MISBAH-UL-HAQ

PAKISTAN

Full name **Misbah-ul-Haq Khan Niazi**
Born **May 28, 1974, Mianwali, Punjab**
Teams **Faisalabad, Sui Northern Gas**
Style **Right-hand bat, occasional legspinner**
Test debut **Pakistan v New Zealand at Auckland 2000-01**
ODI debut **Pakistan v New Zealand at Lahore 2001-02**
T20I debut **Pakistan v Bangladesh at Nairobi 2007-08**

THE PROFILE An orthodox right-hander with a tight technique but inventive in one-dayers, Misbah-ul-Haq (no relation to Inzamam) caught the eye in a one-day tournament in Nairobi in 2002, making 50 in the final against Australia. But then his form slumped: his highest score in three Tests against Australia was 17. Pakistan's abysmal 2003 World Cup gave him another chance, but he did little of note. That seemed to be that, although he was an A-team regular, often as captain. Misbah remained a consistent domestic performer, making 951 runs at 50 in 2004-05, 882 the following season, and capping that with 1108 at 61 in 2006-07, but it was nonetheless a shock when he was given a national contract for 2007-08 and called up for the inaugural World Twenty20 in South Africa. But he was a surprise hit there, and added 464 runs in three Tests against India, including two important centuries. Suddenly, in his mid-thirties but with a first-class average which remains above 50, he was an automatic choice. He played his part in winning the World Twenty20 in England in 2009, but after that had a poor time in Australia, and wasn't required for the tour of England in 2010. That ended in turmoil, with three players being banned for spot-fixing ... and from the ruins strode Misbah, suddenly appointed Test captain. He celebrated with six successive fifties against South Africa and New Zealand then, after a decent World Cup, made a hundred in the West Indies in May 2011. Soon he was the one-day captain too, after Shahid Afridi self-destructed. Misbah is hardly a long-term solution – he's 38 during 2012 – but he does seem an inspired choice as a stopgap.

THE FACTS Misbah-ul-Haq has made six first-class double-centuries, the highest 284 for Sui Northern Gas v Lahore Shalimar in October 2009 ... He also made 208 not out (in a total of 723 for 4) for Punjab v Baluchistan at Sialkot in March 2008 ... He scored 161 and 133, both not out, in successive Tests against India in 2007-08 ... Misbah hit 87 not out, Pakistan's highest score in Twenty20 internationals, against Bangladesh in April 2008 ... He averages 116 in Tests against India, but only 13 against Bangladesh ...

THE FIGURES to 26.09.11   **cricinfo.com**

Batting & Fielding	M	Inns	NO	Runs	HS	Avge	S/R	100	50	4s	6s	Ct	St
Tests	26	46	8	1712	161*	45.05	40.66	3	12	195	16	30	0
ODIs	81	71	18	2308	93*	43.54	78.13	0	17	159	33	41	0
T20Is	34	29	10	652	87*	34.31	113.39	0	3	37	24	11	0
First-class	162	263	32	11933	284	51.65	–	33	61	–	–	164	0

Bowling	M	Balls	Runs	Wkts	BB	Avge	RpO	S/R	5i	10m
Tests	26	0	–	–	–	–	–	–	–	–
ODIs	81	24	30	0	–	–	7.50	–	0	0
T20Is	34	0	–	–	–	–	–	–	–	–
First-class	162	318	242	3	1–2	80.66	4.56	106.00	0	0

AMIT **MISHRA**

Full name	**Amit Mishra**
Born	**November 24, 1982, Delhi**
Teams	**Haryana, Deccan Chargers**
Style	**Right-hand bat, legspinner**
Test debut	**India v Australia at Mohali 2008-09**
ODI debut	**India v South Africa at Dhaka 2002-03**
T20I debut	**India v Zimbabwe at Harare 2010**

THE PROFILE Amit Mishra is a confident cricketer, but even he might have thought his international chance had gone when five years went by after a flirtation with the one-day team early in 2003. The diminutive Mishra, who bowls big loopy legbreaks and has a fizzing googly, took only two wickets in three matches after several players were rested following the World Cup: he was seen as too slow through the air, and went back to the domestic grind. But Mishra remained a consistent force for Haryana, taking 41 first-class wickets in 2004-05 and 46 in 2007-08. He also did well in the inaugural IPL, taking a hat-trick against Adam Gilchrist's Deccan Chargers. Early the following season Mishra took 6 for 81 against New Zealand A, which earned him a Test call-up against Australia a fortnight later after Anil Kumble injured his shoulder. Mishra grabbed his big chance, becoming the first Indian to take a debut five-for since Narendra Hirwani, one of the selectors who finally chose him. The googly accounted for three of his wickets, but the pick was arguably the legbreak which pinned top-scorer Shane Watson in front. Mishra took 14 wickets in three Tests, then six more against England later in 2008. Pragyan Ojha's rise and Harbhajan Singh's continued presence meant Mishra was still a fringe selection, though he had his moments: seven wickets against Bangladesh in January 2010, followed by important strikes in victories over South Africa at Kolkata and Sri Lanka in Colombo. He wasn't required for the 2011 World Cup, then made little impression when replacing the injured Harbhajan in England, although he did collect 84 as a nightwatchman at The Oval.

THE FACTS Mishra took 5 for 71 against Australia at Mohali in October 2008: he was only the sixth Indian to take a five-for on Test debut ... He took a hat-trick in his 5 for 17 for Delhi Daredevils v Deccan Chargers in the first season of the IPL in May 2008 ... Mishra took 6 for 66 for Haryana v Jharkhand in March 2005 ... He came in as nightwatchman in the 2011 Oval Test, and made 84: he has passed 60 three times in first-class cricket, and each time he's been out for 84 ...

THE FIGURES *to 26.09.11*   **ESPNcricinfo.com**

Batting & Fielding	M	Inns	NO	Runs	HS	Avge	S/R	100	50	4s	6s	Ct	St
Tests	13	19	2	392	84	23.05	58.24	0	2	50	2	6	0
ODIs	15	3	1	5	5*	2.50	27.77	0	0	0	0	2	0
T20Is	1	0	–	–	–	–	–	–	–	–	–	0	0
First-class	105	143	20	2506	84	20.37	–	0	11	–	–	54	0

Bowling	M	Balls	Runs	Wkts	BB	Avge	RpO	S/R	5i	10m
Tests	13	3497	1862	43	5–71	43.30	3.19	81.32	1	0
ODIs	15	763	575	19	4–31	30.26	4.52	40.15	0	0
T20Is	1	24	21	1	1–21	21.00	5.25	24.00	0	0
First-class	105	22819	11323	391	6–66	28.95	2.97	58.36	19	1

ABHIMANYU **MITHUN**

Full name	**Abhimanyu Mithun**
Born	**October 25, 1989, Bangalore**
Teams	**Karnataka, Royal Challengers Bangalore**
Style	**Right-hand bat, right-arm fast-medium bowler**
Test debut	**India v Sri Lanka at Galle 2010**
ODI debut	**India v South Africa at Ahmedabad 2009-10**
T20I debut	**No T20Is yet**

THE PROFILE Abhimanyu Mithun spent his early years striving for success in athletics – he was a fine discus thrower – and didn't bowl with a leather ball until he was 17. But three years later, after a remarkably successful debut season in 2009-10, he had forced his way into the national squad. Mithun's build, honed in his father's Bangalore gym, is perfect for a fast bowler: he's 6ft 2ins (188cm) tall, and uses his height to good effect for his favourite weapon, the bouncer. Mithun was snapped up by the Bangalore Royal Challengers before the second IPL in 2009 and, although he didn't do much in his only outing then, he certainly made people sit up when he finally made his Ranji Trophy debut in November: 11 Uttar Pradesh wickets, including a second-innings hat-trick. He made batsmen hop about, and finished with 52 wickets at 23.26 as Karnataka reached the Ranji final for the first time in 12 years. Mithun sat out the home Tests against South Africa, but did play in one of the ensuing one-dayers, although he proved expensive. Still, he went to Sri Lanka in July, and this time played in all three Tests, starting with the early wicket of Tillekeratne Dilshan. After four wickets in the first Test, he managed only two in the other two, but did reveal unexpected tenacity with the bat, playing long defensive knocks in each Test. After that, though, he was sidelined: rather surprisingly overlooked for the South African tour late in 2010, he had played only one more international by September the following year, not even joining the cast of thousands assembled for the various sections of the disastrous tour of England.

THE FACTS Mithun took 6 for 86 and 5 for 95 – including a hat-trick – on his first-class debut for Karnataka v Uttar Pradesh at Meerut in November 2009 ... He took 6 for 71 for Karnataka v Mumbai in the Ranji Trophy final at Mysore in January 2010 ... Mithun's first Test, at Galle in July 2010, was only his 12th first-class match ...

THE FIGURES to 26.09.11   **ESPNcricinfo.com**

Batting & Fielding	M	Inns	NO	Runs	HS	Avge	S/R	100	50	4s	6s	Ct	St
Tests	4	5	0	120	46	24.00	48.19	0	0	16	0	0	0
ODIs	2	2	0	28	24	14.00	71.79	0	0	0	2	0	0
T20Is	0	0	–	–	–	–	–	–	–	–	–	–	–
First-class	25	31	7	435	63*	18.12	53.70	0	1	57	4	5	0

Bowling	M	Balls	Runs	Wkts	BB	Avge	RpO	S/R	5i	10m
Tests	4	720	456	9	4–105	50.66	3.80	80.00	0	0
ODIs	2	72	87	0	–	–	7.25	–	0	0
T20Is	0	0	–	–	–	–	–	–	–	–
First-class	25	4697	2745	93	6–71	29.51	3.50	50.50	4	1

MOHAMMAD ASHRAFUL

Full name	**Mohammad Ashraful**
Born	**July 7, 1984, Dhaka**
Teams	**Dhaka**
Style	**Right-hand bat, legspinner**
Test debut	**Bangladesh v Sri Lanka at Colombo 2001-02**
ODI debut	**Bangladesh v Zimbabwe at Bulawayo 2000-01**
T20I debut	**Bangladesh v Kenya at Nairobi 2007-08**

THE PROFILE In September 2001, Mohammad Ashraful enlivened a terrible mismatch in Colombo by becoming the youngest man – or boy – to make a Test century. Just 17, he broke the long-standing record set by Mushtaq Mohammad of Pakistan in 1960-61. Bangladesh still crashed to heavy defeat, but "Matin" was unbowed, repeatedly dancing down to hit Muttiah Muralitharan and his fellow spinners back over their heads. Inevitably, such a heady early achievement proved hard to live up to, and Ashraful was dropped for England's first visit in October 2003. He returned a better player, but no less flamboyant, producing a glorious unbeaten 158 in defeat against India. Still not 21 when Bangladesh toured England for the first time in 2005, Ashraful confirmed his talent at Cardiff, when his well-paced century set up a stunning one-day victory over Australia. He continued to fire spasmodically: his 87 helped defeat South Africa in the 2007 World Cup, but that was surrounded by more low scores. When Habibul Bashar stood down as captain in May 2007 Ashraful took over – but the results stayed the same, and he looked careworn by the time he was replaced after a dismal World Twenty20 campaign in England in 2009. He celebrated his return to the ranks with a couple of fifties against West Indies and a fine hundred against Zimbabwe, but again indifferent form cost him his place. And again the selectors came back to him, and again Ashraful remained maddeningly inconsistent. After only two outings in the World Cup, he played responsibly for 73 and 39 in the Test defeat by Zimbabwe in August 2011 – but failed to get past 28 in five other innings on that chastening tour.

THE FACTS Only 11 players have made their Test debuts when younger than Ashraful: three of them are from Bangladesh ... He scored 263, putting on 420 with Marshall Ayub, for Dhaka v Chittagong in November 2006 ... Ashraful averages 42.88 in Tests v India, but only 9.12 v England ... His Test batting average is easily the lowest for anyone with five or more centuries: Grant Flower (29.54) is next ... Ashraful's record includes two ODIs for the Asia XI ...

THE FIGURES *to 26.09.11*   **ESPNcricinfo.com**

Batting & Fielding	M	Inns	NO	Runs	HS	Avge	S/R	100	50	4s	6s	Ct	St
Tests	56	109	4	2418	158*	23.02	46.79	5	8	302	21	24	0
ODIs	169	162	13	3395	109	22.78	70.20	3	20	344	29	35	0
T20Is	15	15	0	265	65	17.66	148.04	0	2	27	9	3	0
First-class	109	204	5	5629	263	28.28	–		14	23	–	–	56	0

Bowling	M	Balls	Runs	Wkts	BB	Avge	RpO	S/R	5i	10m
Tests	56	1591	1188	20	2–42	59.40	4.48	79.55	0	0
ODIs	169	685	644	18	3–26	35.77	5.64	38.05	0	0
T20Is	15	138	210	8	3–42	26.25	9.13	17.25	0	0
First-class	109	7036	4263	118	7–99	36.12	3.63	59.62	5	0

MOHAMMAD HAFEEZ

PAKISTAN

Full name	**Mohammad Hafeez**
Born	**October 17, 1980, Sargodha, Punjab**
Teams	**Faisalabad, Sui Northern Gas**
Style	**Right-hand bat, offspinner**
Test debut	**Pakistan v Bangladesh at Karachi 2003**
ODI debut	**Pakistan v Zimbabwe at Sharjah 2002-03**
T20I debut	**Pakistan v England at Bristol 2006**

THE PROFILE Mohammad Hafeez got the first of several Pakistan chances after their abysmal 2003 World Cup. He showed good technique and temperament with the bat, and bowled his Saqlainish offspinners tidily, but was arguably at his most impressive in the field, patrolling the covers with feverish alertness. When Bangladesh toured shortly afterwards he started brightly: 50 on Test debut and 102 in his second match. But then he struggled against South Africa – just 33 runs in five one-day innings – and lost his place. Consistent domestic runs kept Hafeez in contention, but he seemed to be a back number after being dropped again early in 2005. He was not originally chosen for the 2006 England tour, but 180 against Australia A in Darwin in July, while Pakistan struggled to find an opening combination worth the name in England, led to a surprise call-up for the final Test at The Oval, and he made a tidy 95 before the ball-tampering row overshadowed everything. Another century followed against West Indies, but then he was left out for more than two years before a surprise recall for the World Twenty20 in the Caribbean and the one-day portion of the England tour later in 2010. He did well, especially in ODIs, hitting a maiden hundred in New Zealand early in 2011. After a consistent World Cup he was a star in the West Indies, where he made another one-day hundred and proved a surprise bowling hit, accounting for Devon Smith in six successive innings, often taking the new ball so he could get at the opener quickly. And Hafeez confirmed his return with another Test century – his first for almost five years – in Zimbabwe in September.

THE FACTS Mohammad Hafeez scored 50 in his first Test, against Bangladesh at Karachi in August 2003, and added 102 not out in his second, at Peshawar a week later ... He scored 95 in his only Test innings against England (at The Oval in 2006) ... Hafeez scored 180 for Pakistan A v Australia A at Darwin in July 2006 ... He took 8 for 57 (10 for 87 in the match) for Faisalabad v Quetta in December 2004 ...

THE FIGURES *to 26.09.11* 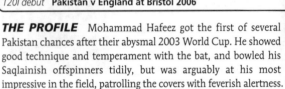 **ESPN cricinfo.com**

Batting & Fielding	M	Inns	NO	Runs	HS	Avge	S/R	100	50	4s	6s	Ct	St
Tests	18	35	2	1052	119	31.87	50.47	3	4	143	6	6	0
ODIs	82	82	4	2132	139*	27.33	68.61	3	11	240	21	27	0
T20Is	24	22	0	491	71	22.31	120.34	0	2	60	11	10	0
First-class	143	241	8	7874	180	33.79	–	17	38	–	–	122	0

Bowling	M	Balls	Runs	Wkts	BB	Avge	RpO	S/R	5i	10m
Tests	18	1512	626	18	4–31	34.77	2.48	84.00	0	0
ODIs	82	3071	2222	66	3–17	33.66	4.34	46.53	0	0
T20Is	24	338	422	19	4–10	22.21	7.49	17.78	0	0
First-class	143	10464	4775	166	8–57	28.76	2.73	63.03	4	1

EOIN **MORGAN**

Full name	**Eoin Joseph Gerard Morgan**
Born	**September 10, 1986, Dublin, Ireland**
Teams	**Middlesex, Kolkata Knight Riders**
Style	**Left-hand bat, occasional right-arm medium-pacer**
Test debut	**England v Bangladesh at Lord's 2010**
ODI debut	**Ireland v Scotland at Ayr 2006**
T20I debut	**England v Netherlands at Lord's 2009**

THE PROFILE Eoin Morgan is an impish batsman capable of inventive and audacious strokeplay: he seems a natural "finisher", a role England struggled to fill for a decade. A compact left-hander, he gained initial recognition with Ireland, playing 23 ODIs for them, although he was disappointing at the 2007 World Cup. He had joined his fellow Dubliner, Ed Joyce, at Middlesex in 2006, and two years later helped them win the Twenty20 Cup. In 2009 he was called up by England. After a quiet start in which his fielding was probably more impressive than his batting, Morgan did well as England won the World Twenty20 in the West Indies early in 2010, then, although not widely viewed as a five-day player, he was a surprise inclusion for the first Test of the home summer, against Bangladesh: he confidently collected his first boundary with a reverse-sweep. He added a gutsy 130 to set up victory over Pakistan in the first Test at Trent Bridge, and finished the season with a fine century to seal a 3-2 victory in a fractious one-day series. When Paul Collingwood retired Morgan wasn't the favourite to replace him, especially after missing the start of the 2011 English season to play in the IPL, but 193 for England Lions against the Sri Lankans won him the place, and he cemented it with three gritty seventies before making 104 against India at Edgbaston ... all this despite adding a curious low squat in the stance. He remained a one-day fixture, scoring two fifties on arriving late at the World Cup after a broken finger. He even captained England – against Ireland – before a shoulder problem (which needed an operation) ended his season.

THE FACTS Morgan is the only player ever to be out (run out, too!) for 99 in his first ODI, against Scotland in August 2006 ... His first 23 ODIs were for Ireland: he made 744 runs at 35.42 for them, including 115 against Canada in Nairobi in February 2007 ... Morgan scored 209 not out – the first double-century for Ireland – against the UAE in Abu Dhabi in February 2007 ... Morgan was the third Irish-born player to score a Test century, after Fred Fane for England in 1905-06 and Australia's Tom Horan (1881-82) ...

THE FIGURES to 26.09.11   **ESP∩cricinfo.com**

Batting & Fielding	M	Inns	NO	Runs	HS	Avge	S/R	100	50	4s	6s	Ct	St
Tests	13	18	1	618	130	36.35	55.87	2	3	70	4	10	0
ODIs	71	69	11	2241	115	38.63	83.24	4	15	197	41	30	0
T20Is	18	18	6	569	85*	47.41	138.78	0	3	58	18	10	0
First-class	64	104	13	3495	209*	38.40	52.37	9	16	–	–	54	1

Bowling	M	Balls	Runs	Wkts	BB	Avge	RpO	S/R	5i	10m
Tests	13	0	–	–	–	–	–	–	–	–
ODIs	71	0	–	–	–	–	–	–	–	–
T20Is	18	0	–	–	–	–	–	–	–	–
First-class	64	97	83	2	2–24	41.50	5.13	48.50	0	0

ALBIE **MORKEL**

Full name	**Johannes Albertus Morkel**
Born	**June 10, 1981, Vereeniging, Transvaal**
Teams	**Titans, Chennai Super Kings**
Style	**Left-hand bat, right-arm fast-medium bowler**
Test debut	**South Africa v Australia at Cape Town 2008-09**
ODI debut	**South Africa v New Zealand at Wellington 2003-04**
T20I debut	**South Africa v New Zealand at Johannesburg 2005-06**

THE PROFILE Albie Morkel, a fast-medium bowler and big-hitting left-handed batsman, was lumbered with the tag of the "new Lance Klusener", and was touted early on by Ray Jennings (his provincial coach, and a former national coach too) as a potential world-class allrounder. It never quite happened, although he does average over 40 in first-class cricket, and scored a half-century in his only Test (he was included after his brother Morne lost form). Most notably, the 20-over game seemed to be tailor-made for Albie's style of play. His huge sixes were a feature of the inaugural World Twenty20 tournament late in 2007, but by 2009-10 the expectation of more rope-clearing every time he came in seemed to be affecting his performances. He eventually lost his one-day place, and was a rather surprising omission from South Africa's 2011 World Cup squad. Morkel responded by being named Titans' player of the season, so an international recall cannot be ruled out. For Easterns (now the Titans) against the touring West Indians at Benoni in 2003-04 Albie defied food poisoning to score a century – putting on 141 for the ninth wicket with his brother – and also took five wickets in the match. He was picked for the senior tour of New Zealand shortly after that, and made his ODI debut there early in 2004: he performed solidly, if unspectacularly, for a while until the selectors looked elsewhere. Morkel was back for the Afro-Asia Cup in June 2007. In the second match, at Chennai, Albie and Morne opened the bowling together for the African XI, the first instance of brothers sharing the new ball in an ODI since Kenya's Martin and Tony Suji did so during the 1999 World Cup.

THE FACTS Morkel made 204 not out, putting on 264 with Justin Kemp, as Titans drew with Western Province Boland in March 2005 after following on ... He took 6 for 36 for Easterns v Griqualand West in December 1999 ... Morkel's brother Morne has also played for South Africa, while another brother, Malan, played for SA Schools ... His record includes two ODIs for the Africa XI, in one of which he opened the bowling with Morne ...

THE FIGURES *to 26.09.11*   **ᴇsᴘⁿcricinfo.com**

Batting & Fielding	M	Inns	NO	Runs	HS	Avge	S/R	100	50	4s	6s	Ct	St
Tests	1	1	0	58	58	58.00	81.69	0	1	10	1	0	0
ODIs	51	38	8	679	97	22.63	100.14	0	2	64	20	14	0
T20Is	31	25	6	443	43	23.31	142.90	0	0	26	29	13	0
First-class	70	101	18	3720	204*	44.81	–	7	21	–	–	28	0

Bowling	M	Balls	Runs	Wkts	BB	Avge	RpO	S/R	5i	10m
Tests	1	192	132	1	1–44	132.00	4.12	192.00	0	0
ODIs	51	1935	1763	50	4–29	35.26	5.46	38.70	0	0
T20Is	31	454	608	18	2–12	33.77	8.03	25.22	0	0
First-class	70	10693	5508	186	6–36	29.61	3.09	57.48	5	0

MORNE **MORKEL**

Full name	**Morne Morkel**
Born	**October 6, 1984, Vereeniging, Transvaal**
Teams	**Titans, Delhi Daredevils**
Style	**Left-hand bat, right-arm fast bowler**
Test debut	**South Africa v India at Durban 2006-07**
ODI debut	**Africa XI v Asia XI at Bangalore 2007**
T20I debut	**South Africa v West Indies at Johannesburg 2007-08**

THE PROFILE Morne Morkel, the taller, faster brother of
Easterns allrounder Albie, has been a hot property ever since his
first-class debut in 2003-04, when he and Albie put on 141
against the West Indians at Benoni. An out-and-out fast bowler,
Morne excelled with 20 wickets at 18.20 apiece in 2004-05, and impressed Allan Donald:
"He gets serious bounce, and he's got really great pace – genuine pace." Morkel used that to
shake up the Indians for the Rest of South Africa in December 2006, bowling Sehwag with
his first ball and adding Laxman, Tendulkar and Dhoni as the tourists lurched to 69 for 5.
That got him into the national frame, and he played in the second Test when Dale Steyn was
ruled out, although three wickets and some handy runs in a crushing victory weren't enough
to keep him in when Steyn was fit again. A stress fracture temporarily halted the rapid rise,
but he returned in 2008 to lead South Africa's attack in England, without ever quite being
at his best as they won the Test series. Early the following year Morne had the unusual
experience of being replaced in the Test side by his brother, but later cemented his place
with seven wickets in a crushing victory over England at Johannesburg, and six more in
another comfortable win over West Indies at Port-of-Spain later in 2010. After that he took
15 in three matches against India at the turn of 2010-11, the seven in the innings victory
in the first Test at Centurion including his 100th in Tests, but he was less effective on
subcontinental pitches at the 2011 World Cup.

THE FACTS Morkel took 6 for 43 and 6 for 48 for Titans v Eagles at Bloemfontein
in March 2009, a week after being dropped from the Test side ... He took 5 for 20 against
India at Centurion in December 2010, his second wicket (Rahul Dravid) being his 100th in
Tests ... Morkel's first three ODIs were for the Africa XI: in one he opened the bowling with
his brother Albie, the first instance of siblings sharing the new ball in an ODI since Kenya's
Martin and Tony Suji did so during the 1999 World Cup ...

THE FIGURES *to 26.09.11*   ᴇꜱᴘñcricinfo.com

Batting & Fielding	M	Inns	NO	Runs	HS	Avge	S/R	100	50	4s	6s	Ct	St
Tests	31	37	4	481	40	14.57	44.91	0	0	74	0	7	0
ODIs	44	18	5	115	25	8.84	76.15	0	0	12	2	15	0
T20Is	17	2	1	2	1*	2.00	40.00	0	0	0	0	1	0
First-class	64	79	10	1148	82*	16.63	47.06	0	4	–	–	27	0

Bowling	M	Balls	Runs	Wkts	BB	Avge	RpO	S/R	5i	10m
Tests	31	6109	3415	113	5–20	30.22	3.35	54.06	4	0
ODIs	44	2173	1771	74	4–21	23.93	4.89	29.36	0	0
T20Is	17	377	395	25	4–17	15.80	6.28	15.08	0	0
First-class	64	11621	6456	238	6–43	27.12	3.33	48.82	11	2

CHRISTOPHER **MPOFU**

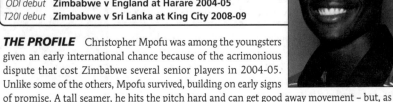
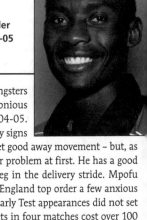

ZIMBABWE

Full name	**Christopher Bobby Mpofu**
Born	**November 27, 1985, Plumtree, Matabeleland**
Teams	**Matabeleland Tuskers**
Style	**Right-hand bat, right-arm fast-medium bowler**
Test debut	**Zimbabwe v Bangladesh at Chittagong 2004-05**
ODI debut	**Zimbabwe v England at Harare 2004-05**
T20I debut	**Zimbabwe v Sri Lanka at King City 2008-09**

THE PROFILE Christopher Mpofu was among the youngsters given an early international chance because of the acrimonious dispute that cost Zimbabwe several senior players in 2004-05. Unlike some of the others, Mpofu survived, building on early signs of promise. A tall seamer, he hits the pitch hard and can get good away movement – but, as with many young quick bowlers, consistency was his major problem at first. He has a good action, although he sometimes collapses over the front leg in the delivery stride. Mpofu made his one-day debut in October 2004, and caused the England top order a few anxious moments although he did not actually take a wicket. His early Test appearances did not set the world alight, and he lost his place after his three wickets in four matches cost over 100 apiece. Mpofu benefited noticeably from Heath Streak's appointment as Zimbabwe's bowling coach in 2009: his action was smoothed out, his outswing became more consistent (although he still has a frustrating propensity to bowl too wide of off stump), and his pace increased. Early in 2010 he took a career-best 7 for 37 against West Indies A, and when Zimbabwe returned to Test cricket in August the following year Mpofu was part of an impressive fast-bowling attack which also included the pacy Kyle Jarvis and left-armer Brian Vitori: they helped set up a fine comeback win over Bangladesh. Mpofu's batting, however, is comically inept: not content with being stumped twice in an afternoon (for a pair) in the first Test against New Zealand in August 2005, in the next match he was run out as he strolled down the pitch to congratulate his partner on reaching a half-century.

THE FACTS Mpofu took 7 for 37 for the Zimbabweans against West Indies A at St George's in Grenada in April 2010 ... He had figures of 8.3-3-8-6 in a one-day match for Matabeleland against Mashonaland at Harare in January 2006 ... Against New Zealand at Harare in August 2005 Mpofu was only the second man to be stumped in both innings for a pair in Tests – the other was England's Bobby Peel, at Sydney in 1894-95 ...

THE FIGURES to 26.09.11   **ESPNcricinfo.com**

Batting & Fielding	M	Inns	NO	Runs	HS	Avge	S/R	100	50	4s	6s	Ct	St
Tests	8	15	6	27	8	3.00	21.42	0	0	2	1	0	0
ODIs	60	33	17	38	6	2.37	22.09	0	0	1	0	10	0
T20Is	9	2	2	7	4*	–	116.66	0	0	0	0	3	0
First-class	68	111	32	669	36	8.46	30.39	0	0	-	-	15	0

Bowling	M	Balls	Runs	Wkts	BB	Avge	RpO	S/R	5i	10m
Tests	8	1160	743	15	4–109	49.53	3.84	77.33	0	0
ODIs	60	2852	2472	67	6–52	36.89	5.20	42.56	1	0
T20Is	9	186	278	7	3–16	39.71	8.96	26.57	0	0
First-class	68	10992	5862	181	7–37	32.38	3.19	60.72	4	0

ABHINAV **MUKUND**

Full name	**Abhinav Mukund**
Born	**January 6, 1990, Madras (now Chennai)**
Teams	**Tamil Nadu**
Style	**Left-hand bat, occasional legspinner**
Test debut	**India v West Indies at Kingston 2011**
ODI debut	**No ODIs yet**
T20I debut	**No T20Is yet**

THE PROFILE Abhinav Mukund is a left-hand opener from Chennai, especially fluent through the off side, who gave early notice of his ability: before turning 20 he had a triple-century, hundreds on Ranji and Irani Trophy debuts, and an opening stand of more than 400 with Murali Vijay, a state team-mate but now a rival for a Test place. At first Mukund was less certain on the leg side, frequently playing around his front pad, but still picked up an impressive quantity of runs. He scored a century in his second first-class match, and was part of the squad that won the Under-19 World Cup in Malaysia in 2008, although that coincided with a dip in form and he didn't actually play. After that, though, he bounced back in style, collecting that triple-century against Maharashtra in November 2008. The run-torrent continued: after four seasons he had a first-class average of 60, and when both Virender Sehwag and Gautam Gambhir missed the West Indian tour which followed the 2011 World Cup Mukund was called up. It was a subdued start, the highlight 62 in the third Test in Dominica, but his 147 runs in the series was double Vijay's output, and Mukund kept his place when Gambhir returned at the start of the England tour. He made a bright start with 49 at Lord's, but a double failure in the second Test cost him his place, and he was sent back to domestic cricket to tighten his technique. But Mukund was unfazed: "The results don't show how much progress I made," he said. "I have definitely got the belief that I could do well, and there's so much that I have learned."

THE FACTS Mukund scored 300 not out for Tamil Nadu v Maharashtra at Nasik in November 2008, in his seventh first-class match, sharing an opening stand of 462 with Murali Vijay (243) ... Mukund hit 257 against Hyderabad in December 2009, and 232 against Saurashtra in November 2010 ... He made 108, his maiden century, in his second first-class match, against Karnataka at Chennai in November 2007 on his Ranji Trophy debut ...

THE FIGURES to 26.09.11   **ESPN**cricinfo.com

Batting & Fielding	M	Inns	NO	Runs	HS	Avge	S/R	100	50	4s	6s	Ct	St
Tests	5	10	0	211	62	21.10	40.73	0	1	21	0	5	0
ODIs	0	0	–	–	–	–	–	–	–	–	–	–	–
T20Is	0	0	–	–	–	–	–	–	–	–	–	–	–
First-class	46	73	4	3708	300*	53.73	54.48	13	10	463	17	35	0

Bowling	M	Balls	Runs	Wkts	BB	Avge	RpO	S/R	5i	10m
Tests	5	12	14	0	–	–	7.00	–	0	0
ODIs	0	0	–	–	–	–	–	–	–	–
T20Is	0	0	–	–	–	–	–	–	–	–
First-class	46	573	346	9	3–5	38.44	3.62	63.66	0	0

MUSHFIQUR RAHIM

BANGLADESH

Full name	**Mohammad Mushfiqur Rahim**
Born	**September 1, 1988, Bogra**
Teams	**Rajshahi**
Style	**Right-hand bat, wicketkeeper**
Test debut	**Bangladesh v England at Lord's 2005**
ODI debut	**Bangladesh v Zimbabwe at Harare 2006**
T20I debut	**Bangladesh v Zimbabwe at Khulna 2006-07**

THE PROFILE A wild-card inclusion for Bangladesh's maiden tour of England in 2005, the diminutive Mushfiqur Rahim was just 16 when he was selected for that daunting trip. He was principally chosen as understudy to long-serving wicketkeeper Khaled Mashud, but he had also shown signs of promise with the bat (a century in an A-team Test in Zimbabwe, and 88 against England Under-19s). He showed more evidence of grit with the full team, with a maiden first-class half-century to soften the pain of defeat against Sussex, followed by a hundred at Northampton. That earned him a call-up – as a batsman – to become the youngest player to appear in a Test at Lord's. Mushfiqur was one of only three players to reach double figures in a disappointing first innings, but a twisted ankle kept him out of the second Test. Two years later he supplanted Mashud for the 2007 World Cup, anchoring the win over India with 56 not out, and soon established himself as the first-choice keeper. He is now one of Bangladesh's most consistent batsmen, and their vice-captain too: he just missed a one-day hundred against Zimbabwe in August 2009, but made sure in Tests with 101 against India at Chittagong in January 2010, Bangladesh's fastest hundred in Tests at the time. There was a near-miss against England at home (95, again at Chittagong), although he was less prolific in England later the same year. After a modest 2011 World Cup with the bat, Mushfiqur bounced back with 126 runs for once out in three one-dayers against Australia, then made a 99-ball hundred in an ODI in Zimbabwe – although it was not enough to prevent another defeat on that embarrassing tour.

THE FACTS Mushfiqur Rahim's hundred for Bangladesh v Northants in 2005 made him the youngest century-maker in English first-class cricket: he was 16 years 261 days old, 211 days younger than Sachin Tendulkar in 1990; the youngest Englishman was 17-year-old Stephen Peters (for Essex in 1996) ... Mushfiqur was stumped for 98 in an ODI in Zimbabwe in August 2009, but made amends with 101 against them two years later ... He had played two Tests before he appeared in a first-class match at home ...

THE FIGURES to 26.09.11   **ESPNcricinfo.com**

Batting & Fielding	M	Inns	NO	Runs	HS	Avge	S/R	100	50	4s	6s	Ct	St
Tests	24	47	3	1195	101	27.15	43.66	1	6	161	8	34	8
ODIs	98	89	16	1875	101	25.68	66.41	1	9	144	19	65	29
T20Is	15	13	4	85	24	9.44	86.73	0	0	5	1	7	7
First-class	49	89	10	2261	115*	28.62	–	3	13	–	–	82	13

Bowling	M	Balls	Runs	Wkts	BB	Avge	RpO	S/R	5i	10m
Tests	24	0	–	–	–	–	–	–	–	–
ODIs	98	0	–	–	–	–	–	–	–	–
T20Is	15	0	–	–	–	–	–	–	–	–
First-class	49	0	–	–	–	–	–	–	–	–

BRENDAN **NASH**

Full name	**Brendan Paul Nash**
Born	**December 14, 1977, Attadale, Western Australia**
Teams	**Jamaica**
Style	**Left-hand bat, left-arm medium-pacer**
Test debut	**West Indies v New Zealand at Dunedin 2008-09**
ODI debut	**West Indies v Bermuda at King City 2008**
T20I debut	**No T20Is yet**

THE PROFILE A smallish but solid left-hander, Brendan Nash played in three Pura Cup finals for Queensland, scoring 96 in one of them, before losing his state contract after a patchy 2006-07 season. After that he decided to try his luck in Jamaica, where his father Paul was born (he swam for Jamaica in the 1968 Mexico Olympics, but emigrated to Australia while his wife was pregnant with Brendan). Nash had a fine first season, helping Jamaica win the Carib Beer Cup title: he scored 422 runs with two centuries, one of them in the final. Although he was less prolific in limited-overs games, it was no great surprise when he was called up to the West Indian squad, although there were murmurs about an Australian "mercenary" muscling his way in. Nash won his first Test cap in New Zealand in December 2008, then proved a reliable middle-order buttress in the home series against England, with a four-hour 55 in the first Test at Kingston, which West Indies won, and a maiden century (batting for 330 minutes in all) at Port-of-Spain, when a draw clinched the series victory. He added 81 in an otherwise disappointing team display at Lord's a couple of months later, and added a second hundred against South Africa in St Kitts in June 2010. The following year, though – soon after being appointed vice-captain – he lost his Test place after a run of poor form. Nash is also a handy containing medium-pacer, and remains a fine fielder: earlier in his career he was Australia's substitute fielder in a Test against West Indies (and dropped his future team-mate Denesh Ramdin).

THE FACTS Nash is generally considered to be the first white man to play for West Indies since Geoff Greenidge in 1972-73 ... He hit 176 for Queensland v New South Wales at Brisbane in October 2002 ... Nash averaged 27 with the bat for Queensland, 42 for Jamaica – and 33 for West Indies ... He scored 96 in Australia's Pura Cup final in 2001-02, and 117 in West Indies' Carib Beer Challenge final in April 2008 ...

THE FIGURES to 26.09.11   **ESPncricinfo.com**

Batting & Fielding	M	Inns	NO	Runs	HS	Avge	S/R	100	50	4s	6s	Ct	St
Tests	21	33	0	1103	114	33.42	43.28	2	8	130	3	6	0
ODIs	9	7	3	104	39*	26.00	73.75	0	0	11	1	1	0
T20Is	0	0	–	–	–	–	–	–	–	–	–	–	–
First-class	81	135	16	4198	207	35.27	–	8	18	–	–	31	0

Bowling	M	Balls	Runs	Wkts	BB	Avge	RpO	S/R	5i	10m
Tests	21	492	247	2	1–21	123.50	3.01	246.00	0	0
ODIs	9	294	224	5	3–56	44.80	4.57	58.80	0	0
T20Is	0	0	–	–	–	–	–	–	–	–
First-class	81	1262	578	17	2–7	34.00	2.74	74.23	0	0

NAZMUL HOSSAIN

Full name	**Mohammad Nazmul Hossain**
Born	**October 5, 1987, Hobigonj**
Teams	**Sylhet**
Style	**Right-hand bat, right-arm fast-medium bowler**
Test debut	**Bangladesh v India at Chittagong 2004-05**
ODI debut	**Bangladesh v South Africa at Edgbaston 2004**
T20I debut	**Bangladesh v West Indies at Basseterre 2009**

THE PROFILE Nazmul Hossain is a hard-working fast bowler with a delivery style not unlike that of Makhaya Ntini, although he is not as quick. He did well at the Under-19 World Cup early in 2004 – although more fuss was made of his faster team-mate, Shahadat Hossain – and was given a premature Test debut later that year, when he was called up to make what was also his first-class debut against India. Only 17, he did not disappoint, claiming the wickets of Gautam Gambhir (for 139) and Harbhajan Singh. After that Nazmul has been seen as more of a one-day specialist – although his style of bowling might have been useful on the early-season pitches the Bangladeshis encountered in England in 2010. He spent 30 months out of the side, but returned in August 2008 a cannier bowler. Early in 2009 his 3 for 30 in the tri-series final at home in Mirpur gave Sri Lanka a severe case of the jitters: chasing a modest 153, they were 6 for 5 after Nazmul's initial burst, but regrouped to win by two wickets. Nazmul sticks to an off-stump line, with the natural angle taking the ball in. But the dangerous one is the delivery which straightens or just moves a shade away – batsmen don't expect that from a bowler with his kind of action. He is also a fine fielder, who pulled off a stunning catch at backward point to remove Zimbabwe's Malcolm Waller in a one-dayer at Chittagong in November 2009. He missed the 2011 World Cup, but remained in the mix and toured Zimbabwe later in the year, although he had few chances to shine on that chastening tour.

THE FACTS Nazmul Hossain was the second Bangladeshi (after Mashrafe Mortaza in 2001-02) to make his first-class debut in a Test match: only three others have done this since 1899 – Graham Vivian of New Zealand (1964-65), Zimbabwe's Ujesh Ranchod (1992-93) and Yasir Ali of Pakistan (2003-04) ... He was 17 years 73 days old at the time of his debut (the fifth-youngest for Bangladesh) ... Nazmul took 5 for 30 for Sylhet at Rajshahi in March 2006 ... His father, an army man, was a Bangladesh football international ...

THE FIGURES to 26.09.11   **ESPNcricinfo.com**

Batting & Fielding	M	Inns	NO	Runs	HS	Avge	S/R	100	50	4s	6s	Ct	St
Tests	1	2	1	8	8*	8.00	88.88	0	0	2	0	0	0
ODIs	35	21	13	35	6*	4.37	27.34	0	0	0	0	5	0
T20Is	2	2	2	3	3*	–	20.00	0	0	0	0	0	0
First-class	31	50	12	384	49	10.10	35.65	0	0	–	–	16	0

Bowling	M	Balls	Runs	Wkts	BB	Avge	RpO	S/R	5i	10m
Tests	1	155	114	2	2–114	57.00	4.41	77.50	0	0
ODIs	35	1523	1302	39	4–40	33.38	5.12	39.05	0	0
T20Is	2	24	33	1	1–15	33.00	8.25	24.00	0	0
First-class	31	4141	1992	65	5–30	30.64	2.88	63.70	2	0

PRAGYAN **OJHA**

Full name **Pragyan Prayash Ojha**
Born **September 5, 1986, Bhubaneshwar**
Teams **Hyderabad, Deccan Chargers, Surrey**
Style **Left-hand bat, left-arm orthodox spinner**
Test debut **India v Sri Lanka at Kanpur 2009-10**
ODI debut **India v Bangladesh at Karachi 2008**
T20I debut **India v Bangladesh at Nottingham 2009**

THE PROFILE A left-arm spinner of teasing flight and pleasing loop, Pragyan Ojha made a stunning start in first-class cricket: for Hyderabad in the Ranji Trophy semi-final in March 2005, he took the first five wickets to fall in eventual champions Railways' first innings, starting with the Test allrounder Sanjay Bangar. Ojha showed his control for Deccan Chargers in the inaugural IPL in 2008: he finished with 11 wickets, then took 21 - four more than anyone else - in 2010. He also made an immediate impact in his first ODI, in the Asia Cup in June 2008, with three outfield catches and an absolute ripper which foxed Bangladesh's Raqibul Hasan. Still seen by the selectors as a one-day specialist, Ojha started the 2009 World Twenty20 in England well, taking a wicket with his first ball and finishing with 4 for 21 against Bangladesh, but was omitted later in the tournament, then missed out on the one-day Compaq Cup in Sri Lanka in September as the selectors tried out legspinner Amit Mishra as Harbhajan Singh's partner. But Ojha did win his first Test cap late in 2009, taking a catch off his first ball in the field, and although his strike-rate was unspectacular he claimed 21 wickets in his first six matches, with seven - including danger men Sangakkara and Jayawardene in both innings - as India squared the series in Sri Lanka in August 2010. Nine wickets followed in two victories over Australia, and a dozen in three Tests against New Zealand ... but then he lost his place after a modest domestic season and hardly featured during 2011, although he added to his experience with a brief stint in English county cricket with Surrey.

THE FACTS Ojha took a wicket (Bangladesh's Shakib Al Hasan) with his first ball in Twenty20 internationals, at Trent Bridge in June 2009, and finished with 4 for 21 ... On his first-class debut, against Railways at Delhi in March 2005, Ojha took the first five wickets to fall, finishing with 5 for 55 ... Ojha was the leading wicket-taker of the third IPL, with 21 ... He took 7 for 114 for Hyderabad v Rajasthan in December 2006: the previous week he took 6 for 84 against Maharashtra ...

THE FIGURES to 26.09.11   **ESPN**cricinfo.com

Batting & Fielding	M	Inns	NO	Runs	HS	Avge	S/R	100	50	4s	6s	Ct	St
Tests	11	13	9	67	18*	16.75	20.87	0	0	4	0	3	0
ODIs	16	9	8	41	16*	41.00	43.61	0	0	3	0	7	0
T20Is	6	1	1	10	10*	–	166.66	0	0	0	1	1	0
First-class	54	71	28	453	35	10.53	31.11	0	0	47	0	18	0

Bowling	M	Balls	Runs	Wkts	BB	Avge	RpO	S/R	5i	10m
Tests	11	3539	1697	42	4–107	40.40	2.87	84.26	0	0
ODIs	16	835	601	20	4–38	30.05	4.31	41.75	0	0
T20Is	6	126	132	10	4–21	13.20	6.28	12.60	0	0
First-class	54	13117	6300	225	7–114	28.00	2.88	58.29	12	1

GRAHAM **ONIONS**

ENGLAND

Full name	**Graham Onions**
Born	**September 9, 1982, Gateshead**
Teams	**Durham**
Style	**Right-hand bat, right-arm fast-medium bowler**
Test debut	**England v West Indies at Lord's 2009**
ODI debut	**England v Australia at Chester-le-Street 2009**
T20I debut	**No T20Is yet**

THE PROFILE   A brisk seam bowler, with a name that is a headline-writer's dream (especially when Durham's keeper Phil Mustard does the catching), Graham Onions first took the eye in 2006, with 54 wickets. He maintained an impressive workload for Durham, and didn't just take wickets on helpful surfaces at Chester-le-Street. He was called up for the late-season ODIs against Pakistan, although he didn't play, but later toured Bangladesh with England A. The following two seasons were more of a struggle – Ottis Gibson sometimes kept him out of the county side in 2007, then he had injury problems – but Onions started 2009 in rare form, and made the early-season Tests against West Indies. He started in fairytale fashion, mopping up the tail with four wickets in seven balls to finish with 5 for 38 at Lord's, bowling at a lively pace and swinging the ball away. He played in three of the Ashes Tests without quite recapturing this form, although he did enliven the second morning at Edgbaston by striking with the first two balls of the day. Although he was left out for the final Test he was at The Oval as the Ashes were recaptured, then returned to Durham as they retained the Championship. He then picked up 11 wickets in three Tests in South Africa – although he will be better remembered for his obstinate batting, twice surviving the last over to stave off defeats. But he also picked up a stress fracture in the back, which ruled him out of the whole of 2010. Onions returned to form and fitness the following year, taking 53 first-class wickets to remind England's established pacemen that he was snapping at their heels.

THE FACTS   Onions took 8 for 101 for Durham v Warwickshire at Edgbaston in May 2007: two years later he took 7 for 38 in the same fixture ... At Edgbaston in July 2009 Onions took wickets with the first two balls of the second day's play against Australia: this is believed to have happened only once before in Test history, when Australia's "Chuck" Fleetwood-Smith did it against England at Melbourne in 1936-37 ...

THE FIGURES *to 26.09.11*   **ESPNcricinfo.com**

Batting & Fielding	M	Inns	NO	Runs	HS	Avge	S/R	100	50	4s	6s	Ct	St
Tests	8	10	7	30	17*	10.00	30.92	0	0	4	0	0	0
ODIs	4	1	0	1	1	1.00	50.00	0	0	0	0	1	0
T20Is	0	0	–	–	–	–	–	–	–	–	–	–	–
First-class	83	109	37	868	41	12.05	51.45	0	0	–	–	21	0

Bowling	M	Balls	Runs	Wkts	BB	Avge	RpO	S/R	5i	10m
Tests	8	1429	869	28	5–38	31.03	3.64	51.03	1	0
ODIs	4	204	185	4	2–58	46.25	5.44	51.00	0	0
T20Is	0	0	–	–	–	–	–	–	–	–
First-class	83	13943	8402	283	8–101	29.68	3.61	49.26	11	0

JACOB **ORAM**

Full name	**Jacob David Philip Oram**
Born	**July 28, 1978, Palmerston North, Manawatu**
Teams	**Central Districts, Rajasthan Royals**
Style	**Left-hand bat, right-arm fast-medium bowler**
Test debut	**New Zealand v India at Wellington 2002-03**
ODI debut	**New Zealand v Zimbabwe at Wellington 2000-01**
T20I debut	**New Zealand v South Africa at Johannesburg 2005-06**

THE PROFILE It's hard to miss Jacob Oram, and not just because of his height of 6ft 6ins (198cm). He is agile in the field, especially at gully, and complements that with solid fast-medium bowling and aggressive batting. Foot problems cost him a season at a vital stage, but he came back strongly in 2002-03 to seal a regular international place. He narrowly missed a century against Pakistan in the Wellington Boxing Day Test of 2003, but made up for that by carving 119 not out against South Africa, then 90 in the second Test, which earned him an England tour in 2004. By then his bowling was starting to lose its sting, and he went down with back trouble shortly after pounding 126 against Australia at Brisbane in November 2004. After nearly 18 months out Oram showed what New Zealand's middle order had been missing, coming in at 38 for 4 at Centurion and making 133, his highest Test score. He missed the start of the 2006-07 Australian one-day series with a hamstring injury, but bucked the team up with some stirring performances when he did get there, including a 71-ball century – NZ's fastest, and his first in ODIs – against Australia at Perth. Oram continued to be a regular member of all New Zealand's sides until 2009, when he retired from Tests to preserve himself for limited-overs games ... and a lucrative IPL contract. He played an important part in New Zealand's run to the semi-final of the 2011 World Cup – not particularly with the bat, but with the ball, collecting 12 wickets, four of them in the shock quarter-final victory over South Africa.

THE FACTS Oram averages 62.00 in Tests against Australia, 52.50 v South Africa – and 10.25 v India ... With the ball in ODIs he averages 23.05 v South Africa, but 74.72 v Australia ... Oram scored his maiden century in only his fourth first-class match, for Central Districts v Canterbury at Christchurch in 1998-99, and his 155 remains his highest score ...

THE FIGURES *to 26.09.11*   **ESPMcricinfo.com**

Batting & Fielding	M	Inns	NO	Runs	HS	Avge	S/R	100	50	4s	6s	Ct	St
Tests	33	59	10	1780	133	36.32	50.38	5	6	209	21	15	0
ODIs	151	108	14	2289	101*	24.35	85.60	1	12	169	75	48	0
T20Is	27	24	5	396	66*	20.84	138.46	0	2	29	20	10	0
First-class	85	136	18	3992	155	33.83	–	8	18	–	–	36	0

Bowling	M	Balls	Runs	Wkts	BB	Avge	RpO	S/R	5i	10m
Tests	33	4964	1983	60	4–41	33.05	2.39	82.73	0	0
ODIs	151	6474	4697	159	5–26	29.54	4.35	40.71	2	0
T20Is	27	387	564	12	3–33	47.00	8.74	32.25	0	0
First-class	85	10670	4158	155	6–45	26.82	2.33	68.83	3	0

TIM **PAINE**

AUSTRALIA

Full name	**Timothy David Paine**
Born	**December 8, 1984, Hobart, Tasmania**
Teams	**Tasmania, Pune Warriors**
Style	**Right-hand bat, wicketkeeper**
Test debut	**Australia v Pakistan at Lord's 2010**
ODI debut	**Australia v Scotland at Edinburgh 2009**
T20I debut	**Australia v England at Manchester 2009**

THE PROFILE A talented top-order batsman and wicket-keeper, Tasmania's Tim Paine was earmarked as next in line behind Brad Haddin when he joined the squad for the one-dayers that followed the Ashes Tests in England in 2009. In the event Paine ended up playing throughout, as Haddin had to have surgery on the finger he broke before the Edgbaston Test. And he did not disappoint, pulling off a couple of quicksilver stumpings to go with some forthright batting from the top of the order, the highlight a fine century at Trent Bridge which included several whips off the pads – stork-like, with the back foot in the air – which fizzed down to fine leg. When Haddin had elbow-tendon trouble in 2010, Paine deputised again, playing his first two Tests against Pakistan in England and generally performing well enough – behind and in front of the stumps – to raise doubts about Haddin's future. There were 11 catches in those two matches, and a fine leg-side stumping to dismiss Salman Butt for 92 at Lord's. But he sat on the bench throughout the 2011 World Cup, then later in the year broke a finger in practice just as Haddin was going through a rough patch with the bat in Sri Lanka. Paine's initial call-up came soon after a strong showing for Australia A, including a six-studded 134 against Pakistan A in July 2009, which followed a season in which he finally elbowed his way past the highly rated Sean Clingeleffer as Tasmania's wicketkeeper in all formats. Paine had made headlines early on in his career, too, extending his maiden first-class century against Western Australia at Perth to 215 in only his fifth match in October 2006.

THE FACTS Paine made 215 (his only first-class century) for Tasmania v Western Australia at Perth in October 2006 ... He scored 111 against England in an ODI at Trent Bridge in September 2009 ... Paine captained Australia at the Under-19 World Cup in Bangladesh in 2003-04, and signed his first contract with Tasmania when he was 16 ...

THE FIGURES *to 26.09.11*   **ESPncricinfo.com**

Batting & Fielding	M	Inns	NO	Runs	HS	Avge	S/R	100	50	4s	6s	Ct	St
Tests	4	8	0	287	92	35.87	43.09	0	2	35	0	16	1
ODIs	26	26	1	737	111	29.48	68.87	1	5	86	5	35	4
T20Is	5	3	0	22	21	7.33	122.22	0	0	2	1	4	0
First-class	46	84	6	2467	215	31.62	44.01	1	18	268	7	129	6

Bowling	M	Balls	Runs	Wkts	BB	Avge	RpO	S/R	5i	10m
Tests	4	0	–	–	–	–	–	–	–	–
ODIs	26	0	–	–	–	–	–	–	–	–
T20Is	5	0	–	–	–	–	–	–	–	–
First-class	46	6	3	0	–	–	3.00	–	0	0

MONTY **PANESAR**

Full name	**Mudhsuden Singh Panesar**
Born	**April 25, 1982, Luton, Bedfordshire**
Teams	**Sussex**
Style	**Left-hand bat, slow left-arm orthodox spinner**
Test debut	**England v India at Nagpur 2005-06**
ODI debut	**England v Australia at Melbourne 2006-07**
T20I debut	**England v Australia at Sydney 2006-07**

THE PROFILE Monty Panesar made himself a cult hero to English crowds enchanted by his enthusiastic celebrations and endearingly erratic fielding. That, and equally amateurish batting, had threatened to hold him back, but when Ashley Giles was ruled out of the 2005-06 Indian tour Panesar received a late summons. He's a throwback to an earlier slow left-armer, Bishan Bedi, who also twirled away for Northants in a patka, teasing and tempting with flight and guile, although Panesar gives it more of a rip. Panesar's arrival was delayed while he finished university but, finally free from studies, he took 46 Championship wickets at 21.54 in 2005. He made his Test debut at Nagpur that winter, picking up Sachin Tendulkar as his first wicket. At home in 2006 he delivered the ball of the season to bowl Younis Khan and set up victory at Leeds; next season he claimed 31 wickets in seven home Tests, and remained the crowd's favourite as Montymania showed no sign of stopping. But, lacking variety, he struggled in Sri Lanka at the end of 2007, and laboured a little in England too, while his antics and frequent appealing rubbed some up the wrong way. By the start of 2009 he had lost his place as England's No. 1 spinner to Graeme Swann (ironically, since Panesar's arrival had hastened Swann's departure from Northamptonshire), and his only contribution to the Ashes series was an unlikely match-saving display with the bat in the first Test. Panesar became a back number after that and lost his England contract, but a move to Sussex seemed to pay off, as he passed 50 wickets for them in both 2010 and 2011, and in between made a second Ashes tour, although he didn't play in the Tests.

THE FACTS Panesar took 7 for 181 for Northamptonshire v Essex at Chelmsford in July 2005 ... He was the first Sikh to play Test cricket for anyone other than India: when Panesar opposed Harbhajan Singh during his debut at Nagpur in 2005-06 it was the first instance of Sikh bowling to Sikh in a Test ... He averages 25.00 with the ball in Tests against West Indies – but 53.57 against India ...

THE FIGURES to 26.09.11   **ESPNcricinfo.com**

Batting & Fielding	M	Inns	NO	Runs	HS	Avge	S/R	100	50	4s	6s	Ct	St
Tests	39	51	17	187	26	5.50	29.44	0	0	20	1	9	0
ODIs	26	8	3	26	13	5.20	28.57	0	0	2	0	3	0
T20Is	1	1	0	1	1	1.00	50.00	0	0	0	0	0	0
First-class	149	191	61	1154	46*	8.87	32.78	0	0	–	–	32	0

Bowling	M	Balls	Runs	Wkts	BB	Avge	RpO	S/R	5i	10m
Tests	39	9042	4331	126	6–37	34.37	2.87	71.76	8	1
ODIs	26	1308	980	24	3–25	40.83	4.49	54.50	0	0
T20Is	1	24	40	2	2–40	20.00	10.00	12.00	0	0
First-class	149	33774	15689	494	7–181	31.75	2.78	68.36	24	3

THARANGA **PARANAVITANA**

SRI LANKA

Full name	**Nishad Tharanga Paranavitana**
Born	**April 15, 1982, Kegalle**
Teams	**Sinhalese Sports Club, Kandurata**
Style	**Left-hand bat, offspinner**
Test debut	**Sri Lanka v Pakistan at Karachi 2008-09**
ODI debut	**No ODIs yet**
T20I debut	**No T20Is yet**

THE PROFILE Tharanga Paranavitana is a tall left-hand opener who scored consistently on the domestic scene before a stellar 2007-08 season established him as a real Test prospect. Paranavitana was the leading runscorer in the top tier of the Premier League with 893, and his 236 against Colombo in the last match helped Sinhalese Sports Club clinch the title. That was his third century of the summer (and the second double of his career), and he added another in the regional competition for Kandurata to finish the first-class season with 1059 runs at 81. All that - and 159 against South Africa A - meant he had to be given a Test chance, and he eventually won his first cap at Karachi early in 2009. The disappointment of a first-ball duck was followed by a chest wound in the terrorist attack on the Sri Lankan team bus in Lahore. Thankfully, Paranavitana was back to full fitness in time for the return series in Sri Lanka, and made his mark with 72 and 49 in a narrow victory at Galle, and 73 in the final Test in Colombo. Leaner times followed against New Zealand, and he was also fined for claiming a catch which replays showed had clearly bounced in front of him. But in July 2010 Paranavitana made a maiden Test century against India at Galle - Murali's last match - and added another in the next game. Back at Galle there was a near-miss (95) against West Indies, then a couple of classy fifties in England in 2011. In Tests he ambles along at a strike rate well below 50, the main reason why he is yet to feature in Sri Lanka's limited-overs teams.

THE FACTS Paranavitana scored 236 (and 80 not out) for Sinhalese Sports Club v Colombo CC in March 2008 ... He made 232 not out for Sinhalese v Tamil Union in February 2007 ... Paranavitana started his Test career (against Pakistan at Karachi in February 2009) with a first-ball duck - just like his opening partner that day, Malinda Warnapura (against Bangladesh in June 2007) ...

THE FIGURES to 26.09.11   **ESPncricinfo.com**

Batting & Fielding	M	Inns	NO	Runs	HS	Avge	S/R	100	50	4s	6s	Ct	St
Tests	22	40	3	1291	111	34.89	43.74	2	8	159	1	17	0
ODIs	0	0	–	–	–	–	–	–	–	–	–	–	–
T20Is	0	0	–	–	–	–	–	–	–	–	–	–	–
First-class	126	209	20	8084	236	42.77	51.78	21	36	–	–	131	0

Bowling	M	Balls	Runs	Wkts	BB	Avge	RpO	S/R	5i	10m
Tests	22	102	86	1	1–26	86.00	5.05	102.00	0	0
ODIs	0	0	–	–	–	–	–	–	–	–
T20Is	0	0	–	–	–	–	–	–	–	–
First-class	126	1679	844	22	4–39	38.36	3.01	76.31	0	0

WAYNE **PARNELL**

Full name	**Wayne Dillon Parnell**
Born	**July 30, 1989, Port Elizabeth, Cape Province**
Teams	**Warriors, Sussex, Pune Warriors**
Style	**Left-hand bat, left-arm fast-medium bowler**
Test debut	**South Africa v England at Johannesburg 2009-10**
ODI debut	**South Africa v Australia at Perth 2008-09**
T20I debut	**South Africa v Australia at Brisbane 2008-09**

THE PROFILE Tall, slim, and waspishly fast, left-armer Wayne Parnell can also bat well, and exhibited strong leadership qualities during a glittering junior career. In the Under-19 World Cup in Malaysia in 2008 he led by example, taking 18 wickets and scoring useful middle-order runs to steer South Africa into the final, where they lost to India. The national selectors were already on alert, and after Parnell tested out the conditions Down Under during an Emerging Players tournament he was drafted for the one-day series in Australia early in 2009. He played only one ODI there, proving a little expensive in a victory over Australia at the WACA, but began to make his presence felt in the return series back home, taking 4 for 25 as the Aussies were rolled for 131 at Centurion. He was rewarded by becoming the youngest South African to be awarded a national contract. Then, after warming up with some useful spells for Kent, Parnell was one of the stars of the World Twenty20 in England in 2009, derailing England (3 for 16) and West Indies (4 for 13) inside 48 hours. He bowled with pace and accuracy during the powerplays and the final overs, at an economy rate of less than six an over, qualities which earned him a big-money IPL contract for 2010 – only for a groin injury, picked up in practice, to stop him appearing. It took him a long time to recover, mentally as well as physically: he played only once in the 2011 World Cup, but a decent IPL season for Pune helped. "I haven't lost my ability," Parnell said. "I may have lost confidence in my ability but I am on track."

THE FACTS In the quarter-final of the Under-19 World Cup in Kuala Lumpur in 2008 Parnell top-scored with 57 from No. 7, then took 6 for 8 as Bangladesh were bowled out for 41 ... He scored 90 for Kent v Glamorgan at Canterbury in May 2009, putting on 151 for the seventh wicket with James Tredwell ... Parnell's best first-class bowling figures of 4 for 7 came in his second match, for Eastern Province v KwaZulu/Natal at Port Elizabeth in November 2006 ...

THE FIGURES to 26.09.11   ᴇsᴘⁿcricinfo.com

Batting & Fielding	M	Inns	NO	Runs	HS	Avge	S/R	100	50	4s	6s	Ct	St
Tests	3	2	0	34	22	17.00	35.41	0	0	6	0	1	0
ODIs	19	8	2	116	49	19.33	70.73	0	0	7	2	2	0
T20Is	11	1	0	14	14	14.00	87.50	0	0	1	0	1	0
First-class	30	37	4	715	90	21.66	51.66	0	3	92	7	9	0

Bowling	M	Balls	Runs	Wkts	BB	Avge	RpO	S/R	5i	10m
Tests	3	306	227	5	2–17	45.40	4.45	61.20	0	0
ODIs	19	950	945	31	5–48	30.48	5.96	30.64	2	0
T20Is	11	245	287	14	4–13	20.50	7.02	17.50	0	0
First-class	30	4721	2709	76	4–7	35.64	3.44	62.11	0	0

MUNAF **PATEL**

Full name **Munaf Musa Patel**
Born **July 12, 1983, Ikhar, Gujarat**
Teams **Baroda, Mumbai Indians**
Style **Right-hand bat, right-arm fast-medium bowler**
Test debut **India v England at Mohali 2005-06**
ODI debut **India v England at Goa 2005-06**
T20I debut **No T20Is yet**

THE PROFILE Few fast men generated as much hype before bowling a ball in first-class cricket as Munaf Patel, from the little town of Ikhar in Gujarat, early in 2003. Kiran More spotted him: soon Patel was being hailed as the fastest bowler in India, although initially he spent more time recovering from injuries than actually playing. He's strongly built, though not overly tall, and bustles up to the crease before releasing in a windmill-whirl of hands. He has a well-directed yorker, and can reverse-swing the ball. In March 2006 he finally received a call from the selectors – now chaired by his old pal More – after taking ten wickets in a match against the England tourists. He finished his first Test with seven more, and struck consistently in the West Indies later in 2006. But then things got harder. He tweaked an ankle in South Africa, and was criticised when it bothered him in the final Test, but was fit in time for the 2007 World Cup. Then it was a back injury, and Patel returned to the Chennai academy – which he calls his "second home" – to remodel his action. In Australia in 2007-08 he sometimes seemed uninterested, and certainly didn't make the batsmen hop about much. He played his first Test for 16 months in New Zealand in March 2009, taking five wickets in a comfortable victory at Hamilton, although his bowling after that was unspectacular, and lacked the fiery pace that earned him those early rave reviews. These days Patel is little more than medium-pace, although he controls the ball well, and played his part as the 2011 World Cup was won – he took 11 wickets and was rarely collared.

THE FACTS Patel's match figures of 7 for 97 were the best on Test debut by an Indian fast bowler, beating Mohammad Nissar's 6 for 135 against England at Lord's in 1932 (Abid Ali, more of a medium-pacer, took 7 for 116 on debut against Australia in 1967-68) ... Patel claimed 6 for 50 for Maharashtra v Railways at Delhi in January 2006 ... He took 5 for 59 and 5 for 32 for the Board President's XI against the England tourists at Vadodara in February 2006 ...

THE FIGURES to 26.09.11   ESPNcricinfo.com

Batting & Fielding	M	Inns	NO	Runs	HS	Avge	S/R	100	50	4s	6s	Ct	St
Tests	13	14	6	60	15*	7.50	42.25	0	0	8	1	6	0
ODIs	70	27	16	74	15	6.72	66.07	0	0	7	1	11	0
T20Is	3	1	0	0	0	0.00	0.00	0	0	0	0	0	0
First-class	54	62	21	617	78	15.04	69.24	0	1	–	–	13	0

Bowling	M	Balls	Runs	Wkts	BB	Avge	RpO	S/R	5i	10m
Tests	13	2658	1349	35	4–25	38.54	3.04	75.94	0	0
ODIs	70	3154	2603	86	4–29	30.26	4.95	36.67	0	0
T20Is	3	60	86	4	2–25	21.50	8.60	15.00	0	0
First-class	54	9839	4661	192	6–50	24.27	2.84	51.24	7	1

SAMIT **PATEL**

Full name	**Samit Rohit Patel**
Born	**November 30, 1984, Leicester**
Teams	**Nottinghamshire**
Style	**Right-hand bat, slow left-arm orthodox spinner**
Test debut	**No Tests yet**
ODI debut	**England v Scotland at Edinburgh 2008**
T20I debut	**England v Sri Lanka at Bristol 2011**

THE PROFILE Samit Patel was long considered a player of great promise, but struggled to produce the goods consistently at first-team level. He has also faced a battle with fitness, which led to him being publicly humiliated by England before the 2011 World Cup: "All we were saying was 'Get into reasonable shape'. It didn't have to be perfect," said the coach Andy Flower in announcing Patel's demotion from the preliminary squad. It seemed to do the trick: he worked hard in the gym, slimmed down, and got his place back, although his early returns weren't spectacular. Patel is a hard-hitting middle-order batsman and a capable slow left-armer who delivers leg-stump darts *à la* Sanath Jayasuriya. He made his debut for Nottinghamshire's 2nd XI in 1999, when only 14. In 2006, he finally began to show signs of realising his potential, hammering 156 not out, with eight sixes, against Middlesex at Lord's – he hurtled from 100 to 150 in just 17 balls. Some of his most eye-catching performances have come in Twenty20 cricket, including a double-wicket maiden against Derbyshire in 2006, but it was in the 50-over game that he first attracted the interest of the selectors. After making 60 not out for the England Lions against South Africa at Derby in August 2008, Patel was called up for the late-season one-day internationals. Replacing his Nottinghamshire team-mate Graeme Swann in the side, he kept the runs down in his first couple of matches, then struck a brisk 31 at The Oval in his first ODI innings, before ruining South Africa's reply with 5 for 41. Suddenly a left-field pick was looking like an inspired one ... but then those fitness concerns intruded.

THE FACTS Patel took 7 for 68 (11 for 111 in the match) for Nottinghamshire v Hampshire at Southampton in July 2011 ... In his fourth ODI he took 5 for 41 against South Africa at The Oval in August 2008 ... He made 176 for Nottinghamshire v Gloucestershire at Bristol in April 2007 ... Patel hit 173, his maiden first-class century, in his fifth match, against Durham UCCE at Durham in April 2006 ...

THE FIGURES *to 26.09.11*   **ESPNcricinfo.com**

Batting & Fielding	M	Inns	NO	Runs	HS	Avge	S/R	100	50	4s	6s	Ct	St
Tests	0	0	–	–	–	–	–	–	–	–	–	–	–
ODIs	16	8	1	146	31	20.85	91.82	0	0	8	4	5	0
T20Is	4	3	1	27	25*	13.50	100.00	0	0	3	0	0	0
First-class	92	145	10	5550	176	41.11	64.41	13	31	–	–	50	0

Bowling	M	Balls	Runs	Wkts	BB	Avge	RpO	S/R	5i	10m
Tests	0	0	–	–	–	–	–	–	–	–
ODIs	16	526	488	14	5–41	34.85	5.56	37.57	1	0
T20Is	4	78	97	4	2–22	24.25	7.46	19.50	0	0
First-class	92	9742	4949	131	7–68	37.77	3.04	74.36	3	1

JAMES **PATTINSON**

Full name	**James Lee Pattinson**
Born	**May 3, 1990, Melbourne**
Teams	**Victoria**
Style	**Left-hand bat, right-arm fast-medium bowler**
Test debut	**No Tests yet**
ODI debut	**Australia v Bangladesh at Mirpur 2010-11**
T20I debut	**No T20Is yet**

THE PROFILE A strong fast bowler who hits the bat hard, James Pattinson will be one of Australia's players to watch over the next few years – or so the selectors thought when they surprised him with a national contract in 2011. He was chosen for the tour of Bangladesh which followed the World Cup, making his one-day international debut in the third match and taking the wicket of top-scorer Imrul Kayes with one that angled away from the left-hander, who was well set with 93. Pattinson remained in the mix for the rest of the year, winning another one-day cap in Sri Lanka in August, when his two wickets (for 41 runs) were again important ones – the experienced pair of Tillekeratne Dilshan and Kumar Sangakkara, Sri Lankan captains present and past. It had been in one-day cricket that Pattinson had shown his early potential: in December 2009 he swung the ball impressively against New South Wales at the SCG, finishing with 6 for 48, the best figures by a Victorian in a domestic one-day game, breaking Graeme Watson's 40-year-old record. Pattinson had already represented Australia's Under-19s, and soon afterwards joined the academy and also played for Australia A. He is the younger brother of Nottinghamshire's Darren Pattinson – with whom he competes for a spot in the Victoria side – who played one Test for England in 2008. Unlike Darren, who was born in Grimsby, James popped out in Melbourne after the family emigrated, so his only passport is an Australian one. James honed his skills against his brother, who is ten years older, in the back yard of their Melbourne home: both of them played for the Dandenong club in the eastern suburbs.

THE FACTS Pattinson took 6 for 48 – the only six wickets to fall – for Victoria v New South Wales in a one-day game at Sydney in December 2009 ... His brother Darren played one Test for England in 2008: they are the first brothers to play international cricket for different full-member countries since the 19th century ...

THE FIGURES to 26.09.11   **ESPncricinfo.com**

Batting & Fielding	M	Inns	NO	Runs	HS	Avge	S/R	100	50	4s	6s	Ct	St
Tests	0	0	–	–	–	–	–	–	–	–	–	–	–
ODIs	2	1	1	0	0*	–	0.00	0	0	0	0	1	0
T20Is	0	0	–	–	–	–	–	–	–	–	–	–	–
First-class	6	7	0	51	31	7.28	28.65	0	0	5	0	4	0

Bowling	M	Balls	Runs	Wkts	BB	Avge	RpO	S/R	5i	10m
Tests	0	0	–	–	–	–	–	–	–	–
ODIs	2	102	80	3	2–41	26.66	4.70	34.00	0	0
T20Is	0	0	–	–	–	–	–	–	–	–
First-class	6	1156	560	19	4–52	29.47	2.90	60.84	0	0

THISARA **PERERA**

Full name	**Narangoda Liyanaarachchilage Thisara Chirantha Perera**
Born	**April 3, 1989, Colombo**
Teams	**Colts, Wayamba, Kochi Tuskers Kerala**
Style	**Left-hand bat, right-arm fast-medium bowler**
Test debut	**Sri Lanka v England at Cardiff 2011**
ODI debut	**Sri Lanka v India at Kolkata 2009-10**
T20I debut	**Sri Lanka v Zimbabwe at Providence 2009-10**

THE PROFILE A big-hitting left-hander who also bowls at a lively pace, Thisara Perera was originally primarily seen as a bowler, taking the new ball for the national under-19 side. He played in the Under-19 World Cup in 2008, and received his first senior call late the following year, replacing the injured Angelo Mathews on tour in India. Perera made his ODI debut there, hammering 31 from just 14 balls at the death. He proved less successful with the ball – none for 66 from nine overs as Gautam Gambhir and Virat Kohli gambolled to centuries. Two matches later he was at it again, slamming 36 from 15 balls to set up another victory, one which improved his bank balance as it led to an IPL contract. He didn't do much – one over for 19 – in his one outing for eventual champions Chennai in 2010, and the following season achieved little more for the Kochi Tuskers. Perera's batting didn't fire in his early ODIs, but his bowling did: 5 for 28 as India were skittled for 103 at Dambulla in August 2010, and not long afterwards he bounced in combatively at Melbourne for another five-for, his victims including Michael Clarke and Brad Haddin. After being a fringe performer at the 2011 World Cup – he played only four matches, but that did include the final, in which he slammed 22 from nine balls and took one expensive wicket – Perera made his Test debut at Cardiff in 2011. He made 25 in the first innings and 20 in the second ... but that was the top score as Sri Lanka crashed to 82 all out and a defeat that had looked impossible when the last day began.

THE FACTS Perera took 5 for 28 as India were bowled out for 103 at Dambulla in August 2010, and 5 for 46 against Australia at Melbourne six weeks later ... He scored 113 not out, with eight sixes, for Colts v Moors in Colombo in December 2009, then took a career-best 5 for 69 when Moors batted ...

THE FIGURES to 26.09.11   **ESɲ**cricinfo.com

Batting & Fielding	M	Inns	NO	Runs	HS	Avge	S/R	100	50	4s	6s	Ct	St
Tests	2	3	0	47	25	15.66	74.60	0	0	8	0	0	0
ODIs	21	15	3	192	36*	16.00	115.66	0	0	20	4	8	0
T20Is	9	7	3	83	24	20.75	140.67	0	0	5	5	3	0
First-class	19	31	6	894	113*	35.76	88.86	1	5	82	37	10	0

Bowling	M	Balls	Runs	Wkts	BB	Avge	RpO	S/R	5i	10m
Tests	2	288	182	2	2–101	91.00	3.79	144.00	0	0
ODIs	21	814	712	33	5–28	21.57	5.24	24.66	2	0
T20Is	9	126	158	6	2–19	26.33	7.52	21.00	0	0
First-class	19	2063	1255	33	5–69	38.03	3.65	62.51	1	0

KEVIN **PIETERSEN**

ENGLAND

Full name	**Kevin Peter Pietersen**
Born	**June 27, 1980, Pietermaritzburg, Natal, South Africa**
Teams	**Surrey**
Style	**Right-hand bat, offspinner**
Test debut	**England v Australia at Lord's 2005**
ODI debut	**England v Zimbabwe at Harare 2004-05**
T20I debut	**England v Australia at Southampton 2005**

THE PROFILE Expansive with bat and explosive with bombast, Kevin Pietersen is not one for the quiet life. Bold-minded and big-hitting, he first ruffled feathers by quitting South Africa – he was disenchanted with the race-quota system – in favour of England, his eligibility coming courtesy of an English mother. He never doubted he would play Test cricket: he has self-confidence in spades and, fortunately, sackfuls of talent too. As soon as he was eligible, he was chosen for a one-day series in Zimbabwe, where he averaged 104. Then, in South Africa, he hammered a robust century in the second match, undeterred by hostile crowds. Test cricket was next. In 2005 he replaced Graham Thorpe, against Australia, at Lord's ... and coolly blasted a brace of fifties. Then, with the Ashes at stake, he hit 158 on the final day at The Oval: "KP" had arrived – and how. The runs kept coming: 158 at Adelaide and 226 against West Indies at Headingley sandwiched two tons in the 2007 World Cup. Late the following year he succeeded Michael Vaughan as captain, starting with a hundred as South Africa were beaten in the Oval Test, then inspiring a one-day landslide. But his captaincy ended in tears after a fallout with the coach, then his form dipped as he battled an Achilles problem. That eventually needed an operation, which kept him out of the last three Ashes Tests in 2009, and indifferent form dogged him the following year too. But just as people were beginning to wonder, Pietersen hammered 227 at Adelaide in December 2010 then, after leaving the World Cup early with a hernia, hit another double-century against India at Lord's and 175 at The Oval to emphasise that he wasn't going anywhere just yet.

THE FACTS Pietersen reached 100 against South Africa at East London in February 2005 in 69 balls, the fastest for England in ODIs ... After 25 Tests he had made 2448 runs, more than anyone else except Don Bradman (3194) ... He averages 64.60 in ODIs v South Africa – but 14.80 v Bangladesh ... Pietersen was out for 158 three times in Tests before going on to 226 against West Indies in May 2007 ... His record includes two ODIs for the World XI ...

THE FIGURES to 26.09.11   **ESPN**cricinfo.com

Batting & Fielding	M	Inns	NO	Runs	HS	Avge	S/R	100	50	4s	6s	Ct	St
Tests	78	133	7	6361	227	50.48	62.64	19	25	766	56	49	0
ODIs	119	108	15	3733	116	40.13	87.15	7	22	353	66	35	0
T20Is	32	32	4	1011	79	36.10	143.20	0	5	101	27	13	0
First-class	173	281	19	13084	254*	49.93	–	41	56	–	–	134	0

Bowling	M	Balls	Runs	Wkts	BB	Avge	RpO	S/R	5i	10m
Tests	78	1071	722	5	1–0	144.40	4.04	214.20	0	0
ODIs	119	382	353	7	2–22	50.42	5.54	54.57	0	0
T20Is	32	30	53	1	1–27	53.00	10.60	30.00	0	0
First-class	173	5959	3460	63	4–31	54.92	3.48	94.58	0	0

KIERON **POLLARD**

Full name **Kieron Adrian Pollard**
Born **May 12, 1987, Cacariqua, Trinidad**
Teams **Trinidad, Mumbai Indians, Somerset, South Australia**
Style **Right-hand bat, right-arm medium-pacer**
Test debut **No Tests yet**
ODI debut **West Indies v South Africa at St George's 2006-07**
T20I debut **West Indies v Australia at Bridgetown 2008**

THE PROFILE Kieron Pollard shot to prominence in 2006-07 when still only 19, with his muscular batting doing much to take Trinidad & Tobago to the final of the inaugural Stanford 20/20 competition: in the semi-final, against Nevis, he clobbered 83 in only 38 balls, and then grabbed a couple of wickets with his medium-pacers. That won him a first-class start against Barbados, and it was a memorable one: he got off the mark with a six, and cleared the boundary six more times on his way to 117. Another hundred, and six more sixes, followed in his third match, and in between he hit 87 off 58 balls – seven sixes this time – in a one-dayer against Guyana. That was followed by his inclusion in West Indies' squad for the 2007 World Cup. The cometary rise almost inevitably tailed off a bit after that: he finished his first Carib Beer season with 420 runs at 42, and played only once in the World Cup itself, as a rather surprise selection in the Super Eight match against South Africa (a must-win encounter which West Indies lost). Pollard spent some time on the sidelines after that, but his big-hitting potential earned him megabucks contracts in the IPL, for Somerset and for South Australia (he thumped 52 off 22 balls against Victoria at Adelaide early in 2010). But while his bank balance rocketed, international success proved elusive: Pollard's first 50 limited-overs internationals featured only one half-century, and although he added three more in the first half of 2011, two of them came against Netherlands and Ireland in the World Cup.

THE FACTS Pollard hit 126 on his first-class debut, for Trinidad & Tobago against Barbados at Crab Hill in January 2007: his innings included 11 fours and seven sixes, one of which got him off the mark ... In his second match he hit 69 in 31 balls, with one four and six sixes, and in his third 117 from 87 balls with 11 fours and six more sixes ... In a Twenty20 match for Somerset in 2010 Pollard failed by just a couple of inches to become only the second person to hit a ball over the Lord's pavilion ...

THE FIGURES *to 26.09.11*   **ESPNcricinfo.com**

Batting & Fielding	M	Inns	NO	Runs	HS	Avge	S/R	100	50	4s	6s	Ct	St
Tests	0	0	–	–	–	–	–	–	–	–	–	–	–
ODIs	43	39	1	826	94	21.73	102.22	0	4	55	36	19	0
T20Is	20	17	2	190	38	12.66	124.18	0	0	17	8	11	0
First-class	21	34	1	1247	174	37.78	–	3	5	–	–	32	0

Bowling	M	Balls	Runs	Wkts	BB	Avge	RpO	S/R	5i	10m
Tests	0	0	–	–	–	–	–	–	–	–
ODIs	43	1289	1126	35	3–27	32.17	5.24	36.82	0	0
T20Is	20	258	360	11	2–22	32.72	8.37	23.45	0	0
First-class	21	643	349	7	2–29	49.85	3.25	91.85	0	0

RICKY **PONTING**

AUSTRALIA

Full name	**Ricky Thomas Ponting**
Born	**December 19, 1974, Launceston, Tasmania**
Teams	**Tasmania**
Style	**Right-hand bat, right-arm medium-pace bowler**
Test debut	**Australia v Sri Lanka at Perth 1995-96**
ODI debut	**Australia v South Africa at Wellington 1994-95**
T20I debut	**Australia v New Zealand at Auckland 2004-05**

THE PROFILE Ricky Ponting played for Tasmania at 17 and Australia at 20, and was unluckily given out for 96 on his Test debut. He plays all the shots with a flourish – and his dead-eye fielding is another plus. A gambler and a buccaneer, Ponting has had setbacks, against probing seam and high-class finger-spin, which he plays with hard hands when off form. In the '90s there were off-field indiscretions, but his growing maturity was acknowledged when he succeeded Steve Waugh as one-day captain in 2002. It was a seamless transition: Ponting led the 2003 World Cup campaign from the front, clouting a coruscating century in the final, and took over in Tests too when Waugh finally stepped down early in 2004. But things changed the following year. A humiliating one-day defeat by Bangladesh caused the first ripples of dissent against his leadership style, and more followed as the Ashes series progressed. The loss of the urn hurt, and the pain lingered. Ponting bounced back by winning 11 of 12 Tests in 2005-06, which was just a warm-up for the following season's Ashes rematch. He led that off with 196 at Brisbane, and remained tight-lipped until the 5-0 whitewash was sealed. His batting never wavered and, after retaining the World Cup in 2007, he sailed past 25,000 international runs during 2010. However, Ashes defeats in 2009 and 2010-11 reopened those old wounds far enough to have Ponting dreaming of a possible return to England in 2013. But he won't be captain, having passed the reins to Michael Clarke after Australia's early elimination from the 2011 World Cup: Ponting returned to the ranks, and scored consistently in Sri Lanka later in the year.

THE FACTS Ponting uniquely scored two hundreds in his 100th Test, against South Africa at Sydney in January 2006 ... His 242 against India at Adelaide in 2003-04 is the highest in a losing cause in a Test (in the next game he made 257, and they won) ... When he was 8, Ponting's grandmother gave him a T-shirt that read "Under this shirt is a Test player" ... His record includes one ODI for the World XI ...

THE FIGURES to 26.09.11   **ESPNcricinfo.com**

Batting & Fielding	M	Inns	NO	Runs	HS	Avge	S/R	100	50	4s	6s	Ct	St
Tests	154	263	28	12487	257	53.13	59.20	39	56	1422	72	181	0
ODIs	367	357	39	13602	164	42.77	80.59	30	81	1218	162	156	0
T20Is	17	16	2	401	98*	28.64	132.78	0	2	41	11	8	0
First-class	257	440	55	21456	257	55.72	–	73	94	–	–	273	0

Bowling	M	Balls	Runs	Wkts	BB	Avge	RpO	S/R	5i	10m
Tests	154	563	261	5	1–0	52.20	2.78	112.60	0	0
ODIs	367	150	104	3	1–12	34.66	4.16	50.00	0	0
T20Is	17	–	–	–	–	–	–	–	–	–
First-class	257	1458	787	14	2–10	56.21	3.23	104.14	0	0

RAYMOND **PRICE**

Full name	**Raymond William Price**
Born	**June 12, 1976, Salisbury (now Harare)**
Teams	**Mashonaland Eagles, Mumbai Indians**
Style	**Right-hand bat, slow left-arm orthodox spinner**
Test debut	**Zimbabwe v Sri Lanka at Harare 1999-2000**
ODI debut	**Zimbabwe v India at Colombo 2002-03**
T20I debut	**Zimbabwe v Sri Lanka at King City 2008-09**

THE PROFILE A slow left-armer who takes wickets with guile and aggression, rather than massive spin, Ray Price has the tenacity and self-belief to compete against the best. He earned high praise by taking seven wickets in only his second Test, against Bangladesh at Harare in April 2001, and generally did well in his early matches, picking up consecutive five-fors against South Africa and India in 2001-02 and 6 for 121 in Australia's first innings at Sydney in October 2003. He almost bowled Zimbabwe to a remarkable victory in the first Test against West Indies in November that year (6 for 73 and 4 for 88), but was denied by the obdurate pair of Ridley Jacobs and Fidel Edwards. He collected nine more wickets in the second match to cap a superb year – 33 wickets in just five Tests. But just as he had established himself, Price was part of the "rebellion" which cost Zimbabwe several senior players in 2004-05. He joined Worcestershire, doing well at first and inspiring suggestions that he might qualify for England. But he rejected the offer of a new contract for 2008, and rejoined the national team as a canny senior pro. Since then he has been successful and parsimonious in one-day cricket, rising to second in the ICC world bowling rankings for a time in 2009: two years later he was a calm presence in Zimbabwe's Test return, wheeling down 50.1 overs (for 2 for 69) in the first innings of their second Test back, against Pakistan at Bulawayo in September 2011. Price suffers from partial deafness, caused by the after-effects of meningitis as a youngster. He is a trained installer of refrigeration and air-conditioning units.

THE FACTS Price took 8 for 35 (12 for 79 in the match) for Midlands against the CFX Academy at Kwekwe in April 2002: later that year he took 8 for 78 against Matabeleland at Bulawayo ... When Matthew Hayden broke the Test record with 380 at Perth in October 2003, Price's figures were 0 for 187: in the next Test, at Sydney, he took 6 for 121 ... His uncle, Nick Price, won three major golf championships, including the British Open in 1994 ...

THE FIGURES *to 26.09.11*   ᴇꜱᴘⁿcricinfo.com

Batting & Fielding	M	Inns	NO	Runs	HS	Avge	S/R	100	50	4s	6s	Ct	St
Tests	20	34	7	238	36	8.81	30.43	0	0	38	0	4	0
ODIs	96	54	14	359	46	8.97	55.65	0	0	25	4	17	0
T20Is	11	6	2	8	3	2.00	38.09	0	0	0	0	3	0
First-class	109	172	30	2395	117*	16.86	–	1	11	–	–	56	0

Bowling	M	Balls	Runs	Wkts	BB	Avge	RpO	S/R	5i	10m
Tests	20	5598	2633	75	6–73	35.10	2.82	74.64	5	1
ODIs	96	5014	3258	97	4–22	33.58	3.89	51.69	0	0
T20Is	11	258	226	13	2–6	17.38	5.25	19.84	0	0
First-class	109	26105	11390	387	8–35	29.43	2.61	67.45	20	3

ASHWELL **PRINCE**

Full name	**Ashwell Gavin Prince**
Born	**May 28, 1977, Port Elizabeth, Cape Province**
Teams	**Warriors**
Style	**Left-hand bat, occasional left-arm spinner**
Test debut	**South Africa v Australia at Johannesburg 2001-02**
ODI debut	**South Africa v Bangladesh at Kimberley 2002-03**
T20I debut	**South Africa v New Zealand at Johannesburg 2005-06**

THE PROFILE A crouching left-hander with a high-batted stance and a Gooch-like grimace, Ashwell Prince was helped into the national team by South Africa's controversial race-quota system, although he quickly justified his selection by top-scoring with a gutsy debut 49 against Australia in 2001-02. That, and a matchwinning 48 in the third Test, seemed to have buried an early reputation as a one-day flasher. But a run of low scores saw him left out for a while, before he bounced back with Test hundreds against outclassed Zimbabwe and almost-outclassed West Indies early in 2005. However, his 119 at Sydney in January 2006 was an altogether better performance after his previous one-sided battles with Shane Warne. Prince did well in the Tests in England in 2008, with centuries at Lord's and Leeds, but by then he was a back number in one-dayers, having been left out after a largely anonymous World Cup. He made a Test-best 162 not out against Bangladesh at Centurion in November 2008, but was then sidelined by a broken thumb. J-P Duminy's stellar arrival meant there was no automatic return for Prince, and he showed what he thought of that by grafting 150 when he was asked to open instead of the injured Graeme Smith against Australia at Cape Town in March 2009. He struggled against Graeme Swann's offspin at the end of the year, but remained in the mix and scored consistently in 2010-11. Long rated highly by Ali Bacher, Prince is strong through the off side, and although his throwing has been hampered by a long-term shoulder injury, he remains a fine fielder in the covers.

THE FACTS Prince became South Africa's first black captain when the injured Graeme Smith missed the series in Sri Lanka in 2006 ... Prince averages 77.75 in Tests against West Indies, but 27.57 v Sri Lanka ... In his first 18 Test innings against Australia, Prince was dismissed 11 times by Shane Warne ... Prince made 254 for Warriors v Titans at Centurion in March 2009, a week before being recalled to the Test side against Australia and hitting 150 ... His record includes three ODIs for the Africa XI ...

THE FIGURES to 26.09.11   ᴇsᴘɴcricinfo.com

Batting & Fielding	M	Inns	NO	Runs	HS	Avge	S/R	100	50	4s	6s	Ct	St
Tests	62	98	16	3556	162*	43.36	43.73	11	10	383	13	42	0
ODIs	52	41	12	1018	89*	35.10	67.77	0	3	77	4	26	0
T20Is	1	1	0	5	5	5.00	83.33	0	0	0	0	0	0
First-class	198	317	44	12034	254	44.08	–	31	55	–	–	135	0

Bowling	M	Balls	Runs	Wkts	BB	Avge	RpO	S/R	5i	10m
Tests	62	96	47	1	1–2	47.00	2.93	96.00	0	0
ODIs	52	12	3	0	–	–	1.50	–	0	0
T20Is	1	–	–	–	–	–	–	–	–	–
First-class	198	276	166	4	2–11	41.50	3.60	69.00	0	0

MATT **PRIOR**

Full name **Matthew James Prior**
Born **February 26, 1982, Johannesburg, South Africa**
Teams **Sussex**
Style **Right-hand bat, wicketkeeper**
Test debut **England v West Indies at Lord's 2007**
ODI debut **England v Zimbabwe at Bulawayo 2004-05**
T20I debut **England v West Indies at The Oval 2007**

THE PROFILE Matt Prior represented England at junior levels, and completed his set by making his Test debut in May 2007, against West Indies at Lord's. He started with a cracking century, the first by a keeper on debut for England. It was full of solid drives and clumping pulls, and seemed to announce a readymade star. He finished that series with 324 runs – but there were already rumbles about his wicketkeeping technique, which didn't seem to matter while England were winning. But then India arrived, and Prior's fumbles were magnified as the visitors stole the series: he dropped Tendulkar and Laxman as India ran up 664 at The Oval. The runs dried up, too, and suddenly Prior's talkativeness behind the stumps, and his footwork, were called into question. Eventually he was dropped. He went back to Hove and sharpened up his technique, and was ready when his replacement (and former Sussex team-mate) Tim Ambrose faltered himself during 2008: Prior returned for the one-dayers against South Africa, and pouched a record-equalling six catches (one of them a one-handed flying stunner) at Trent Bridge. By 2009 he looked even more the part – and even more like his mentor, Alec Stewart – in the Ashes victory. More runs followed in 2010, including an important century to swell the lead over Pakistan at Trent Bridge: Prior was established as England's Test keeper, and emphasised that with an Ashes century at Sydney in January 2011, and two more tons in the home English summer that followed. The only downside was that he lost his one-day place again after the World Cup. Prior was born in South Africa, but moved to England at 11: he says he lost his accent within a week.

THE FACTS Prior was the 17th man to score a century on Test debut for England: he was the fifth to score a century on debut at Lord's, after Australia's Harry Graham, John Hampshire and Andrew Strauss of England, and India's Sourav Ganguly ... Prior equalled the ODI wicketkeeping record with six catches against South Africa at Nottingham in August 2008 ... He made 201 not out for Sussex v Loughborough UCCE at Hove in May 2004 ...

THE FIGURES to 26.09.11   ESrncricinfo.com

Batting & Fielding	M	Inns	NO	Runs	HS	Avge	S/R	100	50	4s	6s	Ct	St
Tests	47	70	13	2549	131*	44.71	66.95	6	18	289	12	144	6
ODIs	68	62	9	1282	87	24.18	76.76	0	3	141	6	71	8
T20Is	10	8	2	127	32	21.16	127.00	0	0	11	5	6	3
First-class	194	299	35	10739	201*	40.67	67.98	26	60	–	–	495	32

Bowling	M	Balls	Runs	Wkts	BB	Avge	RpO	S/R	5i	10m
Tests	47	0	–	–	–	–	–	–	–	–
ODIs	68	0	–	–	–	–	–	–	–	–
T20Is	10	0	–	–	–	–	–	–	–	–
First-class	194	0	–	–	–	–	–	–	–	–

CHETESHWAR **PUJARA**

Full name **Cheteshwar Arvind Pujara**
Born **January 25, 1988, Rajkot, Gujarat**
Teams **Saurashtra, Royal Challengers Bangalore**
Style **Right-hand bat, occasional legspinner**
Test debut **India v Australia at Bangalore 2010-11**
ODI debut **No ODIs yet**
T20I debut **No T20Is yet**

INDIA

THE PROFILE After years of prolific runscoring at domestic and A-team levels, Cheteshwar Pujara finally got an opportunity in a Test match, against Australia in October 2010. He made it count, coming in at No. 3 instead of Rahul Dravid in the second innings and making an excellent 72 in a tricky run-chase. Pujara's game-plan is simple, and he plays within his limitations. His technique is classical: upright at the crease and confident on both sides of the wicket. The son of a former Ranji Trophy player, Pujara was a mighty achiever at age-group cricket: in 2006 he had been the leading scorer at the Under-19 World Cup, and before that had made a triple-century for Saurashtra's Under-14s and 211 in an Under-19 test against England. The runs just kept stacking up: 907 in first-class cricket in 2007-08, and more than 1000 the following season. In 2008-09 he embarked on a spell of scoring Don Bradman would have been hard-pushed to match: two triple-centuries for Saurashtra's Under-22s were followed by one in first-class cricket too, all in the space of little more than a month. The figures couldn't be ignored, and after a double-century while captaining the A team in England Pujara finally got the Test call. He started well, but following two failures in South Africa he injured his knee during IPL4. It needed an operation, and he missed the tours of West Indies and England that followed – but in the light of the continued batting failures in the embarrassing whitewash in England, once fit again Pujara will demand another chance. *The Times of India* likened him to Dravid, with added power: "He is like the Wall, but packs a wallop too."

THE FACTS Pujara scored 386 and 309 in successive matches for Saurashtra Under-22s in the CK Nayudu Trophy in October 2008 ... Less than a month later he made 302 not out in Saurashtra's Ranji Trophy match against Orissa at Rajkot, sharing a stand of 520 with Ravindra Jadeja ... Pujara made his first triple-century shortly before his 13th birthday, for Saurashtra's Under-14s in January 2001 ... Seven of his 14 first-class hundreds have been scores of 150 or more ...

THE FIGURES to 26.09.11   **ESPNcricinfo.com**

Batting & Fielding	M	Inns	NO	Runs	HS	Avge	S/R	100	50	4s	6s	Ct	St
Tests	3	5	0	107	72	21.40	51.69	0	1	12	0	6	0
ODIs	0	0	–	–	–	–	–	–	–	–	–	–	–
T20Is	0	0	–	–	–	–	–	–	–	–	–	–	–
First-class	56	89	15	4130	302*	55.81	–	14	15	–	–	33	0

Bowling	M	Balls	Runs	Wkts	BB	Avge	RpO	S/R	5i	10m
Tests	3	0	–	–	–	–	–	–	–	–
ODIs	0	0	–	–	–	–	–	–	–	–
T20Is	0	0	–	–	–	–	–	–	–	–
First-class	56	153	83	5	2–4	16.60	3.25	30.60	0	0

SURESH **RAINA**

Full name **Suresh Kumar Raina**
Born **November 27, 1986, Ghaziabad, Uttar Pradesh**
Teams **Uttar Pradesh, Chennai Super Kings**
Style **Left-hand bat, occasional offspinner**
Test debut **India v Sri Lanka at Colombo 2010**
ODI debut **India v Sri Lanka at Dambulla 2005**
T20I debut **India v South Africa at Johannesburg 2006-07**

THE PROFILE In April 2005 Suresh Raina strolled in to bat in the domestic one-day final, spanked nine fours and a six in 48 from 33 balls as Uttar Pradesh tied with Tamil Nadu and shared the title, then left to catch the flight home for his school exams. The following season his 620 runs helped UP win the Ranji Trophy for the first time. Electric fielding added zing to India's one-day side, but eventually the runs dried up, and he was dropped early in 2007 after 16 innings without a half-century. A powerful left-hander, he was back a year later and hit two centuries in the Asia Cup in June 2008, against Hong Kong and Bangladesh, then made 53 and 76 in Sri Lanka as India fought back to win the one-day series there. In New Zealand at the start of 2009 he slammed 61 not out from 43 balls in a Twenty20 international then 66 from 39 in a one-dayer, but was underwhelming in the World Twenty20 in England in June. Test cricket seemed to have passed him by, but after a record 98 ODIs he finally made his debut in Sri Lanka the following month, and made up for lost time with a fine 120, adding 62 and 41 not out in the next match. He joined the 2011 World Cup party late, playing only the last four matches – but that included the joyous final, in which he didn't need to bat. After that, though, Raina had a tough time in the Tests in England, his ponderous technique against the short stuff being exposed. He bounced back with runs in the one-day series, but will find his Test place harder to maintain.

THE FACTS Raina played a record 98 ODIs before making his Test debut in July 2010 – then promptly became the 12th Indian to score a century in his first Test ... He captained India in an ODI before he played in a Test ... Raina made 203 for Uttar Pradesh v Orissa at Cuttack in November 2007 ... Raina made 520 runs in the third IPL in 2010, a number exceeded only by Sachin Tendulkar and Jacques Kallis ...

THE FIGURES to 26.09.11   **ESPn**cricinfo.com

Batting & Fielding	M	Inns	NO	Runs	HS	Avge	S/R	100	50	4s	6s	Ct	St
Tests	15	26	2	710	120	29.58	53.46	1	6	91	3	20	0
ODIs	125	106	21	2993	116*	35.21	90.80	3	17	248	68	51	0
T20Is	21	20	3	544	101	32.00	140.93	1	3	46	24	6	0
First-class	67	113	6	4497	203	42.02	59.34	8	31	–	–	74	0

Bowling	M	Balls	Runs	Wkts	BB	Avge	RpO	S/R	5i	10m
Tests	15	891	524	13	2–1	40.30	3.52	68.53	0	0
ODIs	125	638	572	10	2–23	57.20	5.37	63.80	0	0
T20Is	21	24	39	1	1–6	39.00	9.75	24.00	0	0
First-class	67	1917	1011	26	3–31	38.88	3.16	73.73	0	0

RAVI **RAMPAUL**

WEST INDIES

Full name	**Ravindranath Rampaul**
Born	**October 15, 1984, Preysal, Trinidad**
Teams	**Trinidad & Tobago**
Style	**Left-hand bat, right-arm fast-medium bowler**
Test debut	**West Indies v Australia at Brisbane 2009-10**
ODI debut	**West Indies v Zimbabwe at Bulawayo 2003-04**
T20I debut	**West Indies v England at The Oval 2007**

THE PROFILE   Ravi Rampaul is tall and well-built, but his career has been hamstrung by injuries and ill-luck. He made his Trinidad debut in 2002, and 18 wickets in six matches the following season – and an aggressive approach – propelled him to the verge of full international selection. Just 19, he made his ODI debut late in 2003: he was rarely collared, but hardly ran through sides either – in 14 matches he took nine wickets, only once managing more than one, a statistic that was echoed when his Test career eventually started. Nonetheless he was retained for the 2004 England tour, and played three more ODIs before he broke down and returned home ahead of the Tests. Sidelined by shin splints, Rampaul did not play another first-class match until 2006-07, taking 7 for 51 as T&T beat Barbados in the Carib Beer final. That won him another England tour but, restricted by a groin tear, he again missed the Tests, before helping to turn the one-day series around with 4 for 41 in the pivotal second match at Edgbaston. There were still no Tests: he was named to play Bangladesh in July 2009, only for the whole squad to withdraw as a contracts dispute rumbled on. Rampaul finally made his Test debut in Australia late in 2009 – he'd been around so long it was a surprise he was still only 25 – but although he worked up a fair head of steam, success proved elusive at first. He took only four wickets in his first five Tests, but his strike-rate improved in mid-2011 with 21 wickets in five further matches against Pakistan and India.

THE FACTS   Rampaul took 7 for 51 as Trinidad & Tobago beat Barbados in the final of the Carib Beer Challenge at Pointe-à-Pierre in February 2007 ... He took 5 for 51 against India at Chennai in the 2011 World Cup ... In the 2000 World Under-15 Challenge, Rampaul took 7 for 11 against the Netherlands, and opened both the bowling and the batting in the final at Lord's, as West Indies beat Pakistan ... Rampaul played for Ireland in the Friends Provident Trophy in 2008 ...

THE FIGURES *to 26.09.11*   **ESFN**cricinfo.com

Batting & Fielding	M	Inns	NO	Runs	HS	Avge	S/R	100	50	4s	6s	Ct	St
Tests	10	19	7	231	40*	19.25	56.06	0	0	27	7	3	0
ODIs	60	26	5	199	26*	9.47	72.62	0	0	19	5	9	0
T20Is	10	3	2	11	8	11.00	61.11	0	0	0	0	0	0
First-class	48	70	13	855	64*	15.00	–	0	2	–	–	17	0

Bowling	M	Balls	Runs	Wkts	BB	Avge	RpO	S/R	5i	10m
Tests	10	1834	918	25	4-48	36.72	3.00	73.36	0	0
ODIs	60	2426	2027	67	5-51	30.25	5.01	36.20	1	0
T20Is	10	228	343	12	3-17	28.58	9.02	19.00	0	0
First-class	48	7481	4286	141	7-51	30.39	3.43	53.00	6	1

SURAJ **RANDIV**

Full name	**Hewa Kaluhalamullage Suraj Randiv Kaluhalamulla**
Born	**January 30, 1985, Matara**
Teams	**Bloomfield, Ruhuna, Chennai Super Kings**
Style	**Right-hand bat, offspinner**
Test debut	**Sri Lanka v India at Colombo 2010**
ODI debut	**Sri Lanka v India at Nagpur 2009-10**
T20I debut	**Sri Lanka v Zimbabwe at Providence 2009-10**

SRI LANKA

THE PROFILE Suraj Randiv – who changed his name from Mohamed Marshuk Mohamed Suraj in 2009, after converting to Buddhism – has the unenviable task of replacing Muttiah Muralitharan as Sri Lanka's offspinner. A consistent domestic performer, Randiv made his Test debut in July 2010 in the match immediately following Murali's retirement, and matched his predecessor's appetite for hard work by toiling through 73 overs in the first innings, taking 2 for 222. On a more sporting pitch for the third Test, at Colombo's Sara Oval, Randiv hinted at a good future with nine wickets, including all five to fall in the second innings as India successfully chased 257. After that, though, he faded a little: he was not in the original 2011 World Cup squad, although he arrived very late on as a replacement and controversially played in the final. He had a quiet time in England, apart from 5 for 42 in the ODI at Old Trafford, then was dropped after two home Tests against Australia. Randiv actually started as a fast bowler, but switched to offspin at school. He started with the Matara club, but Marvan Atapattu and Mahela Jayawardene spotted him and lured him to the Sinhalese Sports Club in 2004 (he later moved to Bloomfield). Randiv is a tidy bowler – and a better batsman than Murali, with a first-class century as nightwatchman to his name – but doesn't possess the variety of his illustrious predecessor. He took 55 first-class wickets at 15.05 in domestic cricket in 2005-06, including the first of his two nine-wicket hauls, and after a couple of quieter seasons returned to top form with 43 in 2008-09 and 67 (at 20.85) the following season.

THE FACTS Randiv took 2 for 222 in his first Test innings, the most runs ever conceded by a debutant ... He claimed 9 for 62 for Sinhalese SC v Colombo CC in February 2006 ... Randiv took 9 for 109 (the other wicket was a run-out) for Bloomfield v Army in October 2009: earlier in the match he had scored his maiden century after going in as nightwatchman ...

THE FIGURES to 26.09.11   **ESPn** cricinfo.com

Batting & Fielding	M	Inns	NO	Runs	HS	Avge	S/R	100	50	4s	6s	Ct	St
Tests	5	7	1	43	12	7.16	31.38	0	0	6	0	0	0
ODIs	28	15	1	239	56	17.07	71.55	0	1	24	1	6	0
T20Is	7	2	0	8	6	4.00	133.33	0	0	1	0	0	0
First-class	78	108	21	1680	112	19.31	52.19	1	6	–	–	57	0

Bowling	M	Balls	Runs	Wkts	BB	Avge	RpO	S/R	5i	10m
Tests	5	1521	807	19	5–82	42.47	3.18	80.05	1	0
ODIs	28	1269	1008	33	5–42	30.54	4.76	38.45	1	0
T20Is	7	126	139	7	3–20	19.85	6.61	18.00	0	0
First-class	78	14864	8451	334	9–62	25.30	3.41	44.50	24	6

RAQIBUL HASAN

Full name	**Mohammad Raqibul Hasan**
Born	**October 8, 1987, Jamalpur**
Teams	**Barisal**
Style	**Right-hand bat, legspinner**
Test debut	**Bangladesh v South Africa at Centurion 2008-09**
ODI debut	**Bangladesh v South Africa at Chittagong 2007-08**
T20I debut	**Bangladesh v South Africa at Johannesburg 2008-09**

THE PROFILE Raqibul Hasan toured with Bangladesh A before he had played a first-class match, made a hundred on debut, and hit a triple-century – the first in Bangladesh domestic cricket – before he was 20. It was clearly only a matter of time before he played for the senior national team, and he duly made his one-day debut in March 2008, scoring 63 in his second match, against South Africa, and adding 89 against India and 52 against Sri Lanka shortly afterwards. "Nirala" is a complete batsman, with a fine cover-drive, and although he started as more of an accumulator than a dasher, he is capable of upping the tempo in a one-day international, although his best innings include a patient 89 against India at Mirpur in June 2008, and 76 from 95 balls against England at Trent Bridge in July 2010. He looks a natural for Tests, though – that triple-century, an innings of 313 not out in a Barisal total of 712 for 7 (another domestic record) against Sylhet, occupied 11 hours. However, he made a slow start in the five-day game, until a well-played double of 44 and 65 in Grenada helped seal a 2-0 series victory over a depleted West Indian side in July 2009. After that he fell out with the selectors after being overlooked for the World Twenty20 in England in 2010, and announced his retirement – aged only 22 – just before the home series against England ... but wiser counsel prevailed and he was soon back in the fold. He failed to reach 40 in four outings at the 2011 World Cup and two matches against Australia afterwards, and lost his place again – but he'll be back.

THE FACTS Raqibul Hasan scored 313 not out for Barisal v Sylhet at Fatullah in March 2007: he was 19 years 161 days old, the third-youngest triple-centurion in first-class history after Javed Miandad and Wasim Jaffer ... He was selected for the Bangladesh A tour of Zimbabwe in 2004-05 before he had played first-class cricket: on his debut, against Zimbabwe A at Bulawayo, he scored 100 ...

THE FIGURES to 26.09.11   **ESPN**cricinfo.com

Batting & Fielding	M	Inns	NO	Runs	HS	Avge	S/R	100	50	4s	6s	Ct	St
Tests	7	14	0	268	65	19.14	42.27	0	1	34	1	7	0
ODIs	55	54	7	1308	89	27.82	61.32	0	8	102	8	18	0
T20Is	5	5	0	51	18	10.20	82.25	0	0	3	1	1	0
First-class	35	63	2	1932	313*	31.67	–	2	10	–	–	26	0

Bowling	M	Balls	Runs	Wkts	BB	Avge	RpO	S/R	5i	10m
Tests	7	18	5	1	1–0	5.00	1.66	18.00	0	0
ODIs	55	0	–	–	–	–	–	–	–	–
T20Is	5	0	–	–	–	–	–	–	–	–
First-class	35	306	207	5	1–0	41.40	4.05	61.20	0	0

KEMAR **ROACH**

Full name	**Kemar Andre Jamal Roach**
Born	**June 30, 1988, St Lucy, Barbados**
Teams	**Barbados**
Style	**Right-hand bat, right-arm fast-medium bowler**
Test debut	**West Indies v Bangladesh at Kingstown 2009**
ODI debut	**West Indies v Bermuda at King City 2008**
T20I debut	**West Indies v Australia at Bridgetown 2008**

THE PROFILE A genuinely fast bowler with a free-flowing action, Kemar Roach had played only four first-class matches when he was called into the squad for the third Test against Australia at Bridgetown in June 2008. He was only 19, and slightly fortunate still to be around: he had agreed to play in the Birmingham League, but was deemed ineligible as he had not played five first-class games, as required of overseas players by the league's rules. Roach didn't play in Barbados, but he was included for the Twenty20 international shortly afterwards, and took two of the three wickets to fall, dismissing both Australian openers after starting with a nervous beamer. The following year he was one of West Indies' few successes after the senior players withdrew from the series against Bangladesh, taking 13 wickets in the two Tests. Floyd Reifer, his captain then, observed: "He does a lot, especially with the old ball, getting it to move in and out." Roach hit trouble during the ODIs, when he let loose two beamers and was taken off and fined, but he still took ten wickets. When the seniors returned Roach retained his place, winning admirers in Australia in 2009-10 for his hostile pace. He unsettled Ricky Ponting, dismissing him in each of the three Tests, and also smashed him on the elbow at Perth, forcing him to retire hurt. After that eye-catching display Down Under, Roach was one of the star buys at the third IPL auction early in 2010. The rise tailed off a little in 2011, though. After a World Cup hat-trick against the Netherlands, he struggled at home against Pakistan, eventually losing his place when India came calling in June.

THE FACTS Roach took 6 for 48 against Bangladesh at St George's in July 2009, and followed that with 5 for 44 in the first ODI at Roseau ... Roach took a hat-trick – West Indies' first in the World Cup, and only their second in all ODIs – against the Netherlands at Delhi in February 2011 ... He took 7 for 23 (five bowled and two lbw) for Barbados v Combined Colleges and Campuses in Nevis in January 2010 ...

THE FIGURES to 26.09.11   **ESPncricinfo.com**

Batting & Fielding	M	Inns	NO	Runs	HS	Avge	S/R	100	50	4s	6s	Ct	St
Tests	12	19	5	140	29	10.00	30.83	0	0	17	1	6	0
ODIs	28	17	7	83	24	8.30	52.86	0	0	5	1	3	0
T20Is	10	1	1	3	3*	–	150.00	0	0	0	0	1	0
First-class	35	47	10	366	52*	9.89	–	0	1	–	–	16	0

Bowling	M	Balls	Runs	Wkts	BB	Avge	RpO	S/R	5i	10m
Tests	12	2294	1196	40	6–48	29.90	3.12	57.35	2	0
ODIs	28	1384	1102	43	6–27	25.62	4.77	32.18	2	0
T20Is	10	210	248	9	2–25	27.55	7.08	23.33	0	0
First-class	35	5627	3339	101	7–23	33.05	3.56	55.71	4	0

ROBIUL ISLAM

BANGLADESH

Full name	**Sheikh Robiul Islam**
Born	**October 20, 1986, Satkhira**
Teams	**Khulna**
Style	**Right-hand bat, right-arm fast-medium bowler**
Test debut	**Bangladesh v England at Lord's 2010**
ODI debut	**No ODIs yet**
T20I debut	**No T20Is yet**

THE PROFILE A stocky swing bowler from Satkhira, near the Indian border, Robiul Islam bowls at around 80mph, and keeps going well. He made his first-class debut for Khulna in November 2005, and although he failed to strike in his first match he took 5 for 68 in his second, all from among Dhaka's top six. Two quieter seasons followed, but he shot to prominence with 48 wickets at 19.31 in the 2008-09 domestic season – only Suhrawadi Shuvo (59) took more – including eight in a 35-run victory over Sylhet, and nine in the next match, against Barisal. Robiul missed a year through injury, but did enough when he returned early in 2010 – he took ten wickets as Dhaka were thumped – to earn a place on the England tour that followed. He made his Test debut at Lord's, but proved expensive and missed the next game. Not yet seen as a one-day player, he sat out the World Cup, but was back for the A-team tour of South Africa in April 2011, and the senior trip to Zimbabwe a few months later. At Harare in August, he finally took some Test wickets, removing both openers in the first innings, although not before they had put on 102. As Bangladesh slipped to an embarrassing defeat (this was Zimbabwe's first Test for six years), he at least could hold his head up: "The way Robiul bowled, we were all inspired by him," said Shakib Al Hasan, his captain. "The character he showed and the relentless way he kept on bowling was really good. I asked him once if he wanted to stop, but he said one more over. I gave him the ball and he took a wicket."

THE FACTS Robiul Islam took 5 for 30 (and 10 for 92 in the match) for Khulna against Dhaka at Chittagong in February 2010 ... He took 5 for 60 against Sylhet and 5 for 86 v Barisal in successive matches in October 2008 ... He is sometimes referred to on scorecards by his nickname "Shiplu" ...

THE FIGURES *to 26.09.11*   ᴇѕⴖⅽricinfo.com

Batting & Fielding	M	Inns	NO	Runs	HS	Avge	S/R	100	50	4s	6s	Ct	St
Tests	2	4	2	21	12	10.50	77.77	0	0	4	0	2	0
ODIs	0	0	–	–	–	–	–	–	–	–	–	–	–
T20Is	0	0	–	–	–	–	–	–	–	–	–	–	–
First-class	41	62	24	284	23	7.47	47.57	0	0	36	5	19	0

Bowling	M	Balls	Runs	Wkts	BB	Avge	RpO	S/R	5i	10m
Tests	2	396	273	3	2–106	91.00	4.13	132.00	0	0
ODIs	0	0	–	–	–	–	–	–	–	–
T20Is	0	0	–	–	–	–	–	–	–	–
First-class	41	6678	3986	127	5–30	31.38	3.58	52.58	6	1

RILEE **ROSSOUW**

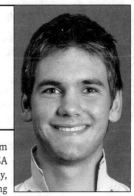

Full name	**Rilee Roscoe Rossouw**
Born	**October 9, 1989, Bloemfontein**
Teams	**Knights**
Style	**Left-hand bat, occasional offspinner**
Test debut	**No Tests yet**
ODI debut	**No ODIs yet**
T20I debut	**No T20Is yet**

THE PROFILE Rilee Rossouw, a free-flowing left-hander from Free State, was long tipped for stardom. After playing for SA Schools he made his first-class debut just after his 18th birthday, scoring 83 against Easterns. The following summer, after stepping up to the full Eagles side, Rossouw finished the campaign as their leading runscorer, with 765. And he rounded off the following season in amazing style, with 319 against the Titans at Centurion, where he shared a record stand of 480 with another highly rated left-hander, Dean Elgar. At 322 minutes it was the fastest triple-century in a domestic match in South Africa (Denis Compton made a faster one for MCC in a tour game in 1948-49), and he came within six of Barry Richards's South African record for runs in one day by a batsman. After that he was a marked man, playing for the national A team in Bangladesh and Sri Lanka. Almost inevitably, his form slipped a little in 2010-11 – 426 runs at less than 30 – but he was recalled to the A team as an injury replacement for a one-day triangular series in Zimbabwe in July 2011, and scored 52 against Australia and 92 against the hosts. Although he missed out on a World Cup spot it seems unlikely that the international arrival of a man described by one onlooker as "better than Jacques Kallis at the same age" will be long delayed. Boeta Dippenaar, the Eagles' captain and a former Test centurymaker himself, has no doubts: "I am prepared to bet my mortgage on it that he will have a long, successful career for South Africa."

THE FACTS Rossouw scored 319 for Eagles v Titans at Centurion in March 2010, all on the first day: it was the second-highest number of runs scored in a day by a South African batsman after Barry Richards (325 in 1970-71) ... During that innings Rossouw shared a South African-record stand of 480 for the second wicket with Dean Elgar ... Rossouw made 131 in a 45-over match against Warriors in November 2008, which helped Eagles clinch the domestic one-day title ...

THE FIGURES to 26.09.11   **cricinfo.com**

Batting & Fielding	M	Inns	NO	Runs	HS	Avge	S/R	100	50	4s	6s	Ct	St
Tests	0	0	–	–	–	–	–	–	–	–	–	–	–
ODIs	0	0	–	–	–	–	–	–	–	–	–	–	–
T20Is	0	0	–	–	–	–	–	–	–	–	–	–	–
First-class	39	69	1	2967	319	43.63	63.46	9	13	431	22	45	0

Bowling	M	Balls	Runs	Wkts	BB	Avge	RpO	S/R	5i	10m
Tests	0	0	–	–	–	–	–	–	–	–
ODIs	0	0	–	–	–	–	–	–	–	–
T20Is	0	0	–	–	–	–	–	–	–	–
First-class	39	5	10	1	1–10	10.00	12.00	5.00	0	0

RUBEL HOSSAIN

BANGLADESH

Full name	**Mohammad Rubel Hossain**
Born	**January 1, 1990, Bagerhat**
Teams	**Chittagong**
Style	**Right-hand bat, right-arm fast-medium bowler**
Test debut	**Bangladesh v West Indies at Kingstown 2009**
ODI debut	**Bangladesh v Sri Lanka at Mirpur 2008-09**
T20I debut	**Bangladesh v South Africa at Johannesburg 2008-09**

THE PROFILE A right-arm fast bowler with a slingy action not unlike Lasith Malinga's, Rubel Hossain began by playing tape-ball cricket in his home town of Bagerhat (in Khulna), before he was discovered during a national search for fast bowlers after getting the highest reading on the speed-gun. Indeed, Rubel's main advantage over his rivals is that he is pacier than most of them. He made his first-class debut in October 2007 against a Khulna side including his hero Mashrafe Mortaza – not that that stopped him letting Mashrafe have a few bouncers. He played in the Under-19 World Cup in Malaysia in February 2008, and later that year made the full national squad. In his first ODI, a rain-affected game against Sri Lanka at Mirpur in January 2009, he helped set up a rare Bangladesh victory with 4 for 33. He toured the Caribbean later in the year, playing in both Tests as Bangladesh pulled off a clean sweep against a depleted West Indian side. Once again he made a decent start: his three first-innings wickets – Ryan Austin, Omar Phillips and Nikita Miller – were, like himself, making their Test debut. But Rubel didn't strike again in the Tests, and went for a few in the subsequent one-dayers: he was left out for a while, then returned to take five expensive wickets in a Test against New Zealand early in 2010, before looking the pick of the pacemen in the home-and-away series against England. After a subdued World Cup – only five wickets on largely spin-friendly pitches – he showed his worth with 11 wickets in the five one-dayers in Zimbabwe later in 2011. Rubel's love of speed also runs to a fascination with motor-bikes.

THE FACTS Rubel Hossain took 5 for 60 for Chittagong at Sylhet in December 2008 ... He took 4 for 33 on his ODI debut as Bangladesh beat Sri Lanka at Mirpur in January 2009 ... Rubel took 5 for 166 (in 29 overs) against New Zealand at Hamilton in February 2010 ... He took 4 for 19 against the Netherlands and 5 for 16 against Scotland on successive days in warm-up games for the World Twenty20 in England in May 2009 ...

THE FIGURES *to 26.09.11*   cricinfo.com

Batting & Fielding	M	Inns	NO	Runs	HS	Avge	S/R	100	50	4s	6s	Ct	St
Tests	9	17	8	67	17	7.44	31.60	0	0	9	0	4	0
ODIs	33	17	9	23	8*	2.87	37.70	0	0	2	0	6	0
T20Is	3	1	1	8	8*	–	160.00	0	0	1	0	1	0
First-class	21	33	11	107	17	4.86	–	0	0	–	–	8	0

Bowling	M	Balls	Runs	Wkts	BB	Avge	RpO	S/R	5i	10m
Tests	9	1554	1156	16	5–166	72.25	4.46	97.12	1	0
ODIs	33	1495	1373	41	4–25	33.48	5.51	36.46	0	0
T20Is	3	62	93	2	1–13	46.50	9.00	31.00	0	0
First-class	21	3190	2265	40	5–60	56.62	4.26	79.75	2	0

JACQUES **RUDOLPH**

Full name	**Jacobus Andries Rudolph**
Born	**May 4, 1981, Springs, Transvaal**
Teams	**Titans, Yorkshire**
Style	**Left-hand bat, occasional legspinner**
Test debut	**South Africa v Bangladesh at Chittagong 2002-03**
ODI debut	**South Africa v India at Dhaka 2002-03**
T20I debut	**South Africa v Australia at Brisbane 2005-06**

THE PROFILE Jacques Rudolph was initially seen by many as a victim of reverse discrimination in South African cricket. His debut double-century – and a record-breaking 429-run stand with Boeta Dippenaar – against Bangladesh in April 2003 came 18 months after he had forced his way into the squad through sheer weight of runs. Twice before he had been expecting to win his first cap, and twice politics intervened. At Centurion in November 2001 the Indians were in dispute with the ICC, who ruled the match unofficial. Then two months later he was named to face Australia at Sydney, but South Africa's board president vetoed his selection, saying there were not enough "players of colour" in the side. But once he finally got in Rudolph became a middle-order fixture for three years. An undemonstrative left-hander, he has neat footwork and balance, and favours the cover-drive. His unbeaten 102 – a classic seven-hour rearguard – saved the Perth Test in December 2005. That was his fifth Test century, but his highest score in five more matches against the Aussies was only 41. After an indifferent run – not helped by a shoulder operation – he was left out for the 2007 World Cup, and threw in his lot with Yorkshire as a Kolpak player. He scored heavily there, and matured as a person. He was due to stay till the end of 2011, but left a year early (although he returned briefly as an overseas player), and – still only 30 – was soon knocking on the door of international selection again. He captained the A team in a triangular series in Zimbabwe in June 2011, and reached 90 three times in his five innings.

THE FACTS Rudolph was the fifth man to score a double-century on Test debut, with 222 not out against Bangladesh at Chittagong in April 2003 ... In that innings he put on 429 for the third wicket with Boeta Dippenaar, a South African Test record ... He scored 228 not out for Yorkshire v Durham in April 2010 ... Occasional legspinner Rudolph took a wicket with his second ball in Tests, dismissing Nasser Hussain for 42 at Headingley in 2003 ... His record includes two ODIs for the Africa XI ...

THE FIGURES to 26.09.11   ESPNcricinfo.com

Batting & Fielding	M	Inns	NO	Runs	HS	Avge	S/R	100	50	4s	6s	Ct	St
Tests	35	63	7	2028	222*	36.21	42.95	5	8	288	6	22	0
ODIs	45	39	6	1174	81	35.57	68.05	0	7	109	5	11	0
T20Is	1	1	1	6	6*	–	85.71	0	0	0	0	0	0
First-class	202	345	23	14681	228*	45.59	–	43	65	–	–	189	0

Bowling	M	Balls	Runs	Wkts	BB	Avge	RpO	S/R	5i	10m
Tests	35	664	432	4	1–1	108.00	3.90	166.00	0	0
ODIs	45	24	26	0	–	–	6.50	–	0	0
T20Is	1	0	–	–	–	–	–	–	–	–
First-class	202	4523	2572	58	5–80	44.34	3.41	77.98	3	0

ANDRE **RUSSELL**

WEST INDIES

Full name	**Andre Dwayne Russell**
Born	**April 29, 1988, Jamaica**
Teams	**Jamaica**
Style	**Right-hand bat, right-arm fast-medium bowler**
Test debut	**West Indies v Sri Lanka at Galle 2010-11**
ODI debut	**West Indies v Ireland at Mohali 2010-11**
T20I debut	**West Indies v Pakistan at Gros Islet 2010-11**

THE PROFILE A bowler with a bit of nip and a big-hitting batsman, Andre Russell showed signs during 2011 of maturing into an international-class allrounder, something West Indies are badly in need of as question-marks persist over the futures of Dwayne Bravo and Chris Gayle. Russell made his international debut against England during the 2011 World Cup. First he dismissed Matt Prior in his second over and Andrew Strauss in his third, finishing with 4 for 49; then, with West Indies struggling to keep up the chase, Russell spanked 49 from 46 balls from No. 8, and only when he and Ramnaresh Sarwan were out in successive overs could England breathe again. Two matches later, though, Russell was left out of the quarter-final against Pakistan, to general surprise. He was back for the home one-dayers that followed, and although he did little against Pakistan and was dropped, on his return he enlivened the third match of the India series by hammering 92 not out after entering at 96 for 7. "This was my biggest innings as it came on a big stage," said Russell, who cheerfully admits that he remains a bowling allrounder: "Bowling is my first choice. I bowl first in the nets and then have a hit. I want to have that balance and enjoy the success." Russell does have a first-class century to his name: it was against Ireland, and included no fewer than ten sixes, nine of them as he sailed past three figures in just 62 balls. He looks like one for the future, although his similarity in style to the current West Indies captain Darren Sammy might limit his opportunities in the short term.

THE FACTS Russell hit 92 not out against India in Antigua in June 2011, the highest score by a No. 9 in any one-day international (the previous-best was 69) ... He reached his maiden first-class century, against Ireland at Spanish Town in April 2010, in just 62 balls, with nine sixes and seven fours ... Russell's two first-class five-fors came in successive matches for West Indies A v India A in England in June 2010 ...

THE FIGURES to 26.09.11   ᴇsᴘncricinfo.com

Batting & Fielding	M	Inns	NO	Runs	HS	Avge	S/R	100	50	4s	6s	Ct	St
Tests	1	1	0	2	2	2.00	22.22	0	0	0	0	1	0
ODIs	8	6	1	172	92*	34.40	118.62	0	1	13	9	3	0
T20Is	4	3	1	18	12*	9.00	105.88	0	0	2	0	0	0
First-class	13	17	1	349	108*	21.81	–	1	0	–	–	5	0

Bowling	M	Balls	Runs	Wkts	BB	Avge	RpO	S/R	5i	10m
Tests	1	138	104	1	1–73	104.00	4.52	138.00	0	0
ODIs	8	364	301	15	4–35	20.06	4.96	24.26	0	0
T20Is	4	60	89	1	1–14	89.00	8.90	60.00	0	0
First-class	13	1491	825	33	5–68	25.00	3.31	45.18	2	0

JESSE **RYDER**

Full name	**Jesse Daniel Ryder**
Born	**August 6, 1984, Masterton, Wellington**
Teams	**Wellington, Pune Warriors**
Style	**Left-hand bat, right-arm medium-pacer**
Test debut	**New Zealand v Bangladesh at Chittagong 2008-09**
ODI debut	**New Zealand v England at Wellington 2007-08**
T20I debut	**New Zealand v England at Auckland 2007-08**

THE PROFILE Jesse Ryder had a troubled childhood, and latterly battled with his weight and demons of his own: just after establishing himself in the one-day side with some promising performances early in 2008, he injured tendons in his hand when he smashed a window in a bar at 5.30am after a tight series victory over England. He missed the Tests, and the England tour which followed. But Ryder, who can also bowl useful gentle seamers, is seriously talented: New Zealand's board had already forgiven him for snubbing their A team (he briefly threatened to try to qualify for England), and gave him several more chances despite continued concerns about his drinking. Ryder gives the ball a good thump: he biffed 79 not out in the second game of that series against England, going run for run with Brendon McCullum in a rollicking opening stand of 165 which won the Hamilton encounter with half the overs unused. He finally made his Test debut in Bangladesh in November 2008, collecting 91 in his second match then three successive fifties against West Indies at home. A maiden Test century followed against India at Hamilton, then he went one better in the second Test at Napier with a superb 201, setting up a massive total of 619 after entering at 23 for 3. Ryder showed his liking for India with more runs in the Tests there late in 2010. Muscle strains mucked up the World Twenty20 in England in 2009, and the following home season, but he was back for the next World Twenty20 in the West Indies early in 2010, and the following year starred with 83 in the shock World Cup quarter-final victory over South Africa.

THE FACTS Ryder scored 236 for Wellington v Central Districts at Palmerston North in March 2005 ... When he scored 201 against India at Napier in March 2009 it was the second time "J. Ryder" had made 201 in a Test – Jack of Australia made 201 not out v England at Adelaide in 1924-25 ... Ryder played two one-day games for Ireland in 2007 before being dumped after missing the plane to the next match ...

THE FIGURES *to 26.09.11*   **ESPN cricinfo.com**

Batting & Fielding	M	Inns	NO	Runs	HS	Avge	S/R	100	50	4s	6s	Ct	St
Tests	16	29	2	1211	201	44.85	54.84	3	6	137	6	10	0
ODIs	35	30	1	1041	107	35.89	90.99	2	5	109	30	13	0
T20Is	17	17	0	330	62	19.41	122.22	0	2	34	14	5	0
First-class	58	94	6	3827	236	43.48	–	9	19	–	–	46	0

Bowling	M	Balls	Runs	Wkts	BB	Avge	RpO	S/R	5i	10m
Tests	16	492	280	5	2–7	56.00	3.41	98.40	0	0
ODIs	35	383	399	11	3–29	36.27	6.25	34.81	0	0
T20Is	17	60	68	2	1–2	34.00	6.80	30.00	0	0
First-class	58	2903	1362	46	4–23	29.60	2.81	63.10	0	0

PAKISTAN

SAEED AJMAL

Full name	**Saeed Ajmal**
Born	**October 14, 1977, Faisalabad, Punjab**
Teams	**Faisalabad, Zarai Taraqiati Bank, Worcestershire**
Style	**Right-hand bat, offspinner**
Test debut	**Pakistan v Sri Lanka at Galle 2009**
ODI debut	**Pakistan v India at Karachi 2008**
T20I debut	**Pakistan v Australia at Dubai 2009**

THE PROFILE Offspinner Saeed Ajmal had been a first-class cricketer for more than ten years when the selectors finally called. Given Pakistan's usual propensity for plucking teenagers from obscurity, he must have thought, at 30, that his chance had gone. However, another impressive domestic season – 38 wickets at 28.63 in 2007-08, plus some decent one-day performances, after 62 wickets at 24.29 the previous term – earned him a place at the Asia Cup in Pakistan in mid-2008. He started with 1 for 47 against India, then strangled Bangladesh with two late strikes in his second match. Ajmal is very much a modern offspinner, tossing in a handy doosra from a high action. His stock ball remains the offie, although it doesn't turn much, but he has a nice rhythmic delivery, and can get a good loop on the ball. He received a jolting setback when his action was reported during a one-day series against Australia in Abu Dhabi early in 2009 – he was also fined after he complained about being complained about – but tests found any elbow flexion was within the permitted 15-degree limit, and he was cleared to resume bowling. He showed his delight by bowling with guile and maturity as Pakistan swept to the World Twenty20 title in England in June, taking 12 wickets (only Umar Gul, with 13, took more) and often bottling up the middle overs. Then he embarked on Test cricket, with 14 wickets in three Tests in Sri Lanka, and two years later claimed 17 in two matches in the West Indies, although doubts about his action were voiced again. Just before that he had done little in the 2011 World Cup, playing only three matches as Pakistan advanced to the semi-final.

THE FACTS Saeed Ajmal took 7 for 63 for Khan Research Laboratories v Zarai Taraqiati Bank in Rawalpindi in December 2008 ... He had unique match figures of 11 for 111 in a Test against West Indies at Providence in May 2011 ... Ajmal claimed 7 for 220 in 63 overs in only his second first-class match, for Faisalabad v Karachi Whites in Karachi in November 1996 ... He had figures of 4.5-3-4-5 for Faisalabad v Karachi Blues at Karachi in January 1998 ...

THE FIGURES *to 26.09.11*

Batting & Fielding	M	Inns	NO	Runs	HS	Avge	S/R	100	50	4s	6s	Ct	St
Tests	12	20	8	153	50	12.75	44.09	0	1	14	2	3	0
ODIs	47	29	13	127	33	7.93	57.99	0	0	8	0	8	0
T20Is	32	12	9	52	21*	17.33	118.18	0	0	4	1	4	0
First-class	98	133	44	1106	53	12.42	–	0	3	–	–	31	0

Bowling	M	Balls	Runs	Wkts	BB	Avge	RpO	S/R	5i	10m
Tests	12	3903	1753	56	6–42	31.30	2.69	69.69	3	1
ODIs	47	2410	1693	63	4–33	26.87	4.21	38.25	0	0
T20Is	32	684	727	45	4–19	16.15	6.37	15.20	0	0
First-class	98	20616	9464	342	7–63	27.67	2.75	60.28	22	2

THILAN **SAMARAWEERA**

Full name **Thilan Thusara Samaraweera**
Born **September 22, 1976, Colombo**
Teams **Sinhalese Sports Club, Wayamba**
Style **Right-hand bat, offspinner**
Test debut **Sri Lanka v India at Colombo 2001-02**
ODI debut **Sri Lanka v India at Sharjah 1998-99**
T20I debut **No T20Is yet**

THE PROFILE Early in 2009, cricket seemed insignificant for
Thilan Samaraweera as he lay in hospital, the most badly injured
of the Sri Lankan players subjected to terrorist attack in Pakistan.
A bullet was lodged in his left thigh, and a distinguished career
hung in the balance – all the more galling as he was in the form of his life, having scored 231
in the first Test at Karachi and 214 in the ongoing one at Lahore. Mercifully, he was soon back
to his best, scoring 159 and 143 in successive Tests against New Zealand at home in August
before settling a few scores with his first one-day international century, after long being
branded too slow for the limited-overs side. In all he made 1234 runs in 11 Tests in 2009 at
72.58, and did well the following year too, although a modest time in England and at home
to Australia cost him his place late in 2011. Even so, this was good stuff for a man who
started out as an offspinner, seemingly destined to play the odd Test in the shadow of Muttiah
Muralitharan. Realising he was on a hiding to nothing there, Samaraweera reinvented himself
as a specialist batsman, starting with a century on Test debut against India in August 2001.
The retirement of Aravinda de Silva helped him secure a middle-order place, where his patient
approach makes him a valuable foil for his more flamboyant colleagues. An adhesive and
well-organised player, Samaraweera has a particular liking for his home ground, the Sinhalese
Sports Club, where he has scored five Test centuries and averages 82. His steady offspin is
rarely used now, although he has a reputation as a partnership-breaker.

THE FACTS Samaraweera was the third Sri Lankan, after Brendon Kuruppu and Romesh
Kaluwitharana, to score a century on Test debut, against India in August 2001 ... Five of his
Test centuries have come at the Sinhalese Sports Club, his home ground in Colombo, where
he averages 82.60 ... He averages 75.00 in Tests against New Zealand, but 24.66 against South
Africa ... Samaraweera's brother Dulip played seven Tests for Sri Lanka in the early 1990s ...

THE FIGURES to 26.09.11   **ESPncricinfo.com**

Batting & Fielding	M	Inns	NO	Runs	HS	Avge	S/R	100	50	4s	6s	Ct	St
Tests	68	108	19	4683	231	52.61	47.94	12	27	548	7	40	0
ODIs	53	42	11	862	105*	27.80	69.29	2	0	76	0	17	0
T20Is	0	0	–	–	–	–	–	–	–	–	–	–	–
First-class	231	325	59	12901	231	48.50	–	33	65	–	–	184	0

Bowling	M	Balls	Runs	Wkts	BB	Avge	RpO	S/R	5i	10m
Tests	68	1315	686	15	4–49	45.73	3.13	87.66	0	0
ODIs	53	702	542	11	3–34	49.27	4.63	63.81	0	0
T20Is	0	0	–	–	–	–	–	–	–	–
First-class	231	17560	8194	349	6–55	23.47	2.79	50.31	15	2

DARREN **SAMMY**

WEST INDIES

Full name	**Darren Julius Garvey Sammy**
Born	**December 20, 1983, Micoud, St Lucia**
Teams	**Windward Islands**
Style	**Right-hand bat, right-arm medium-pacer**
Test debut	**West Indies v England at Manchester 2007**
ODI debut	**West Indies v New Zealand at Southampton 2004**
T20I debut	**West Indies v England at The Oval 2007**

THE PROFILE Darren Julius Garvey Sammy has names invoking images of great leadership – and now needs them, after being thrust into the hot seat of West Indian captain after the board decided to dump Chris Gayle. He was a hard act to follow – especially for someone who was not a regular in the side before his elevation. Sammy did as well as could be expected during the 2011 World Cup, and probably better than that shortly afterwards, squaring a home series with Pakistan (Sammy took 5 for 29 as the tourists slid to defeat in Guyana) then holding No. 1-ranked India to two draws, although victory in a low-scoring first Test at Kingston ultimately gave the Indians the series. Sammy was the first Test cricketer from St Lucia, and is also thought to be Test cricket's only Seventh Day Adventist. He is a handy batsman, a tall, nagging medium-pacer, and a superb fielder. He received a late summons to the Champions Trophy side in England in September 2004 after Jermaine Lawson pulled out injured. In July 2006 Sammy captained St Lucia in the inaugural Stanford 20/20 tournament, and a decent first-class season – 269 runs at 44, plus 16 wickets at less than 20 – earned him a recall for the 2007 England tour. He was drafted into the side for the third Test at Old Trafford, and claimed seven wickets in the second innings – three of them in one over. His pace is unthreatening, but he is accurate and brings the ball down from quite a height and wobbles it around. But he may have to do a little more than that to retain his hold on the captaincy.

THE FACTS Sammy took 7 for 66 in his first Test, against England at Old Trafford in 2007: only Alf Valentine, with 8 for 104 against England at Old Trafford in 1950, has returned better figures on a Test debut for West Indies ... Sammy made 121 for Windward Islands v Barbados at Bridgetown in March 2009 ... He took 5 for 26 (and Sulieman Benn 4 for 6) in a Twenty20 international against Zimbabwe at Port-of-Spain in February 2010 ...

THE FIGURES to 26.09.11   **ESPncricinfo.com**

Batting & Fielding	M	Inns	NO	Runs	HS	Avge	S/R	100	50	4s	6s	Ct	St
Tests	16	28	0	457	48	16.32	57.05	0	0	51	8	19	0
ODIs	63	48	15	670	58*	20.30	96.54	0	2	47	27	31	0
T20Is	23	18	5	158	30	12.15	118.79	0	0	8	8	11	0
First-class	69	115	7	2548	121	23.59	–	1	16	–	–	87	0

Bowling	M	Balls	Runs	Wkts	BB	Avge	RpO	S/R	5i	10m
Tests	16	2992	1347	46	7–66	29.28	2.70	65.04	4	0
ODIs	63	2683	2045	46	4–26	44.45	4.57	58.32	0	0
T20Is	23	417	430	29	5–26	14.82	6.18	14.37	1	0
First-class	69	9997	4402	166	7–66	26.51	2.64	60.22	10	0

MARLON **SAMUELS**

Full name **Marlon Nathaniel Samuels**
Born **January 5, 1981, Kingston, Jamaica**
Teams **Jamaica**
Style **Right-hand bat, offspinner**
Test debut **West Indies v Australia at Adelaide 2000-01**
ODI debut **West Indies v Sri Lanka at Nairobi 2000-01**
T20I debut **West Indies v England at The Oval 2007**

THE PROFILE Marlon Samuels returned to international cricket in 2011 not long after completing a two-year ban for alleged involvement with bookmakers. He protested his innocence, but served his time. At his best Samuels is a classy right-hander, whose composed start in Tests prompted comparisons with Viv Richards, and his return bolstered West Indies' suspect middle order – he made 57 in his first Test back, against Pakistan in St Kitts in May 2011, and 78 not out in his next one, against India. Samuels turns 31 early in 2012, and assuming he can stay out of trouble – and if his sometimes-suspect knees can stand the pace – he should play a big part as West Indies rebuild. His start was exceptional: he flew to Australia for the third Test of the 2000-01 series, only 19 and with just one first-class match under his belt, but showed a beautifully balanced technique, standing still at the crease and moving smoothly into his strokes off either foot, especially while collecting 60 not out and 46 at Melbourne. A combination of over-confidence and arrogance almost got him sent home from India late in 2002, after he defied a team curfew – but he survived, and responded with a disciplined maiden Test century at Kolkata (it was his first one in first-class cricket too). He also excelled in South Africa in 2007-08, making 94 and 40 in the first Test, 51 in the second, and 105 in the third – but that inopportune ban stopped him in his tracks shortly afterwards. Samuels used to bowl some flattish offspin, but has all but given that up after being reported to the ICC on suspicion of throwing.

THE FACTS Samuels scored 257 and then took 5 for 87 – both career-bests – for the West Indians v Queensland in Brisbane in October 2005 ... He scored his maiden first-class century in a Test – 104 v India at Kolkata in October 2002: he was the fifth West Indian to do this, following Clifford Roach, Clairmonte Depeiaza, Gerry Alexander and Bernard Julien ... His brother Robert Samuels, older by ten years, played six Tests and eight ODIs as a left-hand opener, and scored 125 against New Zealand in his second Test ...

THE FIGURES to 26.09.11   ☰ ☰ **cricinfo**.com

Batting & Fielding	M	Inns	NO	Runs	HS	Avge	S/R	100	50	4s	6s	Ct	St
Tests	32	59	5	1567	105	29.01	44.19	2	11	212	7	17	0
ODIs	117	108	18	2698	108*	29.97	74.40	2	19	265	45	31	0
T20Is	10	10	1	201	51	22.33	128.02	0	1	15	10	2	0
First-class	79	135	10	4736	257	37.88	–	9	26	–	–	56	0

Bowling	M	Balls	Runs	Wkts	BB	Avge	RpO	S/R	5i	10m
Tests	32	1596	889	7	2–49	127.00	3.34	228.00	0	0
ODIs	117	3079	2465	57	3–25	43.24	4.80	54.01	0	0
T20Is	10	72	128	2	1–24	64.00	10.66	36.00	0	0
First-class	79	4540	2290	37	5–87	61.89	3.02	122.70	1	0

KUMAR **SANGAKKARA**

Full name	**Kumar Chokshanada Sangakkara**
Born	**October 27, 1977, Matale**
Teams	**Nondescripts, Kandurata, Deccan Chargers**
Style	**Left-hand bat, wicketkeeper**
Test debut	**Sri Lanka v South Africa at Galle 2000**
ODI debut	**Sri Lanka v Pakistan at Galle 2000**
T20I debut	**Sri Lanka v England at Southampton 2006**

THE PROFILE Within months of his debut at 22, Kumar Sangakkara was one of Sri Lanka's most influential players: a talented left-hand strokemaker, a slick wicketkeeper, and a sharp-eyed strategist with an even sharper tongue. From the start his effortless batting oozed class: he possesses the grace of David Gower, but the attitude of an Aussie. At the outset he was happier on the back foot, but a fierce work ethic and a deep interest in the theory of batsmanship helped him, and he is now as comfortable driving through the covers as cutting behind point. He was briefly relieved of keeping duties after the 2003 World Cup: he made more runs, but soon got the gloves back. The extra burden had no obvious effect: he made 185 against Pakistan in March 2006. But there was a change of thinking after that, and Prasanna Jayawardene was given the gloves in Tests. Sangakkara responded with seven hundreds, three of them doubles, in his next nine Tests, including 287 as he and Mahela Jayawardene put on a world-record 624 against South Africa, successive double-centuries against Bangladesh, and a magnificent 192 against Australia at Hobart in November 2007. An astute thinker, he took over as captain early in 2009, and reached the final of the World Twenty20 in England. His batting seemed unaffected: he made five hundreds in his first ten Tests in charge, including three in successive matches against India in 2009 and 2010. He relinquished the captaincy after defeat in the World Cup final, but stayed on as a player to complete 100 Tests later in 2011, by the end of which he was close to 20,000 international runs in all formats.

THE FACTS Sangakkara scored 287, and put on 624 (the highest stand in first-class cricket) with Mahela Jayawardene against South Africa in Colombo in July 2006 ... He also made 270, adding 438 with Marvan Atapattu, against Zimbabwe at Bulawayo in May 2004 ... Sangakkara averages 70.84 in Tests when not the designated wicketkeeper, but 40.48 when lumbered with the gloves ... His record includes three ODIs for the World XI and four for the Asia XI ...

THE FIGURES to 26.09.11   **ESPN**cricinfo.com

Batting & Fielding	M	Inns	NO	Runs	HS	Avge	S/R	100	50	4s	6s	Ct	St
Tests	100	167	12	8651	287	55.81	54.99	25	36	1111	25	166	20
ODIs	301	282	31	9540	138*	38.00	75.50	11	65	933	46	294	78
T20Is	32	31	4	874	78	32.37	119.89	0	6	88	15	14	11
First-class	187	300	23	13240	287	47.79	–	34	60	–	–	327	33

Bowling	M	Balls	Runs	Wkts	BB	Avge	RpO	S/R	5i	10m
Tests	100	78	42	0	–	–	3.23	–	0	0
ODIs	301	0	–	–	–	–	–	–	–	–
T20Is	32	0	–	–	–	–	–	–	–	–
First-class	187	204	112	1	1–13	112.00	3.29	204.00	0	0

RAMNARESH **SARWAN**

Full name   **Ramnaresh Ronnie Sarwan**
Born   **June 23, 1980, Wakenaam Island, Essequibo, Guyana**
Teams   **Guyana**
Style   **Right-hand bat, legspinner**
Test debut   **West Indies v Pakistan at Bridgetown 1999-2000**
ODI debut   **West Indies v England at Nottingham 2000**
T20I debut   **West Indies v South Africa at Johannesburg 2007-08**

THE PROFILE A light-footed right-hander, Ramnaresh Sarwan was brought up in the South American rainforest. After his first Test innings – 84 against Pakistan – the former England captain Ted Dexter was moved to predict a Test average of 50. And on his first tour, to England in 2000, Sarwan justified the hype by topping the averages: his footwork was strikingly confident and precise, and it was a surprise when a horror run of three runs in five innings followed in Australia. He soon put that behind him, although his first Test century took 28 matches. Good times followed – 392 runs against South Africa in 2003-04 then, after a lean run at home against England, an unbeaten 261 against Bangladesh in June 2004. Then came another England tour: despite some patchy form he played a big part as West Indies reached the final of the one-day series then won the Champions Trophy, and carried on his good form in Australia. Sarwan took on the captaincy for the 2007 England tour – but surrendered it after injuring his shoulder early on. Chris Gayle took the reins, but Sarwan was in peerless form at home against England in 2009, collecting 626 runs at 104.33, with three centuries – including a monumental 291 on a Bridgetown featherbed – plus a 94. Another silky hundred followed in the return series, before a back injury disrupted the early part of 2010. Shortly after that he lost his central contract, supposedly on fitness grounds, but was back for the 2011 World Cup and the home Tests that followed – but only 83 runs in four matches saw him dropped for the last one against India in July, leaving renewed question-marks about his future.

THE FACTS Sarwan scored 291 at Bridgetown in 2008-09: only Brian Lara (twice) and Lawrence Rowe (302) have made higher Test scores for West Indies against England (Viv Richards also made 291, at The Oval in 1976) ... Sarwan made 107, 94 and 106 in his previous three Test innings against England in the series ... In ODIs Sarwan averages 61.66 v India – but only 27.05 v Australia ...

THE FIGURES to 26.09.11   **ESPncricinfo.com**

Batting & Fielding	M	Inns	NO	Runs	HS	Avge	S/R	100	50	4s	6s	Ct	St
Tests	87	154	8	5842	291	40.01	46.79	15	31	747	14	53	0
ODIs	173	161	31	5644	115*	43.41	75.76	4	38	466	56	45	0
T20Is	18	16	3	298	59	22.92	104.19	0	2	19	6	7	0
First-class	191	322	22	11822	291	39.40	–	31	62	–	–	137	0

Bowling	M	Balls	Runs	Wkts	BB	Avge	RpO	S/R	5i	10m
Tests	87	2022	1163	23	4–37	50.56	3.45	87.91	0	0
ODIs	173	581	586	16	3–31	36.62	6.05	36.31	0	0
T20Is	18	12	10	2	2–10	5.00	5.00	6.00	0	0
First-class	191	4193	2224	54	6–62	41.18	3.18	77.64	1	0

VIRENDER **SEHWAG**

Full name	**Virender Sehwag**
Born	**October 20, 1978, Delhi**
Teams	**Delhi, Delhi Daredevils**
Style	**Right-hand bat, offspinner**
Test debut	**India v South Africa at Bloemfontein 2001-02**
ODI debut	**India v Pakistan at Mohali 1998-99**
T20I debut	**India v South Africa at Johannesburg 2006-07**

THE PROFILE   Soon after his 2001 Test-debut century Virender Sehwag was being compared to Sachin Tendulkar. It is half-true: Sehwag is also short and square, and plays the straight drive, back-foot punch and whip off the hips identically – but he leaves even Sachin standing when it comes to audacity. He also bowls effective, loopy offspin. Asked to open in England in 2002, Sehwag proved an instant hit, and many pivotal innings followed, including India's first triple-century (brought up, characteristically, with a six), in Pakistan early in 2004. His fitness levels dropped for a while, and he struggled in ODIs – but continued to sparkle in Tests, making 254 (in an opening stand of 410 with Rahul Dravid) at Lahore in January 2006. Then in St Lucia he came excruciatingly close (99 not out) to a century before lunch on the first day, a feat no Indian has yet managed. Dropped after the disastrous 2007 World Cup, Sehwag practised hard, lost a stone, and the following March bounced back with another triple-century, against South Africa. Later that year he carried his bat for 201 at Galle, and overall scored 1462 runs in 2008, at a strike-rate (85.84) unprecedented for an opener. His mould-breaking efforts earned him recognition as *Wisden*'s Leading Cricketer in the World, a title he retained in 2009. Sehwag started the 2011 World Cup with a coruscating 175 against Bangladesh, although his desire to start every innings with a boundary saw productivity drop off after that. Controversially, he delayed a shoulder operation to play in IPL4, and missed the West Indian tour that followed. He returned in England, but looked far short of form and fitness, picking up a pair at Edgbaston as the whitewash loomed.

THE FACTS   Sehwag has made India's highest three Test scores (319, 309 and 293) ... He made 105 on his Test debut, against South Africa in November 2001 ... Sehwag carried his bat for 201 (out of 329, the lowest Test total to include a double-century) against Sri Lanka at Galle in mid-2008 ... His record includes a Test and three ODIs for the World XI, and seven ODIs for the Asia XI ...

THE FIGURES to 26.09.11   ESPncricinfo.com

Batting & Fielding	M	Inns	NO	Runs	HS	Avge	S/R	100	50	4s	6s	Ct	St
Tests	89	154	6	7735	319	52.26	81.69	22	27	1112	85	69	0
ODIs	236	230	9	7760	175	35.11	104.07	14	37	1068	128	87	0
T20Is	14	13	0	313	68	24.07	153.43	0	2	34	14	1	0
First-class	153	255	10	12240	319	49.95	–	36	45	–	–	128	0

Bowling	M	Balls	Runs	Wkts	BB	Avge	RpO	S/R	5i	10m
Tests	89	3249	1643	39	5-104	42.12	3.03	83.30	1	0
ODIs	236	4230	3716	92	4-6	40.39	5.27	45.97	0	0
T20Is	14	6	20	0	–	–	20.00	–	0	0
First-class	153	7988	4143	104	5-104	39.83	3.11	76.80	1	0

SHAFIUL ISLAM

Full name	**Shafiul Islam**
Born	**October 6, 1989, Bogra**
Teams	**Rajshahi**
Style	**Right-hand bat, right-arm fast-medium bowler**
Test debut	**Bangladesh v India at Chittagong 2009-10**
ODI debut	**Bangladesh v Sri Lanka at Dhaka 2009-10**
T20I debut	**Bangladesh v New Zealand at Hamilton 2009-10**

THE PROFILE An enthusiastic medium-pacer, Shafiul Islam's main marks in international cricket so far have, oddly enough, come with bat in hand. Against India in January 2010 his first two scoring shots were big sixes smeared off the legspin of Amit Mishra (his next runs came when he was dropped on the boundary): Shafiul was the first to do this in Tests, although his team-mate Jahurul Islam followed suit against England at Mirpur two months later. During that match, "Suhas" again starred with the bat, making a forthright 53 (from 51 balls, with 11 fours) from No. 10 in a partnership of 74 with Naeem Islam as the total reached 419. Then, in the 2011 World Cup, Shafiul biffed a seemingly nerveless 24 not out in the ninth-wicket stand of 58 with Mahmudullah that spirited Bangladesh to an unlikely victory over England. This partly made up for an uninspiring tournament with the ball – apart from 4 for 21 against Ireland he managed only two other wickets. Still, it is as a bowler that Shafiul is likely to make his mark long term. In 2008-09, his first full season, he took 23 wickets at 22.30 on Bangladesh's usually benign pitches, and received a national call-up after several senior bowlers were injured. He made his one-day debut in the Asia Cup at the start of 2010, and started promisingly – but he proved expensive later on, going for 95 in ten overs against Pakistan (with Shahid Afridi in full flow) in June 2010 and 97 off nine against England a month later. Following the 2011 World Cup Shafiul played against Australia at home and Zimbabwe away, without doing much to dispel the notion that he might just be too hittable in the shorter formats.

THE FACTS Shafiul Islam's first two scoring shots in Test cricket were sixes, off Amit Mishra in two innings at Chittagong in January 2010: he was the first to achieve this in Tests (his team-mate Jahurul Islam soon emulated him) ... Shafiul took 4 for 59 in an ODI against Ireland at Belfast in July 2010, while his best first-class figures of 4 for 38 came for Rajshahi at Khulna in November 2008 ...

THE FIGURES to 26.09.11   **ᴇsᴘᴨcricinfo.com**

Batting & Fielding	M	Inns	NO	Runs	HS	Avge	S/R	100	50	4s	6s	Ct	St
Tests	6	12	1	149	53	13.54	60.08	0	1	24	2	1	0
ODIs	37	20	7	98	24*	7.53	60.12	0	0	11	2	6	0
T20Is	3	2	0	17	16	8.50	77.27	0	0	1	1	1	0
First-class	20	31	7	314	53	13.08	61.44	0	1	43	7	6	0

Bowling	M	Balls	Runs	Wkts	BB	Avge	RpO	S/R	5i	10m
Tests	6	996	569	8	3–86	71.12	3.42	124.50	0	0
ODIs	37	1539	1530	44	4–21	34.77	5.96	34.97	0	0
T20Is	3	54	66	1	1–25	66.00	7.33	54.00	0	0
First-class	20	3031	1543	42	4–38	36.73	3.05	72.16	0	0

SHAHADAT HOSSAIN

Full name **Kazi Shahadat Hossain**
Born **August 7, 1986, Dhaka**
Teams **Dhaka**
Style **Right-hand bat, right-arm fast-medium bowler**
Test debut **Bangladesh v England at Lord's 2005**
ODI debut **Bangladesh v Kenya at Bogra 2005-06**
T20I debut **Bangladesh v Zimbabwe at Khulna 2006-07**

THE PROFILE Shahadat Hossain was discovered at a talent-spotting camp, and whisked away to the Institute of Sports for refinement. "Rajib" has all the necessary attributes for a genuine fast bowler: he is tall and strong, and doesn't put unnecessary pressure on his body, with a slightly open-chested delivery position after a smooth run-up. He is naturally aggressive, and has raw pace. But his Test debut at Lord's in 2005 was a chastening experience, as his 12 overs disappeared for 101. He was just 18 then: after that he did well against Sri Lanka, taking four wickets in an innings twice before going one better in Bogra's inaugural Test in March 2006. Early in 2008 his 6 for 27 at Mirpur gave Bangladesh a rare first-innings lead over South Africa – and an even rarer (if illusory) sniff of victory. In one-day internationals, despite a hat-trick against Zimbabwe, he has been in and out of the side: he played only once in the 2007 World Cup (and was hit around in the sobering defeat by Ireland), and has since generally been viewed as too expensive and erratic for limited-overs games. In Tests, however, he played his part as Bangladesh won an overseas series for the first time, in the Caribbean in mid-2009, and in May 2010 he erased some of the memories of that painful Test debut with 5 for 98 at Lord's, although England still won comfortably in the end. Shahadat was set back by injury after that, and missed the 2011 World Cup – although 5 for 82 for Dhaka against Rajshahi (all but one of his victims a Test player) shortly afterwards suggested he was returning to his best.

THE FACTS Shahadat Hossain's 6 for 27 against South Africa at Mirpur in February 2008 are the best figures by a Bangladesh fast bowler in Tests ... He took Bangladesh's first ODI hat-trick, against Zimbabwe at Harare in August 2006 ... Shahadat averages 26.75 with the ball in Tests against India – but 258.00 v Australia ... He took only two wickets – both against Kenya – in his first six ODIs ...

THE FIGURES to 26.09.11   ᴇꜱᴨɴcricinfo.com

Batting & Fielding	M	Inns	NO	Runs	HS	Avge	S/R	100	50	4s	6s	Ct	St
Tests	29	55	15	394	40	9.85	45.54	0	0	56	3	7	0
ODIs	46	25	15	79	16*	7.90	55.24	0	0	7	1	5	0
T20Is	5	5	3	8	4*	4.00	66.66	0	0	0	0	0	0
First-class	55	92	28	745	40	11.64	–	0	0	–	–	12	0

Bowling	M	Balls	Runs	Wkts	BB	Avge	RpO	S/R	5i	10m
Tests	29	4334	2992	66	6–27	45.33	4.14	65.66	4	0
ODIs	46	1928	1824	42	3–34	43.42	5.67	45.90	0	0
T20Is	5	96	144	4	2–22	36.00	9.00	24.00	0	0
First-class	55	8190	5457	143	6–27	38.16	3.99	57.27	8	0

SHAHID AFRIDI

Full name	**Sahibzada Mohammad Shahid Khan Afridi**
Born	**March 1, 1980, Khyber Agency**
Teams	**Karachi, Habib Bank, Hampshire**
Style	**Right-hand bat, legspinner**
Test debut	**Pakistan v Australia at Karachi 1998-99**
ODI debut	**Pakistan v Kenya at Nairobi 1996-97**
T20I debut	**Pakistan v England at Bristol 2006**

THE PROFILE A flamboyant allrounder introduced to international cricket as a 16-year-old legspinner, Shahid Afridi astonished everyone except himself by pinch-hitting the fastest one-day hundred in his maiden innings. He's a compulsive shotmaker, and although initially that was too often his undoing, he eventually blossomed. A violent century against India in April 2005 (the only faster one in ODIs was Afridi's own) came soon after he walloped 58 in 34 balls to square the Test series at Bangalore. Then came a Test ton against West Indies, important runs against England, and mayhem against India on some flat tracks early in 2006. A typical Afridi assault is laced with lofted drives and short-arm jabs over midwicket. He's at his best when forcing straight, and at his weakest pushing just outside off. With the ball he can get turn as well as lazy drift, but variety is the key: a vicious faster ball and an offbreak too. After an uncertain start in 20-overs cricket – a format which might have been invented with him in mind – Afridi roared back to form in the World Twenty20 in England in 2009, and made a ferocious 51 as Pakistan bossed the final at Lord's. He had retired from Tests in 2006 but returned as captain in 2010, only to quit dramatically after just one match, and two irresponsible shots in a big defeat by Australia at Lord's. His slogging powers seemed to be waning, but his bowling remained potent, as he showed with 21 wickets in the march to the World Cup semi-final in 2011. Not long after that, though, Afridi fell out with the board and was dumped as one-day captain. He immediately retired again ... "provisionally".

THE FACTS In his second match (he hadn't batted in the first) Shahid Afridi hit the fastest hundred in ODIs, from only 37 balls, against Sri Lanka in Nairobi in October 1996 ... Afridi has the highest strike rate – 113.82 runs per 100 balls – of anyone with more than 30 innings in ODIs ... In successive Tests against India in 2006 he hit 103 (from 80 balls) at Lahore, and 156 (128 balls, six sixes) at Faisalabad ... Afridi has hit more sixes in ODIs than anyone else ... Afridi's record includes three ODIs for the Asia XI and two for the World XI ...

THE FIGURES *to 26.09.11*   **ESPNcricinfo.com**

Batting & Fielding	M	Inns	NO	Runs	HS	Avge	S/R	100	50	4s	6s	Ct	St
Tests	27	48	1	1716	156	36.51	86.97	5	8	220	52	10	0
ODIs	325	303	18	6695	124	23.49	113.82	6	31	615	289	107	0
T20Is	43	41	3	683	54*	17.97	144.09	0	3	56	26	12	0
First-class	111	183	4	5631	164	31.45	–	12	30	–	–	75	0

Bowling	M	Balls	Runs	Wkts	BB	Avge	RpO	S/R	5i	10m
Tests	27	3194	1709	48	5–52	35.60	3.21	66.54	1	0
ODIs	325	14056	10782	315	6–38	34.22	4.60	44.62	5	0
T20Is	43	971	1005	53	4–11	18.96	6.21	18.32	0	0
First-class	111	13493	7023	258	6–101	27.22	3.12	52.29	8	0

SHAHRIAR NAFEES

BANGLADESH

Full name	**Shahriar Nafees Ahmed**
Born	**January 25, 1986, Dhaka**
Teams	**Barisal**
Style	**Left-hand bat**
Test debut	**Bangladesh v Sri Lanka at Colombo 2005-06**
ODI debut	**Bangladesh v England at Nottingham 2005**
T20I debut	**Bangladesh v Zimbabwe at Khulna 2006-07**

THE PROFILE A talented left-hand opener, Shahriar Nafees went on Bangladesh's maiden tour of England in 2005, aged 19 and with just five first-class matches behind him. He hadn't fared too badly in those, making 350 runs at 35. That England trip was a case of watching and learning. He did get an opportunity in the one-day series, and made 75 in the last game, against Australia. A Test debut followed in Sri Lanka later that year, and Shahriar made 51 in his second match. Then, in April 2006, he exploded in sensational fashion against the might of Australia, stroking his way to a brilliant hundred, his maiden first-class ton as well as his first in Tests, at Fatullah. His stunning 138, with 19 fours, set up a scarcely believable first-day total of 355 for 5 as the Aussies reeled, and a brisk 79 in the second Test showed this was no flash in the pan. There were also three one-day hundreds against Zimbabwe, and one against Bermuda, but he found life harder against the big boys, being dropped after six innings in the 2007 World Cup produced only 31 runs and a top score of 12. After that Shahriar seemed to have been lost to international cricket, copping a ten-year ban after signing up for the unauthorised Indian Cricket League, but he was the first to be welcomed back after an amnesty. He had another quiet World Cup in 2011, but then spanked 56 and 60 against his old friends Australia to cement his place for a while. He was once considered a captaincy candidate, but it remains to be seen whether that ICL stint will be held against him.

THE FACTS Shahriar Nafees's 138 against Australia at Fatullah in 2005-06 was his maiden century in first-class cricket: his previous-highest score was 97, for the Board President's XI v the touring Zimbabweans in January 2005 ... Shahriar hit four of Bangladesh's first seven ODI hundreds ... He averages 55.50 in ODIs against Zimbabwe, with three hundreds, but only 5.50 v India (and 0 v Canada) ... Shahriar captained Bangladesh Under-19s in a one-day game against England, skippered by Alastair Cook, in 2004 ... His brother, Iftekhar Nayem, has also played first-class cricket ...

THE FIGURES to 26.09.11   ESPNcricinfo.com

Batting & Fielding	M	Inns	NO	Runs	HS	Avge	S/R	100	50	4s	6s	Ct	St
Tests	17	34	0	894	138	26.29	52.83	1	5	131	1	13	0
ODIs	71	71	5	2162	123*	32.75	70.33	4	13	272	7	12	0
T20Is	1	1	0	25	25	25.00	147.05	0	0	3	1	1	0
First-class	49	96	3	2973	138	31.96	58.39	4	20	–	–	29	0

Bowling	M	Balls	Runs	Wkts	BB	Avge	RpO	S/R	5i	10m
Tests	17	0	–	–	–	–	–	–	–	–
ODIs	71	0	–	–	–	–	–	–	–	–
T20Is	1	0	–	–	–	–	–	–	–	–
First-class	49	72	50	0	–	–	4.16	–	0	0

AJMAL **SHAHZAD**

Full name **Ajmal Shahzad**
Born **July 27, 1985, Huddersfield, Yorkshire**
Teams **Yorkshire**
Style **Right-hand bat, right-arm fast-medium bowler**
Test debut **England v Bangladesh at Manchester 2010**
ODI debut **England v Bangladesh at Chittagong 2009-10**
T20I debut **England v Pakistan at Dubai 2009-10**

THE PROFILE Ajmal Shahzad made history in May 2004 when he became the first British-born Asian to play for Yorkshire. Born in Huddersfield and raised in Bradford, Shahzad is a nippy fast bowler and a useful late-order batsman, who excelled at schoolboy level and for Yorkshire's academy sides. Graham Roope, his coach there, said he was "far too mature for most schoolboy opponents of his age". Shahzad endured a couple of sluggish seasons with injuries, and managed only a solitary appearance in 2006 – but he finally allied consistency to his undoubted talent and, given a first-team chance following Tim Bresnan's promotion to the national squad, Shahzad claimed 40 wickets and scored 445 runs for Yorkshire in the 2009 Championship. This was enough to earn him a place on England's Test tour of Bangladesh, much to his own surprise: the decisive factor seems to have been an impressive stint with the England Performance Programme in South Africa a few months earlier, when he caught the eye of the senior management, including Andy Flower, with his pace, control and desire to succeed. "He looks like an impressive young man," said Flower, "and how well he does will be determined by himself." After displaying a happy knack for early strikes – wickets in his first over in both ODIs and Twenty20s – Shahzad made his Test debut against Bangladesh at Old Trafford in June 2010 when Stuart Broad was rested. There were no early breakthroughs this time, but he did take four wickets overall. However, a hamstring injury ended a promising 2011 World Cup, then he endured a difficult season: Yorkshire were relegated, while the advance of Chris Tremlett and Tim Bresnan pushed him down the England pecking order.

THE FACTS Shahzad took two wickets in his first over in Twenty20 internationals, dismissing Imran Nazir third ball and Imran Farhat fifth against Pakistan at Dubai in February 2010 ... The following month he struck with his third ball in ODIs, dismissing Tamim Iqbal of Bangladesh at Chittagong ... Shahzad hit the first ball he received in the World Cup (from Munaf Patel) for six, as England tied their match against India at Bangalore in February 2011 ...

THE FIGURES *to 26.09.11* **ᴇsᴘncricinfo.com**

Batting & Fielding	M	Inns	NO	Runs	HS	Avge	S/R	100	50	4s	6s	Ct	St
Tests	1	1	0	5	5	5.00	41.66	0	0	1	0	2	0
ODIs	11	8	2	39	9	6.50	65.00	0	0	0	3	4	0
T20Is	3	1	1	0	0*	–	0.00	0	0	0	0	1	0
First-class	46	59	16	1155	88	26.86	42.60	0	3	134	18	8	0

Bowling	M	Balls	Runs	Wkts	BB	Avge	RpO	S/R	5i	10m
Tests	1	102	63	4	3–45	15.75	3.70	25.50	0	0
ODIs	11	588	490	17	3–41	28.82	5.00	34.58	0	0
T20Is	3	66	97	3	2–38	32.33	8.81	22.00	0	0
First-class	46	7514	4354	127	5–51	34.28	3.47	59.16	3	0

SHAKIB AL HASAN

Full name	**Shakib Al Hasan**
Born	**March 24, 1987, Magura, Khulna**
Teams	**Khulna, Worcestershire, Kolkata Knight Riders**
Style	**Left-hand bat, slow left-arm orthodox spinner**
Test debut	**Bangladesh v India at Chittagong 2006-07**
ODI debut	**Bangladesh v Zimbabwe at Harare 2006**
T20I debut	**Bangladesh v Zimbabwe at Khulna 2006-07**

THE PROFILE A stylish left-hand batsman and flattish left-arm spinner, Shakib Al Hasan was earmarked for international honours after starring for the Under-19s in 2005. His full debut duly arrived in August 2006: he took a wicket then strolled in at No. 4 to make 30 not out in the matchwinning partnership. From the start Shakib proved remarkably consistent, being dismissed in single figures only once in 18 one-dayers leading up to the 2007 World Cup. The heady start continued in the Caribbean with a half-century in the famous win over India, and another against England. After the World Cup came the inevitable dip – 17 runs in three innings in Sri Lanka – but he soon returned to form. He sealed Bangladesh's 2-0 triumph against West Indies in July 2009, finishing just short of a maiden Test ton in Grenada: by then he had taken over from the injured Mashrafe Mortaza as captain. He looked a natural there, too, and it was a surprise when Mashrafe was briefly reinstated the following year. Shakib's spin bowling – always effective and economical in ODIs – blossomed almost overnight in Tests. After only three wickets in his first six matches, he took 7 for 36 against New Zealand in October 2008, and rubber-stamped his arrival as an international-class allrounder with 13 wickets in those two Tests in the West Indies. He also sailed past 100 one-day wickets in mid-2010, just before becoming the first Bangladeshi to play county cricket. By 2011, with Mashrafe injured again, Shakib seemed entrenched as captain, his own successes contrasting with his team's often woeful performances. However, after the disheartening tour of Zimbabwe in August, Shakib was sacked as skipper, despite doing well himself with bat and ball.

THE FACTS Shakib Al Hasan took 7 for 36, Bangladesh's best bowling figures in Tests, against New Zealand at Chittagong in October 2008 ... He made 100 against New Zealand at Hamilton in February 2010 – and additionally has scored 96 in Tests three times ... Shakib hit 134 not out v Canada in an ODI in Antigua in February 2007 ... He averages 59.66 with the bat in Tests against New Zealand – and 15.12 v South Africa ...

THE FIGURES to 26.09.11   **ESPncricinfo.com**

Batting & Fielding	M	Inns	NO	Runs	HS	Avge	S/R	100	50	4s	6s	Ct	St
Tests	22	42	2	1253	100	31.32	56.54	1	6	166	6	9	0
ODIs	116	112	18	3261	134*	34.69	77.11	5	21	289	21	30	0
T20Is	14	14	0	207	47	14.78	111.89	0	0	17	4	4	0
First-class	56	103	9	3119	129	33.18	–	4	16	–	–	30	0

Bowling	M	Balls	Runs	Wkts	BB	Avge	RpO	S/R	5i	10m
Tests	22	5347	2532	79	7–36	32.05	2.84	67.68	7	0
ODIs	116	5884	4232	144	4–33	29.38	4.31	40.86	0	0
T20Is	14	294	328	17	4–34	19.29	6.69	17.29	0	0
First-class	56	11200	5147	175	7–32	29.41	2.75	64.00	12	0

ISHANT **SHARMA**

Full name   **Ishant Sharma**
Born   **September 2, 1988, Delhi**
Teams   **Delhi, Deccan Chargers**
Style   **Right-hand bat, right-arm fast-medium bowler**
Test debut   **India v Bangladesh at Dhaka 2006-07**
ODI debut   **India v South Africa at Belfast 2007**
T20I debut   **India v Australia at Melbourne 2007-08**

THE PROFILE   Tall fast bowlers have always been a much-prized rarity in Indian cricket. Their earliest Tests featured Mohammad Nissar, a few years ago Abey Kuruvilla flitted across the international scene ... and now there's Ishant Sharma, a lofty 6ft 4ins (193cm). He's regularly above 80mph, with a sharp and deceptive bouncer, delivered from a high arm action. He started to play seriously at 14, but played one-dayers for Delhi in 2005-06 when only 17. The following season he took 4 for 65 from 34 overs on first-class debut, and finished his first term with 29 wickets at 20.10. Early in 2007 he was on the verge of reinforcing the national team in South Africa – flights had been booked and visa arrangements made – but in the end he was left to concentrate on domestic cricket and a youth tour. However, when Munaf Patel was injured again in Bangladesh in May, Sharma finally did get on the plane, and took a wicket in a landslide victory at Dhaka. In Australia at the end of 2007 he looked the real deal, especially in the Perth Test, where he dismissed Ricky Ponting during a sensational spell, and again in the one-dayers as India surprised the hosts to snaffle the series. In 2011 he took 22 wickets in three Tests in the Caribbean, including ten at Bridgetown, but then blew hot and cold in England – listless in the first innings at Lord's, magnificent in the second – before missing the one-day series with an ankle injury. Sharma has been one of the faces of the IPL, if not one of its greatest successes, and – if a worryingly frail-looking physique holds up – should have a long and successful career.

THE FACTS   Ishant Sharma took 7 for 24 (11 for 51 in the match) for Delhi v Orissa at Delhi in November 2008 ... Almost half his ODI wickets (30 out of 64) have been Sri Lankans ... His bowling average in ODIs against Australia is 25.13, but 66.33 against West Indies ... In 2006-07, his first season of first-class cricket, Sharma took 29 wickets at 20.10 for Delhi, then made his Test debut in only his seventh match ...

THE FIGURES to 26.09.11   **ᴇꜱᴘⁿ cricinfo.com**

Batting & Fielding	M	Inns	NO	Runs	HS	Avge	S/R	100	50	4s	6s	Ct	St
Tests	38	55	24	351	31*	11.32	29.05	0	0	40	0	11	0
ODIs	47	16	6	47	13	4.70	34.05	0	0	4	0	12	0
T20Is	11	2	2	8	5*	–	100.00	0	0	1	0	2	0
First-class	60	76	35	416	31*	10.14	29.13	0	0	48	0	17	0

Bowling	M	Balls	Runs	Wkts	BB	Avge	RpO	S/R	5i	10m
Tests	38	7428	4249	123	6–55	34.54	3.43	60.39	3	1
ODIs	47	2153	2056	64	4–38	32.12	5.72	33.64	0	0
T20Is	11	206	291	6	2–34	48.50	8.47	34.33	0	0
First-class	60	11563	6275	207	7–24	30.31	3.25	55.85	5	2

ROHIT **SHARMA**

INDIA

Full name	**Rohit Gurunathan Sharma**
Born	**April 30, 1987, Bansod, Nagpur, Maharashtra**
Teams	**Mumbai, Mumbai Indians**
Style	**Right-hand bat, offspinner**
Test debut	**No Tests yet**
ODI debut	**India v Ireland at Belfast 2007**
T20I debut	**India v England at Durban 2007-08**

THE PROFILE Rohit Sharma made a great start to his first-class career, making 205 against Gujarat in only his fourth match for Mumbai. Earlier in 2006 he had made his first-class debut for India A, and also exuded class in the Under-19 World Cup. Sharma is an adaptable batsman, strong off the back foot, equally happy as accumulator or aggressor. He finished 2006-07 with 600 runs at 40, plus 356 in one-dayers and a 49-ball Twenty20 century against Gujarat, which earned him a national call as the dust settled on India's disastrous World Cup campaign. He made his ODI debut in Ireland, retained his place for the one-day leg of the tour of England that followed, and had a couple of useful innings in the inaugural World Twenty20 in South Africa. Then, during the second season of the IPL in 2009, Sharma's Deccan Chargers entered the last over against Kolkata needing 21 to win – and he hit 26, including a six off the final ball, off Bangladesh's Mashrafe Mortaza. A few matches previously Sharma's seldom-seen offspin had claimed an unlikely hat-trick to derail the Mumbai Indians. In 2009-10 he followed a triple-century for Mumbai with successive one-day hundreds against Zimbabwe and Sri Lanka. He would have had a Test cap, too, except he twisted his ankle during the warm-up before the first match against South Africa at Nagpur in February 2010. The following year he was the unlucky batsman to miss out on World Cup selection, but returned in the Caribbean shortly afterwards and passed 50 in three of his five innings. But in England a first-ball bouncer from Stuart Broad broke his finger in the opening match of the one-day series, and Sharma was on the next plane home.

THE FACTS Rohit Sharma extended his maiden first-class century to 205, for Mumbai v Gujarat in December 2006... He scored 309 not out for Mumbai v Gujarat in December 2009: in his next innings he was out for a duck ... Sharma took a hat-trick (and four wickets in five balls) as Deccan Chargers beat Mumbai Indians in the IPL at Centurion in May 2009 ... He hit 101 not out, off only 45 balls, against Gujarat in a Twenty20 match in April 2007 ...

THE FIGURES to 26.09.11   **ESPNcricinfo.com**

Batting & Fielding	M	Inns	NO	Runs	HS	Avge	S/R	100	50	4s	6s	Ct	St
Tests	0	0	–	–	–	–	–	–	–	–	–	–	–
ODIs	67	63	15	1505	114	31.35	77.25	2	8	101	17	25	0
T20Is	22	19	6	415	79*	31.92	126.91	0	4	33	18	8	0
First-class	43	64	8	3409	309*	60.87	–	10	15	–	–	29	0

Bowling	M	Balls	Runs	Wkts	BB	Avge	RpO	S/R	5i	10m
Tests	0	0	–	–	–	–	–	–	–	–
ODIs	67	329	265	6	2–27	44.16	4.83	54.83	0	0
T20Is	22	36	53	1	1–22	53.00	8.83	36.00	0	0
First-class	43	864	482	10	3–23	48.20	3.34	86.40	0	0

VUSI **SIBANDA**

Full name	**Vusimuzi Sibanda**
Born	**October 10, 1983, Highfields, Harare**
Teams	**Mid West Rhinos**
Style	**Right-hand bat, occasional medium-pacer**
Test debut	**Zimbabwe v West Indies at Harare 2003-04**
ODI debut	**Zimbabwe v West Indies at Bulawayo 2003-04**
T20I debut	**Zimbabwe v Australia at Cape Town 2007-08**

THE PROFILE Vusi Sibanda is a contemporary of Tatenda Taibu, Hamilton Masakadza and Stuart Matsikenyeri. Like them, he comes from the Harare black township of Highfield, and earned a board scholarship to Churchill High School. An opening batsman, Sibanda was one of a clutch of young players promoted to the national team before they were ready, as the dispute that cost Zimbabwe several senior players rumbled on. The player shortage meant he was retained despite modest returns, his continued selection down almost entirely to outstanding potential rather than actual performance. Sibanda has always been a superb timer of the ball, predominantly off the front foot, but was slow to learn how to build a big innings. He showed signs of improvement in the Caribbean in 2006, finishing with 78 and a superb 116 against Bermuda in the tri-series in Trinidad in May. But he continued to struggle against top-class opposition – and fought a similar long battle to get used to contact lenses, rather than glasses. It all came right in 2009-10, when he kicked off a record-breaking domestic season with four centuries in two matches, and went on to score nine in all, a world record. He played only twice in the 2011 World Cup, making 61 against Kenya, but hit form when Bangladesh came calling in August for a tour that included Zimbabwe's first Test for six years. Sibanda started that one off in style, stroking an elegant 78 (and 38 in the second innings as Zimbabwe built their lead), and continued his good form in the one-day series, hitting 96 and 67 in the first two matches to confirm his arrival as an international-class batsman at long last.

THE FACTS Sibanda hit nine centuries in Zimbabwe in 2009-10, the most by a batsman in any overseas season, breaking a record established by Don Bradman (eight in Australia in 1947-48): Sibanda's runs included four centuries in two successive matches, and seven in nine innings overall ... The sequence began with 209 (and 116 not out) for Zimbabwe v Kenya in the Intercontinental Cup at Kwekwe in October 2009, and included a career-best 215 for Mid West Rhinos v Mountaineers at Mutare ...

THE FIGURES *to 26.09.11* ESPNcricinfo.com

Batting & Fielding	M	Inns	NO	Runs	HS	Avge	S/R	100	50	4s	6s	Ct	St
Tests	5	10	0	214	78	21.40	56.76	0	1	30	2	4	0
ODIs	95	94	2	2250	116	24.45	62.77	1	17	249	24	32	0
T20Is	5	5	0	74	29	14.80	104.22	0	0	12	1	1	0
First-class	86	159	7	4892	215	32.18	–	13	20	–	–	85	0

Bowling	M	Balls	Runs	Wkts	BB	Avge	RpO	S/R	5i	10m
Tests	5	0	–	–	–	–	–	–	–	–
ODIs	95	138	148	2	1–12	74.00	6.43	69.00	0	0
T20Is	5	0	–	–	–	–	–	–	–	–
First-class	86	1869	1207	22	4–30	54.86	3.87	84.95	0	0

PETER **SIDDLE**

AUSTRALIA

Full name	**Peter Matthew Siddle**
Born	**November 25, 1984, Traralgon, Victoria**
Teams	**Victoria**
Style	**Right-hand bat, right-arm fast bowler**
Test debut	**Australia v India at Mohali 2008-09**
ODI debut	**Australia v New Zealand at Brisbane 2008-09**
T20I debut	**Australia v New Zealand at Sydney 2008-09**

THE PROFILE Peter Siddle was long considered one of the most dangerous fast bowlers in Australia – but also one of the most fragile. A shoulder reconstruction sidelined him for most of 2006-07, then he dislocated the joint at the start of the following season, and aggravated it again later on. He still finished 2007-08 with 33 wickets in just five matches. He emerged from reconstructive surgery fitter than ever, and was a surprise inclusion for the Indian tour in October 2008, shortly after visiting there with the A team. His first Test wicket was the plum one of Sachin Tendulkar. The burly Siddle has elements of two illustrious predecessors in his make-up: the run-up is reminiscent of Craig McDermott's, while the bustling delivery reminds some of Merv Hughes – and he has a touch of the old Hughes banter, too. In England in 2009 he fought off the challenges of other pacemen to play throughout the series, moving the ball at pace and finishing up with 20 wickets. That included a decisive first-day spell of 5 for 21 to put England on the ropes at Headingley, where Australia won easily. He looked to have booked a spot – but then a stress fracture ruled him out for most of 2010. He returned for the Ashes, and started with a sensational first-day hat-trick on the way to 6 for 54, although he took only eight more wickets in that depressing series. Siddle grew up in Morwell in rural Victoria, and was a promising competitive wood-chopper before concentrating on cricket at 14. "I thought if I was going to play competitive sport I should give it away because I didn't want to chop any toes off!"

THE FACTS Siddle took a Test hat-trick – on his birthday – on the first day of the 2010-11 Ashes series at Brisbane: he finished with a Test-best 6 for 54 ... Siddle took 5 for 21 in the Ashes Test against England at Headingley in 2009 ... He took 9 for 167 in the match in the Pura Cup final against New South Wales at Sydney in March 2008, although Victoria still lost ...

THE FIGURES to 26.09.11   ᴇＳＰＮcricinfo.com

Batting & Fielding	M	Inns	NO	Runs	HS	Avge	S/R	100	50	4s	6s	Ct	St
Tests	23	33	7	436	43	16.76	52.02	0	0	49	2	12	0
ODIs	17	4	2	21	9*	10.50	116.66	0	0	1	0	1	0
T20Is	2	1	1	1	1*	–	100.00	0	0	0	0	0	0
First-class	48	65	14	828	45*	16.23	48.33	0	0	92	4	26	0

Bowling	M	Balls	Runs	Wkts	BB	Avge	RpO	S/R	5i	10m
Tests	23	4856	2467	78	6–54	31.62	3.04	62.25	4	0
ODIs	17	751	581	15	3–55	38.73	4.64	50.06	0	0
T20Is	2	48	58	3	2–24	19.33	7.25	16.00	0	0
First-class	48	9184	4748	168	6–54	28.26	3.10	54.66	9	0

LENDL **SIMMONS**

Full name **Lendl Mark Platter Simmons**
Born **January 25, 1985, Port-of-Spain, Trinidad**
Teams **Trinidad & Tobago**
Style **Right-hand bat, occasional medium-pacer**
Test debut **West Indies v England at Port-of-Spain 2008-09**
ODI debut **West Indies v Pakistan at Faisalabad 2006-07**
T20I debut **West Indies v England at The Oval 2007**

THE PROFILE Lendl Simmons, the nephew of the former Test opener Phil, made a steady rise through the junior ranks, playing in the Under-19 World Cups of 2002 and 2004. An opener, and a fine fielder who can keep wicket, Simmons – named after the top 1980s tennis player Ivan Lendl – made his first-class debut six weeks after his 17th birthday. After passing 500 runs in the previous two domestic seasons, he toured England with West Indies A in 2006. He stepped up to the full one-day side in Pakistan later that year, collecting a duck in his first match but a mature 70 in his second. He struggled after that – only 42 runs in four innings – but retained his place for the 2007 World Cup. He made only one appearance, though, in rather peculiar circumstances: called up in place of a fast bowler for the vital Super Eight match against New Zealand, he batted No. 8 and didn't bowl. A massive 282 against the England tourists early in 2009 finally earned him a Test place, but he failed to set the world alight. Later he hammered 77 off 50 balls against South Africa in the World Twenty20 in England (he had earlier taken four wickets against Sri Lanka), but was then surprisingly dropped again. After nearly two years on the sidelines (save for a forgettable one-day series in Australia early in 2010), Simmons regained his place when new coach Ottis Gibson shuffled the pack after the 2011 World Cup. He did well in limited-overs matches – seven fifties in 12 games against Pakistan and India in the Caribbean – but again failed to nail the big score he needed to consolidate a Test place.

THE FACTS Simmons made 282 for West Indies A v England in St Kitts in January 2009 ... He made 200 (his maiden century) for Trinidad & Tobago v Jamaica in Tobago in February 2006, after being out for 0 in the first innings: in March 2011 he made 204 not out for T&T v Guyana at Providence ... His uncle, Phil Simmons, won 26 Test caps for West Indies between 1988 and 1997 ...

THE FIGURES *to 26.09.11*   ᴇsᴘɴcricinfo.com

Batting & Fielding	M	Inns	NO	Runs	HS	Avge	S/R	100	50	4s	6s	Ct	St
Tests	7	14	0	227	49	16.21	42.74	0	0	22	3	5	0
ODIs	29	28	3	764	77*	30.56	68.33	0	8	62	18	11	0
T20Is	10	10	1	261	77	29.00	123.11	0	2	34	3	4	0
First-class	77	135	10	4189	282	33.51	–	9	17	–	–	86	4

Bowling	M	Balls	Runs	Wkts	BB	Avge	RpO	S/R	5i	10m
Tests	7	192	147	1	1–60	147.00	4.59	192.00	0	0
ODIs	29	60	60	1	1–3	60.00	6.00	60.00	0	0
T20Is	10	36	55	6	4–19	9.16	9.16	6.00	0	0
First-class	77	852	503	13	3–6	38.69	3.54	65.53	0	0

RP SINGH

Full name	**Rudra Pratap Singh**
Born	**December 6, 1985, Rae Bareli, Uttar Pradesh**
Teams	**Uttar Pradesh, Kochi Tuskers Kerala**
Style	**Right-hand bat, left-arm fast-medium bowler**
Test debut	**India v Pakistan at Faisalabad 2005-06**
ODI debut	**India v Zimbabwe at Harare 2005-06**
T20I debut	**India v Scotland at Durban 2007-08**

THE PROFILE One of India's several left-arm seamers, Rudra Pratap Singh first caught the eye at the Under-19 World Cup in 2004, with some intelligent death bowling. After 34 Ranji Trophy wickets for Uttar Pradesh in 2004-05, Singh cracked the Indian one-day squad at the end of 2005, and took two wickets in his second over of international cricket, against Zimbabwe in September. He took four wickets (and the match award) against Sri Lanka in his third game, and three more in his fourth, before being dropped in May 2006 after four barren outings. He had also won the match award on his Test debut on a shirtfront at Faisalabad, where Pakistan ran up 588. He was overlooked for a while, but an early-season stint with Leicestershire paid off in 2007, as he forced his way into the side for the three-Test series in England. He took 5 for 59 in a tidy display of swing bowling at Lord's, knocking over Michael Vaughan in both innings. However, he lost his Test place after three wicketless matches in 2008. Singh was the leading wicket-taker in the second IPL in South Africa early in 2009, and remained in the 50-overs mix for a while, but he seemed to have gone for good when he was ignored after losing his one-day spot later in 2009. However, when injuries struck in England in 2011 "RP" was hustled back for the final Test – his first for three years – but, out of practice, he sent down an embarrassing opening over, and generally looked toothless as England set about completing their whitewash. He looked slightly more at home in the one-dayers that followed, taking 3 for 59 at Lord's.

THE FACTS RP Singh won the Man of the Match award on his Test debut – even though there were six centuries in the match, at Faisalabad in January 2006: Singh took 4 for 89 in Pakistan's first innings of 588 ... He averages 11.00 with the ball in ODIs against New Zealand, but 77.66 against West Indies ... Singh was the leading wicket-taker, with 23, in the second IPL, in South Africa early in 2009 ...

THE FIGURES to 26.09.11   **ESPNcricinfo.com**

Batting & Fielding	M	Inns	NO	Runs	HS	Avge	S/R	100	50	4s	6s	Ct	St
Tests	14	19	3	116	30	7.25	42.02	0	0	16	1	6	0
ODIs	58	20	10	104	23	10.40	42.97	0	0	5	1	13	0
T20Is	10	2	2	3	2*	–	100.00	0	0	0	0	2	0
First-class	63	86	17	692	47	10.02	–	0	0	–	–	28	0

Bowling	M	Balls	Runs	Wkts	BB	Avge	RpO	S/R	5i	10m
Tests	14	2534	1682	40	5–59	42.05	3.98	63.35	1	0
ODIs	58	2565	2343	69	4–35	33.95	5.48	37.17	0	0
T20Is	10	198	225	15	4–13	15.00	6.81	13.20	0	0
First-class	63	11866	6536	215	6–50	30.40	3.30	55.16	18	1

DEVON **SMITH**

Full name	**Devon Sheldon Smith**
Born	**Oct 21, 1981, Hermitage, Sauteurs, St Patrick, Grenada**
Teams	**Windward Islands**
Style	**Left-hand bat, occasional offspinner**
Test debut	**West Indies v Australia at Georgetown 2002-03**
ODI debut	**West Indies v Australia at Kingston 2002-03**
T20I debut	**West Indies v England at The Oval 2007**

THE PROFILE A belligerent left-handed opener whose eye makes up for a lack of footwork, Grenada's Devon Smith made 750 runs in the 2001-02 Busta Cup, and made his Test debut against Australia in Guyana the following year. Smith blazed 62 in his first Test, but bagged a pair in the next. Early in 2004 he dragged West Indies out of a hole with a stroke-filled century against England on the first day of the series at Kingston – but then fractured his thumb in the nets and missed the next two Tests, then was dropped after three failures in the return series in England. It became a similar refrain: he started the 2005-06 Australian tour well, making a hundred against Queensland then 88 in the first Test at Brisbane, but five single-figure scores followed, and the axe fell again. In one-dayers he was originally overshadowed by another Smith, the unrelated Dwayne, but both played in the 2007 World Cup, Devon making 61 in West Indies' last match, the thriller against England, which ensured him another English tour. He made several starts in the Tests there, crunching some classy cover-drives, but got out too often when set, making five scores between 16 and 42 before a double failure at The Oval. A maiden double-century for the Windwards Islands early in 2009 ensured his selection for the Tests against England that followed, but his best score in seven matches was just 55. He kept his name in the frame as captain of West Indies A, and scored a World Cup hundred against Ireland in 2011, but at international level he remains another underachiever in a West Indian side rather too full of them.

THE FACTS Smith made 212 for Windward Islands v Guyana at St George's in January 2009 ... Smith made 181 for West Indies A v Lancashire at Liverpool in July 2002 ... He was dismissed by Pakistan's Mohammad Hafeez in six successive international innings in 2011 (the record is eight, suffered by Ashwell Prince against Shane Warne) ... Smith's 33 Tests include 15 against England and nine against Australia ...

THE FIGURES *to 26.09.11*   ESPncricinfo.com

Batting & Fielding	M	Inns	NO	Runs	HS	Avge	S/R	100	50	4s	6s	Ct	St
Tests	33	58	2	1384	108	24.71	47.46	1	5	196	0	28	0
ODIs	42	40	2	1014	107	26.68	71.20	1	5	105	8	11	0
T20Is	6	6	0	203	61	33.83	126.08	0	2	22	5	1	0
First-class	132	234	9	8220	212	36.53	–	18	37	–	–	124	0

Bowling	M	Balls	Runs	Wkts	BB	Avge	RpO	S/R	5i	10m
Tests	33	6	3	0	–	–	3.00	–	0	0
ODIs	42	17	17	0	–	–	6.00	–	0	0
T20Is	6	0	–	–	–	–	–	–	–	–
First-class	132	444	218	2	1–2	109.00	2.94	222.00	0	0

GRAEME **SMITH**

SOUTH AFRICA

Full name	**Graeme Craig Smith**
Born	**February 1, 1981, Johannesburg, Transvaal**
Teams	**Cape Cobras, Pune Warriors**
Style	**Left-hand bat, occasional offspinner**
Test debut	**South Africa v Australia at Cape Town 2001-02**
ODI debut	**South Africa v Australia at Bloemfontein 2001-02**
T20I debut	**South Africa v New Zealand at Johannesburg 2005-06**

THE PROFILE In March 2003, Graeme Smith became South Africa's youngest captain at 22, when Shaun Pollock was dumped after a disastrous World Cup. A tall, aggressive left-hand opener, Smith had few leadership credentials – and only a handful of caps – but the selectors' faith was instantly justified: in England in 2003 he collected back-to-back double-centuries. Reality bit back the following year, with Test-series defeats in Sri Lanka and India. There was also a run of 11 losses in 12 ODIs, a mixed time in New Zealand, and the start of an ultimately fruitless series against England. Yet Smith continued to crunch runs aplenty: his 125 to square the New Zealand series was a minor epic. He yields to no-one physically, but can be subdued by more insidious means: by the end of 2004, as Matthew Hoggard's inswinger had him frequently fumbling around his front pad, even the runs started to dry up. But he roared back in the Caribbean in 2005, with hundreds in three successive Tests. A baton-charge to 85 squared the home Test series against West Indies at the start of 2008, and later that year Smith achieved what he narrowly missed in 2003 – winning a Test series in England, his unbeaten 154 in a stiff run-chase at Edgbaston being one of the great captain's innings. In 2008-09 he presided over South Africa's first Test-series victory in Australia, although his own contribution to that and the return rubber was hampered by two hand fractures courtesy of Mitchell Johnson. He stood down as one-day captain after a subdued time at the 2011 World Cup, but remains firmly at the helm in Tests.

THE FACTS In the first Test against England in 2003 Smith scored 277 at Birmingham, the highest score by a South African in Tests: in the second he made 259, the highest Test score by a visiting player at Lord's, beating Don Bradman's 254 in 1930 ... He averages 69.26 in Tests against West Indies, but only 32.73 against Australia ... Smith played four matches for Somerset in 2005, scoring 311 against Leicestershire in one of them ... His record includes one Test for the World XI (as captain) and one ODI for the Africa XI ...

THE FIGURES *to 26.09.11*   **ESPNcricinfo.com**

Batting & Fielding	M	Inns	NO	Runs	HS	Avge	S/R	100	50	4s	6s	Ct	St
Tests	91	159	9	7457	277	49.71	60.15	22	29	953	22	119	0
ODIs	172	170	10	6280	141	39.25	81.85	8	43	722	38	94	0
T20Is	31	31	2	958	89*	33.03	129.11	0	5	122	25	18	0
First-class	129	223	14	10644	311	50.92	–	31	39	–	–	174	0

Bowling	M	Balls	Runs	Wkts	BB	Avge	RpO	S/R	5i	10m
Tests	91	1346	832	8	2–145	104.00	3.70	168.25	0	0
ODIs	172	1026	951	18	3–30	52.83	5.56	57.00	0	0
T20Is	31	24	57	0	–	–	14.25	–	0	0
First-class	129	1714	1079	11	2–145	98.09	3.77	155.81	0	0

STEVEN **SMITH**

Full name **Steven Peter Devereux Smith**
Born **June 2, 1989, Sydney**
Teams **New South Wales**
Style **Right-hand bat, legspinner**
Test debut **Australia v Pakistan at Lord's 2010**
ODI debut **Australia v West Indies at Melbourne 2009-10**
T20I debut **Australia v Pakistan at Melbourne 2009-10**

THE PROFILE Steven Smith is a promising young spinner, and also a fine batsman who could eventually slot into the top six, whether his legspin (unsurprisingly less threatening than Shane Warne's at the moment) trains on or not. By the time he was 21 Smith was in all of Australia's senior squads. There were words of caution about his early elevation, but there was no hiding the excitement about a player who gives the ball air, hits it hard, catches it well, and seems unbothered by pressure. Smith became an international player in 2009-10 after starring with New South Wales, striking four Sheffield Shield centuries and finishing the season with career-best figures of 7 for 64. After only 13 first-class matches he was picked for the Test tour of New Zealand, but didn't get to play. He had already been tried in the limited-overs sides, impressing with his attitude, and was used more as a legspinner than a batsman. Two for 78 in his first one-dayer against West Indies doesn't sound very special, but he convinced Ricky Ponting to keep the field up to build pressure: not many 20-year-olds – Smith looks even younger – win arguments like that. His maiden Test series, against Pakistan in England in 2010, was encouraging: there were three wickets in the two games, and a muscular 77 at Headingley. But then he played three Tests in the 2010-11 Ashes without achieving much, and was similarly anonymous in the World Cup, although his fielding stood out. Smith started his state career in 2007-08, making his biggest impact in the Twenty20 Big Bash, in which he took nine wickets at the remarkable average of 5.33.

THE FACTS Smith's first four first-class hundreds – including his highest of 177 for NSW v Tasmania at Hobart – came during the 2009-10 Australian season ... He took 7 for 64 for NSW v South Australia at Adelaide in March 2010, after scoring 100 in the first innings ... Smith played in the Under-19 World Cup in 2008, alongside Phillip Hughes and Josh Hazlewood ...

THE FIGURES to 26.09.11   **ESPN**cricinfo.com

Batting & Fielding	M	Inns	NO	Runs	HS	Avge	S/R	100	50	4s	6s	Ct	St
Tests	5	10	1	259	77	28.77	56.79	0	2	27	2	3	0
ODIs	27	18	4	317	46*	22.64	89.29	0	0	24	3	13	0
T20Is	18	13	3	148	34	14.80	109.62	0	0	11	3	16	0
First-class	23	42	6	1516	177	42.11	60.30	4	6	185	18	28	0

Bowling	M	Balls	Runs	Wkts	BB	Avge	RpO	S/R	5i	10m
Tests	5	372	220	3	3–51	73.33	3.54	124.00	0	0
ODIs	27	827	731	21	3–33	34.80	5.30	39.38	0	0
T20Is	18	285	373	17	3–20	21.94	7.85	16.76	0	0
First-class	23	2988	1975	41	7–64	48.17	3.96	72.87	1	0

TIM **SOUTHEE**

NEW ZEALAND

Full name	**Timothy Grant Southee**
Born	**December 11, 1988, Whangarei**
Teams	**Northern Districts, Essex, Chennai Super Kings**
Style	**Right-hand bat, right-arm fast-medium bowler**
Test debut	**New Zealand v England at Napier 2007-08**
ODI debut	**New Zealand v England at Chester-le-Street 2008**
T20I debut	**New Zealand v England at Auckland 2007-08**

THE PROFILE Few players have made such a remarkable Test debut as 19-year-old Tim Southee in March 2008. First, swinging the ball at a healthy pace, he took 5 for 55 as England were restricted to 253, his victims including Andrew Strauss for 0 and Kevin Pietersen for 129. Later, with New Zealand in a hopeless position, he strolled in and smashed 77 not out from just 40 balls, with nine sixes, five of them off an unamused Monty Panesar. His second Test, at Lord's in May 2008, was rather more mundane – one run, no wickets – then he fell ill. Later that year he shook up the Aussies with three wickets in his first four overs at Brisbane, but leaner times almost inevitably followed, and he was sidelined after ten expensive overs in a one-dayer against India in March 2009. But he was obviously one to watch, and although Test success has proved elusive he has become a consistent one-day wicket-taker: as New Zealand marched to the semi-finals of the 2011 World Cup Southee took 18 wickets, a number exceeded only by Shahid Afridi and Zaheer Khan (21 apiece). Southee made his first-class debut for Northern Districts at 18 in February 2007, and the following season claimed 6 for 68 in a particularly impressive effort against Auckland. He was chosen for the Under-19 World Cup, but had to interrupt his preparations when he was drafted into the senior set-up for the Twenty20 games against England early in 2008. He ended the Under-19 World Cup as the second-highest wicket-taker, with 17, and was named Player of the Tournament. After that he barely had time to unpack before the Test call came.

THE FACTS Southee hit nine sixes in his first Test innings, a number only ever exceeded by four players, none of whom was making his debut: he had earlier become only the sixth New Zealander to take a five-for on Test debut ... He conceded 105 runs in ten overs against India at Christchurch in March 2009, a number exceeded in ODIs only by Australia's Mick Lewis, with 113 v South Africa at Johannesburg in 2005-06 ... Southee took 8 for 27 from 25 overs for Northern Districts v Wellington at Hamilton in November 2009 ...

THE FIGURES to 26.09.11   ☰☰☰ cricinfo.com

Batting & Fielding	M	Inns	NO	Runs	HS	Avge	S/R	100	50	4s	6s	Ct	St
Tests	13	22	4	385	77*	21.38	80.37	0	2	34	22	4	0
ODIs	51	27	8	162	32	8.52	85.26	0	0	9	7	8	0
T20Is	19	7	2	25	12*	5.00	89.28	0	0	2	1	7	0
First-class	35	47	7	662	77*	16.55	71.56	0	3	59	30	8	0

Bowling	M	Balls	Runs	Wkts	BB	Avge	RpO	S/R	5i	10m
Tests	13	2599	1489	35	5–55	42.54	3.43	74.25	1	0
ODIs	51	2466	2152	70	5–33	30.74	5.23	35.22	1	0
T20Is	19	402	570	22	5–18	25.90	8.50	18.27	1	0
First-class	35	7055	3570	116	8–27	30.77	3.03	60.81	5	0

SREESANTH

Full name	**Shanthakumaran Sreesanth**
Born	**February 6, 1983, Kothamangalam, Kerala**
Teams	**Kerala, Kochi Tuskers Kerala**
Style	**Right-hand bat, right-arm fast-medium bowler**
Test debut	**India v England at Nagpur 2005-06**
ODI debut	**India v Sri Lanka at Nagpur 2005-06**
T20I debut	**India v South Africa at Johannesburg 2006-07**

THE PROFILE For three seasons, Sreesanth was little more than a quiz question, as the only Kerala bowler to take a Ranji Trophy hat-trick. He started as a legspinner, idolising Anil Kumble, then once he turned to pace his rise was rapid although, since he played for a weak side, almost unnoticed. Not many bowlers play in the Duleep Trophy in their first season, but Sreesanth did, after taking 22 wickets in his first seven games in 2002-03. A couple of years later, now equipped with a more side-on action and increased pace, a superb display at the Challenger Trophy (trial matches for the national squad) propelled him into the side for the Sri Lanka series. Later he snapped up 6 for 55 against England, still the best one-day figures by an Indian fast bowler at home. Idiosyncratic, with an aggressive approach – to the stumps and the game – he can be expensive, but is also a wicket-taking bowler: in Antigua in June 2006 he fired out Ramnaresh Sarwan and Brian Lara (both for 0) in successive overs. He sometimes rubs opponents up the wrong way, but there is talent among the tantrums: Sreesanth took 19 wickets in the inaugural IPL in 2007-08, although his international form tailed off a little. A back injury in the second IPL didn't help, then more injuries – thigh and knee this time – disrupted the first half of 2010, while the emergence of the tall Abhimanyu Mithun further threatened Sreesanth's Test place. He played in the first and last matches of the 2011 World Cup – failing to take a wicket in either – and was inconsistent on the England tour that followed, disappointing his many fans (and further upsetting his many critics).

THE FACTS Sreesanth took a hat-trick for Kerala v Himachal Pradesh in the Ranji Trophy in November 2004 ... He is only the second Indian Test player from Kerala, after Tinu Yohannan, another fast-medium bowler ... Sreesanth did not score a run in ODIs until his 16th match, although that was only his fourth innings ... He took 19 wickets in the first IPL season in 2008, the same as Shane Warne and exceeded only by Sohail Tanvir (22) ...

THE FIGURES to 26.09.11   **ESPNcricInfo.com**

Batting & Fielding	M	Inns	NO	Runs	HS	Avge	S/R	100	50	4s	6s	Ct	St
Tests	27	40	13	281	35	10.40	52.13	0	0	38	4	5	0
ODIs	53	21	10	44	10*	4.00	36.36	0	0	2	0	7	0
T20Is	10	3	2	20	19*	20.00	142.85	0	0	4	0	2	0
First-class	68	92	28	592	35	9.25	44.27	0	0	–	–	14	0

Bowling	M	Balls	Runs	Wkts	BB	Avge	RpO	S/R	5i	10m
Tests	27	5419	3271	87	5–40	37.59	3.62	62.28	3	0
ODIs	53	2476	2508	75	6–55	33.44	6.07	33.01	1	0
T20Is	10	204	288	7	2–12	41.14	8.47	29.14	0	0
First-class	68	12198	7132	200	5–40	35.66	3.50	60.99	6	0

DALE **STEYN**

SOUTH AFRICA

Full name	**Dale Willem Steyn**
Born	**June 27, 1983, Phalaborwa, Limpopo Province**
Teams	**Titans, Deccan Chargers**
Style	**Right-hand bat, right-arm fast bowler**
Test debut	**South Africa v England at Port Elizabeth 2004-05**
ODI debut	**Africa XI v Asia XI at Centurion 2005-06**
T20I debut	**South Africa v New Zealand at Johannesburg 2007-08**

THE PROFILE Dale Steyn's rise to the South African side was as rapid as his bowling: he was picked for his first Test little more than a year after his first-class debut. A rare first-class cricketer from the Limpopo province close to the Kruger National Park and the Zimbabwe border, Steyn is genuinely fast, and moves the ball away. He played three Tests against England in 2004-05 before returning to domestic cricket, but was recalled in April 2006 and claimed 5 for 47 as New Zealand were routed at Centurion. He had half a season of county cricket with Essex in 2005, and rattled a few helmets for Warwickshire in 2007. But Steyn really came of age in 2007-08, taking 40 wickets in five home Tests against New Zealand and West Indies, then 14 on Bangladesh's traditionally slow tracks. Finally he blew India away with 5 for 23 as they subsided to 76 all out and defeat at Ahmedabad. After a subdued time in England in 2008 – he broke his thumb and missed the last two Tests – Steyn claimed 34 victims in the home-and-away series against Australia, including ten wickets – and a rollicking 76 during a match-turning stand of 180 with J-P Duminy – in the Melbourne win that sealed South Africa's first-ever series win Down Under. He had a quiet 2009, but roared back the following year: after 13 wickets in the last two Tests against England in January, his 7 for 51 helped sink India at Nagpur, then 15 wickets in the Caribbean helped seal a 2-0 series win. Steyn rounded off the year with 21 wickets against India, and had roared past 200 Test wickets at an almost unprecedented strike-rate.

THE FACTS Steyn's strike-rate in Tests has been bettered only by the 19th-century bowlers George Lohmann (34.19 balls per wicket) and John Ferris (37.73), and Shane Bond of New Zealand (38.75) ... Steyn took 8 for 41 (14 for 110 in the match) for Titans v Eagles at Bloemfontein in December 2007 ... He took 10 for 93 and 10 for 91 in successive home Tests against New Zealand in November 2007 ... Steyn made his ODI debut for the Africa XI, and his record includes two matches for them ...

THE FIGURES *to 26.09.11*   **ᴇsᴘɴcricinfo.com**

Batting & Fielding	M	Inns	NO	Runs	HS	Avge	S/R	100	50	4s	6s	Ct	St
Tests	46	58	13	620	76	13.77	42.87	0	1	61	14	13	0
ODIs	54	21	6	136	35	9.06	74.72	0	0	8	4	11	0
T20Is	21	4	2	8	5	4.00	80.00	0	0	0	0	8	0
First-class	87	104	25	1124	82	14.22	49.06	0	3	–	–	19	0

Bowling	M	Balls	Runs	Wkts	BB	Avge	RpO	S/R	5i	10m
Tests	46	9515	5526	238	7–51	23.21	3.48	39.97	16	4
ODIs	54	2627	2238	81	5–50	27.62	5.11	32.43	1	0
T20Is	21	468	531	29	4–9	18.31	6.80	16.13	0	0
First-class	87	16965	9520	392	8–41	24.28	3.36	43.27	24	6

BEN **STOKES**

Full name	**Benjamin Andrew Stokes**
Born	**June 4, 1991, Christchurch, New Zealand**
Teams	**Durham**
Style	**Left-hand bat, right-arm medium-pace bowler**
Test debut	**No Tests yet**
ODI debut	**England v Ireland at Dublin 2011**
T20I debut	**England v West Indies at The Oval 2011**

THE PROFILE Ben Stokes, a well-built youngster with a distinctive mop of bright red hair, was only 18 when he signed for Durham in December 2009. A true allrounder, he had been developing in their academy for some time, and had already made his one-day debut earlier that summer, snaring Mark Ramprakash with his third legal delivery in senior cricket. From there he enjoyed a productive time at the Under-19 World Cup, scoring a century against India, before making 51 on his first-class debut in the pink-ball season opener against MCC in Abu Dhabi: in his sixth match he hit 161 not out against Kent, whose captain Rob Key called him the best young player he had ever seen. Stokes clearly enjoyed his first full Championship season, scoring 740 runs at 46.25, but it was in 2011 that he really began to blossom. In April he took 6 for 68 against Hampshire, then added a brilliant hundred that included five sixes in one Liam Dawson over, and little more than a month later extended his maiden limited-overs hundred to a blazing 150 not out in a CB40 match against Warwickshire. A broken finger hindered his bowling, but he played for England Lions, and then made his full one-day international debut in Dublin. Sterner challenges followed against India, although the weather didn't help his chances of making an impression. But he looks set to have a long run in the one-day side – and may even crack Test cricket soon too. He was born in New Zealand, but came to England in 2003 when his father Ged – who played rugby league for the Kiwis – was appointed coach of Workington's rugby league side.

THE FACTS Stokes hit 150 not out (with seven sixes) in a 40-over game for Durham against Warwickshire at Edgbaston in May 2011 ... The following week he made 185 against Lancashire at Chester-le-Street, sharing a stand of 331 with Dale Benkenstein ... Against Hampshire at Southampton in April 2011 his unbeaten 135 included five successive sixes off Liam Dawson: earlier in the match he took three wickets in an over on the way to career-best figures of 6 for 68 ...

THE FIGURES to 26.09.11   **ESPncricinfo.com**

Batting & Fielding	M	Inns	NO	Runs	HS	Avge	S/R	100	50	4s	6s	Ct	St
Tests	0	0	–	–	–	–	–	–	–	–	–	–	–
ODIs	5	3	0	30	20	10.00	57.69	0	0	1	1	3	0
T20Is	2	1	0	31	31	31.00	134.78	0	0	3	1	0	0
First-class	28	42	5	1615	185	43.64	–	5	6	–	–	17	0

Bowling	M	Balls	Runs	Wkts	BB	Avge	RpO	S/R	5i	10m
Tests	0	0	–	–	–	–	–	–	–	–
ODIs	5	0	–	–	–	–	–	–	–	–
T20Is	2	0	–	–	–	–	–	–	–	–
First-class	28	1398	1046	28	6–68	37.35	4.48	49.92	1	0

ANDREW **STRAUSS**

ENGLAND

Full name	**Andrew John Strauss**
Born	**March 2, 1977, Johannesburg, South Africa**
Teams	**Middlesex**
Style	**Left-hand bat**
Test debut	**England v New Zealand at Lord's 2004**
ODI debut	**England v Sri Lanka at Dambulla 2003-04**
T20I debut	**England v Australia at Southampton 2005**

THE PROFILE A compact left-hander with a preference for pummelling the ball square off the back foot with a crunching cut, Andrew Strauss has worked out a superb technique for Test cricket. He put early problems against Shane Warne behind him to make two hundreds in the epic 2005 Ashes, and added 161 in 2009 to set up England's first victory over Australia at Lord's for 75 years. Calm and urbane, Strauss put the disappointment of being passed over for the 2006-07 Ashes captaincy to bounce back in 2009 and orchestrate the urn's recapture, before presiding over the sensational series victory in 2010-11. His early cricket with Middlesex did not exactly suggest a star in the making, but a 2003 century against Lancashire, with Andrew Flintoff charging in, got the selectors sniffing. After a few one-day caps Strauss was called up against New Zealand in 2004 when Michael Vaughan twisted his knee in the Lord's nets. He responded with a confident century, and was unlucky to miss another in the second innings when Nasser Hussain ran him out. But Hussain had seen enough: with Vaughan set to return, he announced his retirement, confident that Strauss was the real deal. Strauss has been emphasising that almost ever since, responding to being dropped from the one-day team by upping his strike rate, and probably saving his Test career after a poor run with 177 against New Zealand early in 2008. After an early flirtation with captaincy in 2006, when Vaughan and Flintoff were injured, Strauss inherited the armband again early in 2009, after the messy sacking of Kevin Pietersen. It was not a good way to start – but Strauss has hardly put a foot wrong since.

THE FACTS Strauss was the 15th England player to score a century on Test debut ... In July 2006 he became only the third man to make a century on debut as England captain... Strauss has made three of England's five 150-plus scores in ODIs, including 158 v India in the 2011 World Cup, shortly before announcing his retirement from one-dayers ... England never lost a Test in which Strauss scored a century, until he made two at Chennai in December 2008 but India won by six wickets ...

THE FIGURES *to 26.09.11*   **cricinfo.com**

Batting & Fielding	M	Inns	NO	Runs	HS	Avge	S/R	100	50	4s	6s	Ct	St
Tests	89	157	6	6340	177	41.98	49.63	19	25	785	10	107	0
ODIs	127	126	8	4205	158	35.63	80.94	6	27	454	25	57	0
T20Is	4	4	0	73	33	18.25	114.06	0	0	9	0	1	0
First-class	222	390	23	15772	241*	42.97	–	42	69	–	–	205	0

Bowling	M	Balls	Runs	Wkts	BB	Avge	RpO	S/R	5i	10m
Tests	89	0	–	–	–	–	–	–	–	–
ODIs	127	6	3	0	–	–	3.00	–	0	0
T20Is	4	0	–	–	–	–	–	–	–	–
First-class	222	132	142	3	1–16	47.33	6.45	44.00	0	0

174

GRAEME **SWANN**

Full name	**Graeme Peter Swann**
Born	**March 24, 1979, Northampton**
Teams	**Nottinghamshire**
Style	**Right-hand bat, offspinner**
Test debut	**England v India at Chennai 2008-09**
ODI debut	**England v South Africa at Bloemfontein 1999-2000**
T20I debut	**England v New Zealand at Auckland 2007-08**

THE PROFILE Self-confident and gregarious, Graeme Swann is an aggressive offspinner, not afraid to give the ball a real tweak, and also a hard-hitting lower-order batsman. He claimed a place in the revamped England squad which toured South Africa in 1999-2000 under new coach Duncan Fletcher, but Swann found life outside the Test side frustrating, although he bravely continued to give the ball a rip. However, he was less impressive off the field – what some saw as confidence, others interpreted as arrogance or cheek – and slid out of the reckoning. After marking time with Northamptonshire for a while, not helped by Monty Panesar's rise, Swann moved to Nottinghamshire in 2005 – a decision immediately justified when he helped them win the Championship. He was recalled for the Sri Lankan tour late in 2007, and took 4 for 34 in a one-day win at Dambulla, but he was soon on the outer again. However, with Panesar in something of a slump, Swann finally won his first Test cap in India in December 2008, making up for lost time by dismissing Gambhir and Dravid in his first over. He soon developed a reputation for troubling left-handers: over half his 153 Test wickets to date have been lefties, an unprecedented percentage. He also continued his enviable knack of taking wickets in the first over of a spell. Swann was underwhelming in the 2009 Ashes, but after that he blossomed, playing his part in the stunning 2010-11 victory Down Under with 5 for 91 at Adelaide, and spinning England to their 2011 whitewash over India with nine wickets at The Oval. By then he was ranked the No. 3 bowler in the world in Tests – and top in ODIs.

THE FACTS Swann took two wickets in his first over in Test cricket: the only other bowler ever to do this was England's Richard Johnson (against Zimbabwe at Chester-le-Street in 2003) ... Some 52% of Swann's Test wickets have been left-handers, an unprecedented percentage: Mohammad Aamer (48%) is next of bowlers with more than 50 wickets ... Swann took 7 for 33 for Northamptonshire v Derbyshire in June 2003 ... He made 183 for Northants v Gloucestershire at Bristol in August 2002...

THE FIGURES to 26.09.11   **ESPNcricinfo.com**

Batting & Fielding	M	Inns	NO	Runs	HS	Avge	S/R	100	50	4s	6s	Ct	St
Tests	36	40	6	800	85	23.52	81.71	0	4	98	10	32	0
ODIs	60	40	10	430	34	14.33	89.21	0	0	38	3	23	0
T20Is	26	11	8	48	15*	16.00	111.62	0	0	2	0	2	0
First-class	216	291	24	6991	183	26.18	–	4	35	–	–	163	0

Bowling	M	Balls	Runs	Wkts	BB	Avge	RpO	S/R	5i	10m
Tests	36	8903	4410	153	6–65	28.82	2.97	58.18	11	1
ODIs	60	2838	2098	88	5–28	23.84	4.43	32.25	1	0
T20Is	26	534	586	34	3–14	17.23	6.58	15.70	0	0
First-class	216	38801	19390	605	7–33	32.04	2.99	64.13	26	4

TATENDA **TAIBU**

Full name	**Tatenda Taibu**
Born	**May 14, 1983, Harare**
Teams	**Southern Rocks**
Style	**Right-hand bat, wicketkeeper**
Test debut	**Zimbabwe v West Indies at Bulawayo 2001**
ODI debut	**Zimbabwe v West Indies at Harare 2001**
T20I debut	**Zimbabwe v Australia at Cape Town 2007-08**

THE PROFILE Diminutive and light on his feet, Tatenda Taibu is a throwback to the traditional style of wicketkeeper, and he has also become one of Zimbabwe's most dependable batsmen. He was vice-captain in England in 2003, when only 19, and the following year became the youngest Test captain of all time, being a week short of his 21st birthday when he skippered against Sri Lanka. Taibu was plucked from Churchill High School to tour the West Indies and England early in 2000, after impressing the selectors with his natural ability. He had not then played any domestic first-class cricket – his debut for Mashonaland had to be put on hold after he went to the wrong ground – but he was one of Zimbabwe's few bright spots in the 2003 World Cup and the subsequent England tour. In April 2004, he inherited the captaincy when Heath Streak resigned during a damaging dispute, and led a woefully inexperienced side by example in the face of repeated heavy defeats before Zimbabwe withdrew from Test cricket. Taibu had his own battles with authority, briefly threatening to settle in South Africa, but his class meant that he could not be ignored when he returned home. He reclaimed his place in the national side – although not as captain – in August 2007, and hit an ODI century against South Africa in his third match back; he made another ton against them two years later, and has remained a consistent scorer ever since. He made 23 and 59 in Zimbabwe's comeback Test, the victory over Bangladesh in August 2011, and added 44 and 58 in the next Test, against Pakistan, to underline his consistency and value to the side.

THE FACTS Taibu was the youngest Test captain in history – 20 years and 358 days when he skippered against Sri Lanka at Harare in May 2004 ... In his first Test as captain, he took off the pads and took the first wicket to fall, ending an opening stand of 281 by dismissing Sanath Jayasuriya ... For Mashonaland against Midlands at Kwekwe in 2003-04 Taibu scored a career-best 175 not out (after bagging a pair in the previous game) and then took 8 for 43 ... His record includes one ODI for the African XI ...

THE FIGURES to 26.09.11   **ESPICricinfo.com**

Batting & Fielding	M	Inns	NO	Runs	HS	Avge	S/R	100	50	4s	6s	Ct	St
Tests	26	50	3	1457	153	31.00	41.73	1	11	173	6	54	4
ODIs	144	131	21	3238	107*	29.43	67.43	2	20	227	30	113	32
T20Is	15	14	6	232	45*	29.00	99.57	0	0	16	2	6	5
First-class	111	192	20	6694	175*	38.91	–	12	38	–	–	291	29

Bowling	M	Balls	Runs	Wkts	BB	Avge	RpO	S/R	5i	10m
Tests	26	48	27	1	1–27	27.00	3.37	48.00	0	0
ODIs	144	84	61	2	2–42	30.50	4.35	42.00	0	0
T20Is	15	24	41	0	–	–	10.25	–	0	0
First-class	111	924	431	22	8–43	19.59	2.79	42.00	1	0

TAMIM IQBAL

Full name	**Tamim Iqbal Khan**
Born	**March 20, 1989, Chittagong**
Teams	**Chittagong, Nottinghamshire**
Style	**Left-hand bat**
Test debut	**Bangladesh v New Zealand at Dunedin 2007-08**
ODI debut	**Bangladesh v Zimbabwe at Harare 2006-07**
T20I debut	**Bangladesh v Kenya at Nairobi 2007-08**

THE PROFILE A flamboyant left-hander, Tamim Iqbal is particularly strong square of the wicket, and has a good flick shot. Selected for the 2007 World Cup after just four ODIs, he ignited the competition with 51 off 53 balls to ensure Bangladesh's reply to India's modest 191 got off to a flying start. Shrugging off a blow on the neck when he mishooked Zaheer Khan, Tamim jumped down the track and smashed him over midwicket for six ... all this three days before his 18th birthday. He struggled to reproduce this form afterwards: it wasn't until his 18th ODI, in July 2007, that he reached 50 again. But the following year he made a hundred against Ireland, then in August 2009 rounded off a consistent run by hammering 154 – a national one-day record – against Zimbabwe. It was a similar story in Tests: great start (53 and 84 v New Zealand), quieter phase (17 innings with a best of 47), exciting flowering (128 as West Indies were beaten in St Vincent in July 2009). And by 2010 Tamim was clearly Bangladesh's star batsman: a superb 151 forced India to bat again despite amassing 554 at Mirpur in January, then twin eighties at home against England were followed by centuries in both Tests of the return series, at Lord's and Old Trafford. He was rewarded by becoming the first Bangladeshi to be named as one of *Wisden's* Five Cricketers of the Year. Tamim started the 2011 World Cup with another cameo against India, although this time his 70 could not bring victory. He continued to fire fitfully (including during a Twenty20 stint with Nottinghamshire) but the opposition's celebrations whenever he departs cheaply speak volumes for the danger he poses.

THE FACTS Tamim Iqbal hit 154, Bangladesh's highest score in ODIs, against Zimbabwe at Bulawayo in August 2009 ... He scored 53 and 84 on his Test debut, against New Zealand in Dunedin in January 2008 ... Only Sachin Tendulkar and Mohammad Ashraful reached 1000 Test runs at a younger age than Tamim (a week short of his 21st birthday in 2010) ... His brother, Nafees Iqbal, played 11 Tests and 16 ODIs for Bangladesh, while their uncle, Akram Khan, played eight Tests and 44 ODIs ...

THE FIGURES *to 26.09.11*   ᴇꜱᴘᴎcricinfo.com

Batting & Fielding	M	Inns	NO	Runs	HS	Avge	S/R	100	50	4s	6s	Ct	St
Tests	20	38	0	1503	151	39.55	61.87	4	8	210	10	8	0
ODIs	103	103	0	3053	154	29.64	79.81	3	19	345	44	29	0
T20Is	14	14	0	193	32	13.78	93.68	0	0	29	0	2	0
First-class	41	75	1	2986	151	40.35	–	6	20	–	–	20	0

Bowling	M	Balls	Runs	Wkts	BB	Avge	RpO	S/R	5i	10m
Tests	20	24	10	0	–	–	2.50	–	0	0
ODIs	103	6	13	0	–	–	13.00	–	0	0
T20Is	14	0	–	–	–	–	–	–	–	–
First-class	41	132	77	0	–	–	3.50	–	0	0

TANVIR AHMED

Full name	**Tanvir Ahmed**
Born	**December 20, 1978, Kuwait City, Kuwait**
Teams	**Karachi, Sind**
Style	**Right-hand bat, right-arm fast-medium bowler**
Test debut	**Pakistan v South Africa at Abu Dhabi 2010-11**
ODI debut	**Pakistan v West Indies at Bridgetown 2010-11**
T20I debut	**Pakistan v New Zealand at Christchurch 2010-11**

THE PROFILE Tanvir Ahmed had to stand in line for a Test cap. A fast-medium bowler who was born in Kuwait (his father was working there at the time), Tanvir has played for numerous teams in Pakistan, most of them based around Karachi. He first made a mark in 2001-02 with 75 wickets, but did not pass 50 in the following seven seasons. International cricket seemed to have passed him by, but in 2009-10 – by now in his thirties – Tanvir rocketed into contention by topping the domestic wicket-taking lists with 97 at 20.22 apiece. That included 8 for 53 and 5 for 86 for Karachi Blues against Abbottabad, and ten wickets in each of the next two matches as well. "Tanvir's biggest asset is his perseverance," said the former Pakistan captain Rashid Latif. "He pitches the ball up compared to other Pakistani bowlers who bowl short." He could no longer be ignored, and was thrilled when he was selected to tour England in 2010. But he hardly played: his only bowl came in a two-day game against Leicestershire. However, when the new-ball pair Mohammad Asif and Mohammad Aamer were banned after the spot-fixing scandal, Tanvir was finally given a chance. He made his Test debut in Abu Dhabi in November 2010, and made up for lost time by dismissing Alviro Petersen with his third ball. He soon had 3 for 19 – but, with AB de Villiers making 278, South Africa recovered to 584: Tanvir finished with 6 for 120, still a fine effort. He kept his name in the frame by taking eight wickets in two Tests in New Zealand, then hitting an important 57 in victory over West Indies in May 2011.

THE FACTS Tanvir Ahmed was only the second Test cricketer born in Kuwait: Shakeel Ahmed, a left-arm spinner, played one Test for Pakistan, against Australia at Karachi in October 1998 ... Tanvir took the wicket of South Africa's Alviro Petersen with his third ball in a Test, and dismissed Jesse Ryder of New Zealand with his fourth delivery in T20Is ... He took 8 for 53 (13 for 139 in the match) for Karachi Blues at Abbottabad in October 2009 ...

THE FIGURES to 26.09.11   **ESPNcricinfo.com**

Batting & Fielding	M	Inns	NO	Runs	HS	Avge	S/R	100	50	4s	6s	Ct	St
Tests	4	5	1	116	57	29.00	61.70	0	1	21	0	1	0
ODIs	2	1	0	18	18	18.00	150.00	0	0	1	2	1	0
T20Is	1	0	–	–	–	–	–	–	–	–	–	0	0
First-class	108	165	24	2952	90	20.93	–	0	14	–	–	34	0

Bowling	M	Balls	Runs	Wkts	BB	Avge	RpO	S/R	5i	10m
Tests	4	617	393	16	6–120	24.56	3.82	38.56	1	0
ODIs	2	60	83	2	1–38	41.50	8.30	30.00	0	0
T20Is	1	18	13	1	1–13	13.00	4.33	18.00	0	0
First-class	108	20271	11828	421	8–53	28.09	3.50	48.14	24	7

TAUFEEQ UMAR

Full name **Taufeeq Umar**
Born **June 20, 1981, Lahore**
Teams **Lahore, Habib Bank**
Style **Left-hand bat, occasional offspinner**
Test debut **Pakistan v Bangladesh at Multan 2001**
ODI debut **Pakistan v Sri Lanka at Sharjah 2001-02**
T20I debut **No T20Is yet**

THE PROFILE A front-foot player who drives well, the left-hand opener Taufeeq Umar is nonetheless a good cutter. He could not have asked for an easier initiation into international cricket: he started against Bangladesh, and duly notched up a hundred, the eighth Pakistani to score a century on Test debut. But far more impressive were his subsequent performances – 88 against a top-class Australian attack was followed by a flawless 135 against South Africa at Cape Town. On those bouncy pitches, Taufeeq had ample time to play the seamers. He did not get much opportunity in the 2003 World Cup, but proved himself an asset in the home series against South Africa shortly afterwards, with a hundred and three fifties in his four innings. But he was axed a few Tests later after a moderate run, then was in and out – more out – of the team. When he was given a chance, he looked understandably nervous ... but given that Pakistan's openers these days are rarely allowed to settle, the door remained ajar. He seemed to have been dumped for good after a double failure in the 2006 Headingley Test, but was recalled late in 2010, after the disastrous England tour, and initially did well in Tests against South Africa and New Zealand. But after three low scores in the West Indies his international future was on the line – then he was let off twice in the second innings at St Kitts, and went on to make 135, his first Test hundred for more than seven years. Taufeeq seemed to be back ... but then he made only 4 and 8 in the one-off Test against Zimbabwe in September, and had to start looking over his shoulder again.

THE FACTS Taufeeq Umar was the eighth batsman to score a century on Test debut for Pakistan, with 104 against Bangladesh at Multan in August 2001 ... His fifth Test century (against West Indies in May 2011) came more than seven years after his fourth (in October 2003): only Mushtaq Mohammad, with almost nine years between 1962 and 1971, has a longer gap between Test hundreds for Pakistan ...

THE FIGURES to 26.09.11   ᴇꜱᴘᴨcricinfo.com

Batting & Fielding	M	Inns	NO	Runs	HS	Avge	S/R	100	50	4s	6s	Ct	St
Tests	32	60	3	2179	135	38.22	44.12	5	11	310	3	42	0
ODIs	22	22	1	504	81*	24.00	56.31	0	3	51	2	9	0
T20Is	0	0	–	–	–	–	–	–	–	–	–	0	0
First-class	122	210	11	7650	176	38.44	–	16	41	–	–	126	0

Bowling	M	Balls	Runs	Wkts	BB	Avge	RpO	S/R	5i	10m
Tests	32	78	44	0	–	–	3.38	–	0	0
ODIs	22	72	85	1	1–49	85.00	7.08	72.00	0	0
T20Is	0	0	–	–	–	–	–	–	–	–
First-class	122	844	463	13	3–33	35.61	3.29	64.92	0	0

179

BRENDAN **TAYLOR**

Full name	**Brendan Ross Murray Taylor**
Born	**February 6, 1986, Harare**
Teams	**Mid West Rhinos**
Style	**Right-hand bat, occasional wicketkeeper**
Test debut	**Zimbabwe v Sri Lanka at Harare 2004**
ODI debut	**Zimbabwe v Sri Lanka at Bulawayo 2004**
T20I debut	**Zimbabwe v Bangladesh at Khulna 2006-07**

THE PROFILE Brendan Taylor was fast-tracked into the national team at the age of 18 after the withdrawal of several senior players. He shot to international prominence at Cape Town on September 12, 2007, when his ice-cool 60 not out carried Zimbabwe to victory over Australia in the inaugural World Twenty20. Taylor was back where he began as an opening batsman, having briefly moved down the order, and marshalled a tense run-chase with the sort of sang froid that few had ever credited him with. But actually it wasn't the first time he had displayed a calm head in a pressure situation. In August 2006 he smoked 17 from the last over – including a six to win off the last ball – to beat Bangladesh. Early on, Taylor had often showed the ability to build an innings, but was frustratingly dismissed trying to play too aggressively: he passed 90 three times in ODIs before finally reaching 100. In Tests he made 77 against New Zealand in August 2005 when he was 19, but shortly after that Zimbabwe withdrew from Test cricket for six years. When they returned in August 2011, Taylor was captain, having put a chequered disciplinary record behind him. He had been Zimbabwe's outstanding batsman at the 2011 World Cup, his uppercut to third man one of the tournament's enduring images. He celebrated his elevation in style by scoring his first century – and leading Zimbabwe to victory – in their comeback Test, against Bangladesh at Harare. His innings, while disciplined, still featured some of the trademark full-blooded front-foot cover-drives which make him an attractive batsman to watch. Taylor had a spell as wicketkeeper, and is now a reliable slip fielder.

THE FACTS Taylor scored 217 for Mid West Rhinos against Southern Rocks at Masvingo in February 2010 ... After three scores in the nineties, he finally reached his first ODI hundred against Bangladesh at Chittagong in November 2009 ... Taylor made his first Test century in his first match as captain, against Bangladesh at Harare in August 2011 ... He averages 46 in ODIs against India, but only 13 against England ... Taylor averages 39.17 in ODIs in which he has kept wicket, but only 28.48 as a specialist batsman ...

THE FIGURES to 26.09.11   **ESPNcricinfo.com**

Batting & Fielding	M	Inns	NO	Runs	HS	Avge	S/R	100	50	4s	6s	Ct	St
Tests	12	24	1	613	105*	26.65	47.81	1	4	77	2	11	0
ODIs	126	125	11	3675	145*	32.23	69.94	4	23	302	45	63	18
T20Is	11	11	2	244	60*	27.11	118.44	0	2	19	9	4	1
First-class	67	123	7	4552	217	39.24	–	13	18	–	–	81	4

Bowling	M	Balls	Runs	Wkts	BB	Avge	RpO	S/R	5i	10m
Tests	12	42	38	0	–	–	5.42	–	0	0
ODIs	126	396	406	9	3–54	45.11	6.15	44.00	0	0
T20Is	11	30	17	1	1–16	17.00	3.40	30.00	0	0
First-class	67	366	213	4	2–36	53.25	3.49	91.50	0	0

ROSS **TAYLOR**

Full name **Luteru Ross Poutoa Lote Taylor**
Born **March 8, 1984, Lower Hutt, Wellington**
Teams **Central Districts, Rajasthan Royals**
Style **Right-hand bat, offspinner**
Test debut **New Zealand v South Africa at Johannesburg 2007-08**
ODI debut **New Zealand v West Indies at Napier 2005-06**
T20I debut **New Zealand v Sri Lanka at Wellington 2006-07**

THE PROFILE Ross Taylor was singled out for attention from an early age – he captained New Zealand in the 2001-02 Under-19 World Cup – but it was some time before he made the big breakthrough. In March 2005 he extended his maiden first-class century to 184, then began the following season with five sixes in a century against Otago. He then cracked 121 against Wellington, 114 off long-suffering Otago in the semi, then 50 in the final against Canterbury. He rounded off a fine season with 106 as CD won the State Championship final at Wellington. It all led to a call-up for the final two ODIs of West Indies' tour early in 2006, and a regular place the following season. Taylor flogged Sri Lanka – Murali and all – for an unbeaten 128 in only his third match, and showed that was no fluke with an equally muscular 117 against Australia at Auckland in February 2007. A belated Test debut followed in November, and he scored 120 against England in his third match, before entrancing Old Trafford with an unbeaten 154 in the return series in 2008, during which he also took some fine slip catches. Highlights since have included a fine 151 against India at Napier in March 2009, and a defiant 138 against Australia at Hamilton a year later. He also entertained the IPL's crowds with some big hitting. Taylor scored consistently in New Zealand's run to the World Cup semi-final in 2011, the highlight coming against Pakistan – on his 27th birthday – when he broke loose at the end, clattering 55 from the last 13 deliveries he received, to reach 131. After the tournament he was appointed New Zealand's captain after Daniel Vettori stood down.

THE FACTS Only Martin Donnelly and Bevan Congdon (twice) have made higher Test scores for New Zealand in England than Taylor's 154 not out at Manchester in 2008 ... He and Jesse Ryder put on 271, a record for NZ's fourth wicket, against India at Napier in March 2009 ... Taylor made 217 for Central Districts v Otago at Napier in December 2006 ... By September 2011 Taylor had not made a duck in 55 Test innings, the most by anyone in a complete career ...

THE FIGURES to 26.09.11   **ᴇsᴘńcricinfo.com**

Batting & Fielding	M	Inns	NO	Runs	HS	Avge	S/R	100	50	4s	6s	Ct	St
Tests	30	55	1	2221	154*	41.12	60.33	5	12	297	23	52	0
ODIs	107	97	14	3055	131*	36.80	81.37	4	20	249	80	78	0
T20Is	37	34	4	659	63	21.96	116.84	0	3	39	31	23	0
First-class	76	129	3	5054	217	40.11	–	10	29	–	–	95	0

Bowling	M	Balls	Runs	Wkts	BB	Avge	RpO	S/R	5i	10m
Tests	30	90	43	2	2–4	21.50	2.86	45.00	0	0
ODIs	107	42	35	0	–	–	5.00	–	0	0
T20Is	37	–	–	–	–	–	–	–	–	–
First-class	76	660	359	6	2–4	59.83	3.26	110.00	0	0

SACHIN **TENDULKAR**

Full name	**Sachin Ramesh Tendulkar**
Born	**April 24, 1973, Bombay (now Mumbai)**
Teams	**Mumbai, Mumbai Indians**
Style	**Right-hand bat, occasional medium-pace/legspin**
Test debut	**India v Pakistan at Karachi 1989-90**
ODI debut	**India v Pakistan at Gujranwala 1989-90**
T20I debut	**India v South Africa at Johannesburg 2006-07**

THE PROFILE You only have to attend a one-dayer at the Wankhede Stadium, and watch the lights flicker and the floor tremble as the applause echoes around the ground when he comes in, to realise what Sachin Tendulkar means to Mumbai ... and India. Age, and niggling injuries, may have dimmed the light a little – he's now more of an accumulator than an artist – but he is still light-footed with bat in hand, the nearest thing to Bradman, as The Don himself recognised. Sachin seems to have been around for ever: he made his Test debut at 16, shrugging off a blow on the head against Pakistan; captivated England in 1990, with a maiden Test century; and similarly enchanted Australia in 1991-92. Two more big hundreds lit up the 2007-08 series Down Under, and Tendulkar now has 11 Test tons against the Aussies. He leads the list of ODI runscorers by a country mile, and owns the records for most runs, centuries and appearances in Tests too. Early in 2010 he stroked the first ODI double-century, and much of the talk the following year – after an immensely satisfying victory in the 2011 World Cup – was of the quest for 100 international hundreds: he spent the whole of the disappointing England tour stuck on 99. Until he throttled back in his thirties, Tendulkar usually looked to attack: now he's more circumspect, but no less destructive when in form. Small, steady at the crease before a decisive move forward or back, he remains a master, his whipped flick to fine leg an object of wonder. He could have starred as a bowler: he can do offbreaks, leggies or dobbly medium-pacers, although he doesn't bowl much these days.

THE FACTS Tendulkar passed his childhood idol Sunil Gavaskar's record of 34 Test centuries in December 2005: in seven Tests afterwards his highest score was 34 ... No-one is close to his 99 international centuries (Ricky Ponting is next with 69) ... Tendulkar has hit 11 Test centuries against Australia, and nine in ODIs ... His first mention in *Wisden* came when he was 14, after a stand of 664 in a school game with another future Test batsman, Vinod Kambli ...

THE FIGURES to 26.09.11   **ESP**cricinfo.com

Batting & Fielding	M	Inns	NO	Runs	HS	Avge	S/R	100	50	4s	6s	Ct	St
Tests	181	298	32	14965	248*	56.25	–	51	61	1933	64	108	0
ODIs	453	442	41	18111	200*	45.16	86.32	48	95	1981	193	136	0
T20Is	1	1	0	10	10	10.00	83.33	0	0	2	0	1	0
First-class	285	451	48	23884	248*	59.26	–	78	107	–	–	176	0

Bowling	M	Balls	Runs	Wkts	BB	Avge	RpO	S/R	5i	10m
Tests	181	4132	2416	45	3–10	53.68	3.50	91.82	0	0
ODIs	453	8044	6838	154	5–32	44.40	5.10	52.23	2	0
T20Is	1	15	12	1	1–12	12.00	4.80	15.00	0	0
First-class	285	7497	4308	70	3–10	61.54	3.44	107.10	0	0

UPUL **THARANGA**

Full name **Warushavithana Upul Tharanga**
Born **February 2, 1985, Balapitiya**
Teams **Nondescripts, Ruhuna**
Style **Left-hand bat, occasional wicketkeeper**
Test debut **Sri Lanka v India at Ahmedabad 2005-06**
ODI debut **Sri Lanka v West Indies at Dambulla 2005-06**
T20I debut **Sri Lanka v England at Southampton 2006**

THE PROFILE Upul Tharanga's international call-up in July 2005 brightened a year marred by the Indian Ocean tsunami, which washed away his family home in Ambalangoda, a fishing town on the west coast. Tharanga, a wispy left-hander blessed with natural timing, had long been tipped for the big time, playing premier-league cricket at 15 and passing seamlessly through the national age-group squads. He hit 105 against Bangladesh in only his fifth match – he celebrated modestly, aware that stiffer challenges lay ahead – then pummelled 165 against them in his third Test. During 2006 he lit up Lord's with 120 in the first of five successive defeats of England: he added 109 in the last of those, at Headingley, sharing a record opening stand with Sanath Jayasuriya. The feature of those innings was the way he made room to drive through the off side. In the 2007 World Cup Tharanga made 73 in the semi-final, but struggled the following season and lost his place. He emerged from the doldrums in 2008-09, passing 150 twice for the A team in South Africa then making his maiden double-century in a domestic match. In August 2009 he scored 76 in a one-dayer against New Zealand (his first international fifty for more than two years), celebrated with 80 in the next game, and has been a 50-overs regular ever since. He scored two centuries in the 2011 World Cup, against England and Zimbabwe, but made only 2 in the final, and was then hit with a three-month ban after taking a herbal remedy for a shoulder injury which contained a banned drug. He was back later in the year, and stroked another ODI hundred against Australia at Hambantota.

THE FACTS Tharanga and Sanath Jayasuriya put on 286 (in 31.5 overs) against England at Leeds in July 2006, a first-wicket record for all ODIs ... There have been 23 opening stands of 200-plus in ODIs: Tharanga has been involved in a record six of them ... He averages 57.80 in ODIs against England, but 13 against South Africa (and 0 against Ireland) ... Tharanga carried his bat for 265 for Ruhuna v Basnahira South in March 2009 ... His record includes one ODI for the Asia XI ...

THE FIGURES *to 26.09.11*   **ESPNcricinfo.com**

Batting & Fielding	M	Inns	NO	Runs	HS	Avge	S/R	100	50	4s	6s	Ct	St
Tests	15	26	1	713	165	28.52	49.51	1	3	99	5	11	0
ODIs	126	121	7	4064	133	35.64	73.87	12	19	477	18	22	0
T20Is	8	8	0	114	37	14.25	116.32	0	0	10	3	1	0
First-class	83	138	4	4726	265*	35.26	–	10	19	–	–	62	1

Bowling	M	Balls	Runs	Wkts	BB	Avge	RpO	S/R	5i	10m
Tests	15	0	–	–	–	–	–	–	–	–
ODIs	126	0	–	–	–	–	–	–	–	–
T20Is	8	0	–	–	–	–	–	–	–	–
First-class	83	18	4	0	–	–	1.33	–	0	0

RUSTY **THERON**

Full name	**Juan Theron**
Born	**July 24, 1985, Potchefstroom**
Teams	**Warriors**
Style	**Right-hand bat, right-arm fast-medium bowler**
Test debut	**No Tests yet**
ODI debut	**South Africa v Zimbabwe at Bloemfontein 2010-11**
T20I debut	**South Africa v Zimbabwe at Bloemfontein 2010-11**

THE PROFILE Juan "Rusty" Theron – so called because of his thatch of flame-red hair – is a brisk seam bowler from the Eastern Cape who made his name as a last-over specialist in South Africa's Twenty20 competition in 2009-10. His secret is nothing overly complicated: he bowls full and straight most of the time, and mixes things up with the odd slower ball after a bustling, busy run-up. Theron's cricketing prowess was recognised early on: he received a scholarship to Grey High School in Port Elizabeth, a training ground for many notable players such as Graeme and Peter Pollock, Johan Botha and Wayne Parnell. Theron made his first-class debut in November 2005, and took 60 wickets at 18.26 in his first 15 matches, and has been near the top of the Warriors' bowling averages ever since – in first-class matches, and especially in one-day games. It has not all been plain sailing though: in October 2009 his action was reported as suspect, although he was soon cleared. Things got better: that 2009-10 season proved to be the one that launched him into the big time, after he won at least two matches for the Warriors with his last-over heroics, including the semi-final, when the Cobras needed only eight runs but couldn't get them. An IPL contract followed a national one, and in October 2010 Theron made his international debut in Zimbabwe. He claimed 5 for 44 in his second ODI, and 11 wickets overall in the three matches, but missed out on the World Cup. Graeme Smith, though, liked what he saw: "There was a question about the back-up bowling unit, but it's nice to see guys like Rusty coming in and impressing."

THE FACTS Theron won the match award in his second one-day international, after taking 5 for 44 against Zimbabwe at Potchefstroom ... Theron took 7 for 46 in the second innings for Warriors v Eagles at Port Elizabeth in October 2008: he hadn't taken a wicket in the first innings, when Eagles were all out for 28 ... He played for Kings XI Punjab in the 2010 IPL, and won the match award in his first game ...

THE FIGURES to 26.09.11   cricinfo.com

Batting & Fielding	M	Inns	NO	Runs	HS	Avge	S/R	100	50	4s	6s	Ct	St
Tests	0	0	–	–	–	–	–	–	–	–	–	–	–
ODIs	4	1	0	5	5	5.00	100.00	0	0	0	0	4	0
T20Is	5	1	1	1	1*	–	25.00	0	0	0	0	2	0
First-class	42	55	10	606	66	13.46	44.26	0	2	57	7	13	0

Bowling	M	Balls	Runs	Wkts	BB	Avge	RpO	S/R	5i	10m
Tests	0	0	–	–	–	–	–	–	–	–
ODIs	4	194	173	12	5–44	14.41	5.35	16.16	1	0
T20Is	5	119	151	9	4–27	16.77	7.61	13.22	0	0
First-class	42	6722	3176	141	7–46	22.52	2.83	47.67	7	0

LAHIRU **THIRIMANNE**

Full name **Hettige Don Rumesh Lahiru Thirimanne**
Born **September 8, 1989, Moratuwa**
Teams **Ragama, Uva**
Style **Left-hand bat, occ. right-arm medium-pacer**
Test debut **Sri Lanka v England at Southampton 2011**
ODI debut **Sri Lanka v India at Dhaka 2010-11**
T20I debut **No T20Is yet**

THE PROFILE Left-hander Lahiru Thirimanne was long considered one of the best young batsmen in Sri Lanka, and it was no great surprise when he was named in the senior team for a tri-series in Bangladesh early in 2010. He made 22 in his first match, against India at Mirpur, opening against the experienced new-ball attack of Zaheer Khan and Ashish Nehra, but slipped out of the team after two more outings and was not required for the 2011 World Cup. He was back for the England tour that followed, when after Tillekeratne Dilshan broke a finger in the second Test, the match against Essex boiled down to a shootout between Thirimanne and Dinesh Chandimal for the vacant opening spot for the third Test at the Rose Bowl. Chandimal was out for 16 – but Thirimanne booked his place with a fine 104. On his Test debut at 21 he survived an hour for 10 in the first innings, then applied himself well for 38 in the second as Sri Lanka – nearly 200 behind – dug in for the draw. In *The Guardian*, David Hopps wrote: "Thirimanne's hundred against Essex before this Test was his first outside Sri Lanka, but his application against the moving ball suggested that it will not be the last." Dilshan naturally displaced him when the Australians toured later in 2011, but when Thilan Samaraweera was dropped it was Thirimanne who replaced him for the third Test. Thirimanne played in the Under-19 World Cup in 2008, and made his first-class debut later that year. He passed 500 runs in his first season, including a maiden century, and zoomed past 1000 in 2009-10, scoring three more hundreds and averaging over 50.

THE FACTS Thirimanne made 148 (one of four centuries in a total of 720) for Basnahira South against Ruhuna in Colombo in May 2010 ... He scored 108 for Sri Lanka Under-19s against England (whose opening bowler was Steven Finn) in a one-day international in Kuala Lumpur in February 2007 ...

THE FIGURES *to 26.09.11*   ᴇsᴘᴨcricinfo.com

Batting & Fielding	M	Inns	NO	Runs	HS	Avge	S/R	100	50	4s	6s	Ct	St
Tests	2	4	1	80	38	26.66	33.89	0	0	7	0	2	0
ODIs	3	2	0	37	22	18.50	82.22	0	0	4	0	1	0
T20Is	0	0	–	–	–	–	–	–	–	–	–	–	–
First-class	47	81	9	3169	148	44.01	50.13	9	16	329	24	43	0

Bowling	M	Balls	Runs	Wkts	BB	Avge	RpO	S/R	5i	10m
Tests	2	6	7	0	–	–	7.00	–	0	0
ODIs	3	0	–	–	–	–	–	–	–	–
T20Is	0	0	–	–	–	–	–	–	–	–
First-class	47	66	56	0	–	–	5.09	–	0	0

CHRIS **TREMLETT**

Full name	**Christopher Timothy Tremlett**
Born	**September 2, 1981, Southampton, Hampshire**
Teams	**Surrey**
Style	**Right-hand bat, right-arm fast-medium bowler**
Test debut	**England v India at Lord's 2007**
ODI debut	**England v Bangladesh at Nottingham 2005**
T20I debut	**England v India at Durban 2006-07**

THE PROFILE Chris Tremlett has the silent, simmering looks – and impressive sideburns – of a baddie in a spaghetti western, and bangs the ball down from an impressive height at an impressive speed. He has a fine cricket pedigree: his grandfather captained Somerset, while his father also played for Hampshire. But this Tremlett needed no nepotism: he took 4 for 16 on his first-class debut in 2000, and has rarely looked back since, halted only occasionally by niggling injuries (growing pains, perhaps – he's now 6ft 7ins/201cm). In 2005 he almost marked his ODI debut with a hat-trick – the vital ball fell on the stumps without dislodging a bail – then was 12th man in the first four Tests of the epic Ashes series before loss of rhythm led to loss of form. As England's pacemen hit the treatment table in 2007 Tremlett finally got the call. Using his height well, he collected 13 wickets in three Tests against India, including Laxman three times, Dravid and Tendulkar. A side strain forced him home early from New Zealand that winter, after which, amid whispers about his temperament, he became something of a back number. But a move to Surrey revitalised him: he took 48 wickets at 20, a vast improvement on 14 at 40 in 2009. That won him a place on the Ashes tour, and when Stuart Broad broke down Tremlett came in and immediately looked the part, taking 5 for 87 at Perth then 4 for 26 as Australia were routed for 98 on the first day at Melbourne. A six-for followed against Sri Lanka, in front of his old fans at Southampton, but then back and hamstring injuries sidelined him for a time.

THE FACTS Tremlett's grandfather, Maurice, played three Tests for England in 1948: his father, Tim, played for Hampshire ... Chris took two wickets in successive balls on his ODI debut, against Bangladesh in June 2005: the hat-trick ball bounced on top of the stumps but didn't dislodge the bails ... He bagged a pair on his Test debut in July 2007, the first person ever to do this at Lord's ... Tremlett took 6 for 44 for Hampshire v Sussex at Hove in April 2005 ...

THE FIGURES to 26.09.11   **ESPI** cricinfo.com

Batting & Fielding	M	Inns	NO	Runs	HS	Avge	S/R	100	50	4s	6s	Ct	St
Tests	10	11	4	97	25*	13.85	45.75	0	0	10	0	4	0
ODIs	15	11	4	50	19*	7.14	56.17	0	0	2	2	4	0
T20Is	1	0	–	–	–	–	–	–	–	–	–	–	–
First-class	116	150	41	1978	64	18.14	–	0	7	–	–	32	0

Bowling	M	Balls	Runs	Wkts	BB	Avge	RpO	S/R	5i	10m
Tests	10	2560	1258	49	6–48	25.67	2.94	52.24	2	0
ODIs	15	784	705	15	4–32	47.00	5.39	52.26	0	0
T20Is	1	24	45	2	2–45	22.50	11.25	12.00	0	0
First-class	116	20220	10608	386	6–44	27.48	3.14	52.38	9	0

JONATHAN **TROTT**

Full name	**Ian Jonathan Leonard Trott**
Born	**April 22, 1981, Cape Town, South Africa**
Teams	**Warwickshire**
Style	**Right-hand bat, right-arm medium-pacer**
Test debut	**England v Australia at The Oval 2009**
ODI debut	**England v Ireland at Belfast 2009**
T20I debut	**England v West Indies at The Oval 2007**

THE PROFILE The story sounds familiar: aggressive right-hander, born in South Africa, reputation for cockiness on the county circuit. But no, we're not talking Kevin Pietersen here, rather Jonathan Trott, who moved to England in 2003. His grandparents were British, which meant he could play as a non-overseas player for Warwickshire, although he didn't actually become eligible for England until 2006. He was consistent from the start, following up 763 runs from ten matches in 2003 by passing 1000 in each of the next three seasons. His form dipped in 2007 although, contrarily, he was a left-field pick for that summer's two Twenty20 games against West Indies. Trott managed only 9 and 2, and returned post haste to county cricket. But he was soon back in form and, when he continued to make eye-catchingly forthright runs in 2009, he was called up for the fifth and final Test against Australia at The Oval, the first to make his debut for England in an Ashes decider since 1896. He duly silenced the doubters with a seemingly nerveless century. After a quiet time in South Africa, Trott returned to form with 226 against Bangladesh in May 2010, and when Pakistan visited he added 184, sharing a Test-record eighth-wicket stand of 332 with Stuart Broad. And the runs just kept coming: 445 in the Ashes success, including two fine hundreds, and he was then England's leading batsman in the ODI series there and in the World Cup. Another double-century followed against Sri Lanka at Cardiff, before a shoulder injury kept him out for a while. After a successful year in both Test and one-day cricket, Trott was named the ICC's cricketer of the year for 2011.

THE FACTS Trott was the 18th batsman to score a century on Test debut for England ... Trott averages 99.66 in Tests at Lord's, having scored 226 against Bangladesh and 184 against Pakistan in 2010 ... He then he shared a Test-record eighth-wicket stand of 332 with Stuart Broad in that Pakistan game ... Trott took 7 for 39 for Warwickshire v Kent at Canterbury in September 2003 ...

THE FIGURES to 26.09.11   **ESPncricinfo.com**

Batting & Fielding	M	Inns	NO	Runs	HS	Avge	S/R	100	50	4s	6s	Ct	St
Tests	23	38	4	1965	226	57.79	48.51	6	7	215	0	11	0
ODIs	35	34	3	1596	137	51.48	78.35	3	14	121	2	8	0
T20Is	7	7	1	138	51	23.00	95.83	0	1	9	3	0	0
First-class	169	282	34	11206	226	45.18	–	26	54	–	–	157	0

Bowling	M	Balls	Runs	Wkts	BB	Avge	RpO	S/R	5i	10m
Tests	23	264	185	2	1–5	92.50	4.20	132.00	0	0
ODIs	35	183	166	2	2–31	83.00	5.44	91.50	0	0
T20Is	7	0	–	–	–	–	–	–	–	–
First-class	169	4544	2588	57	7–39	45.40	3.41	79.71	1	0

LONWABO **TSOTSOBE**

SOUTH AFRICA

Full name	**Lonwabo Lopsy Tsotsobe**
Born	**March 7, 1984, Port Elizabeth**
Teams	**Warriors, Essex**
Style	**Right-hand bat, left-arm fast-medium**
Test debut	**South Africa v West Indies at Port-of-Spain 2010**
ODI debut	**South Africa v Australia at Perth 2008-09**
T20I debut	**South Africa v Australia at Melbourne 2008-09**

THE PROFILE A tall left-arm swing bowler, Lonwabo Tsotsobe had a dream start to his ODI career in January 2009, when after removing Shaun Marsh he had Ricky Ponting caught behind. Later on he nabbed Mike Hussey and Mitchell Johnson as well, to finish with debut figures of 4 for 50 as South Africa romped to a 4-1 series victory which helped them pinch the No. 1 one-day ranking from the Aussies. This put him in the frame for a Test cap when the Australians toured shortly afterwards, but a knee injury kept him out, allowing Tsotsobe's Warriors team-mate Wayne Parnell – quicker through the air and a better batsman – to take his chance. But in the West Indies early in 2010, with Parnell injured, Tsotsobe did well in the one-dayers and played two of the Tests. Three more caps followed against India at the turn of 2010-11: he took five wickets in the second game. Tsotsobe made his first-class debut for Eastern Province in 2004-05, taking 7 for 44 in his first match. He moved to the Warriors in 2006-07, and again did well, following a solid debut season for them with 49 wickets at 23.59 the following summer, before 12 wickets in two matches against Sri Lanka A in September 2008 earned him that trip to Australia. But he had an unhappy spell at Essex in 2011, being dropped to the second team before a Twitter outburst resulted in him being sent home. He is seen in South Africa as a talisman for the black population – the natural successor to the now-retired Makhaya Ntini – but it remains to be seen whether Tsotsobe is worth his place in the side on merit.

THE FACTS Tsotsobe took 7 for 44 (9 for 96 in the match) on his first-class debut for Eastern Province against Boland at Paarl in November 2004, and took 10 for 72 in the match for EP v South Western Districts in Port Elizabeth in October 2006 ... He took 7 for 39 for Warriors v Lions at Johannesburg in October 2007 ... Tsotsobe's first victim in both Twenty20 internationals and ODIs was the Australian batsman Shaun Marsh ...

THE FIGURES to 26.09.11   **ESPN**cricinfo.com

Batting & Fielding	M	Inns	NO	Runs	HS	Avge	S/R	100	50	4s	6s	Ct	St
Tests	5	5	2	19	8*	6.33	35.84	0	0	2	0	1	0
ODIs	20	6	5	10	4*	10.00	111.11	0	0	2	0	5	0
T20Is	5	1	0	1	1	1.00	14.28	0	0	0	0	0	0
First-class	55	72	30	256	27*	6.09	29.35	0	0	32	3	13	0

Bowling	M	Balls	Runs	Wkts	BB	Avge	RpO	S/R	5i	10m
Tests	5	870	448	9	3–43	49.77	3.08	96.66	0	0
ODIs	20	976	731	39	4–22	18.74	4.49	25.02	0	0
T20Is	5	108	112	7	3–16	16.00	6.22	15.42	0	0
First-class	55	9261	4880	178	7–39	27.41	3.16	52.02	5	1

UMAR AKMAL

Full name	Mohammad Umar Akmal
Born	May 26, 1990, Lahore, Punjab
Teams	Lahore, Sui Northern Gas
Style	Right-hand batsman
Test debut	Pakistan v New Zealand at Dunedin 2009-10
ODI debut	Pakistan v Sri Lanka at Dambulla 2009
T20I debut	Pakistan v Sri Lanka at Colombo 2009

THE PROFILE Umar Akmal, the brother of Pakistan's wicketkeepers Kamran and Adnan Akmal, started his international career with a flourish. Only 19, he hit a run-a-ball 66 in only his second one-dayer, in Sri Lanka in August 2009, and bettered that with a superb century in the next match. He entered with Pakistan a wobbly 130 for 4 in the 26th over, and hurtled to his hundred from just 70 balls: he outscored Younis Khan in a stand of 176, and looked comfortable from the start. He refused to be tied down, swinging his seventh delivery – from Ajantha Mendis – over long-on for the first of four sixes. In November 2009 Akmal marked his Test debut, in New Zealand, with 129 and 75, and he continued to look the part throughout 2010, scoring consistently in all three formats, although impetuosity often got the better of him. People started to lose patience, though, as he kept trying the big shots too soon and the tall scores refused to come: in 15 further Tests after his debut to September 2011 he reached 30 11 times but never progressed beyond 79, while in almost 50 ODIs he had failed to add to that century in his third one. But his obvious talent – and a shortage of alternatives – kept him in the side. Akmal's international start mirrored his domestic one. In a triumphant 2007-08 season, he amassed 855 runs at 77.72 in nine Quaid-e-Azam Trophy matches, at an impressive strike-rate of 90.18. He extended his maiden century – in his sixth match – to 248 (off 225 balls) against Karachi Blues, and two matches later clattered 186 not out from 170 balls against Quetta.

THE FACTS Umar Akmal made 129 and 75 on his Test debut, against New Zealand at Dunedin in November 2009: only KS Ranjitsinhji, with 216 for England v Australia in 1896, scored more runs in his debut Test yet finished on the losing side ... Umar made 248 for Sui Northern Gas v Karachi Blues in December 2007 ... He hit a century, from only 70 balls, in his fourth ODI, against Sri Lanka in Colombo in August 2009 ... His brothers Kamran and Adnan Akmal have also kept wicket for Pakistan, as Umar did in an emergency in Dubai in 2010 ...

THE FIGURES to 26.09.11   cricinfo.com

Batting & Fielding	M	Inns	NO	Runs	HS	Avge	S/R	100	50	4s	6s	Ct	St
Tests	16	30	2	1003	129	35.82	65.98	1	6	117	17	12	0
ODIs	45	40	6	1285	102*	37.79	86.29	1	8	100	21	18	0
T20Is	24	23	4	621	64	32.68	120.11	0	4	45	18	20	1
First-class	47	80	7	3361	248	46.04	71.64	7	20	412	53	41	0

Bowling	M	Balls	Runs	Wkts	BB	Avge	RpO	S/R	5i	10m
Tests	16	0	–	–	–	–	–	–	–	–
ODIs	45	0	–	–	–	–	–	–	–	–
T20Is	24	0	–	–	–	–	–	–	–	–
First-class	47	6	10	0	–	–	10.00	–	0	0

UMAR GUL

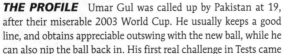

PAKISTAN

Full name	**Umar Gul**
Born	**April 14, 1984, Peshawar, North-Western Frontier Province**
Teams	**Peshawar, Habib Bank, Sussex**
Style	**Right-hand bat, right-arm fast-medium bowler**
Test debut	**Pakistan v Bangladesh at Karachi 2003-04**
ODI debut	**Pakistan v Zimbabwe at Sharjah 2002-03**
T20I debut	**Pakistan v Kenya at Nairobi 2007-08**

THE PROFILE Umar Gul was called up by Pakistan at 19, after their miserable 2003 World Cup. He usually keeps a good line, and obtains appreciable outswing with the new ball, while he can also nip the ball back in. His first real challenge in Tests came against India at Lahore in April 2004. Disparaged by some as the "Peshawar Rickshaw" to Shoaib Akhtar's "Rawalpindi Express", Gul tore through India's imposing top order, moving the ball both ways off the seam at a sharp pace. His 5 for 31 gave Pakistan the early initiative, and they went on to level the series. Stress fractures in the back then kept him out for two years, but he did well in England in 2006, particularly enjoying the conditions at Headingley. Nine wickets followed against West Indies at Lahore, but then he injured his knee. He was back for the 2007 World Cup, and was one of the few to return with reputation intact, but injuries intruded again before he started 2009 with a superb six-for against Sri Lanka on a Lahore batting paradise. Gul has proved a Twenty20 star, usually coming on after the initial overs and firing in yorkers on demand. He was the leading wicket-taker in the first two World Twenty20s, and it was a blow when a shoulder injury ruled him out of the third one in 2010. But in England later that year he revealed unexpected talent with the bat and bowled with his old fire, then led the attack well at the 2011 World Cup, although he misfired badly in the semi-final defeat by India. He missed the tour of Zimbabwe in September, but was expected to return for sterner challenges.

THE FACTS Umar Gul was the first bowler to take five wickets in a Twenty20 international, with 5 for 6 against New Zealand at The Oval in June 2009: he also took 4 for 8 against Australia in Dubai in May 2009 ... He took 6 for 42 in an ODI against England at The Oval in September's 2010 ... Gul's best first-class figures are 8 for 78 for Peshawar v Karachi Urban in October 2005 ... He took 5 for 46 on his first-class debut, for Pakistan International Airlines v ADBP at Karachi in 2000-01 ...

THE FIGURES to 26.09.11   **ESPN cricinfo.com**

Batting & Fielding	M	Inns	NO	Runs	HS	Avge	S/R	100	50	4s	6s	Ct	St
Tests	35	50	7	496	65*	11.53	52.87	0	1	57	18	7	0
ODIs	90	42	12	284	34*	9.46	64.84	0	0	24	6	11	0
T20Is	34	15	6	86	30	9.55	104.87	0	0	5	5	10	0
First-class	66	84	13	939	65*	13.22	–	0	1	–	–	15	0

Bowling	M	Balls	Runs	Wkts	BB	Avge	RpO	S/R	5i	10m
Tests	35	7328	4302	125	6–135	34.41	3.52	58.62	4	0
ODIs	90	4268	3618	134	6–42	27.00	5.08	31.85	2	0
T20Is	34	697	752	47	5–6	16.00	6.47	14.82	1	0
First-class	66	12967	7507	266	8–78	28.22	3.47	48.74	14	1

PROSPER **UTSEYA**

Full name	**Prosper Utseya**
Born	**March 26, 1985, Harare**
Teams	**Mountaineers**
Style	**Right-hand bat, offspinner**
Test debut	**Zimbabwe v Sri Lanka at Harare 2004**
ODI debut	**Zimbabwe v Sri Lanka at Bulawayo 2004**
T20I debut	**Zimbabwe v Bangladesh at Khulna 2006-07**

THE PROFILE A diminutive offspinner, Prosper Utseya was unexpectedly thrust into the national team in 2004, aged 19, after several senior players withdrew as a damaging dispute rumbled on. Utseya made 45 in his first Test, but failed to take a wicket, and it soon became clear that the selectors considered him a one-day specialist. He was given a long run in the 50-overs side, but failed to make a consistent mark with either bat or ball ... until the West Indian tour early in 2006, when his mature bowling was a rare highlight. His flight was widely praised, and at times his economy rate was remarkable, which became a trademark. Utseya was consistently able to stifle the runs in the middle overs, and he provided two of the series highlights – comprehensively beating Brian Lara with successive deliveries in the first match in Trinidad, and taking a remarkable diving, juggling boundary catch in the second. In 2006 Utseya took over as captain, and at first continued to keep the runs down. But as opponents grew used to his flattish delivery his economy-rate diminished a little, and after a disappointing World Twenty20 campaign in May 2010 he resigned as skipper. Ironically, as his bowling had lost its sparkle his batting had improved, to the point where he made a dozen successive double-figure scores in ODIs in 2010-11. He might struggle to take wickets at international level, but Utseya is a force to be reckoned with in domestic cricket. His spin partnership with Timycen Maruma has brought their teams several titles: in 2008-09 his ten-wicket haul helped Easterns clinch the Logan Cup with a thrilling one-wicket victory in a low-scoring contest against Northerns.

THE FACTS Utseya has played more than 130 ODIs – but only one Test, in May 2004 ... He took 7 for 56 (11 for 110 in the match) for Easterns v Centrals in Harare in April 2009: in his next game he had match figures of 10 for 93 against Northerns in the Logan Cup final ... Utseya made 115 not out from No. 9 for Zimbabwe against a South African XI at Potchefstroom in November 2007...

THE FIGURES *to 26.09.11*   **espncricinfo.com**

Batting & Fielding	M	Inns	NO	Runs	HS	Avge	S/R	100	50	4s	6s	Ct	St
Tests	1	2	0	45	45	22.50	77.58	0	0	5	1	2	0
ODIs	135	109	40	1146	68*	16.60	59.53	0	3	72	15	42	0
T20Is	14	9	4	38	13*	7.60	71.69	0	0	2	0	5	0
First-class	69	117	7	2350	115*	21.36	42.01	1	13	–	–	27	0

Bowling	M	Balls	Runs	Wkts	BB	Avge	RpO	S/R	5i	10m
Tests	1	72	55	0	–	–	4.58	–	0	0
ODIs	135	6927	4891	106	4–38	46.14	4.23	65.34	0	0
T20Is	14	317	322	16	3–25	20.12	6.09	19.81	0	0
First-class	69	12289	5533	188	7–56	29.43	2.70	65.36	8	2

DANIEL **VETTORI**

Full name	**Daniel Luca Vettori**
Born	**January 27, 1979, Auckland**
Teams	**Northern Districts, Royal Challengers Bangalore**
Style	**Left-hand bat, left-arm orthodox spinner**
Test debut	**New Zealand v England at Wellington 1996-97**
ODI debut	**New Zealand v Sri Lanka at Christchurch 1996-97**
T20I debut	**New Zealand v Kenya at Durban 2007-08**

THE PROFILE Daniel Vettori, the first slow left-armer to take 300 Test wickets, has been arguably the best bowler of his type in international cricket for almost a decade – an assessment reinforced by his selection for the World XI in Australia late in 2005 – and the only cloud on his horizon is a susceptibility to injury, particularly in the bowler's danger area of the back. He seemed to have recovered from one stress fracture, which led to a dip in form in 2003, but after a couple of matches for Warwickshire in 2006 he was on the plane home nursing another one. Vettori has usually been fit since, though, which was just as well for New Zealand as he carried a huge burden as captain (until standing down after the 2011 World Cup), key batsman and senior bowler. His early Tests in charge were notable for some superb personal performances: two fifties and nine wickets to stave off an embarrassing defeat by Bangladesh in October 2008, and two similar allround efforts which could not prevent defeat in Sri Lanka the following August. Vettori still has the enticing flight and guile that made him New Zealand's youngest Test player at 18 in 1996-97, and he remains economical in 50- and 20-over games. After his mini-slump he returned to form in England in 2004, then butchered Bangladesh with 20 wickets in two Tests. He has improved his batting – after starting at No. 11, blinking nervously through his glasses – to the point that his six centuries include New Zealand's fastest in Tests, an 82-ball effort against the admittedly hopeless Zimbabweans at Harare in August 2005.

THE FACTS Vettori made his first-class debut at 17 in 1996-97, for Northern Districts against the England tourists: his maiden first-class victim was Nasser Hussain ... Three weeks later Vettori became NZ's youngest-ever Test player, at 18 years 10 days: his first wicket was Hussain again ... Vettori averages 23.62 with the ball in Tests against Sri Lanka, but 69.66 v South Africa ... His record includes a Test and four ODIs for the World XI ...

THE FIGURES *to 26.09.11* **ESPN**cricinfo.com

Batting & Fielding	M	Inns	NO	Runs	HS	Avge	S/R	100	50	4s	6s	Ct	St
Tests	105	161	23	4167	140	30.19	57.72	6	22	509	16	57	0
ODIs	272	172	51	2105	83	17.39	81.93	0	4	156	14	77	0
T20Is	28	20	6	187	38	13.35	109.35	0	0	13	2	8	0
First-class	157	229	31	6014	140	30.37	–	9	32	–	–	81	0

Bowling	M	Balls	Runs	Wkts	BB	Avge	RpO	S/R	5i	10m
Tests	105	26860	11724	345	7–87	33.98	2.61	77.85	19	3
ODIs	272	12903	8880	282	5–7	31.48	4.12	45.75	2	0
T20Is	28	649	580	35	4–20	16.57	5.36	18.54	0	0
First-class	157	37585	16637	519	7–87	32.05	2.65	72.41	29	3

MURALI **VIJAY**

Full name	**Murali Vijay Krishna**
Born	**April 1, 1984, Chennai**
Teams	**Tamil Nadu, Chennai Super Kings**
Style	**Right-hand bat, occasional offspinner**
Test debut	**India v Australia at Nagpur 2008-09**
ODI debut	**India v West Indies at Roseau 2011**
T20I debut	**India v Afghanistan at Gros Islet 2008-09**

THE PROFILE   All batsmen want to go into their first Test in good form, and Murali Vijay was in better nick than most: when Gautam Gambhir was banned against Australia in November 2008, Vijay was hoicked out of a Ranji Trophy match in which he'd scored 243. While the Ranji game went on without him, Vijay made a very sound debut, sharing useful opening stands of 98 and 116 with Virender Sehwag as India set about what became a series-clinching 172-run victory. Vijay helped in the field too, running out Matthew Hayden and Michael Hussey, and taking a catch at short leg. Once Gambhir returned Vijay sat out the Tests in New Zealand early in 2009, but later that year made 87 in an opening stand of 221 with Sehwag against Sri Lanka in Mumbai. His next five Tests did not produce anything special, but he remained a consistent runscorer for Tamil Nadu – and upped his short game in the 2010 IPL, hammering a 46-ball hundred against Rajasthan Royals, and 458 runs overall as Chennai Super Kings lifted the title for the first time. Tall and solid, Vijay was an instant success in first-class cricket, despite being a late starter (he only switched to "proper" cricket from the soft-ball variety at 17): he hit 179 against Andhra in his second match, and finished his first season (2006-07) with 628 runs at 52 – only two others made more. There was no second-season dip, either: 667 runs, including a double-century against Saurashtra. But he had a quiet time in the West Indies in mid-2011, scoring only 72 runs in six Test innings, and found himself overtaken in the pecking order by his state team-mate Abhinav Mukund.

THE FACTS   Vijay made 243 for Tamil Nadu v Maharashtra in November 2008, sharing an opening stand of 462 with Abhinav Mukund (300 not out) ... Vijay also scored 230 not out for Tamil Nadu v Saurashtra in December 2007: this time the opening stand with Mukund was worth 256 ... He hit a 46-ball century against Rajasthan Royals in the 2010 IPL ... Vijay made 179 against Andhra in his second first-class match, at Chennai in December 2006 ...

THE FIGURES *to 26.09.11*   ≡sɪˈn cricinfo.com

Batting & Fielding	M	Inns	NO	Runs	HS	Avge	S/R	100	50	4s	6s	Ct	St
Tests	12	20	0	609	139	30.45	48.48	1	2	68	3	10	0
ODIs	11	11	0	196	33	17.81	61.82	0	0	23	1	6	0
T20Is	7	7	0	122	48	17.42	98.38	0	0	8	6	3	0
First-class	43	71	2	3309	243	47.95	49.08	8	14	386	45	44	0

Bowling	M	Balls	Runs	Wkts	BB	Avge	RpO	S/R	5i	10m
Tests	12	0	–	–	–	–	–	–	–	–
ODIs	11	0	–	–	–	–	–	–	–	–
T20Is	7	0	–	–	–	–	–	–	–	–
First-class	43	186	118	1	1–16	118.00	3.80	186.00	0	0

BRIAN **VITORI**

Full name	**Brian Vitalis Vitori**
Born	**February 22, 1990, Masvingo**
Teams	**Southern Rocks**
Style	**Left-hand bat, left-arm fast-medium bowler**
Test debut	**Zimbabwe v Bangladesh at Harare 2011**
ODI debut	**Zimbabwe v Bangladesh at Harare 2011**
T20I debut	**No T20Is yet**

THE PROFILE Like his near-namesake Daniel Vettori, Brian Vitori is a left-hander: unlike the New Zealander, though, this Vitori likes to bowl fast, and can move the ball in to the right-hander at a decent pace. He is a stocky youngster from the southern province of Masvingo, and is one of the products of Zimbabwe's new franchise system. "I started playing street cricket when I was eight, at primary school," he says. He played a few one-day matches for Masvingo early in 2006 with mixed results – hardly surprising given that he was barely 16 – but the new system, created in 2008, offered him an opportunity to improve under the guidance of the former Surrey and England batsman Monte Lynch, who recommended that he take part in a national training camp early in 2011. Vitori had just taken 25 wickets in the season for Southern Rocks – a reasonable return, although his average (37.16) was nothing to write home about. But Alan Butcher, Zimbabwe's new coach and an old county colleague of Lynch's, was also impressed: "I knew we had found someone special, who could be good for Zimbabwe cricket going forward." Butcher kept Vitori under wraps until Bangladesh toured in August 2011, for a series that included Zimbabwe's first Test for six years. He made an immediate impact, taking five wickets in a joyous victory, moving the ball around at a waspish pace, and seemed to work well in concert with the rapid right-armer Kyle Jarvis. Vitori then showed this was no fluke by taking five wickets in each of his first two ODIs, a unique feat, to leave Zimbabweans licking their lips at the prospect of a combative new-ball partnership at last.

THE FACTS Vitori took five wickets in each of his first two ODIs, an unprecedented feat (Ryan Harris of Australia took two in his first three): he had ten wickets after two ODIs, another record (previously eight) … Only six bowlers had previously taken a five-for on ODI debut … Vitori took 6 for 55 for Southern Rocks against Mountaineers at Masvingo in March 2011 …

THE FIGURES to 26.09.11   **ESPncricinfo.com**

Batting & Fielding	M	Inns	NO	Runs	HS	Avge	S/R	100	50	4s	6s	Ct	St
Tests	2	3	0	33	14	11.00	75.00	0	0	5	1	1	0
ODIs	5	1	1	3	3*	–	100.00	0	0	0	0	0	0
T20Is	0	0	–	–	–	–	–	–	–	–	–	–	–
First-class	20	29	10	132	16*	6.94	39.63	0	0	14	2	5	0

Bowling	M	Balls	Runs	Wkts	BB	Avge	RpO	S/R	5i	10m
Tests	2	390	240	5	4–66	48.00	3.69	78.00	0	0
ODIs	5	279	200	12	5–20	16.66	4.30	23.25	2	0
T20Is	0	0	–	–	–	–	–	–	–	–
First-class	20	2664	1716	45	6–55	38.13	3.86	59.20	1	0

WAHAB RIAZ

Full name	**Wahab Riaz**
Born	**June 28, 1985, Lahore**
Teams	**Lahore, National Bank, Kent**
Style	**Right-hand bat, left-arm fast-medium bowler**
Test debut	**Pakistan v England at The Oval 2010**
ODI debut	**Pakistan v Zimbabwe at Sheikhupura 2007-08**
T20I debut	**Pakistan v Bangladesh at Karachi 2007-08**

THE PROFILE Wahab Riaz initially benefited from Pakistan's chronic luck with fast bowlers. With Shoaib Akhtar and Mohammad Asif missing more often than not, for various weird and wonderful reasons, and with Umar Gul prone to injury, Riaz made it into the national squad quicker than he might have expected. He made a good start early in 2008, taking two good wickets (Tatenda Taibu and Sean Williams of Zimbabwe) in his first one-day international, and adding five more scalps in two games against Bangladesh. But then reality intruded, in the shape of India's batsmen: two days after he'd beaten up the Banglas, Riaz was knocked about himself, taking 2 for 86 in 9.2 overs before being removed from the attack for sending down two beamers. He faded from the scene for a couple of years before returning to the limelight in England in 2010, taking four wickets at The Oval in his first nine overs in Tests, and finishing with 5 for 63. He also hung around for a while as nightwatchman. He is a bustling bowler whose stock ball is the one angled away from the right-hander, and he is a bit sharper than he looks: at The Oval the speedo was often nudging 90mph. However, in six more Tests by May 2011 Riaz did not exactly set the world alight, and it was a similar story in ODIs too. He had a quiet time at the World Cup before taking 5 for 46 – in vain – against India in the semi-final (despite three sleepless nights beforehand), then embarked on a successful county stint with Kent. He remains in the frame, although the rise of Junaid Khan, a younger left-armer, might threaten his place.

THE FACTS Wahab Riaz took a wicket (Zimbabwe's Tatenda Taibu) with his third ball in international cricket, in an ODI at Sheikhupura in February 2008 ... He was the ninth Pakistani to take a five-for on Test debut, with 5 for 63 against England at The Oval in 2010 ... Riaz's best first-class figures are 6 for 64, for National Bank v Customs in Karachi in December 2007: he took 6 for 76 (11 for 190 in the match) for Hyderabad at Sialkot in April 2004 ...

THE FIGURES to 26.09.11   **ESP̄Ncricinfo.com**

Batting & Fielding	M	Inns	NO	Runs	HS	Avge	S/R	100	50	4s	6s	Ct	St
Tests	7	9	3	57	27	9.50	34.75	0	0	6	0	1	0
ODIs	22	15	4	80	21	7.27	86.02	0	0	6	3	6	0
T20Is	6	4	2	54	30*	27.00	135.00	0	0	3	3	1	0
First-class	77	107	19	1269	68	14.42	–	0	3	–	–	24	0

Bowling	M	Balls	Runs	Wkts	BB	Avge	RpO	S/R	5i	10m
Tests	7	986	580	17	5–63	34.11	3.52	58.00	1	0
ODIs	22	1013	896	38	5–46	23.57	5.30	26.65	1	0
T20Is	6	84	89	4	2–24	22.25	6.35	21.00	0	0
First-class	77	13059	7400	251	6–64	29.48	3.39	52.02	10	2

DAVID **WARNER**

AUSTRALIA

Full name	**David Andrew Warner**
Born	**October 27, 1986, Paddington, Sydney**
Teams	**New South Wales, Delhi Daredevils**
Style	**Left-hand bat, occasional legspinner**
Test debut	**No Tests yet**
ODI debut	**Australia v South Africa at Hobart 2008-09**
T20I debut	**Australia v South Africa at Melbourne 2008-09**

THE PROFILE A diminutive and dangerous opener, David Warner exploded onto the international scene in January 2009. His astonishing 89 from 43 balls, wielding the bat more like a club, on his Twenty20 debut against South Africa at the MCG was all the more remarkable as he was the first man to play for the full Australian side before playing first-class cricket since 1877. His surprise selection capped an eventful couple of months in which he also earned an IPL contract and a deal to use a two-sided bat. The rewards came after he began the season by smashing nine sixes in 165 not out – a NSW one-day record – against Tasmania in Sydney, and showed it was no fluke with 97 from 54 balls against the luckless islanders the following week. He finished with 390 one-day runs at a strike-rate of 129, and did eventually make his first-class debut for NSW. Warner struggled in ODIs after a muscular 69 in his second game, and hasn't played since a duck against Scotland in August 2009. Since then he has been pigeonholed as a Twenty20 blaster, with predictably volatile results: highlights have included 67 from 29 balls against West Indies at Sydney in February 2010, and 72 from 42 against India at Bridgetown in the World Twenty20 three months later. Both innings included seven sixes. He is improving his first-class record, though, and in July 2011 knuckled down for 7½ hours for 211 for Australia A in Zimbabwe. He's also an excellent fielder, who came on as a substitute in the Perth Test against South Africa in 2005-06. A keen surfer, he was sent home from the Australian academy in 2007 for general untidiness.

THE FACTS Warner was the first man since John Hodges and Tom Kendall in the first Test of all in 1876-77 to represent Australia in a full international without having previously played first-class cricket: Warner won the match award for his 89 from 43 balls (seven fours and six sixes) on T20I debut against South Africa in January 2009 ... He finally made his first-class debut for New South Wales in March 2009 ... Warner scored 211 for Australia A v Zimbabwe A at Harare in July 2011 ...

THE FIGURES *to 26.09.11*   **ESPNcricinfo.com**

Batting & Fielding	M	Inns	NO	Runs	HS	Avge	S/R	100	50	4s	6s	Ct	St
Tests	0	0	–	–	–	–	–	–	–	–	–	–	–
ODIs	7	7	0	106	69	15.14	77.37	0	1	8	3	1	0
T20Is	27	27	0	775	89	28.70	144.32	0	5	78	33	15	0
First-class	9	15	1	747	211	53.35	69.16	2	2	85	13	5	0

Bowling	M	Balls	Runs	Wkts	BB	Avge	RpO	S/R	5i	10m
Tests	0	0	–	–	–	–	–	–	–	–
ODIs	7	0	–	–	–	–	–	–	–	–
T20Is	27	0	–	–	–	–	–	–	–	–
First-class	9	139	79	1	1–0	79.00	3.41	139.00	0	0

B-J **WATLING**

Full name	**Bradley-John Watling**
Born	**July 9, 1985, Durban, South Africa**
Teams	**Northern Districts**
Style	**Right-hand bat, occasional wicketkeeper**
Test debut	**New Zealand v Pakistan at Napier 2009-10**
ODI debut	**New Zealand v Sri Lanka at Dambulla 2010**
T20I debut	**New Zealand v Pakistan at Dubai 2009-10**

THE PROFILE A right-hand opening batsman who can also keep wicket, Bradley-John (usually known just by his initials) Watling spent his early years in South Africa before his family moved to New Zealand when he was ten. He was part of the squad for the Under-19 World Cup in Bangladesh in 2003-04 before making it to the Northern Districts team, but in 2006-07 – his third season – he made 564 runs at 37.60, and passed 500 again in 2009-10 and 2010-11. He also did well in one-dayers, and was rewarded with a place in New Zealand's squad against Pakistan in November 2009. He made his Black Caps in the Twenty20 games in Dubai – a slight surprise, since he is not regarded at home as a terribly fast scorer (his overall one-day strike-rate is a modest 68 per 100 balls). However, that didn't bother Daniel Vettori: "He plays pace well, lets the ball come to him, and in the middle overs he is very adept at turning the strike over against spin. I've actually opened with him a few times ... but that's not why he made the team!" When Pakistan toured New Zealand later in 2009 Watling made his debut in the third Test at Napier, making an undefeated 60 in the second innings, and after a couple of quiet matches he resisted the Australian attack for more than two hours in making 46 at Hamilton. But he slipped out of the national side after a modest Indian tour late in 2010: he missed the following year's World Cup, although another good domestic season rescued his national contract. Watling is also a reliable stand-in keeper, although Peter McGlashan (who has also played for NZ's Twenty20 side) usually takes the gloves for Northern Districts.

THE FACTS Watling's highest score of 164 not out came as Northern Districts chased down 384 to beat Wellington by nine wickets at Whangarei in March 2011, after conceding a first-innings lead of 175 ... His first three first-class hundreds all came at Otago's expense ... Watling made 145 not out in the final of the NZC one-day competition against Auckland in February 2010 ...

THE FIGURES to 26.09.11   **ESPN**cricinfo.com

Batting & Fielding	M	Inns	NO	Runs	HS	Avge	S/R	100	50	4s	6s	Ct	St
Tests	5	10	2	203	60*	25.37	41.76	0	1	26	1	7	0
ODIs	7	6	0	84	55	14.00	54.90	0	1	10	0	4	0
T20Is	2	2	0	29	22	14.50	64.44	0	0	2	0	2	0
First-class	55	100	6	3045	164*	32.39	40.01	6	14	–	–	59	0

Bowling	M	Balls	Runs	Wkts	BB	Avge	RpO	S/R	5i	10m
Tests	5	0	–	–	–	–	–	–	–	–
ODIs	7	0	–	–	–	–	–	–	–	–
T20Is	2	0	–	–	–	–	–	–	–	–
First-class	55	47	39	2	2–31	19.50	4.97	23.50	0	0

SHANE **WATSON**

AUSTRALIA

Full name **Shane Robert Watson**
Born **June 17, 1981, Ipswich, Queensland**
Teams **New South Wales, Rajasthan Royals**
Style **Right-hand bat, right-arm fast-medium bowler**
Test debut **Australia v Pakistan at Sydney 2004-05**
ODI debut **Australia v South Africa at Centurion 2001-02**
T20I debut **Australia v South Africa at Johannesburg 2005-06**

THE PROFILE To conquer international cricket, Shane Watson first had to beat his fragile body. Despite an athletic figure made for photoshoots, Watson's frame was so brittle it threatened to break him. He refused to give up, despite back stress fractures, hamstring strains, calf and hip trouble, a dislocated shoulder and a suspected heart attack that turned out to be food poisoning. He changed his training, and gave up alcohol, but not his dream. It finally paid off when he was promoted to open in the middle of the 2009 Ashes. Many would have been uncomfortable with the elevation from the middle order, but Watson was used to reinventing himself. In his first eight Tests in the new role he scored seven fifties and a 120. His first Test century was a long time coming, but after two nineties (and an 89) he finally reached three figures against Pakistan at the MCG in December 2009 ... thanks to a single from a dropped catch. He had earned some luck. At the crease he is an aggressive brute with a broad chest, a right-handed disciple of Matthew Hayden. He's had some purple patches in ODIs – successive centuries in the semi and final of the 2009 Champions Trophy, and a rollicking 161 not out against England at Melbourne in January 2011, which was just a warm-up for an astonishing undefeated 185 – with a record 15 sixes – to bully Bangladesh three months later. As a bowler he is willing and speedy, if not quite as good as he thinks he is: he is prone to verbal exchanges with batsmen, but does pick up handy wickets – 11 of them in two Tests against Pakistan in England in 2010.

THE FACTS Watson made 185 not out, Australia's highest score in ODIs, against Bangladesh at Mirpur in April 2011: the innings included an ODI-record 15 sixes ... He hit 201 in the 2005-06 Pura Cup final demolition of Victoria before retiring hurt: uniquely, four batsmen passed 150 in Queensland's 900 for 6 ... Watson played for Hampshire, alongside Shane Warne: in 2005 he scored 203 not out for them against Warwickshire at the Rose Bowl ...

THE FIGURES to 26.09.11   **ESPr cricinfo.com**

Batting & Fielding	M	Inns	NO	Runs	HS	Avge	S/R	100	50	4s	6s	Ct	St
Tests	30	54	2	2040	126	39.23	50.89	2	15	276	10	22	0
ODIs	138	119	24	4122	185*	43.38	89.55	6	25	414	91	47	0
T20Is	24	23	2	522	81	24.85	153.98	0	5	40	32	8	0
First-class	97	171	18	7008	203*	45.80	–	17	38	–	–	79	0

Bowling	M	Balls	Runs	Wkts	BB	Avge	RpO	S/R	5i	10m
Tests	30	3051	1495	50	6–33	29.90	2.94	61.02	2	0
ODIs	138	4953	4016	138	4–36	29.10	4.86	35.89	0	0
T20Is	24	321	420	17	4–15	24.70	7.85	18.88	0	0
First-class	97	9228	5068	180	7–69	28.15	3.29	51.26	6	1

CHANAKA **WELAGEDARA**

Full name	**Uda Walawwe Mahim Bandaralage Chanaka Asanga Welagedara**
Born	**March 20, 1981, Matale**
Teams	**Tamil Union, Wayamba**
Style	**Right-hand bat, left-arm fast-medium bowler**
Test debut	**Sri Lanka v England at Galle 2007-08**
ODI debut	**Sri Lanka v India at Rajkot 2009-10**
T20I debut	**Sri Lanka v New Zealand at Providence 2009-10**

THE PROFILE   Chanaka Welagedara is a brisk left-armer with a sturdy action, who is shaping up as the long-term replacement for Chaminda Vaas. Welagedara, whose array of initials outdoes even Vaas's, swings the ball in nicely, and traps a lot of batsmen lbw. He had problems at first with consistency – against India at home in mid-2010 he sprayed the ball around and proved expensive. A few months earlier, he had reduced India to 31 for 3 at Ahmedabad without the aid of a fielder. He later dismissed Rahul Dravid too – but not before he had made 177. Shortly afterwards Welagedara took 5 for 66 against India in a one-dayer in Bangladesh, again removing the top three before proving costly later on. He was dropped after only three wickets in four Tests following nine in his first two, but after missing the 2011 World Cup he was back for the ensuing England tour. After missing the opening Test he added a spark to the attack in the second at Lord's, dismissing Andrew Strauss early on and finishing with five wickets in the match. Welagedara was a late starter to cricket, not playing seriously until he was 17. When he came to Colombo from Matale (a hill-country town not far from Kandy) in 2000 he was soon chosen for the national Pace Academy, headed by the former Test fast bowler Rumesh Ratnayake. Welagedara bowled Moors to the Premier League title in 2002-03, with 34 wickets at 24.14. An ankle injury, requiring an operation, kept him out for 18 months until the end of 2006, but he made his Test debut against England the following December and took four wickets, three of them top-five batsmen.

THE FACTS   Welagedara took 5 for 34 (10 for 95 in the match) for a Sri Lanka Cricket XI v Tamil Nadu in the Gopalan Trophy match in Colombo in September 2007 ... He took 5 for 66 in an ODI against India at Mirpur in January 2010 ... Welagedara scored 76 for Moors v Sinhalese SC in Colombo in October 2009 ...

THE FIGURES to 26.09.11   **ESPncricinfo.com**

Batting & Fielding	M	Inns	NO	Runs	HS	Avge	S/R	100	50	4s	6s	Ct	St
Tests	11	12	3	48	8	5.33	46.15	0	0	6	0	3	0
ODIs	10	3	2	4	2*	4.00	44.44	0	0	0	0	2	0
T20Is	2	1	1	2	2*	–	66.66	0	0	0	0	0	0
First-class	84	100	36	612	76	9.56	41.57	0	1	–	–	18	0

Bowling	M	Balls	Runs	Wkts	BB	Avge	RpO	S/R	5i	10m
Tests	11	1899	1280	27	4–87	47.40	4.04	70.33	0	0
ODIs	10	457	433	15	5–66	28.86	5.68	30.46	1	0
T20Is	2	36	61	1	1–21	61.00	10.16	36.00	0	0
First-class	84	11657	6972	231	5–34	30.18	3.58	50.46	6	1

CAMERON **WHITE**

AUSTRALIA

Full name	**Cameron Leon White**
Born	**August 18, 1983, Bairnsdale, Victoria**
Teams	**Victoria, Deccan Chargers**
Style	**Right-hand bat, legspinner**
Test debut	**Australia v India at Bangalore 2008-09**
ODI debut	**Australia v World XI at Melbourne 2005-06**
T20I debut	**Australia v England at Sydney 2006-07**

THE PROFILE Cameron "Bear" White long seemed destined to play a significant role for Australia. Only the precise nature of it baffled admirers. Nagging legspinner? Solid middle-order bat? Intuitive skipper? Or a bit of all three? The over-eager Shane Warne comparisons that accompanied his arrival died away long ago. Indeed, White is a peculiarly unAustralian leggie – tall and robust, relying on changes of pace and a handy wrong'un rather than prodigious turn or flight. "There's no flippers or anything exciting like that," he once admitted with a self-deprecating smile. Victoria's youngest-ever captain at 20, he won rave reviews for his handling of more experienced colleagues. White played his first ODIs against the World XI late in 2005, but made little impact and lost his national contract after a mediocre season. But he batted wonderfully for Somerset in 2006 (David Hookes, the late Victorian coach, always felt his best chance of representing Australia was to earn a top-six spot), feasting on county bowlers and smashing a Twenty20 ton in 55 balls. That preceded a better home season, and he was recalled for the one-day series at the start of 2007: his bowling lacked control, and batting opportunities were limited. He toured India late in 2008, but did little in four Tests there, and returned even more firmly pigeonholed as a one-day player. But back in England late in 2009 he followed mature one-day innings of 53 and 42 with a fine maiden century at Southampton, and added another one against Pakistan at Brisbane early in 2010. Soon after that White was appointed Australia's Twenty20 captain ... and a few months later was dropped from the 50-overs side after an underwhelming World Cup.

THE FACTS White made 260 not out for Somerset v Derbyshire in August 2006, the highest individual score in the fourth innings of any first-class match, beating a record formerly held by Hansie Cronje and Denis Compton ... White took 6 for 66 (10 for 136 in the match) for Victoria v Western Australia at Melbourne in March 2003 ... Ten of his 16 first-class centuries were scored in 24 matches for Somerset ...

THE FIGURES to 26.09.11   **ESPN**cricinfo.com

Batting & Fielding	M	Inns	NO	Runs	HS	Avge	S/R	100	50	4s	6s	Ct	St
Tests	4	7	2	146	46	29.20	44.24	0	0	15	1	1	0
ODIs	87	73	15	2037	105	35.12	80.48	2	11	142	45	37	0
T20Is	27	26	8	565	85*	31.38	139.50	0	3	30	34	15	0
First-class	113	189	24	6933	260*	42.01	–	16	32	–	–	107	0

Bowling	M	Balls	Runs	Wkts	BB	Avge	RpO	S/R	5i	10m
Tests	4	558	342	5	2–71	68.40	3.67	111.60	0	0
ODIs	87	331	351	12	3–5	29.25	6.36	27.58	0	0
T20Is	27	24	25	1	1–11	25.00	6.25	24.00	0	0
First-class	113	11820	6945	172	6–66	40.37	3.52	68.72	2	1

KANE **WILLIAMSON**

Full name	**Kane Stuart Williamson**
Born	**August 8, 1990, Tauranga**
Teams	**Northern Districts, Gloucestershire**
Style	**Right-hand bat, offspinner**
Test debut	**New Zealand v India at Ahmedabad 2010-11**
ODI debut	**New Zealand v India at Dambulla 2010**
T20I debut	**No T20Is yet**

THE PROFILE Well balanced, with an enviably perpendicular bat in defence, Kane Williamson is probably the most exciting batting talent New Zealand have unearthed since Martin Crowe in the early 1980s. He had a smooth ride through age-group cricket and made his first-class debut at 17 in December 2007. A slow start (2 and 0) was followed next season by innings of 82, 73 and 98 in his next four matches, and the seemingly inevitable maiden century came up in his tenth. He finished 2008-09 with 812 runs at 50.75, and collected 614 more the following season – at a slightly lower average (47.23) but with two eye-catching big scores, 170 against Wellington and 192 against Auckland. All this propelled him into the squad for the second Test against Australia at Hamilton in March 2010, and although he didn't play in the end it was a clear sign that his entry would not be long delayed. He made a quiet start in one-day internationals – a ninth-ball duck, courtesy of a peach from Praveen Kumar, in his first game, and another blob in his next match before finally getting off the mark in his third. But then he made 108 against Bangladesh, before marking his Test debut with a seemingly nerveless 131 against India at Ahmedabad in November 2010. He looked set for another in his second Test, too, before being cut off by an unlucky lbw for 69 in Hyderabad. He was a consistent scorer as New Zealand advanced to the semi-finals of the 2011 World Cup, and looked capable of some handy spells of offspin as well. He added to his experience with a county season for Gloucestershire in 2011.

THE FACTS Williamson was the youngest of the eight New Zealanders to score a century on his Test debut, with 131 v India at Ahmedabad in November 2010 ... He made 192 for Northern Districts against Auckland at Whangarei in March 2010: in the previous match (at Wellington) he scored 170 ... He hit 75 and 151 against England in an Under-19 Test at Worcester in August 2008 ... Williamson scored more first-class runs before he had turned 20 than Martin Crowe (1428 to 1127) ...

THE FIGURES to 26.09.11   **ESPM**cricinfo.com

Batting & Fielding	M	Inns	NO	Runs	HS	Avge	S/R	100	50	4s	6s	Ct	St
Tests	5	9	0	299	131	33.22	42.83	1	2	28	0	1	0
ODIs	15	14	2	352	108	29.33	68.48	1	0	22	3	3	0
T20Is	0	0	–	–	–	–	–	–	–	–	–	–	–
First-class	38	65	2	2558	192	40.60	54.58	6	13	320	12	37	0

Bowling	M	Balls	Runs	Wkts	BB	Avge	RpO	S/R	5i	10m
Tests	5	240	176	2	1–45	88.00	4.40	120.00	0	0
ODIs	15	156	133	1	1–2	133.00	5.11	156.00	0	0
T20Is	0	0	–	–	–	–	–	–	–	–
First-class	38	3094	1790	37	5–75	48.37	3.47	83.62	1	0

CHRIS **WOAKES**

ENGLAND

Full name	**Christopher Roger Woakes**
Born	**March 2, 1989, Birmingham**
Teams	**Warwickshire**
Style	**Right-hand bat, right-arm fast-medium bowler**
Test debut	**No Tests yet**
ODI debut	**England v Australia at Sydney 2010-11**
ODI debut	**England v Australia at Adelaide 2010-11**

THE PROFILE   A tall quick bowler and a handy batsman, Chris Woakes hit the headlines in his first international, a Twenty20 game at Adelaide, when he kept his cool to hit the winning run off the last ball, after earlier striking the pacy Shaun Tait for a big six: not for nothing did the England coach Andy Flower describe him beforehand as "a serious batter". He almost did it again in the next game, keeping England in touch by hammering Brett Lee over long-on for six in the final over, but history didn't quite repeat itself there. Then, in only his second ODI, Woakes ripped through Australia's middle order to take 6 for 45 at Brisbane – although, just to ruin the fairytale, England eventually lost by 51 runs. It looked as if a star had been born – but, rather perplexingly, Woakes soon slid from view. He missed out on initial selection for the World Cup, then more surprisingly lost out to the uncapped Jade Dernbach when a replacement was needed. Woakes played only three full internationals in the 2011 home season, the ODI against Ireland and two Twenty20s, although he remained an England Lions regular. At county level Woakes remains a considerable force. He seems to like playing Hampshire: his first two first-class hundreds came against them – 131 at Southampton in 2009, and 135 at Edgbaston in 2010, both not out – then in August 2011 he took a career-best 7 for 20 against them at Edgbaston as Warwickshire continued their ultimately unsuccessful bid for the Championship title. Woakes played a big part in that success, with 56 wickets and 78 in all matches – his only problem being that none of them came for England.

THE FACTS   Woakes took 6 for 45 against Australia at Brisbane in his second ODI, in January 2011: only Paul Collingwood (6 for 31 against Bangladesh at Trent Bridge in 2005) has recorded better figures for England ... Woakes took 5 for 18, including a hat-trick, in a first-class match for England Lions v Guyana at Providence in March 2011 ... He has hit four first-class centuries, two of them against Hampshire: in August 2011 he took a career-best 7 for 20 against them at Edgbaston ...

THE FIGURES *to 26.09.11*   **ESFN cricinfo.com**

Batting & Fielding	M	Inns	NO	Runs	HS	Avge	S/R	100	50	4s	6s	Ct	St
Tests	0	0	–	–	–	–	–	–	–	–	–	–	–
ODIs	4	4	2	39	19*	19.50	73.58	0	0	2	0	1	0
T20Is	3	3	2	37	19*	37.00	123.33	0	0	1	2	1	0
First-class	61	81	21	2002	136*	33.36	–	4	8	–	–	32	0

Bowling	M	Balls	Runs	Wkts	BB	Avge	RpO	S/R	5i	10m
Tests	0	0	–	–	–	–	–	–	–	–
ODIs	4	194	169	7	6–45	24.14	5.22	27.71	1	0
T20Is	3	60	94	2	1–29	47.00	9.40	30.00	0	0
First-class	61	10695	5487	223	7–20	24.60	3.07	47.95	12	3

REECE **YOUNG**

Full name **Reece Alan Young**
Born **September 15, 1979, Auckland**
Teams **Canterbury**
Style **Right-hand bat, wicketkeeper**
Test debut **New Zealand v Pakistan at Hamilton 2011**
ODI debut **No ODIs yet**
T20I debut **No T20Is yet**

THE PROFILE Wicketkeeper Reece Young chipped away on the domestic scene for Auckland for a decade, seemingly without much hope of dislodging Brendon McCullum from behind the stumps in the national side. He was also hamstrung by often playing alongside Gareth Hopkins – McCullum's international understudy – who usually kept wicket for Auckland. But everything changed in 2010. First Young moved to Canterbury: "In Auckland, I was batting up the order, but I wasn't keeping consistently," he said. "That was the reason for leaving: to forge my own path. Down here I get to bat up the order and keep wickets consistently." McCullum, wary of overtaxing a suspect back, had just decided he would no longer keep wicket in Tests, which coincided with the selectors dumping Hopkins, who had struggled to impose himself with the bat on his occasional international appearances. Young's first senior tour was actually before this, to Sri Lanka in 2009. He didn't get into the side, although he was allowed to keep wicket in the second innings of the second Test after McCullum fell ill. His call-up had followed a productive domestic season in which he was Auckland's leading batsman with 557 runs at 50.63. He continued that form in his first season for Canterbury – 534 runs at 44, and 26 catches behind the stumps. It all led to a summons for New Zealand's first Test after McCullum hung up the gloves, at home to Pakistan early in 2011. Young did little wrong behind the stumps, or in front of them, scoring 57 and sharing a partnership of 138 with Daniel Vettori in the second Test at Wellington. The upshot was a national contract – replacing Hopkins on the list – for 2011-12.

THE FACTS Young has scored six first-class centuries, the highest 126 not out for Auckland against Canterbury in April 2010, in his last match for Auckland before joining Canterbury ... Young kept wicket in a Test (in Sri Lanka in August 2009) before he played in one ... He took six catches in an innings for Auckland v Wellington in March 2003 ...

THE FIGURES to 26.09.11   **ESPNcricinfo.com**

Batting & Fielding	M	Inns	NO	Runs	HS	Avge	S/R	100	50	4s	6s	Ct	St
Tests	2	4	0	103	57	25.75	36.91	0	1	11	0	3	0
ODIs	0	0	–	–	–	–	–	–	–	–	–	–	–
T20Is	0	0	–	–	–	–	–	–	–	–	–	–	–
First-class	106	147	25	3782	126*	31.00	–	6	23	–	–	292	5

Bowling	M	Balls	Runs	Wkts	BB	Avge	RpO	S/R	5i	10m
Tests	2	–	–	–	–	–	–	–	–	–
ODIs	0	0	–	–	–	–	–	–	–	–
T20Is	0	0	–	–	–	–	–	–	–	–
First-class	106	42	68	1	1–65	68.00	9.71	42.00	0	0

YOUNIS KHAN

PAKISTAN

Full name	**Mohammad Younis Khan**
Born	**Nov 29, 1977, Mardan, North-West Frontier Province**
Teams	**NWFP, Peshawar, Habib Bank**
Style	**Right-hand bat, occasional legspinner**
Test debut	**Pakistan v Sri Lanka at Rawalpindi 1999-2000**
ODI debut	**Pakistan v Sri Lanka at Karachi 1999-2000**
T20I debut	**Pakistan v England at Bristol 2006**

THE PROFILE Younis Khan is a fearless middle-order batsman, as befits his Pathan ancestry. He plays with a flourish, and is especially strong in the arc from backward point to extra cover; he is prone to getting down on one knee and driving extravagantly. But this flamboyance is coupled with grit. He started with a century on Test debut, early in 2000, and scored well in bursts after that, including 153 against West Indies in Sharjah. He lost his place shortly after the 2003 World Cup following a modest run, but was soon back in favour, and made another century against Sri Lanka. He remained a heavy runmaker, especially against India: in March 2005 he hit 147 and 267 in successive Tests against them, then early the following year made 199, 83, 194, 0 and 77, before scoring consistently in England too, with 173 at Leeds. He flirted with the captaincy – theatrically resigning more than once – and started his reign as fulltime skipper with 313 in 760 minutes against Sri Lanka on a Karachi featherbed early in 2009. Later that year he led Pakistan to victory in the World Twenty20 in England ... but retired from 20-over cricket immediately afterwards. Not much later he resigned as Test captain too, then was banned for unspecified offences during the disastrous Australian tour that followed. He missed the 2010 England tour – possibly a blessing in disguise – but was welcomed back afterwards, scoring a century against South Africa in his first Test back, at Dubai in November. He had a quiet World Cup in 2011, then missed the West Indian tour after his brother died. But Younis made it to Zimbabwe in September, and hit form straight away.

THE FACTS Younis Khan scored 313, Pakistan's third triple-century in Tests, against Sri Lanka at Karachi in February 2009 ... He averages 88.06 in Tests against India – and more than 31 against everyone else ... Younis was the seventh Pakistani to score a century on Test debut, with 107 against Sri Lanka in February 2000 ... Against India at home early in 2006 he shared successive stands of 319, 142, 242, 0 and 158 with Mohammad Yousuf ... At Lahore in that series Younis became the sixth batsman to be out for 199 in a Test ...

THE FIGURES to 26.09.11   ᴇsᴘᴨcricinfo.com

Batting & Fielding	M	Inns	NO	Runs	HS	Avge	S/R	100	50	4s	6s	Ct	St
Tests	68	121	9	5719	313	51.06	53.05	17	24	683	29	75	0
ODIs	226	217	21	6442	144	32.86	75.49	6	44	509	52	116	0
T20Is	25	23	3	442	51	22.10	121.42	0	2	31	12	12	0
First-class	156	254	30	11364	313	50.73	–	35	47	–	–	166	0

Bowling	M	Balls	Runs	Wkts	BB	Avge	RpO	S/R	5i	10m
Tests	68	660	407	7	2–23	58.14	3.70	94.28	0	0
ODIs	226	260	260	3	1–3	86.66	6.00	86.66	0	0
T20Is	25	22	18	3	3–18	6.00	4.90	7.33	0	0
First-class	156	2928	1705	38	4–52	44.86	3.49	77.05	0	0

YUVRAJ SINGH

Full name	**Yuvraj Singh**
Born	**December 12, 1981, Chandigarh**
Teams	**Punjab, Pune Warriors**
Style	**Left-hand bat, left-arm orthodox spinner**
Test debut	**India v New Zealand at Mohali 2003-04**
ODI debut	**India v Kenya at Nairobi 2000-01**
T20I debut	**India v Scotland at Durban 2007-08**

THE PROFILE Yuvraj Singh made a lordly entry into international cricket at 18, toppling Australia in the ICC Knockout of October 2000 with a blistering 84 in his first innings and some scintillating fielding. He supplements those skills with loopy left-arm spin, with which he took two hat-tricks in IPL2 in 2009. While his ability to hit the ball long and clean was instantly recognised, at first he was troubled by quality spin, and temporarily lost his place. But in 2002 he swung the series against Zimbabwe India's way with two matchwinning innings, then went to England and played key roles in three run-chases, culminating at Lord's where his stand with Mohammad Kaif set up a memorable victory over England. It still took another 15 months, and an injury to Sourav Ganguly, for Yuvraj to get a Test look-in. But in his third match, on a Lahore greentop, he stroked a stunning first-day century off 110 balls. A troublesome knee injury briefly threatened to keep him out of the 2007 World Cup, but later that year he smashed Stuart Broad for six sixes in an over during the inaugural World Twenty20 in South Africa. A scintillating 169 against Pakistan at Bangalore in December 2007 seemed to have nailed down a Test place at last ... but a string of modest scores followed, and he was out again by the middle of 2008. He remained a one-day regular – and a fearsome sight (for bowlers, at least) in Twenty20 games – and was a star with bat and ball as the 2011 World Cup was won, lifting four match awards. However, in England afterwards he broke a finger after making 62 in the first innings of his only Test, at Trent Bridge.

THE FACTS Yuvraj hit England's Stuart Broad for six sixes in an over during the World Twenty20 at Durban in September 2007 ... He played 73 ODIs before winning his first Test cap ... He averages 63.55 in Tests against Pakistan, but 9.14 v Australia ... Yuvraj hit 358 for Punjab Under-19s against Bihar's in December 1999 ... His father, fast bowler Yograj Singh, played one Test in 1980-81 ... Yuvraj's record includes three ODIs for the Asia XI ...

THE FIGURES to 26.09.11   **ESPNcricinfo.com**

Batting & Fielding	M	Inns	NO	Runs	HS	Avge	S/R	100	50	4s	6s	Ct	St
Tests	35	54	6	1709	169	35.60	58.34	3	10	238	17	31	0
ODIs	274	252	38	8051	139	37.62	87.58	13	49	827	144	84	0
T20Is	23	22	4	567	70	31.50	151.60	0	5	34	38	6	0
First-class	97	155	18	6114	209	44.62	–	18	30	–	–	93	0

Bowling	M	Balls	Runs	Wkts	BB	Avge	RpO	S/R	5i	10m
Tests	35	823	483	9	2–9	53.66	3.52	91.44	0	0
ODIs	274	4832	4060	109	5–31	37.24	5.04	44.33	1	0
T20Is	23	144	194	8	3–23	24.25	8.08	18.00	0	0
First-class	97	2113	1211	21	3–25	57.66	3.43	100.61	0	0

AFGHANISTAN

Mohammad Nabi

Mohammad Shahzad

Noor Ali

The improbable rise of war-torn Afghanistan as a cricket power was one of the great feelgood stories of 2008 and 2009. Starting in the lowly backwaters of world cricket's fifth division in May 2008, they won in Jersey to progress up the ladder a notch. They topped Division Four, too, in Tanzania, then emerged from Division Three, in Argentina at the end of January 2009. That put them into the World Cup qualifying series in South Africa, where they finished just one win short of a fairytale appearance in the main event itself in 2011. The decision to reduce the number of associate nations in the World Cup from six in 2007 to four next time ultimately cost Afghanistan a place, as they finished sixth – but that did bring the considerable consolation (and considerable funding) of official one-day international status for the next four years. They celebrated by walloping Scotland in their first ODI, and later in the year shared a short series in the unfamiliar surroundings of the Netherlands. They were also holding their own in the ICC's first-class Intercontinental Cup competition: also in Holland, Noor Ali became only the fourth man – after Test players in Arthur Morris of Australia, India's Nari Contractor and Aamer Malik of Pakistan – to score two centuries on his first-class debut. They qualified for the World Twenty20 in the West Indies early in 2010, and did not look out of place despite losing to India and South Africa. Some more impressive Intercontinental Cup performances followed, and by the end of the year the players were starting to bemoan their lack of opportunities against the senior Test nations in 50-overs matches. Afghanistan's cricketers still have hurdles to overcome – it's difficult to imagine many teams wanting to tour there in the current climate, so home matches will be difficult – but they have coped admirably with everything that has been thrown at them so far.

Afghanistan's ODI records as at 26.09.11

Highest total	295-8	v Scotland at Benoni 2008-09
Lowest total	88	v Kenya at Nairobi 2010-11
Most runs	652	Mohammad Shahzad (avge. 43.46)
Highest score	118	Moh'd Shahzad v Canada at Sharjah 2009-10
Most wickets	25	Samiullah Shenwari (avge. 25.36)
Best bowling	4-24	Shapoor Zadran v Netherlands at Amstelveen 2009
Most matches	18	(four different players)
World Cup record	Have not qualified yet	
Overall ODI record	Played 18: Won 11, Lost 7	

AFGHANISTAN

ASGHAR STANIKZAI, Mohammad February 22, 1987, Kabul
RHB, RFM: 18 ODIs, 366 runs at 24.40, HS 64; 2 wickets at 42.00, BB 1-22.
Middle-order batsman who made 102 against Bahrain in July 2008.

DAWLAT ZADRAN March 19, 1988, Khost
RHB, RFM: 2 ODIs, 0 runs at 0.00, HS 0*; 4 wickets at 18.50, BB 3-49.
Hit for two sixes in his first ODI over – v Canada – but took 9 wickets in his next one.

GULBODIN NAIB January 1, 1988, Loger
RHB, RFM: 1 ODI, 0 runs at 0.0, HS 0.
Out second ball on ODI debut – and didn't get a bowl.

HAMID HASSAN June 1, 1987, Bati Kot, Nangrahar
RHB, RFM: 14 ODIs, 42 runs at 7.00, HS 17; 24 wickets at 21.91, BB 4-26.
Fast bowler who took 5-23 against Ireland in World Cup qualifier in South Africa in April 2009.

JAVED AHMADI January 2, 1992, Kunduz
RHB, OB: 6 ODIs, 67 runs at 13.40, HS 35; 0 wicket for 16.
Batsman who appeared in the Under-19 World Cup in New Zealand in 2010.

KARIM SADIQ Khan February 18, 1984, Nangrahar
RHB, OB, WK: 16 ODIs, 290 runs at 22.30, HS 114*, 1x100: 2 wickets at 41.00, BB 2-28.
Scored 114 against Scotland at Ayr in August 2010.*

KHALIQ DAD Noori January 1, 1984, Baghlan
RHB, RFM: 6 ODIs, 40 runs at 13.33, HS 20; 9 wickets at 16.66, BB 3-30.
Medium-pacer whose brother, Allah Dad, has also played for Afghanistan.

MIRWAIS ASHRAF June 30, 1988, Kunduz
RHB, RFM: 9 ODIs, 71 runs at 11.83, HS 17; 11 wickets at 23.09, BB 4-35.
Medium-pacer who took 4-35 v Kenya in Nairobi in October 2010.

MOHAMMAD NABI Eisakhil March 7, 1985, Loger
RHB, OB: 18 ODIs, 429 runs at 35.75, HS 62; 14 wickets at 39.07, BB 4-31.
Hard-hitting batsman who spent some time on the MCC cricket staff at Lord's.

MOHAMMAD SHAHZAD Mohammadi July 15, 1991, Nangrahar
RHB, WK: 16 ODIs, 652 runs at 43.46, HS 118, 3x100; 19 ct, 5 st.
Scored Afghanistan's first ODI hundred. against the Netherlands at Amstelveen in his second match.

NAWROZ MANGAL, Khan November 28, 1984, Kabul
RHB, OB: 18 ODIs, 384 runs at 27.42, HS 70*; 7 wickets at 26.42, BB 3-35.
Afghanistan's captain during their astonishing rise. Took 5-24 v Malaysia in 2008.

NOOR ALI Zadran July 10, 1988, Khost
RHB, RM: 13 ODIs, 362 runs at 30.16, HS 114, 1x100.
Made 130 and 100 on first-class debut, for Afghanistan v Zimbabwe A in August 2009.*

SAMIULLAH SHENWARI December 31, 1987, Nangrahar
RHB, LBG: 18 ODIs, 300 runs at 30.00, HS 82; 25 wickets at 25.36, BB 4-31.
Improving legspinner who took 4-28 v Bermuda in World Cup qualifier in 2009.

SHABIR NOORI February 23, 1992, Nangrahar
RHB, OB: 8 ODIs, 169 runs at 21.12, HS 94.
Solid batsman who scored 94 against Canada at King City in August 2011.

SHAPOOR ZADRAN July 8, 1987, Loger
LHB, LFM: 13 ODIs, 18 runs at 4.50, HS 17; 17 wickets at 27.70, BB 4-24.
Left-armer who took 4-24 – including 3 for 1 in 8 balls – on ODI debut v Netherlands in Aug 2009.

CANADA

Nitish Kumar   Jimmy Hansra   Zubin Surkari

Cricket has long been played in Canada: the first-ever international match was not England v Australia but Canada v the United States, in New York in 1844. But although the series continued fitfully over the years, cricket never quite took hold in north America – although the States had several handy teams around the turn of the 20th century, and the Canadians have long hosted visits by strong touring sides. Don Bradman made one such trip in the 1930s, and nominated the Brockton Point ground in Vancouver as the most beautiful he'd ever seen. In 1954 a Canadian side toured England, playing several first-class matches. In a portent of things to come, that team included several players who had moved to Canada from the West Indies for better job prospects. After a quiet period, Canadian cricket received a shot in the arm when they qualified for the 1979 World Cup in England, although the inexperienced team was embarrassed by the hosts, being hustled out for 45 at Old Trafford. Canada missed out on World Cup qualification until 2002-03, when a side largely made up of expats – and a few journeymen who happened to have been born in Canada – gave a decent account of themselves. John Davison, who had hovered on the fringes of the Victoria and South Australia sides, returned for the land of his birth and shocked everyone by hammering a century in 67 balls – the fastest in the World Cup at the time – against West Indies. Sri Lanka proved rather more ruthless, bowling them out for 36. Canada qualified again in 2007 and 2011, without upsetting any apple-carts. Their administration has been striving hard to become more professional, and in 2009 the first central contracts were introduced. Whether to accept them was simple for some, like the hard-hitting batsman Rizwan Cheema, who was serving behind the counter in a fast-food joint – and harder for others, like the wicketkeeper/batsman Ashish Bagai, was had been carving out a career in banking. The Canadians deserve some success, although the paucity of home-grown talent remains a worry.

Canada's ODI records as at 11.09.11

Highest total	312-4	v Ireland at Nairobi 2006-07
Lowest total	36	v Sri Lanka at Paarl 2002-03
Most runs	1961	A Bagai (avge. 38.45)
Highest score	137*	A Bagai v Scotland at Nairobi 2006-07
Most wickets	42	H Osinde (avge. 31.04)
Best bowling	5-27	A Codrington v Bangladesh at Durban 2002-03
Most matches	60	A Bagai (2003–2011)
World Cup record		First phase 1979, 2002-03, 2006-07, 2010-11
Overall ODI record		Played 68: Won 17, Lost 50, No result 1

CANADA

BAGAI, Ashish January 26, 1982, Delhi, India
RHB, WK: 60 ODIs, 1961 runs at 38.45, HS 137*, 2x100; 58 ct 9 st.
Tidy wicketkeeper/batsman who captained in 2011 World Cup: hundreds v Scotland and Ireland.

BAIDWAN, Harvir Singh July 31, 1987, Chandigarh, India
RHB, RM: 26 ODIs, 201 runs at 20.10, HS 33; 40 wickets at 27.12, BB 3-19.
Tidy medium-pacer who has a good economy rate (just above five an over) in ODIs.

BALAJI RAO, Wandavasti Dorakanti March 4, 1978, Chennai, India
LHB, LB: 10 ODIs, 59 runs at 7.37, HS 24; 12 wickets at 37.33, BB 4-57.
Combative legspinner who took 4-57 v Zimbabwe in the 2011 World Cup.

BHATTI, Umar January 4, 1984, Lahore, Pakistan
LHB, LM: 36 ODIs, 378 runs at 17.18, HS 46; 33 wickets at 34.81, BB 4-45.
Left-armer who took a hat-trick against Ireland in 2007 Intercontinental Cup final.

DESAI, Parth Ajaykumar December 11, 1990, Navsari, Gujarat, India
RHB, SLA: 12 ODIs, 8 runs at 2.66, HS 3*; 11 wickets at 41.00, BB 3-35.
Young spinner who took 3-35 against Ireland in 2010.

DHANIRAM, Sunil October 17, 1968, Port Mourant, Berbice, Guyana
LHB, SLA: 44 ODIs, 915 runs at 24.72, HS 92; 41 wickets at 30.24, BB 5-32.
Former Guyana allrounder whose brother Sudesh has played for the United States.

GORDON, Tyson George January 31, 1982, St Mary, Jamaica
LHB, RFM: 5 ODIs, 27 runs at 5.40, HS 9; 0 wicket for 25.
Batsman who made his ODI debut against Sri Lanka in the 2011 World Cup.

GUNASEKERA, Ruvindu July 20, 1991, Colombo, Sri Lanka
LHB: 10 ODIs, 247 runs at 24.70, HS 71.
Batsman who played his first ODI at 17: in 2010 hit 71 and 59 v Ireland on successive days.

JYOTI, Sandeep December 14, 1973, Shimla, India
RHB, OB: 14 ODIs, 264 runs at 22.00, HS 117; 1 wicket at 90.00, BB 1-26.
Entertaining batsman who scored 117 against Scotland at Aberdeen in 2009.

KHURRAM CHOHAN February 22, 1980, Lahore, Pakistan
RHB, RFM: 21 ODIs, 136 runs at 13.60, HS 35*; 27 wickets at 30.03, BB 4-26.
Medium-pacer who took eight wickets in successive matches against Afghanistan in 2010.

KUMAR, Nitish Roenik May 21, 1994, Scarborough, Ontario
RHB: 8 ODIs, 79 runs at 11.28, HS 38.
Precocious batsman who made his ODI debut at 15.

OSINDE, Henry October 17, 1978, Uganda
RHB, RFM: 40 ODIs, 63 runs at 4.20, HS 21*; 42 wickets at 31.04, BB 4-26.
Experienced opening bowler who took 4-26 v Kenya in the 2011 World Cup.

PATEL, Hiral August 10, 1991, Ahmedabad, India
RHB, SLA: 16 ODIs, 355 runs at 22.18, HS 62; 8 wickets at 32.50, BB 4-28.
Aggressive batsman who hit 54 against Australia in the 2011 World Cup.

RIZWAN CHEEMA August 15, 1978, Pakistan
RHB, RM: 29 ODIs, 671 runs at 24.85, HS 94; 31 wickets at 30.61, BB 3-25.
Big-hitting batsman with an ODI strike-rate of 116.29 – and 33 sixes.

SURKARI, Zubin Eruch February 26, 1980, Toronto, Ontario
RHB: 23 ODIs, 328 runs at 17.26, HS 49.
Captained Canada on his ODI debut, against Bermuda in 2008.

IRELAND

| George Dockrell | Kevin O'Brien | Paul Stirling |

Cricket in Ireland was once so popular that Oliver Cromwell banned it in 1656. Since then, it has been something of a minority sport, although there have been occasional big days, as in 1969 when the West Indians were skittled for 25 on a boggy pitch at Sion Mills in County Tyrone (rumours that the visitors enjoyed lavish hospitality at a nearby Guinness brewery the night before are thought to be unfounded). Cricket continued as an amateur pastime until the 1990s, when the Irish board left the auspices of the English one and attained independent ICC membership. Ireland became eligible to play in the World Cup, and narrowly missed out on the 1999 tournament, when they lost a playoff to Scotland. They made no mistake for 2007, though, winning the ICC Trophy (handily, it was played in Ireland) to ensure qualification. A change of captain to the Australian-born Trent Johnston ushered in a new, more professional set-up, and Ireland travelled to the Caribbean hopeful of making a mark. No-one, though, was quite prepared for what happened – except maybe Johnston himself, who packed enough for a seven-week stay when most were expecting a quiet return home in a week or two. In their first World Cup match, Ireland tied with Zimbabwe, then went one better on a Sabina Park greentop on St Patrick's Day, hanging on to beat Pakistan and eliminate one of the pre-tournament favourites. Ireland sailed on to the Super Eights, where they beat Bangladesh too. In 2011, the highlight of several good performances was a stunning victory over England, thanks to Kevin O'Brien's 50-ball hundred. But the better Irish players are already with English counties (Ed Joyce and Eoin Morgan have already played for England, and others are trying to follow suit), and the others struggle to fit in ever-increasing international commitments around a steady job. Irish cricket is striving – against considerable odds – to build on World Cup success by planning a proper first-class structure.

Ireland's ODI records *as at 11.09.11*

Highest total	329-7	v England at Bangalore 2010-11
Lowest total	77	v Sri Lanka at St George's 2006-07
Most runs	1606	WTS Porterfield (avge. 31.49)
Highest score	177	PR Stirling v Canada at Toronto 2010
Most wickets	55	DT Johnston (avge. 32.12)
Best bowling	5-14	DT Johnston v Canada at Centurion 2008-09
Most matches	62	KJ O'Brien (2006-2011)
World Cup record		Super Eights 2006-07, first phase 2010-11
Overall ODI record		Played 68: Won 30, Lost 34, Tied 1, No result 3

IRELAND

BOTHA, Andre Cornelius September 12, 1975, Johannesburg, South Africa
LHB, RM: 42 ODIs, 666 runs at 19.58, HS 56; 42 wickets at 27.00, BB 4-19.
Former South African provincial player: made 186 for Ireland v Scotland in August 2007.

CUSACK, Alex Richard October 29, 1980, Brisbane, Australia
RHB, RFM: 40 ODIs, 629 runs at 26.20, HS 71; 38 wickets at 23.81, BB 5-20.
Man of the Match on ODI debut for 36* and 3-15 v South Africa at Belfast in June 2007.

DOCKRELL, George Henry July 22, 1992, Dublin
RHB, SLA: 24 ODIs, 60 runs at 10.00, HS 19; 29 wickets at 28.31, BB 4-35.
Precocious slow left-armer now plying his trade for Somerset.

JOHNSTON, David Trent April 29, 1974, Wollongong, NSW, Australia
RHB, RFM: 55 ODIs, 620 runs at 19.37, HS 45*; 55 wickets at 32.12, BB 5-14.
Inspirational captain (and innovative chicken dancer) during Ireland's 2007 World Cup run.

JONES, Nigel Geoffrey April 22, 1982, Timaru, New Zealand
RHB, RM: 14 ODIs, 74 runs at 14.80, HS 25*; 10 wickets at 23.40, BB 2-19.
Former New Zealander who appears to bowl off the wrong foot.

JOYCE, Edmund Christopher September 22, 1978, Dublin
LHB: 26 ODIs (17 for England), 675 runs at 25.96, HS 107, 1×100.
Played for England in the 2006-07 World Cup, and Ireland in the 2010-11 one.

MOONEY, John Francis February 10, 1982, Dublin
LHB, RM: 39 ODIs, 641 runs at 25.64, HS 55; 29 wickets at 30.10, BB 4-63.
Left-hander with a mean reverse-sweep; his brother Paul played for Ireland too.

O'BRIEN, Kevin Joseph March 4, 1984, Dublin
RHB, RFM: 62 ODIs, 1582 runs at 32.95, HS 142, 2×100; 48 wickets at 30.79, BB 4-71.
Well-built allrounder whose 50-ball century led to victory over England at the 2011 World Cup.

O'BRIEN, Niall John November 8, 1981, Dublin
LHB, WK: 47 ODIs, 1142 runs at 26.55, HS 72; 35 ct, 7 st.
Feisty keeper who has played for Kent and Northants: made 72 in World Cup win over Pakistan.

PORTERFIELD, William Thomas Stuart September 6, 1984, Londonderry
RHB: 54 ODIs, 1606 runs at 31.49, HS 112*, 5×100.
Solid opener: made two ODI hundreds in three days early in 2007; took over as captain in 2008.

POYNTER, Andrew David April 25, 1987, Hammersmith, London
RHB, OB: 15 ODIs, 200 runs at 22.22, HS 78.
Clontarf batsman who played once for Middlesex in 2005: 78 v Afghanistan in 2010.

RANKIN, William Boyd July 5, 1984, Derry
LHB, RFM: 33 ODIs, 34 runs at 8.50, HS 7*; 40 wickets at 31.80, BB 3-32.
Tall fast bowler who did well at the 2007 World Cup and played for England Lions in 2011.

STIRLING, Paul Robert September 3, 1990, Belfast
RHB: 33 ODIs, 1323 runs at 41.34, HS 177, 4×100; 16 wickets at 37.87, BB 4-11.
Batsman on Middlesex's books who slammed 177 against Canada in September 2010.

WHITE, Andrew Roland July 3, 1980, Newtownards, Co. Down
RHB, OB: 54 ODIs, 731 runs at 18.74, HS 79; 25 wickets at 25.00, BB 4-44.
Offspinner, formerly with Northants, who hit 152* on first-class debut, for Ireland v Holland in 2004.

WILSON, Gary Craig February 5, 1986, Dundonald, Northern Ireland
RHB, WK: 33 ODIs, 808 runs at 26.93, HS 113, 1×100; 20 ct, 6 st.
Handy keeper-batsman who is on the Surrey staff; scored 113 v Holland in Dublin in 2010.

KENYA

Tanmay Mishra   *Collins Obuya*   *Seren Waters*

The British Empire spread cricket to Kenya: the first notable match was played there in 1899, and English-style country clubs still flourish in Nairobi, which can claim one cricket record – six different grounds there have staged official one-day internationals, more than any other city. Strong MCC teams have made several visits to East Africa – one of them, in the early 1960s, unearthed Basharat Hassan, who went on to enjoy a long career with Nottinghamshire. Kenyan players formed the backbone of the East African side in the first World Cup, in 1975, but soon after that they struck out on their own, joining the ICC in their own right in 1981. Kenyan cricket continued to improve quietly until they qualified for the World Cup in 1995-96, where they amazed everyone by upsetting West Indies in a group game. Players reared on hard pitches struggled in early-season England at the 1999 Cup, but the 2003 version was different: it was held in Africa, and some of the matches were played in Kenya. Helped by outside events (England refused to go to Zimbabwe, while New Zealand boycotted Nairobi for security reasons), the Kenyans progressed to the semi-finals. It seemed like the start of a golden era: instead it ushered in a depressing time, marked by player strikes and arguments about administration. Peace broke out in time for the 2007 World Cup, but with several players approaching the veteran stage – many of them come from the same Luo tribe, which is why so many of their surnames begin with O – the results were poor, and by then Ireland had comfortably usurped them as the leading non-Test nation. More haggling over money intruded in 2010, before a resolution in time for the following year's World Cup. But more disappointing results there led to a clearout of the old guard, meaning farewells to stalwarts like Steve Tikolo – once seen as the best batsman outside Test cricket – and the chunky allrounder Thomas Odoyo, the first bowler from a non-Test nation to take 100 wickets in one-day internationals.

Kenya's ODI records *as at 11.09.11*

Highest total	347-3	v Bangladesh at Nairobi 1997-98
Lowest total	69	v New Zealand at Chennai 2010-11
Most runs	3362	SO Tikolo (avge. 29.49)
Highest score	144	KO Otieno v Bangladesh at Nairobi 1997-98
Most wickets	137	TM Odoyo (avge. 29.71)
Best bowling	5-24	CO Obuya v Sri Lanka at Nairobi 2002-03
Most matches	130	SO Tikolo (1996-2011)
World Cup record		Semi-finalists 2002-03; first phase 1995-96, 1999, 2006-07, 2010-11
Overall ODI record		Played 142: Won 38, Lost 99, No result 5

KENYA

KAMANDE, James Kabatha   December 12, 1978, Muranga
RHB, OB: 86 ODIs, 1055 runs at 17.29, HS 74; 48 wickets at 45.18, BB 4-36.
Former medium-pacer who now bowls offspin, after his action was reported to the ICC.

MISHRA, Tanmay   December 22, 1986, Mumbai, India
RHB, RM: 34 ODIs, 863 runs at 30.82, HS 72; 0 wicket for 6.
Talented batsman who returned to Kenya in 2010 after studying in India.

NGOCHE, James Otieno   January 29, 1988, Kenya
RHB, OB: 12 ODIs, 33 runs at 4.71, HS 21*; 15 wickets at 25.80, BB 3-18.
Offspinner who took 3-18 against Scotland in 2010.

NGOCHE , Shem Obado   June 6, 1989, Kenya
RHB, SLA: 8 ODIs, 15 runs at 2.50, HS 7*; 5 wickets at 45.60, BB 2-28.
Slow left-armer who faced three balls at the 2011 World Cup – and was dismissed by all three.

OBANDA, Alex Ouma   December 25, 1987, Nairobi
RHB: 40 ODIs, 1137 runs at 32.48, HS 96*.
Strokeplaying batsman who was stranded four short of a century against Zimbabwe in Feb 2009.

OBUYA, Collins Omondi   July 27, 1981, Nairobi
RHB, LB: 92 ODIs, 1760 runs at 25.88, HS 98*; 30 wickets at 51.73, BB 5-24.
Made 98 v Australia in the 2011 World Cup – and took over as captain afterwards.*

OBUYA, David Oluoch   August 14, 1979, Nairobi
RHB, WK: 71 ODIs, 1307 runs at 19.50, HS 93; 36 ct, 5 st.
Opener, wicketkeeper, and brother of Collins Obuya and Kennedy Otieno.

ODHIAMBO, Nehemiah Ngoche   August 7, 1983, Nairobi, Kenya
RHB, RFM: 59 ODIs, 481 runs at 12.65, HS 66; 63 wickets at 35.09, BB 4-61.
Fast bowler who took 5-20 in T20 v Scotland in Feb 2010; three brothers have played for Kenya.

ODHIAMBO, Nelson Mandela   March 21, 1989, Kenya
RHB, RFM: 5 ODIs, 34 runs at 11.33, HS 29; 4 wickets at 47.25, BB 1-22.
Seamer who opened the bowling in an ODI with his uncle, Thomas Odoyo.

ODOYO, Thomas Migai   May 12, 1978, Nairobi
RHB, RFM: 134 ODIs (5 for Africa), 2418 runs (23.94), HS 111*; 141 wkts (29.98), BB 4-25.
Hard-hitting allrounder: the first bowler from a non-Test nation to take 100 wickets in ODIs.

OTIENO, Elijah Asoyo   January 3, 1988, Nairobi
RHB, RFM: 22 ODIs, 40 runs at 4.44, HS 11; 17 wickets at 46.00, BB 3-39.
Promising young seamer – but with the bat collected five ducks in his first seven first-class innings.

OUMA, Maurice Akumu   November 8, 1982, Kiambli
RHB, WK: 72 ODIs, 1291 runs at 19.86, HS 61; 46 ct, 10 st.
Handy striker who often opens: took over as captain in 2009 but resigned in 2010.

PATEL, Rakep Rajendra   July 12, 1989, Nairobi
RHB, OB: 27 ODIs, 366 runs at 16.63, HS 92; 0 wicket for 61.
Promising batsman who hit 92 against the Netherlands in February 2010.

WATERS, Seren Robert   April 11, 1990, Nairobi
RHB: 18 ODIs, 337 runs at 18.72, HS 74.
Young batsman who scored 74 v South Africa in November 2008 while still a schoolboy.

THE NETHERLANDS

Ryan ten Doeschate

Tom de Grooth

Alexei Kervezee

Cricket was brought to The Netherlands by British soldiers during the Napoleonic War: by 1881 there was a Dutch team, and two years later a national board, comprising 18 clubs, four of which still exist. A league system has long flourished, and there has been a tradition of foreign players coming over to coach. Dutch cricket received a boost in 1964 when Australia visited after an Ashes tour and lost by three wickets, and more noses were tweaked in 1989, with a win over England A. West Indies (1991) and South Africa (1994) also succumbed – it's safe to say they were more relaxed than they might have been for an official international – and another strongish England side was beaten in 1993. The Netherlands qualified for their first World Cup three years later, and weren't disgraced, and they were there again in 2003, when they beat Namibia. They just scraped in to the 2007 tournament, winning a playoff against the UAE, but again managed a consolation win, this time over Scotland, which made up for being pummelled by South Africa and Australia. Perhaps their biggest moment, though, came in the first match of the World Twenty20 in 2009, when they embarrassed England – at Lord's, too. Standout performers in recent years have included Roland Lefebvre, who played for Somerset and Glamorgan, and Bas Zuiderent, who had a spell with Sussex. Essex's Ryan ten Doeschate hammered four centuries in three ICC Intercontinental Cup games in 2006, while the Australian Tom Cooper, whose mother is Dutch, made a stunning start in 2010. Ten Doeschate hit two fine centuries in the 2011 World Cup, including 119 as the Netherlands nearly embarrassed England again. The local players are very keen, but there are not that many of them, fans are thin on the ground, and there's really no chance of a proper first-class competition. The future might not be too bright but, for the Dutch one-day team at least, it's certainly orange.

The Netherlands' ODI records *as at 11.09.11*

Highest total	315-8	v Bermuda at Rotterdam 2007
Lowest total	80	v West Indies at Dublin 2007
Most runs	1541	RN ten Doeschate (avge. 67.00)
Highest score	134*	KJJ van Noortwijk v Namibia at Bloemfontein 2002-03
Most wickets	55	RN ten Doeschate (avge. 24.12)
Best bowling	4-23	E Schiferli v Kenya at Potchefstroom 2008-09
Most matches	57	B Zuiderent (1996-2011)
World Cup record		Eliminated in first round 1995-96, 2002-03, 2006-07 and 2010-11
Overall ODI record		Played 65: Won 23, Lost 40, No result 2

THE NETHERLANDS

ADEEL RAJA August 15, 1980, Lahore, Pakistan
RHB, OB: 21 ODIs, 28 runs at 2.80, HS 8*; 17 wickets at 40.58, BB 4-42.
Returned in 2010 after failing a drugs test in 2007.

BARRESI, Wesley May 3, 1984, Johannesburg, South Africa
RHB: 17 ODIs, 377 runs at 25.13, HS 64*.
Hard-hitting batsman who formerly played for Easterns in South Africa.

BORREN, Peter William August 21, 1983, Christchurch, New Zealand
RHB, RM: 47 ODIs, 724 runs at 19.05, HS 96; 40 wickets at 33.50, BB 3-30.
Combative allrounder who made 105 and 96 v Canada in 2006: appointed captain in 2010.

BUKHARI, Mudassar December 26, 1983, Gujrat, Pakistan
RHB, RFM: 35 ODIs, 420 runs at 17.50, HS 71; 41 wickets at 27.58, BB 3-17.
Primarily a bowler, he scored 71 (after opening) and took 3-24 against Ireland in July 2007.

BUURMAN, Atse F. March 21, 1982, The Netherlands
RHB, WK: 17 ODIs, 140 runs at 15.55, HS 34; 17 ct, 3 st.
Found a permanent place after the retirement of long-serving wicketkeeper Jeroen Smits in 2009.

COOPER, Tom Lexley William November 26, 1986, Wollongong, NSW, Australia
RHB, OB: 18 ODIs, 864 runs at 54.00, HS 101, 1×100; 9 wickets at 33.22, BB 2-19.
Hard-hitting batsman who uniquely passed 50 in his first three ODIs, then made 101 in his fifth.

de GROOTH, Tom Nico May 14, 1979, The Hague
RHB, OB: 29 ODIs, 440 runs at 17.60, HS 97; 1 wicket at 2.00, BB 1-2.
Made 98 (v Scotland), 196 and 97 (v Bermuda) in successive matches in August 2007.

KERVEZEE, Alexei Nicolaas September 11, 1989, Walvis Bay, Namibia
RHB, RM: 37 ODIs, 794 runs at 24.81, HS 92; 0 wickets for 34.
World Cup debut at 17, later made 98 v Canada, and joined Worcestershire in 2007.

KRUGER, Bradley Peter September 17, 1988, Pretoria, South Africa
RHB, RFM: 5 ODIs, 32 runs at 10.66, HS 15; 3 wickets at 43.66, BB 3-21.
Seamer who took 3-21 in his first ODI, against Canada in 2010.

LOOTS, Bernadus Pieters April 19, 1979, Prieska, South Africa
RHB, RM: 7 ODIs, 16 runs at 5.33, HS 9*; 6 wickets at 47.83, BB 3-16.
Seamer who took wickets with his 2nd and 3rd balls in ODIs (against Ireland in 2010).

SEELAAR, Pieter Marinus July 2, 1987, Schiedam
RHB, SLA: 29 ODIs, 92 runs at 10.22, HS 34*; 30 wickets at 35.20, BB 3-22.
Tidy spinner who took 5-57 in Intercontinental Cup match v Kenya at Amstelveen in 2008.

SZWARCZYNSKI, Eric Stefan February 13, 1983, Vanderbijlpark, South Africa
RHB: 33 ODIs, 805 runs at 26.83, HS 84*.
Batsman whose favourite player is Allan Donald: made 84 v Canada in July 2010.*

ten DOESCHATE, Ryan Neil June 30, 1980, Port Elizabeth, South Africa
RHB, RFM: 33 ODIs, 1541 runs at 67.00, HS 119, 5×100; 55 wickets at 24.12, BB 4-31.
Allrounder who reached 1000 ODI runs quicker than anyone bar Viv Richards and Gordon Greenidge.

WESTDIJK, Berend Arnold March 5, 1985, The Hague
RHB, RFM: 4 ODIs, 1 run at 0.50, HS 1*; 1 wicket at 195.00, BB 1-56.
Medium-pacer whose first three ODIs were during the 2011 World Cup.

ZUIDERENT, Bastiaan March 3, 1977, Utrecht
RHB: 57 ODIs, 1097 runs at 23.84, HS 77*.
Orthodox opener who had a spell with Sussex: has played in all four of Holland's World Cups.

SCOTLAND

Richie Berrington *Gordon Drummond* *Kyle Coetzer*

Cricket crept over the border from England in the mid-18th century: soldiers played it near Perth in 1750, although the first recorded match in Scotland was not till 1785. More recently there has long been a strong amateur league system in the country, although – just as in Ireland – international aspirations have always been handicapped by the absence of a proper professional set-up, which has meant that the better players have always migrated south. One of them, the Ayr-born Mike Denness, captained England, while one of the few bowlers to trouble Don Bradman in 1930 was the Scottish legspinner Ian Peebles. More recently, offspinner Peter Such (born in Helensburgh) played for England, while Gavin Hamilton (born in Broxburn) also won an England Test cap after impressing for Scotland at the 1999 World Cup. Unfortunately, Hamilton bagged a pair, and was soon back playing for Scotland: he hit his maiden ODI century in 2008. At the 2007 World Cup, Hamilton appeared alongside another former England player in Dougie Brown, the combative allrounder who had a long career with Warwickshire and played nine ODIs in 1997-98. Scotland left the auspices of the English board and joined the ICC in 1994, but they failed to win a match – or reach 200 – in any of their World Cup games in 1999 or 2007. They also competed in the English counties' limited-overs league for many years, without managing more than the occasional upset, and the team failed to qualify for the World Twenty20 in 2010 or the following year's World Cup. The main problem lying in the way of Scotland's advancement – apart from the weather – remains the lack of a sound domestic structure which might support first-class cricket; local support is also patchy, despite the sterling efforts of a few diehards. Until this is addressed – if it ever can be – Scotland will continue to suffer from a player drain to English counties.

Scotland's ODI records *as at 11.09.11*

Highest total	323-5	v Ireland at Edinburgh 2011
Lowest total	68	v West Indies at Leicester 1999
Most runs	1231	GM Hamilton (avge. 35.17)
Highest score	123*	RR Watson v Canada at Mombasa 2006-07
Most wickets	41	JAR Blain (avge. 28.60)
Best bowling	5-9	JH Davey v Afghanistan at Ayr 2010
Most matches	43	NFI McCallum (2006-2011)
World Cup record		Eliminated in first round 1999 and 2006-07
Overall ODI record		Played 54: Won 18, Lost 33, No result 3

SCOTLAND

BERRINGTON, Richard Douglas   April 3, 1987, Pretoria, South Africa
RHB, RFM: 20 ODIs, 387 runs at 22.76, HS 84; 11 wickets at 42.90, BB 2-14.
Handy allrounder who made 84 against the Netherlands in June 2010.

COETZER, Kyle James   April 14, 1984, Aberdeen
RHB, RM: 9 ODIs, 384 runs at 48.00, HS 89*; 1 wicket at 125.00, BB 1-35.
Attractive batsman who is on Durham's books, and scored two first-class hundreds for them in 2007.

DAVEY, Joshua Henry   August 3, 1990, Aberdeen
RHB, RM: 8 ODIs, 147 runs at 21.00, HS 48*; 13 wickets at 16.92, BB 5-9.
Batsman on Middlesex's books: took 5-9 v Afghanistan at Ayr in August 2010.

DRUMMOND, Gordon David   April 21, 1980, Meigle, Perthshire
RHB, RFM: 25 ODIs, 207 runs at 23.00, HS 35*; 23 wickets at 34.52, BB 4-41.
Watsonians fast bowler who took 4-41 v Canada in July 2009: appointed captain in 2010.

GOUDIE, Gordon   August 12, 1987, Aberdeen
RHB, RFM: 14 ODIs, 40 runs at 6.66, HS 17*; 21 wickets at 23.95, BB 5-73.
West of Scotland fast bowler who took 5-73 against Australia in 2009.

HAQ Khan, Rana Majid   February 11, 1983, Paisley
LHB, OB: 31 ODIs, 445 runs at 18.54, HS 71; 38 wickets at 31.47, BB 4-28.
Hard-hitting allrounder, who plays for Ferguslie: took 4-28 v West Indies at Clontarf in 2007.

LYONS, Ross Thomas   December 8, 1984, Greenock
LHB, SLA: 25 ODIs, 90 runs at 22.50, HS 28; 20 wickets at 45.05, BB 3-21.
Slow left-armer who dismissed Shahid Afridi in his first ODI.

MacLEOD, Calum Scott   November 15, 1988, Glasgow
RHB, RFM: 8 ODIs, 80 runs at 13.33, HS 35; 3 wickets at 46.33, BB 2-46.
Fast bowler once on Warwickshire's books, whose bowling action has been under scrutiny.

MAIDEN, Gregor Ian   July 22, 1979, Glasgow
RHB, WK: 7 ODIs, 84 runs at 21.00, HS 31; 5 ct.
Grange allrounder tried as Scotland's wicketkeeper in 2011.

MOMMSEN, Preston Luke   October 14, 1987, Durban, South Africa
RHB, OB: 10 ODIs, 204 runs at 20.40, HS 80; 6 wickets at 14.66, BB 3-26.
Prolific schoolboy batsman who qualified for Scotland in 2010.

NEL, Johann Dewald   June 6, 1980, Klerksdorp, South Africa
RHB, RFM: 19 ODIs, 31 runs at 15.50, HS 11*; 14 wickets at 46.35, BB 4-25.
Fast bowler who dismissed Inzamam-ul-Haq on his ODI debut, and both Australia's openers in 2009.

PARKER, Matthew Archibald   March 2, 1990, Dundee
LHB, RFM: 10 ODIs, 59 runs at 9.83, HS 22; 12 wickets at 27.25, BB 4-33.
Fast bowler who took 5-47 v Warwickshire in 2011.

SHARIF, Safyaan   May 24, 1991, Huddersfield
RHB, RFM: 3 ODIs, 10 runs, HS 9*; 5 wickets at 23.80, BB 4-27.
Dunfermline fast bowler who took 4-27 on ODI debut, v Netherlands in 2011.

WATSON, Ryan Robert   November 12, 1976, Salisbury (now Harare), Zimbabwe
RHB, RM: 35 ODIs, 956 runs at 30.83, HS 123*, 1×100; 12 wickets at 44.00, BB 3-18.
Chunky batsman, at school with SA's Graeme Smith, who hit 123 v Canada in Mombasa in 2006-07.*

WATTS, David Fraser   June 5, 1979, King's Lynn, Norfolk
RHB: 36 ODIs, 974 runs at 28.64, HS 101, 1×100.
Banker-turned-batsman who scored 171 v Denmark in 2006, and 101 v Canada in July 2009.*

OFFICIALS

ALEEM DAR

Aleem Dar played 17 first-class matches as an offspinning allrounder, but never surpassed the 39 he scored in his first innings, for Railways in February 1987. He took up umpiring in 1998-99, and stood in his first ODI the following season. He officiated at the 2003 World Cup, and a year later was the first Pakistani to join the ICC's elite panel. Calm and unobtrusive, he soon established a good reputation, and it was no surprise when he was chosen to stand in the 2007 World Cup final. What was a surprise was his part in the chaos in the dark at the end, for which all the officials were excluded from the World Twenty20 championships later in the year. But he was soon back in favour, and stood in the World Twenty20 final in Barbados in 2010 and the World Cup final in Mumbai in April 2011. Unlike most of his colleagues, he continues to play, and made 82 in a club game the day after umpiring a Test in Mumbai in November 2004.

Born *June 6, 1968, Jhang, Pakistan.* **Tests** 67, **ODIs** 146, **T20Is** 18

ASAD RAUF

Asad Rauf was a right-hand batsman who enjoyed a solid if unspectacular first-class career in Pakistan in the 1980s, four times making more than 600 runs in a season and scoring three centuries, the highest 130 for Railways against National Bank in November 1981. He umpired his first first-class match in 1998-99, and stood in his first ODI early in 2000. It took a bit longer to crack the Test scene, but he advanced rapidly once he did, joining the ICC's elite panel in April 2006. A former offspinner himself, he is more prepared than some to give spinners lbws when batsmen prop forward hiding bat behind pad.

Born *May 12, 1956, Lahore, Pakistan.* **Tests** 38, **ODIs** 90, **T20Is** 17

DAVID **BOON**

David Boon, and his trademark bushy moustache, were Australian legends: he scored 7,422 runs in more than 100 Tests between 1984 and 1996, and was also a feared presence at short leg. He soon became a national selector, and also worked in cricket administration in his native Tasmania before replacing his fellow Aussie Alan Hurst as a match referee in 2011.

Born *December 29, 1960, Launceston, Tasmania, Australia. No international matches as a referee yet*

BILLY **BOWDEN**

Some eccentrics are born. Others thrust eccentricity upon themselves. Brent "Billy" Bowden shot to fame with a zany array of embellished signals and a preposterous eye for showmanship. Bowden turned to umpiring after the onset of arthritis in his early twenties, and earned a reputation for giving batsmen out with a curiously bent finger. The most celebrated of his antics is the hop-on-one-leg-and-reach-for-Jesus signal for six. For all the embellishments, though, his decision-making is usually spot-on.

Born *April 11, 1963, Henderson, Auckland, New Zealand.* **Tests** *68,* **ODIs** *160,* **T20Is** *19*

CHRIS **BROAD**

It was a classic case of poacher turned gamekeeper when Chris Broad became a match referee: he had several jousts with authority during a 25-Test career in the 1980s. A tall, angular left-hander, Broad did well in Australia, scoring four Test hundreds there. After a back injury hastened his retirement, he tried his hand at TV commentary, then in 2003 became a match referee keen on enforcing the Code of Conduct. His son, Stuart, made his England debut in 2006.

Born *September 29, 1957, Knowle, Bristol, England.* **Tests** *47,* **ODIs** *191,* **T20Is** *39*

ALAN **BUTCHER**

Alan Butcher played with distinction for Surrey and then Glamorgan – he was around for so long he once played against his son, the England batsman Mark – and won one England cap, opening with Geoff Boycott against India in 1979. After various coaching roles he took over the Zimbabwean national team in time for the 2011 World Cup, and oversaw their successful return to Test cricket against Bangladesh in August of that year.

Born *January 7, 1954, Croydon, Surrey, England. Appointed Zimbabwe's coach in 2011*

JEFF **CROWE**

Jeff Crowe might have played for Australia – he had several successful Sheffield Shield seasons in Adelaide – but he eventually returned to New Zealand, winning 39 Test caps, six as captain. Although he was often overshadowed by his younger brother Martin, Jeff managed three Test centuries of his own. After retirement he had a spell as New Zealand's manager, before becoming a referee in 2003. He oversaw the World Cup finals of 2007 and 2011.

Born *September 14, 1958, Auckland, New Zealand.* **Tests** *46,* **ODIs** *155,* **T20Is** *24*

OFFICIALS

STEVE **DAVIS**

Steve Davis played club cricket in Adelaide before turning to umpiring. He had a rapid rise: appointed to the Australian first-class list in 1990-91, he joined the national panel two years later and stood in his first ODI the same season. He stood in three matches in the 2007 World Cup, and in the final two Tests in his native England in 2008, against South Africa, shortly after being elevated to the elite panel. He was one of the umpires in Lahore early the following year and was lucky to survive the terrorist attack on the Sri Lankan team coach.

Born *April 9, 1952, London, England.* **Tests** *32,* **ODIs** *105,* **T20Is** *14*

KUMAR **DHARMASENA**

Kumar Dharmasena played 31 Tests for Sri Lanka as a brisk offspinner who could bat a bit. He took 69 wickets, with a best of 6 for 72 against New Zealand at Galle in 1998, and also claimed 138 wickets in 141 ODIs. After retiring in 2006 he was fast-tracked into umpiring, standing in his first ODI less than three years later, and joined the ICC's elite panel in 2011.

Born *April 24, 1971, Colombo, Sri Lanka.* **Tests** *3,* **ODIs** *30,* **T20Is** *3*

BILLY **DOCTROVE**

Billy Doctrove played club cricket in Dominica for a number of years, but his first love was football, particularly Liverpool, which explains his odd nickname "Toshack". In 1995 he became Dominica's first FIFA referee, and officiated in a number of internationals in the Caribbean, including a World Cup qualifier between Guyana and Grenada. In 1997 he quit football to concentrate on cricket umpiring, and stood in his first Test in 2000. He joined the international panel in 2004 and the elite one in 2006, but his first forays at the highest level were uninspiring, and he found himself embroiled in the Pakistan ball-tampering furore at The Oval in 2006, as the "other umpire" to Darrell Hair. He grew in stature, though, and stood in the first two Tests of the 2009 Ashes series. The following year he umpired the final of the World Twenty20 in Barbados.

Born *July 3, 1955, Marigot, Dominica.* **Tests** *33,* **ODIs** *109,* **T20Is** *17*

MARAIS **ERASMUS**

The solidly built Marais Erasmus was a handy allrounder for Boland in South African domestic cricket, averaging just under 30 with the bat and also taking 131 wickets with some energetic medium-pace. That included 6 for 22 as the New Zealanders were bundled out for an embarrassing 86 on a sporting Paarl pitch in December 1994. Erasmus turned to umpiring on retirement and, once he reached the ICC's reserve list, was speedily promoted: he stood in his first ODI in Kenya in 2007. Three years later he was appointed to the ICC's elite panel, and stood in his first Test in Bangladesh in January 2010.

Born *February 27, 1964, George, Cape Province, South Africa.* **Tests** *6,* **ODIs** *36,* **T20Is** *12*

DUNCAN **FLETCHER**

Duncan Fletcher was a gutsy allrounder for Zimbabwe in pre-Test days – he scored 69 not out and took four wickets when they upset Australia in the 1983 World Cup – and after a successful coaching career had a mixed time in charge of England, when the euphoric 2005 Ashes victory was followed by the 2006-07 whitewash Down Under. Fletcher replaced Gary Kirsten as India's coach after the 2011 World Cup, and endured a chastening return to England, which overshadowed his achievement in becoming the first international coach to oversee 100 Tests.

Born *September 27, 1948, Salisbury (now Harare), Zimbabwe. Appointed India's coach in 2011*

ANDY **FLOWER**

Andy Flower was often a lone beacon of class in an underpowered Zimbabwe side. A compact left-hander strong on the sweep, Flower scored 4,794 Tests runs at 51, and nearly 7,000 in ODIs. A deep thinker, Flower was hounded out of Zimbabwe after he and Henry Olonga wore black armbands mourning the "death of democracy" there during the 2003 World Cup. Flower moved to England, where he did well for Essex, then joined the England coaching set-up, taking over as fulltime coach in time for the successful 2009 Ashes series and oversaw England's impressive climb to No. 1 in the world Test rankings.

Born *April 28, 1968, Cape Town, South Africa. Appointed England coach in 2009*

OTTIS **GIBSON**

Fast bowler Ottis Gibson was unlucky that his best years coincided with the pomp of Curtly Ambrose and Courtney Walsh: Gibson played only two Tests, and a few ODIs, in the 1990s. Still, he carved out a successful career in county cricket for Glamorgan, Leicestershire and for Durham. It was an inspired move: he made a career-best 155 for his new county in 2006, and the following year took all ten wickets in an innings against Hampshire. That winter he joined the England coaching staff, but early in 2010 Gibson was persuaded to return home and take on the big task of returning West Indies to Test cricket's top table.

Born *March 16, 1969, Sion Hill, St Peter, Barbados. Appointed West Indies coach in 2010*

OFFICIALS

IAN **GOULD**

UMPIRE

Ian "Gunner" Gould was a combative wicketkeeper/batsman who scored nearly 9000 runs and made more than 700 dismissals in first-class cricket. He started with Middlesex, then moved to Sussex, who he captained to the NatWest Trophy in 1986. Although he never won a Test cap, he did appear in 18 ODIs, all of them in 1983, including that year's World Cup in England. He joined the English first-class umpires' panel in 2002, was promoted to the international panel in April 2006, joined the elite panel three years later, and immediately looked at home.

Born *August 19, 1957, Taplow, Buckinghamshire, England.* **Tests** *21,* **ODIs** *65,* **T20Is** *15*

TONY **HILL**

UMPIRE

Tony Hill came into umpiring without any background in first-class cricket, but soon established himself as a competent and reliable official, being appointed to the ICC's international panel in 1998 – he stood in an ODI against Zimbabwe that March – and to the full elite panel in 2009, although he had umpired the occasional Test since 2001-02. At Lord's in 2010, for England's Test against Pakistan, Hill formed an all-Kiwi umpiring partnership with Billy Bowden. A keen golfer, he is a regional training officer and mentor for umpires in the Northern Districts.

Born *June 26, 1951, Auckland, New Zealand.* **Tests** *25,* **ODIs** *87,* **T20Is** *16*

RICHARD **KETTLEBOROUGH**

UMPIRE

Richard Kettleborough had an unspectacular career as a batsman with Yorkshire and Middlesex, the highlight 108 for his native county against Essex in 1996. He became a first-class umpire in 2006, when only 33, and soon made a mark as a calm official who usually got things right. He stood in his first internationals in 2009, and joined the ICC's elite panel in 2011.

Born *March 15, 1973, Sheffield, Yorkshire, England.* **Tests** *5,* **ODIs** *17,* **T20Is** *3*

GARY **KIRSTEN**

COACH

A gritty left-hander, Gary Kirsten worked out his strengths and played to them superbly in a career that brought him 7289 runs in 101 Tests for South Africa, with 21 centuries. Kirsten's methodical approach helped when he turned to coaching, first as a batting consultant, then as director of his own coaching academy in Cape Town. In December 2007 he succeeded Greg Chappell in the hot seat as coach of India. He took them to World Cup glory in 2011 before returning home to coach South Africa.

Born *November 23, 1967, Cape Town, South Africa. Appointed South Africa coach in 2011*

STUART **LAW**

Stuart Law was a prolific batsman for Queensland – and in county cricket for Lancashire and Essex – and was unlucky that a surfeit of great batsmen restricted him to one Test for Australia (in which he scored 54 not out). He finally stopped playing in 2009, with 79 first-class hundreds and an average over 50, and moved into coaching: after a spell as Sri Lanka's assistant he succeeded his fellow Australian Jamie Siddons as Bangladesh's coach in 2011.

Born *October 18, 1968, Herston, Brisbane, Queensland, Australia. Appointed Bangladesh's coach in 2011*

RANJAN **MADUGALLE**

A stylish right-hander, Ranjan Madugalle won 21 Test caps, the first of them in Sri Lanka's inaugural Test, against England in 1981-82, when he top-scored with 65. He also made 103 against India in Colombo in 1985, and captained Sri Lanka twice. Not long after retiring, he became one of the first match refs, and was appointed the ICC's chief referee in 2001. His easy-going exterior and charming personality are a mask for someone who has a reputation as a strict disciplinarian.

Born *April 22, 1959, Kandy, Sri Lanka.* **Tests** *128,* **ODIs** *265,* **T20Is** *46*

ROSHAN **MAHANAMA**

Roshan Mahanama was part of the winning team in the 1996 World Cup, and the following year made 225 as he and Sanath Jayasuriya put on 576, then a record Test partnership, as Sri Lanka ran up 952 for 6 (another record) against India in Colombo. An attacking right-hander who made four Test centuries, he was also a fine fielder. He was jettisoned after the 1999 World Cup and quit not long afterwards. He joined the ICC's referees panel in 2003.

Born *May 31, 1966, Colombo, Sri Lanka.* **Tests** *32,* **ODIs** *171,* **T20Is** *13*

TIM **NIELSEN**

Tim Nielsen had a hard act to follow, replacing John Buchanan after his incredibly successful stint as Australia's coach. Nielsen, a talented wicketkeeper-batsman for South Australia whose international hopes were stymied by the perpetual presence under the Baggy Green of Ian Healy, had been around for part of the Buchanan era as assistant coach and computer analyst. Nielsen's arrival coincided with the retirements of several senior players, and his rebuilt side lost to India and South Africa before surrendering the Ashes in 2009 and losing at home to England in 2010-11.

Born *May 5, 1968, Forest Gate, London, England. Appointed Australia coach in 2007*

OFFICIALS

REFEREE

ANDY **PYCROFT**

A fine batsman, especially strong off the back foot, Andy Pycroft was a Zimbabwe regular throughout the 1980s, although he was slightly past his peak when they gained Test status in 1992-93. Still, he played in their first three Tests, scoring 60 against New Zealand at Harare in the last of them. The first and last of his 20 ODIs produced famous wins: over Australia in the 1983 World Cup and England in the 1991-92 one. After retiring from playing he was successively a Zimbabwean selector, team manager, and coach. He also found time to fit in the occasional spot of commentary. Outside cricket he was an attorney-at-law for 17 years, which stood him in good stead when he joined the ICC's referees' panel. His first Test as a referee was at Lord's – England v West Indies in May 2009 – and two months later he oversaw Bangladesh's victory over a makeshift West Indian side in the Caribbean.

Born *June 6, 1956, Salisbury (now Harare), Zimbabwe.* **Tests** *18,* **ODIs** *33,* **T20Is** *8*

COACH

RUMESH **RATNAYAKE**

Rumesh Ratnayake was a fast-medium bowler with an easy, slippery action who took 73 wickets in 23 Tests for Sri Lanka between 1983 and 1992. He wasn't quite your archetypal fast bowler, once fainting at the sight of blood after hitting the batsman. After a spell as a development officer with the Asian Cricket Council, Ratnayake was appointed Sri Lanka's interim coach in July 2011.

Born *January 2, 1964, Colombo, Sri Lanka. Appointed Sri Lanka's interim coach in 2011*

REFEREE

JAVAGAL **SRINATH**

Arguably the fastest bowler India has ever produced, Javagal Srinath took 236 wickets in Tests, and 315 more in ODIs. He was tall, and usually slanted the ball in. Unusually for a quick bowler, he did better in India than overseas, his bowling average of 26 at home being four runs lower than his overall one. He went out at the top: his last international match was the 2003 World Cup final. Sadly, there was no fairytale farewell – Srinath was caned (0 for 87) as Australia ran out easy winners. He was not long away from the international arena, though: after a spell as a commentator he joined the referees' panel in 2006. "I'll have to concentrate more than I did during my playing days," he observed wryly.

Born *August 31, 1969, Mysore, Karnataka, India.* **Tests** *17,* **ODIs** *105,* **T20Is** *16*

SIMON **TAUFEL**

Simon Taufel came young to umpiring: he was only 24 when he stood in his first Sheffield Shield match, and still under 30 – and younger than some of the players – when he made his Test debut on Boxing Day 2000. He started after being forced to retire from Sydney club cricket with a back injury. Calm and collected, he leaves little to chance, regularly running laps of the ground to keep fit and often standing in the nets to familiarise himself with players' techniques. He joined the ICC's elite panel in 2003, and stood in the World Cup final in Mumbai in April 2011.

Born *January 21, 1971, St Leonards, Sydney, Australia.* **Tests** *69,* **ODIs** *167,* **T20Is** *22*

ROD **TUCKER**

Allrounder Rod Tucker played 100 first-class matches for Tasmania over ten years from 1988-89. His seven hundreds included a satisfying 165 against his native NSW in March 1991. He was also a handy medium-pacer who took 123 wickets. On his first morning as a first-class umpire, in December 2004, South Australia were bowled out for 29, but by January 2009 he was standing in his first ODI. He officiated in the World Twenty20s of 2009 and 2010, in between making his Test debut in New Zealand, and was appointed to the ICC's elite panel in 2010.

Born *August 28, 1964, Auburn, Sydney, Australia.* **Tests** *12,* **ODIs** *24,* **T20Is** *8*

WAQAR YOUNIS

One of the most fearsome fast bowlers in world cricket in the 1990s, Waqar Younis took 373 wickets in Tests and 416 in ODIs, many of them with his trademark inswinging yorker, which batsmen ruefully described as being "Waqared". He was also an early – and deadly – exponent of reverse swing. In March 2006 he was appointed Pakistan's bowling coach, then early in 2010 – after another calamitous tour of Australia – Waqar inherited the hot seat as national coach. A return to England, where he had had conspicuous success with Surrey, was soured when Pakistan's players were accused of "spot-fixing" during the final Test at Lord's.

Born *November 16, 1971, Vehari, Punjab, Pakistan. Appointed Pakistan coach in 2010*

JOHN **WRIGHT**

John Wright was an adhesive left-hand opener for New Zealand in 82 Tests between 1978 and 1993, scoring 5,334 runs. Since retirement he has held a variety of high-profile coaching positions, notably having a successful stint in charge of India, and once back home it was something of a surprise that it was some time before he was appointed as New Zealand's national coach – he finally took over the hot seat in December 2010, their fourth coach in less than three years.

Born *July 5, 1954, Darfield, Canterbury, New Zealand. Appointed New Zealand's coach in 2010*

OVERALL RECORDS

Test Matches

Most appearances

181	SR Tendulkar *I*	
168	SR Waugh *A*	
157	R Dravid *I**	
156	AR Border *A*	
154	RT Ponting *A*	
145	JH Kallis *SA**	
145	SK Warne *A*	
139	MV Boucher *SA**	
133	M Muralitharan *SL**	
133	AJ Stewart *E*	

*The records for Boucher, Dravid, Kallis and Muralitharan include one Test for the World XI

Most runs

			Avge
14965	SR Tendulkar *I*		56.25
12775	R Dravid *I**		53.00
12487	RT Ponting *A*		53.13
11953	BC Lara *WI**		52.88
11947	JH Kallis *SA**		57.43
11174	AR Border *A*		50.56
10927	SR Waugh *A*		51.06
10122	SM Gavaskar *I*		51.12
9852	DPMD J'wardene *SL*		52.40
9367	S Chanderpaul *WI*		49.04

*The records for Dravid, Kallis and Lara include one Test for the World XI

Most wickets

			Avge
800	M Muralitharan *SL**		22.72
708	SK Warne *A*		25.41
619	A Kumble *I*		29.65
563	GD McGrath *A*		21.64
519	CA Walsh *WI*		24.44
434	Kapil Dev *I*		29.64
431	RJ Hadlee *NZ*		22.29
421	SM Pollock *SA*		23.11
414	Wasim Akram *P*		23.62
406	Harbhajan Singh *I*		32.22

*Muralitharan's record includes one Test (5 wkts) for the World XI.
CEL Ambrose (WI; 405) also passed 400

Highest scores

400*	BC Lara	WI v Eng at St John's	2003-04
380	ML Hayden	Aust v Zim at Perth	2003-04
375	BC Lara	WI v Eng at St John's	1993-94
374	DPMD Jayawardene	SL v SA at Colombo	2006
365*	GS Sobers	WI v Pak at Kingston	1957-58
364	L Hutton	Eng v Aust at The Oval	1938
340	ST Jayasuriya	SL v India at Colombo	1997-98
337	Hanif Mohammad	Pak v WI at Bridgetown	1957-58
336*	WR Hammond	Eng v NZ at Auckland	1932-33
334*	MA Taylor	Aust v Pak at Peshawar	1998-99
334	DG Bradman	Aust v Eng at Leeds	1930

In all 24 scores of 300 or more have been made in Tests

Best innings bowling

10-53	JC Laker	Eng v Aust at Manchester	1956
10-74	A Kumble	India v Pak at Delhi	1998-99
9-28	GA Lohmann	Eng v SA at Jo'burg	1895-96
9-37	JC Laker	Eng v Aust at Manchester	1956
9-51	M Muralitharan	SL v Zim at Kandy	2001-02
9-52	RJ Hadlee	NZ v Aust at Brisbane	1985-86
9-56	Abdul Qadir	Pak v Eng at Lahore	1987-88
9-57	DE Malcolm	Eng v SA at The Oval	1994
9-65	M Muralitharan	SL v Eng at The Oval	1998
9-69	JM Patel	India v Aust at Kanpur	1959-60

There have been seven further instances of a bowler taking nine wickets in an innings

Record wicket partnerships

1st	415	ND McKenzie (226) and GC Smith (232)	South Africa v Bangladesh at Chittagong	2007-08
2nd	576	ST Jayasuriya (340) and RS Mahanama (225)	Sri Lanka v India at Colombo	1997-98
3rd	624	KC Sangakkara (287) and DPMD Jayawardene (374)	Sri Lanka v South Africa at Colombo	2006
4th	437	DPMD Jayawardene (240) and TT Samaraweera (231)	Sri Lanka v Pakistan at Karachi	2008-09
5th	405	SG Barnes (234) and DG Bradman (234)	Australia v England at Sydney	1946-47
6th	351	DPMD Jayawardene (275) and HAPW Jayawardene (154*)	Sri Lanka v India at Ahmedabad	2009-10
7th	347	DS Atkinson (219) and CC Depeiaza (122)	West Indies v Australia at Bridgetown	1954-55
8th	332	IJL Trott (184) and SCJ Broad (169)	England v Pakistan at Lord's	2010
9th	195	MV Boucher (78) and PL Symcox (108)	South Africa v Pakistan at Johannesburg	1997-98
10th	151	BF Hastings (110) and RO Collinge (68*)	New Zealand v Pakistan at Auckland	1972-73
	151	Azhar Mahmood (128*) and Mushtaq Ahmed (59)	Pakistan v South Africa at Rawalpindi	1997-98

Figures to 26.09.11. Updated records can be found at **www.cricinfo.com/ci/engine/records**

Test Matches OVERALL RECORDS

Most catches

Fielders
207	R Dravid	I/World
181	RT Ponting	A
181	ME Waugh	A
172	DPMD Jayawardene	SL
171	SP Fleming	NZ

Most dismissals

Wicketkeepers   Ct/St
521	MV Boucher	
	SA/World	499/22
416	AC Gilchrist A	379/37
395	IA Healy A	366/29
355	RW Marsh A	343/12
270	PJL Dujon WI	265/5

Highest team totals

952-6d	Sri Lanka v India at Colombo	1997-98
903-7d	Eng v Australia at The Oval	1938
849	Eng v WI at Kingston	1929-30
790-3d	WI v Pakistan at Kingston	1957-58
765-6d	Pak v Sri Lanka at Karachi	2008-09
760-7d	SL v India at Ahmedabad	2009-10
758-8d	Aust v WI at Kingston	1954-55
756-5d	Sri Lanka v SA at Colombo	2006
751-5d	WI v England at St John's	2003-04
749-9d	WI v England at Bridgetown	2008-09

There have been 10 further totals of more than 700, three by Australia and India, and one each by England, Pakistan, Sri Lanka and West Indies

Lowest team totals

Completed innings
26	NZ v Eng at Auckland	1954-55
30	SA v Eng at Pt Elizabeth	1895-96
30	SA v Eng at Birmingham	1924
35	SA v Eng at Cape Town	1898-99
36	Aust v Eng at B'ham	1902
36	SA v Aust at M'bourne	1931-32
42	Aust v Eng at Sydney	1887-88
42	NZ v Aust at W'ton	1945-46
42*	India v England at Lord's	1974
43	SA v Eng at Cape Town	1888-89

* One batsmen absent hurt. There have been seven further totals of less than 50, the most recent West Indies' 47 v England at Kingston in 2003-04

Best match bowling

19-90	JC Laker	Eng v Aust at Manchester	1956
17-159	SF Barnes	Eng v SA at Jo'burg	1913-14
16-136	ND Hirwani	India v WI at Madras	1987-88
16-137	RAL Massie	Aust v England at Lord's	1972
16-220	M Muralitharan	SL v England at The Oval	1998
15-28	J Briggs	Eng v SA at Cape Town	1888-89
15-45	GA Lohmann	Eng v SA at Pt Elizabeth	1895-96
15-99	C Blythe	Eng v SA at Leeds	1907
15-104	H Verity	England v Aust at Lord's	1934
15-123	RJ Hadlee	NZ v Aust at Brisbane	1985-86

Hirwani and Massie were making their Test debuts. W Rhodes (15-124) and Harbhajan Singh (15-217) also took 15 wickets in a match

Most centuries

		Tests
51	SR Tendulkar India	181
40	JH Kallis South Africa/World XI	145
39	RT Ponting Australia	154
35	R Dravid India/World XI	157
34	SM Gavaskar India	125
34	BC Lara West Indies/World XI	131
32	SR Waugh Australia	168
30	ML Hayden Australia	94
29	DG Bradman Australia	52
29	DPMD Jayawardene Sri Lanka	122

Tendulkar had scored 99 centuries in international cricket by September 2011

Test match results

	Played	Won	Lost	Drawn	Tied	% win
Australia	733	342	192	197	2	46.65
Bangladesh	69	3	60	6	0	4.34
England	915	326	261	328	0	35.62
India	455	110	143	201	1	24.17
New Zealand	364	68	147	149	0	18.68
Pakistan	359	109	100	150	0	30.36
South Africa	358	125	124	109	0	34.91
Sri Lanka	204	61	72	71	0	29.90
West Indies	473	153	156	163	1	32.34
Zimbabwe	85	9	50	26	0	10.58
World XI	1	0	1	0	0	0.00
TOTAL	2008	1306	1306	700	2	

OVERALL RECORDS *One-day Internationals*

Most appearances

453	SR Tendulkar	*I*
445	ST Jayasuriya	*SL*
378	Inzamam-ul-Haq	*P*
367	RT Ponting	*A*
356	Wasim Akram	*P*
352	DPMD Jayawardene	*SL*
350	M Muralitharan	*SL*
344	R Dravid	*I*
334	M Azharuddin	*I*
325	Shahid Afridi	*P*
325	SR Waugh	*A*

Six further men have played in more than 300 ODIs

Most runs

		Avge
18111	SR Tendulkar *I*	45.16
13602	RT Ponting *A*	42.77
13430	ST Jayasuriya *SL*	32.36
11739	Inzamam-ul-Haq *P*	39.52
11363	SC Ganguly *I*	41.02
11227	JH Kallis *SA*	45.45
10889	R Dravid *I*	39.16
10405	BC Lara *WI*	40.48
9913	DPMD Jayawardene *SL*	33.48
9720	Mohammad Yousuf *P*	41.71

AC Gilchrist (9619), KC Sangakkara (9540), M Azharuddin (9378) and PA de Silva (9284) also reached 9000 runs

Most wickets

		Avge
534	M Muralitharan *SL*	23.08
502	Wasim Akram *P*	23.52
416	Waqar Younis *P*	23.84
400	WPUJC Vaas *SL*	27.53
393	SM Pollock *SA*	24.50
381	GD McGrath *A*	22.02
357	B Lee *A*	22.89
337	A Kumble *I*	30.89
323	ST Jayasuriya *SL*	36.75
315	Shahid Afridi *P*	34.22
315	J Srinath *I*	28.08

Eleven other bowlers have passed 250 wickets in ODIs

Highest scores

200*	SR Tendulkar	India v SA at Gwalior	2009-10
194*	CK Coventry	Zim v Bangladesh at Bulawayo	2008-09
194	Saeed Anwar	Pakistan v India at Chennai	1996-97
189*	IVA Richards	W Indies v England at Manchester	1984
189	ST Jayasuriya	Sri Lanka v India at Sharjah	2000-01
188*	G Kirsten	SA v UAE at Rawalpindi	1995-96
186*	SR Tendulkar	India v NZ at Hyderabad	1999-2000
185*	SR Watson	Aust v Bangladesh at Mirpur	2010-11
183*	MS Dhoni	India v Sri Lanka at Jaipur	2005-06
183	SC Ganguly	India v Sri Lanka at Taunton	1999

SR Tendulkar has scored 48 ODI centuries, RT Ponting 30, ST Jayasuriya 28, SC Ganguly 22, HH Gibbs 21, Saeed Anwar 20, CH Gayle and BC Lara 19

Best innings bowling

8-19	WPUJC Vaas	SL v Zimbabwe at Colombo	2001-02
7-15	GD McGrath	Aust v Namibia at P'stroom	2002-03
7-20	AJ Bichel	Aust v Eng at Port Elizabeth	2002-03
7-30	M Muralitharan	Sri Lanka v India at Sharjah	2000-01
7-36	Waqar Younis	Pakistan v England at Leeds	2001
7-37	Aqib Javed	Pakistan v India at Sharjah	1991-92
7-51	WW Davis	West Indies v Australia at Leeds	1983
6-12	A Kumble	India v West Indies at Calcutta	1993-94
6-13	BAW Mendis	Sri Lanka v India at Karachi	2008
6-14	GJ Gilmour	Australia v England at Leeds	1975
6-14	Imran Khan	Pakistan v India at Sharjah	1984-85
6-14	MF Maharoof	Sri Lanka v W Indies at Mumbai	2006-07

Waqar Younis took five in an innings 13 times and Muralitharan 10

Record wicket partnerships

1st	286	WU Tharanga (109) and ST Jayasuriya (152)	Sri Lanka v England at Leeds	2006
2nd	331	SR Tendulkar (186*) and R Dravid (153)	India v New Zealand at Hyderabad	1999-2000
3rd	237*	R Dravid (104*) and SR Tendulkar (140*)	India v Kenya at Bristol	1999
4th	275*	M Azharuddin (153*) and A Jadeja (116*)	India v Zimbabwe at Cuttack	1997-98
5th	223	M Azharuddin (111*) and A Jadeja (119)	India v Sri Lanka at Colombo	1997-98
6th	218	DPMD Jayawardene (107) and MS Dhoni (139*)	Asia XI v Africa XI at Chennai	2007
7th	130	A Flower (142*) and HH Streak (56)	Zimbabwe v England at Harare	2001-02
8th	138*	JM Kemp (110*) and AJ Hall (56*)	South Africa v India at Cape Town	2006-07
9th	132	AD Mathews (77*) and SL Malinga (56)	Sri Lanka v Australia at Melbourne	2010-11
10th	106*	IVA Richards (189*) and MA Holding (12*)	West Indies v England at Manchester	1984

One-day Internationals **OVERALL RECORDS**

Most catches

Fielders

183	DPMD Jayawardene *SL*	
156	M Azharuddin *I*	
156	RT Ponting *A*	
136	SR Tendulkar *I*	
133	SP Fleming *NZ*	

Most dismissals

Wicketkeepers   *Ct/St*

472	AC Gilchrist *A*	417/55
421	MV Boucher *SA*	399/22
353	KC Sangakkara *SL*	275/78
287	Moin Khan *P*	214/73
241	MS Dhoni *I*	181/60

Most sixes

289	Shahid Afridi *P*	
270	ST Jayasuriya *SL*	
193	SR Tendulkar *I*	
190	SC Ganguly *I*	
169	CH Gayle *WI*	
162	RT Ponting *A*	
153	CL Cairns *NZ*	
149	AC Gilchrist *A*	
144	Inzamam-ul-Haq *P*	
144	Yuvraj Singh *I*	

Eleven others have hit 100 sixes

Highest team totals

443-9	**SL** v N'lands at Amstelveen	2006
438-9	**SA** v Aust at Johannesburg	2005-06
434-4	**Australia** v SA at Jo'burg	2005-06
418-5	**SA** v Zim at P'stroom	2006-07
414-7	**India** v SL at Rajkot	2009-10
413-5	**Ind** v Bermuda at P-o-Spain	2006-07
411-8	**SL** v India at Rajkot	2009-10
402-2	**NZ** v Ireland at Aberdeen	2008
401-3	**India** v SA at Gwalior	2009-10
399-6	**SA** v Zim at Benoni	2010-11

All these totals were made in 50 overs except SA's 438-9, when the winning run came off the fifth ball of the 50th over

Best strike rate

Runs per 100 balls   *Runs*

113.82	Shahid Afridi *P*	6695
104.07	V Sehwag *I*	7760
99.43	IDS Smith *NZ*	1055
96.94	AC Gilchrist *A*	9619
96.66	RL Powell *WI*	2085
96.08	PR Stirling *Ire*	1349
95.07	Kapil Dev *I*	3783
93.71	JR Hopes *A*	1326
92.76	HM Amla *SA*	2462
92.44	A Symonds *A*	5088

Qualification: 1000 runs

Lowest team totals

Completed innings

35	**Zim** v SL at Harare	2003-04
36	**Canada** v SL at Paarl	2002-03
38	**Zim** v SL at Colombo	2001-02
43	**Pak** v WI at Cape Town	1992-93
44	**Zim** v B'desh at Ch'gong	2009-10
45	**Can** v Eng at Manchester	1979
45	**Nam** v Aust at P'stroom	2002-03
54	**India** v SL at Sharjah	2000-01
54	**WI** v SA at Cape Town	2003-04
55	**SL** v WI at Sharjah	1986-87

The lowest total successfully defended in a non-rain-affected ODI is 125, by India v Pakistan (87) at Sharjah in 1984-85

Most economical bowlers

Runs per over   *Wkts*

3.09	J Garner *WI*	146
3.28	RGD Willis *E*	80
3.30	RJ Hadlee *NZ*	158
3.32	MA Holding *WI*	142
3.37	SP Davis *A*	44
3.40	AME Roberts *WI*	87
3.48	CEL Ambrose *WI*	225
3.53	MD Marshall *WI*	157
3.54	ARC Fraser *E*	47
3.55	MR Whitney *A*	46

Qualification: 2000 balls bowled

One-day international results

	Played	Won	Lost	Tied	No result	% win
Australia	773	480	260	8	25	64.70
Bangladesh	252	69	181	0	2	27.60
England	567	274	267	7	19	50.63
India	783	383	360	5	35	51.53
Kenya	144	38	101	0	5	27.33
New Zealand	611	263	311	5	32	45.85
Pakistan	752	404	326	6	16	55.29
South Africa	459	287	155	5	12	64.76
Sri Lanka	638	301	308	3	26	49.42
West Indies	657	342	286	5	24	54.42
Zimbabwe	401	106	281	5	9	27.67
Others (see below)	353	115	226	1	11	33.77
TOTAL	**3195**	**3062**	**3062**	**25**	**108**	

Others: Afghanistan (P18, W11, L7), Africa XI (P6, W1, L4, NR1), Asia XI (P7, W4, L2, NR1), Bermuda (P35, W7, L28), Canada (P68, W17, L50, NR1), East Africa (P3, L3), Hong Kong (P4, L4), Ireland (P68, W30, L34, T1, NR3), Namibia (P6, L6), Netherlands (P67, W25, L40, NR2), Scotland (P54, W18, L33, NR3), UAE (P11, W1, L10), USA (P2, L2), World XI (P4, W1, L3).

Most appearances

43	Shahid Afridi	P
40	BB McCullum	NZ
38	Kamran Akmal	P
37	LRPL Taylor	NZ
35	PD Collingwood	E
35	DPMD Jayawardene	SL
34	MJ Clarke	A
34	TM Dilshan	SL
34	Misbah-ul-Haq	P
34	Shoaib Malik	P
34	Umar Gul	P

The first Twenty20 international was played in New Zealand in February 2005

Most runs

			Avge
1100	BB McCullum	NZ	33.33
1011	KP Pietersen	E	36.10
958	GC Smith	SA	33.03
953	DPMD Jayawardene	SL	31.76
874	KC Sangakkara	SL	32.37
866	TM Dilshan	SL	32.07
775	DA Warner	A	28.70
704	Kamran Akmal	P	23.46
683	Shadid Afridi	P	17.97
659	LRPL Taylor	NZ	21.96

The highest batting average (min. 200 runs) is 51.33, by ML Hayden (Aust)

Most wickets

			Avge
53	Shahid Afridi	P	18.96
47	Umar Gul	P	16.00
45	Saeed Ajmal	P	16.15
39	BAW Mendis	SL	10.89
37	SCJ Broad	E	22.18
37	SL Malinga	SL	20.08
36	MG Johnson	A	20.11
35	DL Vettori	NZ	16.57
33	GP Swann	E	16.60
29	DJG Sammy	WI	13.82
29	DW Steyn	SA	18.31

Seven further bowlers have taken 25 or more wickets

Highest Scores

117	CH Gayle	WI v SA at Johannesburg	2007-08
116*	BB McCullum	NZ v A at Christchurch	2009-10
104*	TM Dilshan	SL v A at Pallekele	2011
101	SK Raina	India v SA at Gros Islet	2010
100	DPMD J'wardene	SL v Zim at Providence	2010
98*	RT Ponting	A v NZ at Auckland	2004-05
98*	DPMD J'wardene	SL v WI at Bridgetown	2010
98	CH Gayle	WI v India at Bridgetown	2010
96*	TM Dilshan	SL v WI at The Oval	2009
96*	JP Duminy	SA v Zim at Kimberley	2010-11
96	DR Martyn	A v SA at Brisbane	2005-06

Ponting's innings is the highest score on T20I debut

Best innings bowling

6-16	BAW Mendis	SL v Australia at Pallekele	2011
5-6	Umar Gul	Pakistan v NZ at The Oval	2009
5-18	TG Southee	NZ v Pakistan at Auckland	2010-11
5-19	R McLaren	SA v WI at N Sound	2010
5-20	NN Odhiambo	Ken v Scot at Nairobi	2009-10
5-26	DJG Sammy	WI v Zim at P-o-Spain	2009-10
4-6	SJ Benn	WI v Zim at P-o-Spain	2009-10
4-7	MR Gillespie	NZ v Kenya at Durban	2007-08
4-8	Umar Gul	Pak v Australia at Dubai	2009-09
4-9	DW Steyn	SA v WI at Port Elizabeth	2007-08

Umar Gul has taken four wickets in an innings four times, BAW Mendis and Shahid Afridi three

Record wicket partnerships

1st	170	GC Smith (88) and LL Bosman (94)	South Africa v England at Centurion	2009-10
2nd	166	DPMD Jayawardene (98*) and KC Sangakkara (68)	Sri Lanka v West Indies at Bridgetown	2010
3rd	120*	HH Gibbs (90*) and JM Kemp (46*)	South Africa v West indies at Johannesburg	2007-08
4th	112*	KP Pietersen (43*) and EJG Morgan (67*)	England v Pakistan at Dubai	2009-10
5th	119*	Shoaib Malik (52*) and Misbah-ul-Haq (66*)	Pakistan v Australia at Johannesburg	2007-08
6th	101*	CL White (85*) and MEK Hussey (39*)	Australia v Sri Lanka at Bridgetown	2010
7th	91	PD Collingwood (79) and MH Yardy (23*)	England v West Indies at The Oval	2007
8th	61	SK Raina (61*) and Harbhajan Singh (21)	India v New Zealand at Christchurch	2008-09
9th	44	SL Malinga (27) and CRD Fernando (21)	Sri Lanka v New Zealand at Auckland	2006-07
10th	31*	Wahab Riaz (30*) and Shoaib Akhtar (8*)	Pakistan v New Zealand at Auckland	2010-11

Figures to 26.09.11. Updated records can be found at www.cricinfo.com/ci/engine/records

Most catches

Fielders

23	**LRPL Taylor** *NZ*	
22	**AB de Villiers** *SA*	
18	**MEK Hussey** *A*	
18	**GC Smith** *SA*	
17	**DJ Hussey** *A*	

Most dismissals

Wicketkeepers   *Ct/St*

45	**Kamran Akmal** *P*	17/28
25	**KC Sangakkara** *SL*	14/11
21	**D Ramdin** *WI*	19/2
20	**BB McCullum** *NZ*	16/4
19	**MV Boucher** *SA*	18/1

Highest team totals

260-6	**Sri Lanka** v Kenya at Jo'burg	2007-08
241-6	**SA** v England at Centurion	2009-10
221-5	**Aust** v England at Sydney	2006-07
218-4	**India** v England at Durban	2007-08
215-5	**Sri Lanka** v India at Nagpur	2009-10
214-5	**Australia** v NZ at Auckland	2004-05
214-6	**NZ** v Aust at Christchurch	2009-10
214-4	**Aust** v NZ at Christchurch	2009-10
211-4	**India** v Sri Lanka at Mohali	2009-10
211-5	**SA** v Scotland at The Oval	2009

There have been nine further totals of 200 or more

Lowest team totals

Completed innings

67	**Kenya** v Ireland at Belfast	2008
68	**Ireland** v WI at Providence	2010
70	**Bermuda** v Can at Belfast	2008
73	**Kenya** v NZ at Durban	2007-08
74	**India** v Aus at M'bourne	2007-08
75	**Can** v Zim at King City	2008-09
78	**B'desh** v NZ at Hamilton	2009-10
79	**Aust** v Eng at Southampton	2005
80	**Afgh** v SA at Bridgetown	2010
80	**NZ** v Pak at Christchurch	2010-11

West Indies scored 79-7 in 20 overs v Zimbabwe at Port-of-Spain in 2009-10

Most sixes

39	**BB McCullum** *NZ*	
38	**Yuvraj Singh** *I*	
34	**CH Gayle** *WI*	
34	**CL White** *NZ*	
33	**DA Warner** *A*	
32	**SR Watson** *A*	
31	**LRPL Taylor** *NZ*	
29	**JA Morkel** *SA*	
27	**DJ Hussey** *A*	
27	**KP Pietersen** *E*	

Yuvraj's sixes included 6 in one over

Best strike rate

Runs per 100 balls   *Runs*

169.34	**A Symonds** *A*	337
159.82	**CD McMillan** *NZ*	187
153.98	**SR Watson** *A*	522
153.43	**V Sehwag** *I*	313
151.67	**YK Pathan** *I*	226
151.60	**Yuvraj Singh** *I*	567
150.32	**MEK Hussey** *A*	457
148.04	**Moh'd Ashraful** *B*	265
147.48	**LE Bosman** *SA*	323
144.49	**CH Gayle** *WI*	617

Qualification: 100 balls faced

Meanest bowlers

Runs per over   *Wkts*

4.88	**TM Odoyo** *Kenya*	6
5.25	**RW Price** *Zim*	13
5.36	**DL Vettori** *NZ*	35
5.38	**GH Dockrell** *Ire*	12
5.40	**JAR Blain** *Scot*	6
5.41	**AC Botha** *Ire*	21
5.45	**JD Nel** *Scot*	12
5.56	**HA Varaiya** *Ken*	5
5.59	**BAW Mendis** *SL*	39
5.60	**H Osinde** *Can*	6

Qualification: 120 balls bowled

Twenty20 international results

	Played	Won	Lost	Tied	No Result	% win
Australia	43	22	19	1	1	53.57
Bangladesh	16	3	13	0	0	18.75
England	40	20	18	0	2	52.63
India	30	16	12	1	1	56.89
New Zealand	43	19	21	3	0	47.67
Pakistan	48	29	18	1	0	61.45
South Africa	38	25	13	0	0	65.78
Sri Lanka	37	23	14	0	0	62.16
West Indies	32	13	17	2	0	42.42
Others (see below)	89	29	54	2	4	35.29
TOTAL	**208**	**199**	**199**	**5**	**4**	

Other teams: Afghanistan (P8, W4, L4), Bermuda (P3, L3), Canada (P11, W3, L7, T1), Ireland (P17, W7, L8, NR2), Kenya (P12, W4, L8), Netherlands (P10, W6, L3, NR1), Scotland (P12, W2, L9, NR1), Zimbabwe (P16, W3, L12, T1). Matches decided by bowlouts are shown as tied

AUSTRALIA
Test Match Records

Most appearances

168	SR Waugh
156	AR Border
154	RT Ponting
145	SK Warne
128	ME Waugh
124	GD McGrath
119	IA Healy
107	DC Boon
105	JL Langer
104	MA Taylor

ML Hayden (103) also won more than 100 caps

Most runs

		Avge
12487	RT Ponting	53.13
11174	AR Border	50.56
10927	SR Waugh	51.06
8625	ML Hayden	50.73
8029	ME Waugh	41.81
7696	JL Langer	45.27
7525	MA Taylor	43.49
7422	DC Boon	43.65
7110	GS Chappell	53.86
6996	DG Bradman	99.94

RN Harvey (6149) also reached 6000 Test runs

Most wickets

		Avge
708	SK Warne	25.41
563	GD McGrath	21.64
355	DK Lillee	23.92
310	B Lee	30.81
291	CJ McDermott	28.63
259	JN Gillespie	26.13
248	R Benaud	27.03
246	GD McKenzie	29.78
228	RR Lindwall	23.03
216	CV Grimmett	24.21

MG Hughes (212), SCG MacGill (208) & JR Thomson (200) also reached 200

Highest scores

380	ML Hayden	v Zimbabwe at Perth	2003-04
334*	MA Taylor	v Pakistan at Peshawar	1998-99
334	DG Bradman	v England at Leeds	1930
311	RB Simpson	v England at Manchester	1964
307	RM Cowper	v England at Melbourne	1965-66
304	DG Bradman	v England at Leeds	1934
299*	DG Bradman	v South Africa at Adelaide	1931-32
270	DG Bradman	v England at Melbourne	1936-37
268	GN Yallop	v Pakistan at Melbourne	1983-84
266	WH Ponsford	v England at The Oval	1934

At the time of his retirement in 1948 DG Bradman had made eight of Australia's highest ten Test scores

Best innings bowling

9-121	AA Mailey	v England at Melbourne	1920-21
8-24	GD McGrath	v Pakistan at Perth	2004-05
8-31	FJ Laver	v England at Manchester	1909
8-38	GD McGrath	v England at Lord's	1997
8-43	AE Trott	v England at Adelaide	1894-95
8-53	RAL Massie	v England at Lord's	1972
8-59	AA Mallett	v Pakistan at Adelaide	1972-73
8-61	MG Johnson	v South Africa at Perth	2008-09
8-65	H Trumble	v England at The Oval	1902
8-71	GD McKenzie	v West Indies at Melbourne	1968-69
8-71	SK Warne	v England at Brisbane	1994-95

Trott and Massie were making their Test debuts

Record wicket partnerships

1st	382	WM Lawry (210) and RB Simpson (205)	v West Indies at Bridgetown	1964-65
2nd	451	WH Ponsford (266) and DG Bradman (244)	v England at The Oval	1934
3rd	315	RT Ponting (206) and DS Lehmann (160)	v West Indies at Port-of-Spain	2002-03
4th	388	WH Ponsford (181) and DG Bradman (304)	v England at Leeds	1934
5th	405	SG Barnes (234) and DG Bradman (234)	v England at Sydney	1946-47
6th	346	JHW Fingleton (136) and DG Bradman (270)	v England at Melbourne	1936-37
7th	217	KD Walters (250) and GJ Gilmour (101)	v New Zealand at Christchurch	1976-77
8th	243	MJ Hartigan (116) and C Hill (160)	v England at Adelaide	1907-08
9th	154	SE Gregory (201) and JM Blackham (74)	v England at Sydney	1894-95
10th	127	JM Taylor (108) and AA Mailey (46*)	v England at Sydney	1924-25

Figures to 26.09.11. Updated records can be found at www.cricinfo.com/ci/engine/records

Test Match Records

AUSTRALIA

Most catches

	Fielders	
181	RT Ponting	
181	ME Waugh	
157	MA Taylor	
156	AR Border	
128	ML Hayden	

Most dismissals

	Wicketkeepers	Ct/St
416	AC Gilchrist	379/37
395	IA Healy	366/29
355	RW Marsh	343/12
187	ATW Grout	163/24
131	BJ Haddin	128/3

Highest team totals

758-8d	v West Indies at Kingston	1954-55
735-6d	v Zimbabwe at Perth	2003-04
729-6d	v England at Lord's	1930
701	v England at The Oval	1934
695	v England at The Oval	1930
674-6d	v England at Cardiff	2009
674	v India at Adelaide	1947-48
668	v West Indies at Bridgetown	1954-55
659-8d	v England at Sydney	1946-47
656-8d	v England at Manchester	1964

Australia have reached 600 on 29 occasions, 16 of them against England

Lowest team totals

	Completed innings	
36	v England at Birmingham	1902
42	v England at Sydney	1887-88
44	v England at The Oval	1896
53	v England at Lord's	1896
58*	v England at Brisbane	1936-37
60	v England at Lord's	1888
63	v England at The Oval	1882
65	v England at The Oval	1912
66*	v England at Brisbane	1928-29
68	v England at The Oval	1886

*One or more batsmen absent. Australia's lowest total against anyone other than England is 75, v South Africa at Durban in 1949-50

Best match bowling

16-137	RAL Massie	v England at Lord's	1972
14-90	FR Spofforth	v England at The Oval	1882
14-199	CV Grimmett	v South Africa at Adelaide	1931-32
13-77	MA Noble	v England at Melbourne	1901-02
13-110	FR Spofforth	v England at Melbourne	1878-79
13-148	BA Reid	v England at Melbourne	1990-91
13-173	CV Grimmett	v South Africa at Durban	1935-36
13-217	MG Hughes	v West Indies at Perth	1988-89
13-236	AA Mailey	v England at Melbourne	1920-21
12-87	CTB Turner	v England at Sydney	1887-88

Massie was playing in his first Test, Grimmett (1935-36) in his last – he took 10 or more wickets in each of his last three

Hat-tricks

FR Spofforth	v England at Melbourne	1878-79
H Trumble	v England at Melbourne	1901-02
H Trumble	v England at Melbourne	1903-04
TJ Matthews	v South Africa at Manchester	1912
TJ Matthews	v South Africa at Manchester	1912
LF Kline	v South Africa at Cape Town	1957-58
MG Hughes	v West Indies at Perth	1988-89
DW Fleming	v Pakistan at Rawalpindi	1994-95
SK Warne	v England at Melbourne	1994-95
GD McGrath	v West Indies at Perth	2000-01
PM Siddle	v England at Brisbane	2010-11

Fleming was playing in his first Test, Trumble (1903-04) in his last. Matthews took two in the same Test

Australia's Test match results

	Played	Won	Lost	Drawn	Tied	% win
v Bangladesh	4	4	0	0	0	100.00
v England	326	133	102	91	0	40.79
v India	78	34	20	23	1	43.58
v New Zealand	50	26	7	17	0	52.00
v Pakistan	57	28	12	17	0	49.12
v South Africa	83	47	18	18	0	56.62
v Sri Lanka	23	14	1	8	0	60.86
v West Indies	108	52	32	23	1	48.14
v Zimbabwe	3	3	0	0	0	100.00
v World XI	1	1	0	0	0	100.00
TOTAL	733	342	192	197	2	46.65

Figures to 26.09.11. Updated records can be found at www.cricinfo.com/ci/engine/records

AUSTRALIA — One-day International Records

Most appearances

366	RT Ponting
325	SR Waugh
286	AC Gilchrist
273	AR Border
249	GD McGrath
244	ME Waugh
232	MG Bevan
208	DR Martyn
205	B Lee
203	MJ Clarke

A total of 25 Australians have played in more than 100 ODIs

Most runs

		Avge
13487	RT Ponting	42.54
9595	AC Gilchrist	35.93
8500	ME Waugh	39.35
7569	SR Waugh	32.90
6912	MG Bevan	53.58
6551	MJ Clarke	45.81
6524	AR Border	30.62
6131	ML Hayden	44.10
6068	DM Jones	44.61
5964	DC Boon	37.04

DR Martyn (5346) and A Symonds (5088) also reached 5000 runs

Most wickets

		Avge
380	GD McGrath	21.98
357	B Lee	22.89
291	SK Warne	25.82
203	CJ McDermott	24.71
195	SR Waugh	34.67
174	NW Bracken	24.36
163	MG Johnson	25.30
156	GB Hogg	26.84
142	JN Gillespie	25.42
138	SR Watson	29.10

Five further Australians have taken 100 wickets

Highest scores

185*	SR Watson	v Bangladesh at Mirpur	2010-11
181*	ML Hayden	v New Zealand at Hamilton	2006-07
173	ME Waugh	v West Indies at Melbourne	2000-01
172	AC Gilchrist	v Zimbabwe at Hobart	2003-04
164	RT Ponting	v South Africa at Johannesburg	2005-06
161*	SR Watson	v England at Melbourne	2010-11
158	ML Hayden	v West Indies at North Sound	2006-07
156	A Symonds	v New Zealand at Wellington	2005-06
154	AC Gilchrist	v Sri Lanka at Melbourne	1998-99
151	A Symonds	v Sri Lanka at Sydney	2005-06

Ponting has scored 29 hundreds, ME Waugh 18, Gilchrist 16 and Hayden 10

Best innings bowling

7-15	GD McGrath	v Namibia at Potchefstroom	2002-03
7-20	AJ Bichel	v England at Port Elizabeth	2002-03
6-14	GJ Gilmour	v England at Leeds	1975
6-31	MG Johnson	v Sri Lanka at Pallekele	2011
6-39	KH MacLeay	v India at Nottingham	1983
5-13	SP O'Donnell	v New Zealand at Christchurch	1989-90
5-14	GD McGrath	v West Indies at Manchester	1999
5-14	JR Hopes	v Ireland at Dublin	2010
5-15	GS Chappell	v India at Sydney	1980-81
5-16	CG Rackemann	v Pakistan at Adelaide	1983-84

DK Lillee took 5-34 against Pakistan at Leeds in the 1975 World Cup, the first five-wicket haul in ODIs

Record wicket partnerships

1st	212	GR Marsh (104) and DC Boon (111)	v India at Jaipur	1986-87
2nd	252*	SR Watson (136*) and RT Ponting (111*)	v England at Centurion	2009-10
3rd	234*	RT Ponting (140*) and DR Martyn (88*)	v India at Johannesburg	2002-03
4th	237	RT Ponting (124) and A Symonds (151)	v Sri Lanka at Sydney	2005-06
5th	220	A Symonds (156) and MJ Clarke (82*)	v New Zealand at Wellington	2005-06
6th	165	MEK Hussey (109*) and BJ Haddin (70)	v West Indies at Kuala Lumpur	2006-07
7th	123	MEK Hussey (73) and B Lee (57)	v South Africa at Brisbane	2005-06
8th	119	PR Reiffel (58) and SK Warne (55)	v South Africa at Port Elizabeth	1993-94
9th	88	SE Marsh (110) and DE Bollinger (30)	v England at Hobart	2010-11
10th	63	SR Watson (35*) and AJ Bichel (28)	v Sri Lanka at Sydney	2002-03

AUSTRALIA

Most catches

Fielders

155	RT Ponting	
127	AR Border	
111	SR Waugh	
108	ME Waugh	
92	MEK Hussey	

Most dismissals

Wicketkeepers		*Ct/St*
470	AC Gilchrist	416/54
233	IA Healy	194/39
132	BJ Haddin	124/8
124	RW Marsh	120/4
49	WB Phillips	42/7

Highest team totals

434-4	v South Africa at Johannesburg	2005-06
377-6	v South Africa at Basseterre	2006-07
368-5	v Sri Lanka at Sydney	2005-06
361-8	v Bangladesh at Mirpur	2010-11
359-2†	v India at Johannesburg	2002-03
359-5	v India at Sydney	2003-04
358-5	v Netherlands at Basseterre	2006-07
350-4	v India at Hyderabad	2009-10
349-6	v New Zealand at St George's	2006-07
348-6	v New Zealand at C'church	1999-2000

† In World Cup final. All scores made in 50 overs

Lowest team totals

Completed innings

70	v England at Birmingham	1977
70	v New Zealand at Adelaide	1985-86
91	v West Indies at Perth	1986-87
93	v S Africa at Cape Town	2005-06
101	v England at Melbourne	1978-79
101	v India at Perth	1991-92
107	v W Indies at Melbourne	1981-82
109	v England at Sydney	1982-83
120	v Pakistan at Hobart	1996-97
124	v New Zealand at Sydney	1982-83

Australia scored 101-9 in a 30-overs match against West Indies at Sydney in 1992-93 – and won

Most sixes

159	RT Ponting	
148	AC Gilchrist	
103	A Symonds	
91	SR Watson	
87	ML Hayden	
68	SR Waugh	
66	MEK Hussey	
64	DM Jones	
57	ME Waugh	
54	BJ Haddin	

Ponting (3) and Gilchrist (1) also hit sixes for the World XI

Best strike rate

Runs per 100 balls		*Runs*
99.00	MG Johnson	693
96.89	AC Gilchrist	9595
93.71	JR Hopes	1326
92.44	A Symonds	5504
89.55	SR Watson	4122
89.35	DJ Hussey	940
88.16	IJ Harvey	715
88.07	MEK Hussey	4287
87.51	BJ Hodge	516
85.71	WB Phillips	852

Qualification: 500 runs

Most economical bowlers

Runs per over		*Wkts*
3.37	SP Davis	44
3.55	MR Whitney	46
3.58	DK Lillee	103
3.65	GF Lawson	88
3.65	TM Alderman	88
3.87	GD McGrath	380
3.92	PR Reiffel	106
3.94	CG Rackemann	82
3.94	RM Hogg	85
4.03	CJ McDermott	203

Qualification: 2000 balls bowled

Australia's one-day international results

	Played	Won	Lost	Tied	No Result	% win
v Bangladesh	19	18	1	0	0	94.73
v England	113	67	42	2	2	61.26
v India	105	61	36	0	8	62.88
v New Zealand	124	85	34	0	5	71.42
v Pakistan	86	52	30	1	3	63.25
v South Africa	77	39	35	3	0	52.59
v Sri Lanka	77	50	24	0	3	67.56
v West Indies	125	63	57	2	3	52.45
v Zimbabwe	28	26	1	0	1	96.29
v others *(see below)*	19	19	0	0	0	100.00
TOTAL	**773**	**480**	**260**	**8**	**25**	**64.70**

Other teams: Canada (P2, W2), Ireland (P2, W2), Kenya (P5, W5), Namibia (P1, W1), Netherlands (P2, W2), Scotland (P3, W3), USA (P1, W1), World XI (P3, W3).

BANGLADESH *Test Match Records*

Most appearances

56	Mohammad Ashraful
50	Habibul Bashar
44	Khaled Mashud
40	Javed Omar
36	Mashrafe Mortaza
33	Mohammad Rafique
29	Shahadat Hossain
24	Mushfiqur Rahim
24	Rajin Saleh
22	Shakib Al Hasan

Habibul Bashar missed only two of Bangladesh's first 52 Tests

Most runs

		Avge
3026	Habibul Bashar	30.87
2418	Mohammad Ashraful	23.02
1720	Javed Omar	22.05
1503	Tamim Iqbal	39.55
1409	Khaled Mashud	19.04
1253	Shakib Al Hasan	31.32
1195	Mushfiqur Rahim	27.15
1141	Rajin Saleh	25.93
1059	Mohammad Rafique	18.57
942	Junaid Siddique	26.91

Habibul Bashar reached 2000 runs for Bangladesh before anyone else had made 1000

Most wickets

		Avge
100	Mohammad Rafique	40.76
79	Shakib Al Hasan	32.05
78	Mashrafe Mortaza	41.52
66	Shahadat Hossain	45.33
41	Enamul Haque jnr	39.24
36	Tapash Baisya	59.36
28	Manjural Islam	57.32
23	Mahmudullah	36.26
20	Mohammad Ashraful	59.40
18	Abdur Razzak	65.83
18	Enamul Haque snr	57.05

Moh'd Rafique completed the 1000-run 100-wicket double in his last Test

Highest scores

158*	Moh'd Ashraful	v India at Chittagong	2004-05
151	Tamim Iqbal	v India at Mirpur	2009-10
145†	Aminul Islam	v India at Dhaka	2000-01
138	Shahriar Nafees	v Australia at Fatullah	2005-06
136	Moh'd Ashraful	v Sri Lanka at Chittagong	2005-06
129*	Moh'd Ashraful	v Sri Lanka at Colombo	2007
128	Tamim Iqbal	v West Indies at Kingstown	2009
121	Nafees Iqbal	v Zimbabwe at Dhaka	2004-05
119	Javed Omar	v Pakistan at Peshawar	2003-04
115	Mahmudullah	v New Zealand at Hamilton	2009-10

† On debut. Mohammad Ashraful has scored five Test centuries, Tamim Iqbal four, and Habibul Bashar three

Best innings bowling

7-36	Shakib Al Hasan	v NZ at Chittagong	2008-09
7-95	Enamul Haque jnr	v Zimbabwe at Dhaka	2004-05
6-27	Shahadat Hossain	v South Africa at Dhaka	2007-08
6-45	Enamul Haque jnr	v Zim at Chittagong	2004-05
6-77	Moh'd Rafique	v South Africa at Dhaka	2002-03
6-81	Manjural Islam	v Zim at Bulawayo	2000-01
6-99	Shakib Al Hasan	v SA at Centurion	2008-09
6-122	Moh'd Rafique	v New Zealand at Dhaka	2004-05
6-132	Naimur Rahman	v India at Dhaka	2000-01
5-36	Moh'd Rafique	v Pakistan at Multan	2003-04

Mohammad Rafique and Shakib Al Hasan took five wickets in an innings on seven occasions, Shahadat Hossain four, and Enamul Haque jnr three

Record wicket partnerships

1st	185	Tamim Iqbal (103) and Imrul Kayes (75)	v England at Lord's	2010
2nd	200	Tamim Iqbal (151) and Junaid Siddique (55)	v India at Mirpur	2009-10
3rd	130	Javed Omar (119) and Mohammad Ashraful (77)	v Pakistan at Peshawar	2003-04
4th	120	Habibul Bashar (77) and Manjural Islam Rana (35)	v West Indies at Kingstown	2004
5th	144	Mehrab Hossain jnr (83) and Mushfiqur Rahim (79)	v New Zealand at Chittagong	2008-09
6th	191	Mohammad Ashraful (129*) and Mushfiqur Rahim (80)	v Sri Lanka at Colombo	2007
7th	145	Shakib Al Hasan (87) and Mahmudullah (115)	v New Zealand at Hamilton	2009-10
8th	113	Mushfiqur Rahim (79) and Naeem Islam (38)	v England at Chittagong	2009-10
9th	77	Mashrafe Mortaza (79) and Shahadat Hossain (31)	v India at Chittagong	2006-07
10th	69	Mohammad Rafique (65) and Shahadat Hossain (3*)	v Australia at Chittagong	2005-06

Figures to 26.09.11. Updated records can be found at **www.cricinfo.com/ci/engine/records**

Test Match Records **BANGLADESH**

Fielders

24	**Mohammad Ashraful**
22	**Habibul Bashar**
14	**Rajin Saleh**
13	**Imrul Kayes**
13	**Shahriar Nafees**

Most dismissals

Wicketkeepers   *Ct/St*

87	**Khaled Mashud**	78/9
41	**Mushfiqur Rahim**	33/8
4	**Mohammad Salim**	3/1
2	**Mehrab Hossain**	2/0

Highest team totals

488	v Zimbabwe at Chittagong	2004-05
427	v Australia at Fatullah	2005-06
419	v England at Mirpur	2009-10
416	v West Indies at Gros Islet	2004
413	v Sri Lanka at Mirpur	2008-09
408	v New Zealand at Hamilton	2009-10
400	v India at Dhaka	2000-01
382	v England at Lord's	2010
361	v Pakistan at Peshawar	2003-04
345	v West Indies at Kingstown	2009

The 400 against India came in Bangladesh's inaugural Test

Lowest team totals

Completed innings

62	v Sri Lanka at Colombo	2007
86	v Sri Lanka at Colombo	2005-06
87	v West Indies at Dhaka	2002-03
89	v Sri Lanka at Colombo	2007
90	v Sri Lanka at Colombo	2001-02
91	v India at Dhaka	2000-01
96	v Pakistan at Peshawar	2003-04
97	v Australia at Darwin	2003
102	v South Africa at Dhaka	2002-03
104	v Eng at Chester-le-Street	2005

The lowest all-out total by the opposition is 154, by Zimbabwe at Chittagong in 2004-05 (Bangladesh's first Test victory)

Best match bowling

12-200	**Enamul Haque jnr**	v Zimbabwe at Dhaka	2004-05
9-97	**Shahadat Hossain**	v South Africa at Dhaka	2007-08
9-115	**Shakib Al Hasan**	v NZ at Chittagong	2008-09
9-160	**Moh'd Rafique**	v Australia at Fatullah	2005-06
8-110	**Mahmudullah**	v W Indies at Kingstown	2009
8-129	**Shakib Al Hasan**	v W Indies at St George's	2009
7-105	**Khaled Mahmud**	v Pakistan at Multan	2003-04
7-116	**Moh'd Rafique**	v Pakistan at Multan	2003-04
7-174	**Shakib Al Hasan**	v India at Chittagong	2009-10
6-77	**Moh'd Rafique**	v South Africa at Dhaka	2002-03

Khaled Mahmud took only six other wickets in 11 more Tests

Hat-tricks

Alok Kapali	v Pakistan at Peshawar	2003-04

Alok Kapali's figures were 2.1-1-3-3; he ended Pakistan's innings by dismissing Shabbir Ahmed, Danish Kaneria and Umar Gul. He took only three other Test wickets.

Two bowlers have taken hat-tricks against Bangladesh: AM Blignaut for Zimbabwe at Harare in 2003-04, and JEC Franklin for New Zealand at Dhaka in 2004-05.

Shahadat Hossain and Abdur Razzak have taken ODI hat-tricks for Bangladesh

Bangladesh's Test match results

	Played	Won	Lost	Drawn	Tied	% win
v Australia	4	0	4	0	0	0.00
v England	8	0	8	0	0	0.00
v India	7	0	6	1	0	0.00
v New Zealand	9	0	8	1	0	0.00
v Pakistan	6	0	6	0	0	0.00
v South Africa	8	0	8	0	0	0.00
v Sri Lanka	12	0	12	0	0	0.00
v West Indies	6	2	3	1	0	33.33
v Zimbabwe	9	1	5	3	0	11.11
TOTAL	**69**	**3**	**60**	**6**	**0**	**4.34**

Figures to 26.09.11. Updated records can be found at **www.cricinfo.com/ci/engine/records**

BANGLADESH One-day International Records

Most appearances

167	Mohammad Ashraful
126	Khaled Mashud
124	Abdur Razzak
123	Mohammad Rafique
118	Mashrafe Mortaza
116	Shakib Al Hasan
111	Habibul Bashar
103	Tamim Iqbal
98	Mushfiqur Rahim
85	Aftab Ahmed

Habibul Bashar captained in 69 ODIs, Shakib Al Hasan in 47, and Mohammad Ashraful in 38

Most runs

		Avge
3395	Moh'd Ashraful	22.93
3261	Shakib Al Hasan	34.69
3053	Tamim Iqbal	29.64
2168	Habibul Bashar	21.68
2162	Shahriar Nafees	32.75
1954	Aftab Ahmed	24.73
1875	Mushfiqur Rahim	25.68
1818	Khaled Mashud	21.90
1318	Mahmudullah	30.65
1312	Javed Omar	23.85

Eight further batsmen have scored 1000 runs in ODIs for Bangladesh

Most wickets

		Avge
175	Abdur Razzak	27.77
150	Mashrafe Mortaza	30.34
144	Shakib Al Hasan	29.38
119	Mohammad Rafique	38.75
67	Khaled Mahmud	42.76
61	Syed Rasel	33.62
59	Tapash Baisya	41.55
44	Shafiul Islam	34.77
42	Shahadat Hossain	43.42
41	Rubel Hossain	33.48

Mohammad Rafique completed the 1000-run/100-wicket double in ODIs as well as Tests

Highest scores

154	Tamim Iqbal	v Zimbabwe at Bulawayo	2009
134*	Shakib Al Hasan	v Canada at St John's	2006-07
129	Tamim Iqbal	v Ireland at Dhaka	2007-08
125	Tamim Iqbal	v England at MIrpur	2009-10
123*	Shahriar Nafees	v Zimbabwe at Jaipur	2006
118*	Shahriar Nafees	v Zimbabwe at Harare	2006-07
115	Alok Kapali	v India at Karachi	2008
109	Moh'd Ashraful	v UAE at Lahore	2008
108*	Rajin Saleh	v Kenya at Fatullah	2005-06
108	Shakib Al Hasan	v Pakistan at Multan	2007-08

Shakib Al Hasan has scored five ODI hundreds, Shahriar Nafees four, Mohammad Ashraful and Tamim Iqbal three

Best bowling figures

6-26	Mashrafe Mortaza	v Kenya at Nairobi	2006
5-29	Abdur Razzak	v Zimbabwe at Mirpur	2009-10
5-30	Abdur Razzak	v Zimbabwe at Mirpur	2010-11
5-31	Aftab Ahmed	v NZ at Dhaka	2004-05
5-33	Abdur Razzak	v Zimbabwe at Bogra	2006-07
5-42	Farhad Reza	v Ireland at Dhaka	2007-08
5-47	Moh'd Rafique	v Kenya at Fatullah	2005-06
4-14	Abdur Razzak	v Zimbabwe at Mirpur	2010-11
4-16	Tapash Baisya	v West Indies at Kingstown	2004
4-16	Rajin Saleh	v Zimbabwe at Harare	2006

Aftab Ahmed took only seven more wickets in 84 other matches

Record wicket partnerships

1st	170	Shahriar Hossain (68) and Mehrab Hossain (101)	v Zimbabwe at Dhaka	1998-99
2nd	160	Imrul Kayes (66) and Junaid Siddique (97)	v Pakistan at Dambulla	2010
3rd	141	Mohammad Ashraful (109) and Raqibul Hassan (83)	v United Arab Emirates at Lahore	2008
4th	175*	Rajin Saleh (108*) and Habibul Bashar (64*)	v Kenya at Fatullah	2005-06
5th	119	Shakib Al Hasan (52) and Raqibul Hassan (63)	v South Africa at Dhaka	2007-08
6th	123*	Al Sahariar (62*) and Khaled Mashud (53*)	v West Indies at Dhaka	1999-2000
7th	101	Mushfiqur Rahim (86) and Naeem Islam (43)	v New Zealand at Dunedin	2009-10
8th	70*	Khaled Mashud (35*) and Mohammad Rafique (41*)	v New Zealand at Kimberley	2002-03
9th	97	Shakib Al Hasan (108) and Mashrafe Mortaza (38)	v Pakistan at Multan	2007-08
10th	54*	Khaled Mashud (39*) and Tapash Baisya (22*)	v Sri Lanka at Colombo	2005-06

Figures to 26.09.11. Updated records can be found at www.cricinfo.com/ci/engine/records

Most catches

Fielders

36	Mashrafe Mortaza	
35	Mohammad Ashraful	
30	Shakib Al Hasan	
29	Aftab Ahmed	
29	Tamim Iqbal	

Most dismissals

Wicketkeepers   *Ct/St*

126	Khaled Mashud	91/35
94	Mushfiqur Rahim	65/29
13	Dhiman Ghosh	9/4
4	Jahurul Islam	4/0

Highest team totals

320-8	v Zimbabwe at Bulawayo	2009
313-6	v Zimbabwe at Bulawayo	2009
301-7	v Kenya at Bogra	2005-06
300-8	v UAE at Lahore	2008
296-6	v India at Mirpur	2009-10
295-6	v Australia at Mirpur	2010-11
293-7	v Ireland at Dhaka	2007-08
285-7	v Pakistan at Lahore	2007-08
283-6	v India at Karachi	2008
283-9	v India at Mirpur	2010-11

Bangladesh passed 300 for the first time in their 119th one-day international

Lowest team totals

Completed innings

58	v West Indies at Mirpur	2010-11
74	v Australia at Darwin	2008
76	v Sri Lanka at Colombo	2002
76	v India at Dhaka	2002-03
77	v NZ at Colombo	2002-03
78	v S Africa at Mirpur	2010-11
86	v NZ at Chittagong	2004-05
87*	v Pakistan at Dhaka	1999-2000
92	v Zimbabwe at Nairobi	1997-98
93	v S Africa at Birmingham	2004
93	v NZ at Queenstown	2007-08

* One batsman absent hurt

Most sixes

49	Aftab Ahmed
44	Tamim Iqbal
40	Mashrafe Mortaza
29	Mohammad Ashraful
29	Mohammad Rafique
21	Shakib Al Hasan
19	Mushfiqur Rahim
15	Abdur Razzak
13	Mahmudullah
12	Naeem Islam

Best strike rate

Runs per 100 balls   *Runs*

86.46	Mashrafe Mortaza	1163
83.04	Aftab Ahmed	1954
79.81	Tamim Iqbal	3053
77.11	Shakib Al Hasan	3261
71.81	Mohammad Rafique	1190
70.78	Abdur Razzak	613
70.33	Shahriar Nafees	2162
70.21	Mohammad Ashraful	3395
69.58	Mahmudullah	1318
68.85	Alok Kapali	1183

Qualification: 500 runs

Most economical bowlers

Runs per over   *Wkts*

4.31	Shakib Al Hasan	144
4.39	Mohammad Rafique	119
4.42	Mushfiqur Rahman	19
4.49	Abdur Razzak	175
4.63	Mashrafe Mortaza	150
4.63	Syed Rasel	61
4.80	Naeem Islam	33
4.84	Manjural Islam	24
4.95	Naimur Rahman	10
5.07	Khaled Mahmud	67

Qualification: 1000 balls bowled

Bangladesh's one-day international results

	Played	Won	Lost	Tied	No Result	% win
v Australia	19	1	18	0	0	5.26
v England	15	2	13	0	0	13.33
v India	23	2	21	0	0	8.69
v New Zealand	21	5	16	0	0	23.80
v Pakistan	26	1	25	0	0	3.84
v South Africa	14	1	13	0	0	7.14
v Sri Lanka	29	2	27	0	0	6.89
v West Indies	17	3	12	0	2	20.00
v Zimbabwe	56	30	26	0	0	53.57
v others (see below)	32	22	10	0	0	68.75
TOTAL	252	69	181	0	2	27.60

Other teams: Bermuda (P2, W2), Canada (P2, W1, L1), Hong Kong (P1, W1), Ireland (P7, W5, L2), Kenya (P14, W8, L6), Netherlands (P2, W1, L1), Scotland (P3, W3), UAE (P1, W1).

ENGLAND
Test Match Records

133	AJ Stewart	
118	GA Gooch	
117	DI Gower	
115	MA Atherton	
114	MC Cowdrey	
108	G Boycott	
102	IT Botham	
100	GP Thorpe	
96	N Hussain	
95	APE Knott	

Cowdrey was the first man to reach 100 Tests, in 1968

Most runs

		Avge
8900	GA Gooch	42.58
8463	AJ Stewart	39.54
8231	DI Gower	44.25
8114	G Boycott	47.72
7728	MA Atherton	37.69
7624	MC Cowdrey	44.06
7249	WR Hammond	58.45
6971	L Hutton	56.67
6806	KF Barrington	58.67
6744	GP Thorpe	44.66

KP Pietersen (6361) and AJ Strauss (6340) have also passed 6000 runs

Most wickets

		Avge
383	IT Botham	28.40
325	RGD Willis	25.20
307	FS Trueman	21.57
297	DL Underwood	25.83
252	JB Statham	24.84
248	MJ Hoggard	30.50
240	JM Anderson	30.57
236	AV Bedser	24.89
234	AR Caddick	29.91
229	D Gough	28.39

SJ Harmison (222), A Flintoff (219) and JA Snow (202) also took more than 200 wickets

Highest scores

364	L Hutton	v Australia at The Oval	1938
336*	WR Hammond	v New Zealand at Auckland	1932-33
333	GA Gooch	v India at Lord's	1990
325	A Sandham	v West Indies at Kingston	1929-30
310*	JH Edrich	v New Zealand at Leeds	1965
294	AN Cook	v India at Birmingham	2011
287	RE Foster	v Australia at Sydney	1903-04
285*	PBH May	v West Indies at Birmingham	1957
278	DCS Compton	v Pakistan at Nottingham	1954
262*	DL Amiss	v West Indies at Kingston	1973-74

Foster was playing in his first Test, Sandham in his last

Best innings bowling

10-53	JC Laker	v Australia at Manchester	1956
9-28	GA Lohmann	v South Africa at Johannesburg	1895-96
9-37	JC Laker	v Australia at Manchester	1956
9-57	DE Malcolm	v South Africa at The Oval	1994
9-103	SF Barnes	v S Africa at Johannesburg	1913-14
8-7	GA Lohmann	v S Africa at Port Elizabeth	1895-96
8-11	J Briggs	v South Africa at Cape Town	1888-89
8-29	SF Barnes	v South Africa at The Oval	1912
8-31	FS Trueman	v India at Manchester	1952
8-34	IT Botham	v Pakistan at Lord's	1978

Botham also scored 108 in England's innings victory

Record wicket partnerships

1st	359	L Hutton (158) and C Washbrook (195)	v South Africa at Johannesburg	1948-49
2nd	382	L Hutton (364) and M Leyland (187)	v Australia at The Oval	1938
3rd	370	WJ Edrich (189) and DCS Compton (208)	v South Africa at Lord's	1947
4th	411	PBH May (285*) and MC Cowdrey (154)	v West Indies at Birmingham	1957
5th	254	KWR Fletcher (113) and AW Greig (148)	v India at Bombay	1972-73
6th	281	GP Thorpe (200*) and A Flintoff (137)	v New Zealand at Christchurch	2001-02
7th	197	MJK Smith (96) and JM Parks (101*)	v West Indies at Port-of-Spain	1959-60
8th	332	IJL Trott (184) and SCJ Broad (169)	v Pakistan at Lord's	2010
9th	163*	MC Cowdrey (128*) and AC Smith (69*)	v New Zealand at Wellington	1962-63
10th	130	RE Foster (287) and W Rhodes (40*)	v Australia at Sydney	1903-04

Figures to 26.09.11. Updated records can be found at **www.cricinfo.com/ci/engine/records**

Test Match Records

ENGLAND

Most catches

Fielders

120	IT Botham
120	MC Cowdrey
110	WR Hammond
107	AJ Strauss
105	GP Thorpe

Most dismissals

Wicketkeepers		*Ct/St*
269	APE Knott	250/19
241	AJ Stewart	227/14
219	TG Evans	173/46
174	RW Taylor	167/7
165	RC Russell	153/12

Highest team totals

903-7d	v Australia at The Oval	1938
849	v West Indies at Kingston	1929-30
710-7d	v India at Birmingham	2011
658-8d	v Australia at Nottingham	1938
654-5	v South Africa at Durban	1938-39
653-4d	v India at Lord's	1990
652-7d	v India at Madras	1984-85
644	v Australia at Sydney	2010-11
636	v Australia at Sydney	1928-29
633-5d	v India at Birmingham	1979

England have made nine other totals of 600 or more

Lowest team totals

Completed innings

45	v Australia at Sydney	1886-87
46	v WI at Port-of-Spain	1993-94
51	v WI at Kingston	2008-09
52	v Australia at The Oval	1948
53	v Australia at Lord's	1888
61	v Aust at Melbourne	1901-02
61	v Aust at Melbourne	1903-04
62	v Australia at Lord's	1888
64	v NZ at Wellington	1977-78
65*	v Australia at Sydney	1894-95

*One batsman absent

Best match bowling

19-90	JC Laker	v Australia at Manchester	1956
17-159	SF Barnes	v S Africa at Johannesburg	1913-14
15-28	J Briggs	v S Africa at Cape Town	1888-89
15-45	GA Lohmann	v S Africa at Port Elizabeth	1895-96
15-99	C Blythe	v South Africa at Leeds	1907
15-104	H Verity	v Australia at Lord's	1934
15-124	W Rhodes	v Australia at Melbourne	1903-04
14-99	AV Bedser	v Australia at Nottingham	1953
14-102	W Bates	v Australia at Melbourne	1882-83
14-144	SF Barnes	v South Africa at Durban	1913-14

Barnes took ten or more wickets in a match a record seven times for England

Hat-tricks

W Bates	v Australia at Melbourne	1882-83
J Briggs	v Australia at Sydney	1891-92
GA Lohmann	v S Africa at Port Elizabeth	1895-96
JT Hearne	v Australia at Leeds	1899
MJC Allom	v New Zealand at Christchurch	1929-30
TWJ Goddard	v S Africa at Johannesburg	1938-39
PJ Loader	v West Indies at Leeds	1957
DG Cork	v West Indies at Manchester	1995
D Gough	v Australia at Sydney	1998-99
MJ Hoggard	v West Indies at Bridgetown	2003-04
RJ Sidebottom	v New Zealand at Hamilton	2007-08
SCJ Broad	v India at Nottingham	2011

England's Test match results

	Played	Won	Lost	Drawn	Tied	% win
v Australia	326	102	133	91	0	31.28
v Bangladesh	8	8	0	0	0	100.00
v India	103	38	19	46	0	36.89
v New Zealand	94	45	8	41	0	47.87
v Pakistan	71	22	13	36	0	30.98
v South Africa	138	56	29	53	0	40.57
v Sri Lanka	24	9	6	9	0	37.50
v West Indies	145	43	53	49	0	29.65
v Zimbabwe	6	3	0	3	0	50.00
TOTAL	**915**	**326**	**261**	**328**	**0**	**35.62**

Figures to 26.09.11. Updated records can be found at **www.cricinfo.com/ci/engine/records**

ENGLAND
One-day International Records

Most appearances

197	PD Collingwood	
170	AJ Stewart	
158	D Gough	
151	JM Anderson	
138	A Flintoff	
127	AJ Strauss	
125	GA Gooch	
123	ME Trescothick	
122	AJ Lamb	
120	GA Hick	

Six further men have played 100 or more ODIs for England

Most runs

		Avge
5092	PD Collingwood	35.36
4677	AJ Stewart	31.60
4335	ME Trescothick	37.37
4290	GA Gooch	36.98
4205	AJ Strauss	35.63
4010	AJ Lamb	39.31
3846	GA Hick	37.33
3715	KP Pietersen	40.82
3637	NV Knight	40.41
3293	A Flintoff	31.97

IR Bell (3232) and DI Gower (3170) have also passed 3000 runs in ODIs

Most wickets

		Avge
234	D Gough	26.29
204	JM Anderson	30.89
168	A Flintoff	23.61
145	IT Botham	28.54
137	SCJ Broad	27.08
115	PAJ DeFreitas	32.82
111	PD Collingwood	38.68
88	GP Swann	23.84
80	RGD Willis	24.60
76	JE Emburey	30.86
76	SJ Harmison	32.64

Nine further bowlers have taken 50 wickets in ODIs for England

Highest scores

167*	RA Smith	v Australia at Birmingham	1993
158	DI Gower	v New Zealand at Brisbane	1982-83
158	AJ Strauss	v India at Bangalore	2010-11
154	AJ Strauss	v Bangladesh at Birmingham	2010
152	AJ Strauss	v Bangladesh at Nottingham	2005
142*	CWJ Athey	v New Zealand at Manchester	1986
142	GA Gooch	v Pakistan at Karachi	1987-88
137	DL Amiss	v India at Lord's	1975
137	ME Trescothick	v Pakistan at Lord's	2001
137	IJL Trott	v Australia at Sydney	2010-11

Trescothick scored 12 centuries in ODIs, Gooch 8, Gower and KP Pietersen 7, and Strauss 6

Best innings bowling

6-31	PD Collingwood	v B'desh at Nottingham	2005
6-45	CR Woakes	v Australia at Brisbane	2010-11
5-15	MA Ealham	v Zim at Kimberley	1999-2000
5-19	A Flintoff	v WI at Gros Islet	2008-09
5-20	VJ Marks	v NZ at Wellington	1983-84
5-21	C White	v Zim at Bulawayo	1999-2000
5-23	SCJ Broad	v S Africa at Nottingham	2008
5-23	JM Anderson	v SA at Port Elizabeth	2009-10
5-26	RC Irani	v India at The Oval	2002
5-28	GP Swann	v Aust at Chester-le-Street	2009

Collingwood also scored 112 in the same match.*
All Ealham's five wickets were lbw, an ODI record

Record wicket partnerships

1st	200	ME Trescothick (114*) and VS Solanki (106)	v South Africa at The Oval	2003
2nd	250	AJ Strauss (154) and IJL Trott (110)	v Bangladesh at Birmingham	2010
3rd	213	GA Hick (86*) and NH Fairbrother (113)	v West Indies at Lord's	1991
4th	226	AJ Strauss (100) and A Flintoff (123)	v West Indies at Lord's	2004
5th	174	A Flintoff (99) and PD Collingwood (79*)	v India at The Oval	2004
6th	150	MP Vaughan (90*) and GO Jones (80)	v Zimbabwe at Bulawayo	2004-05
7th	110	PD Collingwood (100) and C White (48)	v Sri Lanka at Perth	2002-03
8th	99*	RS Bopara (43*) and SCJ Broad (45*)	v India at Manchester	2007
9th	100	LE Plunkett (56) and VS Solanki (39*)	v Pakistan at Lahore	2005-06
10th	53	JM Anderson (20*) and ST Finn (35)	v Australia at Brisbane	2010-11

Figures to 26.09.11. Updated records can be found at www.cricinfo.com/ci/engine/records

One-day International Records ENGLAND

Most catches

Fielders

108	PD Collingwood	
64	GA Hick	
57	AJ Strauss	
46	A Flintoff	
45	GA Gooch/ME Tres'thick	

Most dismissals

Wicketkeepers		*Ct/St*
163	AJ Stewart	148/15
77	MJ Prior	69/8
72	GO Jones	68/4
47	RC Russell	41/6
43	CMW Read	41/2

Highest team totals

391-4	v Bangladesh at Nottingham	2005
363-7	v Pakistan at Nottingham	1992
347-7	v Bangladesh at Birmingham	2010
340-6	v New Zealand at Napier	2007-08
338-8	v India at Bangalore	2010-11
334-4	v India at Lord's	1975
333-6	v Australia at Sydney	2010-11
333-9	v Sri Lanka at Taunton	1983
328-7	v West Indies at Birmingham	2009
327-4	v Pakistan at Lahore	2005-06
327-8	v Ireland at Bangalore	2010-11

England have reached 300 on 16 other occasions

Lowest team totals

Completed innings

86	v Australia at Manchester	2001
88	v SL at Dambulla	2003-04
89	v NZ at Wellington	2001-02
93	v Australia at Leeds	1975
94	v Aust at Melbourne	1978-79
101	v NZ at Chester-le-Street	2004
103	v SA at The Oval	1999
104	v SL at Colombo	2007-08
107	v Zim at Cape Town	1999-2000
110	v Aust at Melbourne	1998-99
110	v Aust at Adelaide	2006-07

The lowest totals against England are 45 by Canada (1979), and 70 by Australia (1977)

Most sixes

92	A Flintoff*	
74	PD Collingwood	
65	KP Pietersen*	
44	IT Botham	
41	GA Hick	
41	ME Trescothick	
30	AJ Lamb	
26	OA Shah	
26	AJ Stewart	
25	AJ Strauss	

*Also hit one six for the World XI

Best strike rate

Runs per 100 balls		*Runs*
92.83	C Kieswetter	674
92.54	TT Bresnan	608
90.50	EJG Morgan	1497
89.29	LJ Wright	701
89.14	A Flintoff	3293
87.30	KP Pietersen	3715
85.21	ME Trescothick	4335
83.83	PAJ DeFreitas	690
80.94	AJ Strauss	4205
79.10	IT Botham	2113

Qualification: 500 runs

Most economical bowlers

Runs per over		*Wkts*
3.28	RGD Willis	80
3.54	ARC Fraser	47
3.79	GR Dilley	48
3.84	AD Mullally	63
3.96	IT Botham	145
3.96	PAJ DeFreitas	115
4.01	AR Caddick	69
4.08	MA Ealham	67
4.10	JE Emburey	76
4.17	GC Small	58

Qualification: 2000 balls bowled

England's one-day international results

	Played	Won	Lost	Tied	No result	% win
v Australia	113	42	67	2	2	38.73
v Bangladesh	15	13	2	0	0	86.66
v India	76	33	38	2	3	46.57
v New Zealand	70	29	35	2	4	45.45
v Pakistan	68	38	28	0	2	57.57
v South Africa	45	19	23	1	2	45.34
v Sri Lanka	50	26	24	0	0	52.00
v West Indies	83	38	41	0	4	48.10
v Zimbabwe	30	21	8	0	1	72.41
v others (see below)	17	15	1	0	1	93.75
TOTAL	**567**	**274**	**267**	**7**	**19**	**50.66**

Other teams: Canada (P2, W2), East Africa (P1, W1), Ireland (P5, W4, L1), Kenya (P2, W2), Namibia (P1, W1), Netherlands (P3, W3), Scotland (P2, W1, NR1), United Arab Emirates (P1, W1).

INDIA

Test Match Records

Most appearances

181	SR Tendulkar
156	R Dravid
132	A Kumble
131	Kapil Dev
127	VVS Laxman
125	SM Gavaskar
116	DB Vengsarkar
113	SC Ganguly
99	M Azharuddin
98	Harbhajan Singh

Gavaskar played 106 consecutive matches between 1974-75 and 1986-87

Most runs

		Avge
14965	SR Tendulkar	56.25
12752	R Dravid	53.35
10122	SM Gavaskar	51.12
8328	VVS Laxman	46.26
7652	V Sehwag	52.41
7212	SC Ganguly	42.17
6868	DB Vengsarkar	42.13
6215	M Azharuddin	45.03
6080	GR Viswanath	41.74
5248	Kapil Dev	31.05

Tendulkar has scored 51 centuries, Dravid 35, Gavaskar 34, Azharuddin 22 and Sehwag 22

Most wickets

		Avge
619	A Kumble	29.65
434	Kapil Dev	29.64
406	Harbhajan Singh	32.22
273	Z Khan	31.78
266	BS Bedi	29.74
242	BS Chandrasekhar	29.74
236	J Srinath	30.49
189	EAS Prasanna	30.38
162	MH Mankad	32.32
156	S Venkataraghavan	36.11

In all 17 Indians have taken 100 wickets in Tests

Highest scores

319	V Sehwag	v South Africa at Chennai	2007-08
309	V Sehwag	v Pakistan at Multan	2003-04
293	V Sehwag	v Sri Lanka at Mumbai	2009-10
281	VVS Laxman	v Australia at Kolkata	2000-01
270	R Dravid	v Pakistan at Rawalpindi	2003-04
254	V Sehwag	v Pakistan at Lahore	2005-06
248*	SR Tendulkar	v Bangladesh at Dhaka	2004-05
241*	SR Tendulkar	v Australia at Sydney	2003-04
239	SC Ganguly	v Pakistan at Bangalore	2007-08
236*	SM Gavaskar	v West Indies at Madras	1983-84

Sehwag and Tendulkar have scored six double-centuries, Dravid five, and Gavaskar four

Best innings bowling

10-74	A Kumble	v Pakistan at Delhi	1998-99
9-69	JM Patel	v Australia at Kanpur	1959-60
9-83	Kapil Dev	v WI at Ahmedabad	1983-84
9-102	SP Gupte	v W Indies at Kanpur	1958-59
8-52	MH Mankad	v Pakistan at Delhi	1952-53
8-55	MH Mankad	v England at Madras	1951-52
8-61	ND Hirwani	v W Indies at Madras	1987-88
8-72	S Venkataraghavan	v N Zealand at Delhi	1964-65
8-75	ND Hirwani	v W Indies at Madras	1987-88
8-76	EAS Prasanna	v NZ at Auckland	1975-76

Hirwani's two performances were in the same match, his Test debut

Record wicket partnerships

1st	413	MH Mankad (231) and P Roy (173)	v New Zealand at Madras	1955-56
2nd	344*	SM Gavaskar (182*) and DB Vengsarkar (157*)	v West Indies at Calcutta	1978-79
3rd	336	V Sehwag (309) and SR Tendulkar (194*)	v Pakistan at Multan	2003-04
4th	353	SR Tendulkar (241*) and VVS Laxman (178)	v Australia at Sydney	2003-04
5th	376	VVS Laxman (281) and R Dravid (180)	v Australia at Calcutta	2000-01
6th	298*	DB Vengsarkar (164*) and RJ Shastri (121*)	v Australia at Bombay	1986-87
7th	259*	VVS Laxman (143*) and MS Dhoni (132*)	v South Africa at Kolkata	2009-10
8th	161	M Azharuddin (109) and A Kumble (88)	v South Africa at Calcutta	1996-97
9th	149	PG Joshi (52*) and RB Desai (85)	v Pakistan at Bombay	1960-61
10th	133	SR Tendulkar (248*) and Z Khan (75)	v Bangladesh at Dhaka	2004-05

Figures to 26.09.11. Updated records can be found at **www.cricinfo.com/ci/engine/records**

Test Match Records

Most catches

Fielders

206	R Dravid	
127	VVS Laxman	
108	SM Gavaskar	
108	SR Tendulkar	
105	M Azharuddin	

Most dismissals

Wicketkeepers		*Ct/St*
198	MS Dhoni	173/25
198	SMH Kirmani	160/38
130	KS More	110/20
107	NR Mongia	99/8
82	FM Engineer	66/16

Highest team totals

726-9d	v Sri Lanka at Mumbai	2009-10
707	v Sri Lanka at Colombo	2010
705-7d	v Australia at Sydney	2003-04
676-7	v Sri Lanka at Kanpur	1986-87
675-5d	v Pakistan at Multan	2003-04
664	v England at The Oval	2007
657-7d	v Australia at Kolkata	2000-01
644-7d	v West Indies at Kanpur	1978-79
643-6d	v South Africa at Kolkata	2009-10
642	v Sri Lanka at Kampur	2009-10

India have reached 600 on 12 further occasions

Lowest team totals

Completed innings

42*	v England at Lord's	1974
58	v Australia at Brisbane	1947-48
58	v England at Manchester	1952
66	v S Africa at Durban	1996-97
67	v Aust at Melbourne	1947-48
75	v West Indies at Delhi	1987-88
76	v SA at Ahmedabad	2007-08
81*	v NZ at Wellington	1975-76
81	v W Indies at Bridgetown	1996-97
82	v England at Manchester	1952

*One or more batsmen absent

Best match bowling

16-136	ND Hirwani	v West Indies at Madras	1987-88
15-217	Harbhajan Singh	v Australia at Chennai	2000-01
14-124	JM Patel	v Australia at Kanpur	1959-60
14-149	A Kumble	v Pakistan at Delhi	1998-99
13-131	MH Mankad	v Pakistan at Delhi	1952-53
13-132	J Srinath	v Pakistan at Calcutta	1998-99
13-181	A Kumble	v Australia at Chennai	2004-05
13-196	Harbhajan Singh	v Australia at Kolkata	2000-01
12-104	BS Chandrasekhar	v Australia at Melbourne	1977-78
12-108	MH Mankad	v England at Madras	1951-52

Hirwani's feat was on his Test debut

Hat-tricks

Harbhajan Singh   v Australia at Kolkata   2000-01

The wickets of RT Ponting, AC Gilchrist and SK Warne, as India fought back to win after following on.

IK Pathan   v Pakistan at Karachi   2005-06

Salman Butt, Younis Khan and Mohammad Yousuf with the fourth, fifth and sixth balls of the match – Pakistan still won the match by 341 runs.

India had never conceded a hat-trick in a Test match until SCJ Broad took one for England at Nottingham in 2011

India's Test match results

	Played	Won	Lost	Drawn	Tied	% win
v Australia	78	20	34	23	1	25.64
v Bangladesh	7	6	0	1	0	85.71
v England	103	19	38	46	0	18.44
v New Zealand	50	16	9	25	0	32.00
v Pakistan	59	9	12	38	0	15.25
v South Africa	27	7	12	8	0	25.92
v Sri Lanka	35	14	6	15	0	40.00
v West Indies	85	12	30	43	0	14.11
v Zimbabwe	11	7	2	2	0	63.63
TOTAL	**455**	**110**	**143**	**201**	**1**	**24.17**

Figures to 26.09.11. Updated records can be found at **www.cricinfo.com/ci/engine/records**

One-day International Records

Most appearances

453	SR Tendulkar
340	R Dravid
334	M Azharuddin
308	SC Ganguly
271	Yuvraj Singh
269	A Kumble
229	J Srinath
227	Harbhajan Singh
226	V Sehwag
225	Kapil Dev

Robin Singh played 136 ODIs for India – but only one Test match

Most runs

		Avge
18111	SR Tendulkar	45.16
11221	SC Ganguly	40.95
10768	R Dravid	39.15
9378	M Azharuddin	36.92
7959	Yuvraj Singh	37.54
7482	V Sehwag	35.45
6111	MS Dhoni	48.88
5359	A Jadeja	37.47
4413	NS Sidhu	37.08
4091	K Srikkanth	29.01

G Gambhir (4073) has also scored more than 4000 runs in ODIs

Most wickets

		Avge
334	A Kumble	30.83
315	J Srinath	28.08
288	AB Agarkar	27.85
260	Z Khan	29.51
255	Harbhajan Singh	33.52
253	Kapil Dev	27.45
196	BKV Prasad	32.30
157	M Prabhakar	28.87
155	A Nehra	31.60
154	SR Tendulkar	44.26

IK Pathan (152), RJ Shastri (129), Yuvraj Singh (108) and SC Ganguly (100) also reached 100 wickets

Highest scores

200*	SR Tendulkar	v South Africa at Gwalior	2009-10
186*	SR Tendulkar	v N Zealand at Hyderabad	1999-2000
183*	MS Dhoni	v Sri Lanka at Jaipur	2005-06
183	SC Ganguly	v Sri Lanka at Taunton	1999
175*	Kapil Dev	v Zimbabwe at Tunbridge Wells	1983
175	SR Tendulkar	v Australia at Hyderabad	2009-10
175	V Sehwag	v Bangladesh at Mirpur	2010-11
163*	SR Tendulkar	v NZ at Christchurch	2008-09
159*	D Mongia	v Zimbabwe at Guwahati	2001-02
153*	M Azharuddin	v Zimbabwe at Cuttack	1997-98
153*	SC Ganguly	v New Zealand at Gwalior	1999-2000
153	R Dravid	v N Zealand at Hyderabad	1999-2000

Tendulkar has scored 48 centuries, Ganguly 22 and Sehwag 14

Best bowling figures

6-12	A Kumble	v West Indies at Calcutta	1993-94
6-23	A Nehra	v England at Durban	2002-03
6-27	M Kartik	v Australia at Mumbai	2007-08
6-42	AB Agarkar	v Australia at Melbourne	2003-04
6-55	S Sreesanth	v England at Indore	2005-06
6-59	A Nehra	v Sri Lanka at Colombo	2005
5-6	SB Joshi	v South Africa at Nairobi	1999-2000
5-15	RJ Shastri	v Australia at Perth	1991-92
5-16	SC Ganguly	v Pakistan at Toronto	1997-98
5-21	Arshad Ayub	v Pakistan at Dhaka	1988-89
5-21	N Chopra	v West Indies at Toronto	1999-2000

Agarkar took four wickets in an ODI innings 12 times

Record wicket partnerships

1st	258	SC Ganguly (111) and SR Tendulkar (146)	v Kenya at Paarl	2001-02
2nd	331	SR Tendulkar (186*) and R Dravid (153)	v New Zealand at Hyderabad	1999-2000
3rd	237*	R Dravid (104*) and SR Tendulkar (140*)	v Kenya at Bristol	1999
4th	275*	M Azharuddin (153*) and A Jadeja (116*)	v Zimbabwe at Cuttack	1997-98
5th	223	M Azharuddin (111*) and A Jadeja (119)	v Sri Lanka at Colombo	1997-98
6th	158	Yuvraj Singh (120) and MS Dhoni (67*)	v Zimbabwe at Harare	2005-06
7th	102	HK Badani (60*) and AB Agarkar (53)	v Australia at Melbourne	2003-04
8th	84	Harbhajan Singh (49) and P Kumar (40*)	v Australia at Vadodara	2009-10
9th	126*	Kapil Dev (175*) and SMH Kirmani (24*)	v Zimbabwe at Tunbridge Wells	1983
10th	64	Harbhajan Singh (41*) and L Balaji (18)	v England at The Oval	2004

Figures to 26.09.11. Updated records can be found at **www.cricinfo.com/ci/engine/records**

One-day International Records

INDIA

Most catches

Fielders

156	M Azharuddin	
136	SR Tendulkar	
124	R Dravid	
99	SC Ganguly	
85	A Kumble	

Most dismissals

		Ct/St
Wicketkeepers		
235	MS Dhoni	178/57
154	NR Mongia	110/44
90	KS More	63/27
86	R Dravid	72/14
36	SMH Kirmani	27/9

Highest team totals

414-7	v Sri Lanka at Rajkot	2009-10
413-5	v Bermuda at Port-of-Spain	2006-07
401-3	v South Africa at Gwalior	2009-10
392-4	v N Zealand at Christchurch	2008-09
387-5	v England at Rajkot	2008-09
376-2	v N Zealand at Hyderabad	1999-2000
374-4	v Hong Kong at Karachi	2008
373-6	v Sri Lanka at Taunton	1999
370-4	v Bangladesh at Mirpur	2010-11
363-5	v Sri Lanka at Colombo	2008-09

All scored in 50 overs

Lowest team totals

Completed innings

54	v Sri Lanka at Sharjah	2000-01
63	v Australia at Sydney	1980-81
78	v Sri Lanka at Kanpur	1986-87
79	v Pakistan at Sialkot	1978-79
88	v NZ at Dambulla	2010
91	v South Africa at Durban	2006-07
100	v WI at Ahmedabad	1993-94
100	v Australia at Sydney	1999-2000
103	v Sri Lanka at Colombo	2008-09
103	v Sri Lanka at Dambulla	2010

The lowest score against India is Zimbabwe's 65 at Harare in 2005

Most sixes

193	SR Tendulkar
189	SC Ganguly
142	Yuvraj Singh
123	V Sehwag
120	MS Dhoni
85	A Jadeja
77	M Azharuddin
68	SK Raina
67	Kapil Dev
44	NS Sidhu

Dhoni hit 10 sixes in one innings

Best strike rate

Runs per 100 balls		Runs
113.60	YK Pathan	810
104.17	V Sehwag	7482
95.07	Kapil Dev	3783
91.92	RV Uthappa	786
90.80	SK Raina	2993
89.43	SB Joshi	584
87.32	Yuvraj Singh	7959
87.15	MS Dhoni	6111
86.38	G Gambhir	4073
86.32	SR Tendulkar	18111

Qualification: 500 runs

Most economical bowlers

Runs per over		Wkts
3.71	Kapil Dev	253
3.95	Maninder Singh	66
4.05	Madan Lal	73
4.21	RJ Shastri	129
4.27	M Prabhakar	157
4.29	Harbhajan Singh	255
4.29	A Kumble	334
4.33	M Amarnath	46
4.36	SLV Raju	63
4.44	SB Joshi	69
4.44	J Srinath	315

Qualification: 2000 balls bowled

India's one-day international results

	Played	Won	Lost	Tied	No result	% win
v Australia	105	36	61	0	8	37.11
v Bangladesh	23	21	2	0	0	91.30
v England	76	38	33	2	3	53.42
v New Zealand	88	46	37	0	5	55.42
v Pakistan	120	47	69	0	4	40.51
v South Africa	66	24	40	0	2	37.50
v Sri Lanka	129	68	50	0	11	57.62
v West Indies	101	42	56	1	2	42.92
v Zimbabwe	51	39	10	2	0	78.43
v others (see below)	24	22	2	0	0	91.66
TOTAL	783	383	360	5	35	51.53

Other teams: Bermuda (P1, W1), East Africa (P1, W1), Hong Kong (P1, W1), Ireland (P2, W2), Kenya (P13, W11, L2), Namibia (P1, W1), Netherlands (P2, W2), Scotland (P1, W1), United Arab Emirates (P2, W2).

NEW ZEALAND *Test Match Records*

Most appearances

111	SP Fleming
104	DL Vettori
86	RJ Hadlee
82	JG Wright
81	NJ Astle
78	AC Parore
77	MD Crowe
63	IDS Smith
62	CL Cairns
61	BE Congdon
61	CS Martin

Vettori also played for the World XI against Australia in October 2005

Most runs

		Avge
7172	SP Fleming	40.06
5444	MD Crowe	45.36
5334	JG Wright	37.82
4702	NJ Astle	37.02
4159	DL Vettori	30.35
3448	BE Congdon	32.22
3428	JR Reid	33.28
3389	BB McCullum	37.24
3320	CL Cairns	33.53
3124	RJ Hadlee	27.16

CD McMillan (3116) also scored more than 3000 runs

Most wickets

		Avge
431	RJ Hadlee	22.29
344	DL Vettori	33.75
218	CL Cairns	29.40
199	CS Martin	34.66
160	DK Morrison	34.68
130	BL Cairns	32.92
123	EJ Chatfield	32.17
116	RO Collinge	29.25
111	BR Taylor	26.60
102	JG Bracewell	35.81

RC Motz (100) also took 100 Test wickets. Vettori also took one wicket for the World XI

Highest scores

299	MD Crowe	v Sri Lanka at Wellington	1990-91
274*	SP Fleming	v Sri Lanka at Colombo	2002-03
267*	BA Young	v Sri Lanka at Dunedin	1996-97
262	SP Fleming	v South Africa at Cape Town	2005-06
259	GM Turner	v West Indies at Georgetown	1971-72
239	GT Dowling	v India at Christchurch	1967-68
230*	B Sutcliffe	v India at Delhi	1955-56
225	BB McCullum	v India at Hyderabad	2010-11
224	L Vincent	v Sri Lanka at Wellington	2004-05
223*	GM Turner	v West Indies at Kingston	1971-72

There have been six other double-centuries, two by MS Sinclair and one each by NJ Astle, MP Donnelly, SP Fleming and JD Ryder

Best innings bowling

9-52	RJ Hadlee	v Australia at Brisbane	1985-86
7-23	RJ Hadlee	v India at Wellington	1975-76
7-27	CL Cairns	v West Indies at Hamilton	1999-2000
7-52	C Pringle	v Pakistan at Faisalabad	1990-91
7-53	CL Cairns	v Bangladesh at Hamilton	2001-02
7-65	SB Doull	v India at Wellington	1998-99
7-74	BR Taylor	v West Indies at Bridgetown	1971-72
7-74	BL Cairns	v England at Leeds	1983
7-87	SL Boock	v Pakistan at Hyderabad	1984-85
7-87	DL Vettori	v Australia at Auckland	1999-2000

Hadlee took five or more wickets in an innings 36 times: the next-best for New Zealand is 19, by DL Vettori

Record wicket partnerships

1st	387	GM Turner (259) and TW Jarvis (182)	v West Indies at Georgetown	1971-72
2nd	241	JG Wright (116) and AH Jones (143)	v England at Wellington	1991-92
3rd	467	AH Jones (186) and MD Crowe (299)	v Sri Lanka at Wellington	1990-91
4th	271	LRPL Taylor (151) and JD Ryder (201)	v India at Napier	2008-09
5th	222	NJ Astle (141) and CD McMillan (142)	v Zimbabwe at Wellington	2000-01
6th	339	MJ Guptill (189) and BB McCullum (185)	v Bangladesh at Hamilton	2009-10
7th	225	CL Cairns (158) and JDP Oram (90)	v South Africa at Auckland	2003-04
8th	256	SP Fleming (262) and JEC Franklin (122*)	v South Africa at Cape Town	2005-06
9th	136	IDS Smith (173) and MC Snedden (22)	v India at Auckland	1989-90
10th	151	BF Hastings (110) and RO Collinge (68*)	v Pakistan at Auckland	1972-73

Figures to 26.09.11. Updated records can be found at **www.cricinfo.com/ci/engine/records**

Test Match Records   **NEW ZEALAND**

Most catches

Fielders

171	SP Fleming	
71	MD Crowe	
70	NJ Astle	
64	JV Coney	
57	DL Vettori	

Most dismissals

Wicketkeepers   *Ct/St*

201	AC Parore	194/7
176	IDS Smith	168/8
172	BB McCullum	161/11
96	KJ Wadsworth	92/4
59	WK Lees	52/7

Highest team totals

671-4	v Sri Lanka at Wellington	1990-91
630-6d	v India at Chandigarh	2003-04
619-9d	v India at Napier	2008-09
595	v South Africa at Auckland	2003-04
593-8d	v South Africa at Cape Town	2005-06
586-7d	v Sri Lanka at Dunedin	1996-97
563	v Pakistan at Hamilton	2003-04
561	v Sri Lanka at Napier	2004-05
553-7d	v Australia at Brisbane	1985-86
553-7d	v Bangladesh at Hamilton	2009-10

671-4 is the record score in any team's second innings in a Test match

Lowest team totals

Completed innings

26	v England at Auckland	1954-55
42	v Australia at Wellington	1945-46
47	v England at Lord's	1958
54	v Australia at Wellington	1945-46
65	v England at Christchurch	1970-71
67	v England at Leeds	1958
67	v England at Lord's	1978
70	v Pakistan at Dacca	1955-56
73	v Pakistan at Lahore	2001-02
74	v W Indies at Dunedin	1955-56
74	v England at Lord's	1958

26 is the lowest all-out total by any team in a Test match

Best match bowling

15-123	RJ Hadlee	v Australia at Brisbane	1985-86
12-149	DL Vettori	v Australia at Auckland	1999-2000
12-170	DL Vettori	v Bangladesh at Chittagong	2004-05
11-58	RJ Hadlee	v India at Wellington	1975-76
11-102	RJ Hadlee	v West Indies at Dunedin	1979-80
11-152	C Pringle	v Pakistan at Faisalabad	1990-91
11-155	RJ Hadlee	v Australia at Perth	1985-86
11-169	DJ Nash	v England at Lord's	1994
11-180	CS Martin	v South Africa at Auckland	2003-04
10-88	RJ Hadlee	v India at Bombay	1988-89

Hadlee took 33 wickets at 12.15 in the three-Test series in Australia in 1985-86

Hat-tricks

PJ Petherick	v Pakistan at Lahore	1976-77
JEC Franklin	v Bangladesh at Dhaka	2004-05

*Petherick's hat-trick was on Test debut: he dismissed Javed Miandad (who had made 163 on **his** debut), Wasim Raja and Intikhab Alam. Petherick won only five more Test caps.*

Franklin is one of only five men to have scored a century and taken a hat-trick in Tests: the others are J Briggs of England, Abdul Razzaq and Wasim Akram of Pakistan, and IK Pathan of India

New Zealand's Test match results

	Played	Won	Lost	Drawn	Tied	% win
v Australia	50	7	26	17	0	14.00
v Bangladesh	9	8	0	1	0	88.88
v England	94	8	45	41	0	8.51
v India	50	9	16	25	0	18.00
v Pakistan	50	7	23	20	0	14.00
v South Africa	35	4	20	11	0	11.42
v Sri Lanka	26	9	7	10	0	34.61
v West Indies	37	9	10	18	0	24.32
v Zimbabwe	13	7	0	6	0	53.84
TOTAL	**364**	**68**	**147**	**149**	**0**	**18.68**

Figures to 26.09.11. Updated records can be found at **www.cricinfo.com/ci/engine/records**

NEW ZEALAND One-day International Records

Most appearances

279	SP Fleming
268	DL Vettori
250	CZ Harris
223	NJ Astle
214	CL Cairns
197	CD McMillan
192	BB McCullum
188	SB Styris
179	AC Parore
151	JDP Oram

Fleming (1), Vettori (4) and Cairns (1) also played in official ODIs for the World XI

Most runs

		Avge
8007	SP Fleming	32.41
7090	NJ Astle	34.92
4881	CL Cairns	29.22
4707	CD McMillan	28.18
4704	MD Crowe	38.55
4483	SB Styris	32.48
4379	CZ Harris	29.00
4037	BB McCullum	28.83
3891	JG Wright	26.46
3314	AC Parore	25.68

Astle scored 16 centuries: Fleming is next with eight. Fleming also scored 30 runs and Cairns 69 for the World XI

Most wickets

		Avge
274	DL Vettori	31.75
203	CZ Harris	37.50
200	CL Cairns	32.78
192	KD Mills	26.03
159	JDP Oram	29.54
158	RJ Hadlee	21.56
147	SE Bond	20.88
140	EJ Chatfield	25.84
137	SB Styris	35.32
126	DK Morrison	27.53

MC Snedden (114), GR Larsen (113), DR Tuffey (110) and C Pringle (103) also took 100 wkts. Vettori also took 8 wkts, and Cairns 1, for the World XI

Highest scores

172	L Vincent	v Zimbabwe at Bulawayo	2005-06
171*	GM Turner	v East Africa at Birmingham	1975
166	BB McCullum	v Ireland at Aberdeen	2008
161	JAH Marshall	v Ireland at Aberdeen	2008
145*	NJ Astle	v USA at The Oval	2004
141	SB Styris	v Sri Lanka at Bloemfontein	2002-03
140	GM Turner	v Sri Lanka at Auckland	1982-83
141	SB Styris	v Sri Lanka at Bloemfontein	2002-03
139	JM How	v England at Napier	2007-08
131*	LRPL Taylor	v Pakistan at Pallekele	2010-11
131	BB McCullum	v Pakistan at Abu Dhabi	2009-10

Turner's 171 was the highest score in the first World Cup*

Best bowling figures

6-19	SE Bond	v India at Bulawayo	2005-06
6-23	SE Bond	v Australia at Port Elizabeth	2002-03
6-25	SB Styris	v West Indies at Port-of-Spain	2001-02
5-7	DL Vettori	v Bangladesh at Queenstown	2007-08
5-22	MN Hart	v West Indies at Margao	1994-95
5-22	AR Adams	v India at Queenstown	2002-03
5-23	RO Collinge	v India at Christchurch	1975-76
5-23	SE Bond	v Australia at Wellington	2006-07
5-25	RJ Hadlee	v Sri Lanka at Bristol	1983
5-25	SE Bond	v Australia at Adelaide	2001-02
5-25	KD Mills	v South Africa at Durban	2007-08

In all Hadlee took five wickets in an ODI on five occasions

Record wicket partnerships

1st	274	JAH Marshall (161) and BB McCullum (166)	v Ireland at Aberdeen	2008
2nd	156	L Vincent (102) and NJ Astle (81)	v West Indies at Napier	2005-06
3rd	181	AC Parore (96) and KR Rutherford (108)	v India at Baroda	1994-95
4th	190	LRPL Taylor (95) and SB Styris (89)	v India at Dambulla	2010
5th	148	RG Twose (80*) and CL Cairns (60)	v Australia at Cardiff	1999
6th	165	CD McMillan (117) and BB McCullum (86*)	v Australia at Hamilton	2006-07
7th	123	NT Broom (71) and JDP Oram (83)	v Bangladesh at Napier	2009-10
8th	94	JEC Franklin (72*) and NL McCullum (43)	v India at Vadodara	2010-11
9th	83	KD Mills (54) and TG Southee (32)	v India at Christchurch	2008-09
10th	65	MC Snedden (40) and EJ Chatfield (19*)	v Sri Lanka at Derby	1983

Figures to 26.09.11. Updated records can be found at **www.cricinfo.com/ci/engine/records**

Most catches

Fielders

132	SP Fleming
96	CZ Harris
83	NJ Astle
78	LRPL Taylor
75	DL Vettori

Most dismissals

Wicketkeepers		Ct/St
221	BB McCullum	207/14
136	AC Parore	111/25
85	IDS Smith	80/5
37	TE Blain	36/1
30	LK Germon	21/9
30	WK Lees	28/2

Highest team totals

402-2	v Ireland at Aberdeen	2008
397-5	v Zimbabwe at Bulawayo	2005-06
363-5	v Canada at St Lucia	2006-07
358-6	v Canada at Mumbai	2010-11
350-9	v Australia at Hamilton	2006-07
349-9	v India at Rajkot	1999-2000
348-8	v India at Nagpur	1995-96
347-4	v USA at The Oval	2004
340-5	v Australia at Auckland	2006-07
340-7	v England at Napier	2007-08

The 397-5 came from 44 overs; all the others were from 50, except 350-9 (49.3), and 340-5 (48.4)

Lowest team totals

Completed innings

64	v Pakistan at Sharjah	1985-86
73	v Sri Lanka at Auckland	2006-07
74	v Aust at Wellington	1981-82
74	v Pakistan at Sharjah	1989-90
94	v Aust at Christchurch	1989-90
97	v Aust at Faridabad	2003-04
103	v India at Chennai	2010-11
105	v Aust at Auckland	2005-06
108	v Pakistan at Wellington	1992-93
110	v Pakistan at Auckland	1993-94

The lowest totals against New Zealand are 69, by Kenya at Chennai in 2010-11, and 70, by Australia at Adelaide in 1985-86

Most sixes

151	CL Cairns
115	BB McCullum
86	NJ Astle
84	CD McMillan
80	LRPL Taylor
75	JDP Oram
68	SB Styris
63	SP Fleming
43	CZ Harris
41	BL Cairns

CL Cairns also hit 2 for the World XI

Best strike rate

Runs per 100 balls		Runs
104.88	BL Cairns	987
99.43	IDS Smith	1055
90.99	JD Ryder	1041
88.74	BB McCullum	4037
85.60	JDP Oram	2289
83.76	CL Cairns	4881
81.76	DL Vettori	2053
81.37	LRPL Taylor	3055
80.74	KD Mills	843
79.75	MJ Guptill	1572

Qualification: 500 runs

Most economical bowlers

Runs per over		Wkts
3.30	RJ Hadlee	158
3.57	EJ Chatfield	140
3.76	GR Larsen	113
4.06	BL Cairns	89
4.12	DL Vettori	274
4.14	W Watson	74
4.17	DN Patel	45
4.17	JV Coney	54
4.28	SE Bond	147
4.28	CZ Harris	203

Qualification: 2000 balls bowled

New Zealand's one-day international results

	Played	Won	Lost	Tied	No result	% win
v Australia	124	34	85	0	5	28.57
v Bangladesh	21	16	5	0	0	76.19
v England	70	35	29	2	4	54.54
v India	88	37	46	0	5	44.57
v Pakistan	89	35	51	1	2	40.80
v South Africa	52	18	30	0	4	37.50
v Sri Lanka	74	35	34	1	4	50.71
v West Indies	51	20	24	0	7	45.45
v Zimbabwe	29	20	7	1	1	73.21
v others (see below)	13	13	0	0	0	100.00
TOTAL	**611**	**263**	**311**	**5**	**32**	**45.85**

Other teams: Canada (P3, W3), East Africa (P1, W1), Ireland (P2, W2), Kenya (P2, W2), Netherlands (P1, W1), Scotland (P2, W2), United Arab Emirates (P1, W1), United States of America (P1, W1).

PAKISTAN
Test Match Records

Most appearances

124	Javed Miandad
119	Inzamam-ul-Haq
104	Wasim Akram
103	Salim Malik
90	Mohammad Yousuf
88	Imran Khan
87	Waqar Younis
81	Wasim Bari
78	Zaheer Abbas
76	Mudassar Nazar

Inzamam-ul-Haq also played one Test for the World XI

Most runs

			Avge
8832	Javed Miandad		52.57
8829	Inzamam-ul-Haq		50.16
7530	Mohammad Yousuf		52.29
5768	Salim Malik		43.69
5719	Younis Khan		51.06
5062	Zaheer Abbas		44.79
4114	Mudassar Nazar		38.09
4052	Saeed Anwar		45.52
3931	Majid Khan		38.92
3915	Hanif Mohammad		43.98

Mohammad Yousuf was known as Yousuf Youhana until September 2005

Most wickets

		Avge
414	Wasim Akram	23.62
373	Waqar Younis	23.56
362	Imran Khan	22.81
261	Danish Kaneria	34.79
236	Abdul Qadir	32.80
208	Saqlain Mushtaq	29.83
185	Mushtaq Ahmed	32.97
178	Shoaib Akhtar	25.69
177	Sarfraz Nawaz	32.75
171	Iqbal Qasim	28.11

Five further bowlers have taken 100 wickets

Highest scores

337	Hanif Mohammad	v WI at Bridgetown	1957-58
329	Inzamam-ul-Haq	v NZ at Lahore	2001-02
313	Younis Khan	v Sri Lanka at Karachi	2008-09
280*	Javed Miandad	v India at Hyderabad	1982-83
274	Zaheer Abbas	v Eng at Birmingham	1971
271	Javed Miandad	v NZ at Auckland	1988-89
267	Younis Khan	v India at Bangalore	2004-05
260	Javed Miandad	v England at The Oval	1987
257*	Wasim Akram	v Zim at Sheikhupura	1996-97
240	Zaheer Abbas	v England at The Oval	1974

Wasim Akram's innings included 12 sixes, a record for any Test innings

Best innings bowling

9-56	Abdul Qadir	v England at Lahore	1987-88
9-86	Sarfraz Nawaz	v Australia at Melbourne	1978-79
8-58	Imran Khan	v Sri Lanka at Lahore	1981-82
8-60	Imran Khan	v India at Karachi	1982-83
8-69	Sikander Bakht	v India at Delhi	1979-80
8-164	Saqlain Mushtaq	v England at Lahore	2000-01
7-40	Imran Khan	v England at Leeds	1987
7-42	Fazal Mahmood	v India at Lucknow	1952-53
7-49	Iqbal Qasim	v Australia at Karachi	1979-80
7-52	Intikhab Alam	v NZ at Dunedin	1972-73
7-52	Imran Khan	v Eng at Birmingham	1982

Wasim Akram took five or more wickets in a Test innings on 25 occasions, Imran Khan 23, Waqar Younis 22

Record wicket partnerships

1st	298	Aamer Sohail (160) and Ijaz Ahmed (151)	v West Indies at Karachi	1997-98
2nd	291	Zaheer Abbas (274) and Mushtaq Mohammad (100)	v England at Birmingham	1971
3rd	451	Mudassar Nazar (231) and Javed Miandad (280*)	v India at Hyderabad	1982-83
4th	350	Mushtaq Mohammad (201) and Asif Iqbal (175)	v New Zealand at Dunedin	1972-73
5th	281	Javed Miandad (163) and Asif Iqbal (166)	v New Zealand at Lahore	1976-77
6th	269	Mohammad Yousuf (223) and Kamran Akmal (154)	v England at Lahore	2005-06
7th	308	Waqar Hasan (189) and Imtiaz Ahmed (209)	v New Zealand at Lahore	1955-56
8th	313	Wasim Akram (257*) and Saqlain Mushtaq (79)	v Zimbabwe at Sheikhupura	1996-97
9th	190	Asif Iqbal (146) and Intikhab Alam (51)	v England at The Oval	1967
10th	151	Azhar Mahmood (128*) and Mushtaq Ahmed (59)	v South Africa at Rawalpindi	1997-98

Figures to 26.09.11. Updated records can be found at **www.cricinfo.com/ci/engine/records**

Test Match Records

PAKISTAN

Most catches

Fielders

93	Javed Miandad
81	Inzamam-ul-Haq
75	Younis Khan
65	Majid Khan
65	Mohammad Yousuf
65	Salim Malik

Most dismissals

Wicketkeepers		Ct/St
228	Wasim Bari	201/27
206	Kamran Akmal	184/22
147	Moin Khan	127/20
130	Rashid Latif	119/11
104	Salim Yousuf	91/13

Highest team totals

765-6d	v Sri Lanka at Karachi	2008-09
708	v England at The Oval	1987
699-5	v India at Lahore	1989-90
679-7d	v India at Lahore	2005-06
674-6	v India at Faisalabad	1984-85
657-8d	v West Indies at Bridgetown	1957-58
652	v India at Faisalabad	1982-83
643	v New Zealand at Lahore	2001-02
636-8d	v England at Lahore	2005-06
624	v Australia at Adelaide	1983-84

Pakistan have made four other scores of 600 or more, and one of 599-7d

Lowest team totals

Completed innings

53*	v Australia at Sharjah†	2002-03
59	v Australia at Sharjah†	2002-03
62	v Australia at Perth	1981-82
72	v Australia at Perth	2004-05
72	v England at Birmingham	2010
74	v England at Lord's	2010
77*	v West Indies at Lahore	1986-87
80	v England at Nottingham	2010
87	v England at Lord's	1954
90	v England at Manchester	1954
90	v Sri Lanka at Colombo	2009

* One batsman retired hurt or absent hurt.
† Same match

Best match bowling

14-116	Imran Khan	v Sri Lanka at Lahore	1981-82
13-101	Abdul Qadir	v England at Lahore	1987-88
13-114	Fazal Mahmood	v Australia at Karachi	1956-57
13-135	Waqar Younis	v Zimbabwe at Karachi	1993-94
12-94	Fazal Mahmood	v India at Lucknow	1952-53
12-94	Danish Kaneria	v Bangladesh at Multan	2001-02
12-99	Fazal Mahmood	v England at The Oval	1954
12-100	Fazal Mahmood	v West Indies at Dacca	1958-59
12-130	Waqar Younis	v NZ at Faisalabad	1990-91
12-165	Imran Khan	v Australia at Sydney	1976-77

Imran Khan took ten or more wickets in a match six times, Abdul Qadir, Waqar Younis and Wasim Akram five each

Hat-tricks

Wasim Akram	v Sri Lanka at Lahore	1998-99
Wasim Akram	v Sri Lanka at Dhaka	1998-99
Abdul Razzaq	v Sri Lanka at Galle	1999-2000
Mohammad Sami	v Sri Lanka at Lahore	2001-02

Wasim Akram's hat-tricks came in successive matches: he also took Pakistan's first two hat-tricks in one-day internationals.

RS Kaluwitharana was the first victim in both Wasim Akram's first hat-trick and in Abdul Razzaq's

Pakistan's Test match results

	Played	Won	Lost	Drawn	Tied	% win
v Australia	57	12	28	17	0	21.05
v Bangladesh	6	6	0	0	0	100.00
v England	71	13	22	36	0	18.30
v India	59	12	9	38	0	20.33
v New Zealand	50	23	7	20	0	46.00
v South Africa	18	3	8	7	0	16.66
v Sri Lanka	37	15	9	13	0	40.54
v West Indies	46	16	15	15	0	34.78
v Zimbabwe	15	9	2	4	0	60.00
TOTAL	359	109	100	150	0	30.36

Figures to 26.09.11. Updated records can be found at www.cricinfo.com/ci/engine/records

PAKISTAN
One-day International Records

Most appearances

375	Inzamam-ul-Haq
356	Wasim Akram
320	Shahid Afridi
283	Salim Malik
281	Mohammad Yousuf
262	Waqar Younis
258	Abdul Razzaq
250	Ijaz Ahmed
247	Saeed Anwar
233	Javed Miandad

Younis Khan (226) and Moin Khan (219) also played in more than 200 ODIs

Most runs

		Avge
11701	Inzamam-ul-Haq	39.53
9554	Mohammad Yousuf	42.08
8824	Saeed Anwar	39.21
7381	Javed Miandad	41.70
7170	Salim Malik	32.88
6658	Shahid Afridi	23.77
6564	Ijaz Ahmed	32.33
6442	Younis Khan	32.86
5841	Rameez Raja	32.09
5204	Shoaib Malik	34.01

Abdul Razzaq (5014) and Aamer Sohail (4780) also scored more than 4000 runs

Most wickets

		Avge
502	Wasim Akram	23.52
416	Waqar Younis	23.84
313	Shahid Afridi	34.25
288	Saqlain Mushtaq	21.78
266	Abdul Razzaq	31.54
241	Shoaib Akhtar	24.70
182	Aqib Javed	31.43
182	Imran Khan	26.61
161	Mushtaq Ahmed	33.29
135	Shoaib Malik	36.34

Six further bowlers have taken 100 wickets for Pakistan ODIs

Highest scores

194	Saeed Anwar	v India at Chennai	1996-97
160	Imran Nazir	v Zimbabwe at Kingston	2006–07
144	Younis Khan	v Hong Kong at Colombo	2004
143	Shoaib Malik	v India at Colombo	2004
141*	Mohammad Yousuf	v Zim at Bulawayo	2002-03
140	Saeed Anwar	v India at Dhaka	1997-98
139*	Ijaz Ahmed	v India at Lahore	1997-98
139*	Mohammad Hafeez	v Zimbabwe at Harare	2011
137*	Inzamam-ul-Haq	v N Zealand at Sharjah	1993-94
137	Ijaz Ahmed	v England at Sharjah	1998-99

Saeed Anwar scored 20 centuries, Mohammad Yousuf 15, Ijaz Ahmed and Inzamam-ul-Haq 10

Best innings bowling

7-36	Waqar Younis	v England at Leeds	2001
7-37	Aqib Javed	v India at Sharjah	1991-92
6-14	Imran Khan	v India at Sharjah	1984-85
6-16	Shoaib Akhtar	v New Zealand at Karachi	2001-02
6-18	Azhar Mahmood	v W Indies at Sharjah	1999-2000
6-26	Waqar Younis	v Sri Lanka at Sharjah	1989-90
6-27	Naved-ul-Hasan	v India at Jamshedpur	2004-05
6-30	Waqar Younis	v N Zealand at Auckland	1993-94
6-35	Abdul Razzaq	v Bangladesh at Dhaka	2001-02
6-38	Shahid Afridi	v Australia at Dubai	2008-09

Waqar Younis took five or more wickets in an innings 13 times (the ODI record), Saqlain Mushtaq and Wasim Akram 6

Record wicket partnerships

1st	228*	Mohammad Hafeez (139*) and Imran Farhat (75*)	v Zimbabwe at Harare	2011
2nd	263	Aamer Sohail (134) and Inzamam-ul-Haq (137*)	v New Zealand at Sharjah	1993-94
3rd	230	Saeed Anwar (140) and Ijaz Ahmed (117)	v India at Dhaka	1997-98
4th	206	Shoaib Malik (128) and Mohammad Yousuf (87)	v India at Centurion	2009-10
5th	176	Younis Khan (89) and Umar Akmal (102*)	v Sri Lanka at Colombo	2009
6th	144	Imran Khan (102*) and Shahid Mahboob (77)	v Sri Lanka at Leeds	1983
7th	124	Mohammad Yousuf (91*) and Rashid Latif (66)	v Australia at Cardiff	2001
8th	100	Fawad Alam (63*) and Sohail Tanvir (59)	v Hong Kong at Karachi	2008
9th	73	Shoaib Malik (52*) and Mohammad Sami (46)	v South Africa at Centurion	2006-07
10th	103	Mohammad Aamer (73*) and Saeed Ajmal (33)	v New Zealand at Abu Dhabi	2009-10

Figures to 26.09.11. Updated records can be found at www.cricinfo.com/ci/engine/records

One-day International Records

PAKISTAN

Most catches

Fielders

113	Inzamam-ul-Haq	
111	Younis Khan	
107	Shahid Afridi	
90	Ijaz Ahmed	
88	Wasim Akram	

Most dismissals

Wicketkeepers		*Ct/St*
287	Moin Khan	214/73
220	Rashid Latif	182/38
161	Kamran Akmal	136/25
103	Salim Yousuf	81/22
62	Wasim Bari	52/10

Highest team totals

385-7	v Bangladesh at Dambulla	2010
371-9	v Sri Lanka at Nairobi	1996-97
353-6	v England at Karachi	2005-06
351-4	v South Africa at Durban	2006-07
349	v Zimbabwe at Kingston	2006-07
347-5	v Zimbabwe at at Karachi	2007-08
344-5	v Zimbabwe at Bulawayo	2002-03
344-8	v India at Karachi	2003-04
343-5	v Hong Kong at Colombo	2004
338-5	v Sri Lanka at Swansea	1983

Pakistan have reached 300 on 43 further occasions

Lowest team totals

Completed innings

43	v W Indies at Cape Town	1992-93
71	v W Indies at Brisbane	1992-93
74	v England at Adelaide	1991-92
75	v Sri Lanka at Lahore	2008-09
81	v West Indies at Sydney	1992-93
85	v England at Manchester	1978
87	v India at Sharjah	1984-85
89	v S Africa at Mohali	2006-07
107	v S Africa at Cape Town	2006-07
108	v Australia at Nairobi	2002-03

Against India in 1984-85 Pakistan were chasing only 126 to win

Most sixes

287	Shahid Afridi
143	Inzamam-ul-Haq
124	Abdul Razzaq
121	Wasim Akram
97	Saeed Anwar
87	Ijaz Ahmed
87	Mohammad Yousuf
61	Moin Khan
59	Shoaib Malik
52	Younis Khan

Afridi hit 2 other sixes in official ODIs

Best strike rate

Runs per 100 balls		*Runs*
113.73	Shahid Afridi	6658
89.60	Manzoor Elahi	741
88.33	Wasim Akram	3717
86.29	Umar Akmal	1285
84.80	Zaheer Abbas	2572
84.51	Naved-ul-Hasan	524
84.31	Kamran Akmal	2924
81.90	Abdul Razzaq	5014
81.30	Moin Khan	3266
81.01	Imran Nazir	1895

Qualification: 500 runs

Most economical bowlers

Runs per over		*Wkts*
3.63	Sarfraz Nawaz	63
3.71	Akram Raza	38
3.89	Imran Khan	182
3.89	Wasim Akram	502
4.06	Abdul Qadir	132
4.14	Arshad Khan	56
4.14	Tauseef Ahmed	55
4.24	Mudassar Nazar	111
4.26	Mushtaq Ahmed	161
4.28	Aqib Javed	182

Qualification: 2000 balls bowled

Pakistan's one-day international results

	Played	Won	Lost	Tied	No result	% win
v Australia	86	30	52	1	3	36.74
v Bangladesh	26	25	1	0	0	96.15
v England	68	28	38	0	2	42.42
v India	120	69	47	0	4	59.48
v New Zealand	89	51	35	1	2	59.19
v South Africa	57	18	38	0	1	32.14
v Sri Lanka	121	71	46	1	3	60.59
v West Indies	120	52	66	2	0	44.16
v Zimbabwe	44	40	2	1	1	94.18
v others (see below)	21	20	1	0	0	95.23
TOTAL	752	404	326	6	16	55.29

Other teams: Canada (P2, W2), Hong Kong (P2, W2), Ireland (P3, W2, L1), Kenya (P6, W6), Namibia (P1, W1),
Netherlands (P3, W3), Scotland (P2, W2), United Arab Emirates (P2, W2).

SOUTH AFRICA *Test Match Records*

Most appearances

144	JH Kallis
138	MV Boucher
108	SM Pollock
101	G Kirsten
101	M Ntini
90	HH Gibbs
90	GC Smith
72	AA Donald
70	DJ Cullinan
68	WJ Cronje

Kallis, Boucher and Smith all also played one Test for the World XI against Australia

Most runs

		Avge
11864	JH Kallis	57.31
7445	GC Smith	50.30
7289	G Kirsten	45.27
6167	HH Gibbs	41.95
5295	MV Boucher	30.96
4741	AB de Villiers	47.41
4554	DJ Cullinan	44.21
3897	HM Amla	46.95
3781	SM Pollock	32.31
3714	WJ Cronje	36.41

Kallis (83 runs), Smith (12) and Boucher (17) also played one Test for the World XI against Australia

Most wickets

		Avge
421	SM Pollock	23.11
390	M Ntini	28.82
330	AA Donald	22.25
269	JH Kallis	31.98
238	DW Steyn	23.21
170	HJ Tayfield	25.91
134	PR Adams	32.87
123	TL Goddard	26.22
123	A Nel	31.86
116	PM Pollock	24.18

Four other bowlers have also taken 100 wickets. Kallis also took one wicket for the World XI

Highest scores

278*	AB de Villiers	v Pakistan at Abu Dhabi	2010-11
277	GC Smith	v England at Birmingham	2003
275*	DJ Cullinan	v New Zealand at Auckland	1998-99
275	G Kirsten	v England at Durban	1999-2000
274	RG Pollock	v Australia at Durban	1969-70
259	GC Smith	v England at Lord's	2003
255*	DJ McGlew	v New Zealand at Wellington	1952-53
253*	HM Amla	v India at Nagpur	2009-10
236	EAB Rowan	v England at Leeds	1951
232	GC Smith	v Bangladesh at Chittagong	2007-08

Smith's 277 and 259 were in consecutive matches

Best innings bowling

9-113	HJ Tayfield	v England at Johannesburg	1956-57
8-53	GB Lawrence	v N Zealand at Johannesburg	1961-62
8-64	L Klusener	v India at Calcutta	1996-97
8-69	HJ Tayfield	v England at Durban	1956-57
8-70	SJ Snooke	v England at Johannesburg	1905-06
8-71	AA Donald	v Zimbabwe at Harare	1995-96
7-23	HJ Tayfield	v Australia at Durban	1949-50
7-29	GF Bissett	v England at Durban	1927-28
7-37	M Ntini	v W Indies at Port-of-Spain	2004-05
7-51	DW Steyn	v India at Nagpur	2009-10

Klusener was making his Test debut

Record wicket partnerships

1st	415	ND McKenzie (226) and GC Smith (232)	v Bangladesh at Chittagong	2007-08
2nd	315*	HH Gibbs (211*) and JH Kallis (148*)	v New Zealand at Christchurch	1998-99
3rd	429*	JA Rudolph (222*) and HH Dippenaar (177*)	v Bangladesh at Chittagong	2002-03
4th	249	JH Kallis (177) and G Kirsten (137)	v West Indies at Durban	2003-04
5th	267	JH Kallis (147) and AG Prince (131)	v West Indies at St John's	2004-05
6th	271	AG Prince (162*) and MV Boucher (117)	v Bangladesh at Centurion	2008-09
7th	246	DJ McGlew (255*) and ARA Murray (109)	v New Zealand at Wellington	1952-53
8th	150	ND McKenzie (103) and SM Pollock (111)	v Sri Lanka at Centurion	2000-01
	150	G Kirsten (130) and M Zondeki (59)	v England at Leeds	2003
9th	195	MV Boucher (78) and PL Symcox (108)	v Pakistan at Johannesburg	1997-98
10th	107*	AB de Villiers (278*) and M Morkel (35*)	v Pakistan at Abu Dhabi	2010-11

Figures to 26.09.11. Updated records can be found at **www.cricinfo.com/ci/engine/records**

Test Match Records SOUTH AFRICA

Most catches

Fielders

162	JH Kallis	
116	GC Smith	
94	HH Gibbs	
83	AB de Villiers	
83	G Kirsten	

Most dismissals

Wicketkeepers   Ct/St

519	MV Boucher	497/22
152	DJ Richardson	150/2
141	JHB Waite	124/17
56	DT Lindsay	54/2
51	HB Cameron	39/12

Highest team totals

682-6d	v England at Lord's	2003
658-9d	v West Indies at Durban	2003-04
651	v Australia at Cape Town	2008-09
622-9d	v Australia at Durban	1969-70
621-5d	v New Zealand at Auckland	1998-99
620-4d	v India at Centurion	2010-11
620-7d	v Pakistan at Cape Town	2002-03
620	v Australia at Johannesburg	1966-67
604-6d	v West Indies at Centurion	2003-04
600-3d	v Zimbabwe at Harare	2001-02

The 620 was scored in the second innings of the match

Lowest team totals

Completed innings

30	v Eng at Port Elizabeth	1895-96
30	v Eng at Birmingham	1924
35	v Eng at Cape Town	1898-99
36	v Aust at Melbourne	1931-32
43	v Eng at Cape Town	1888-89
45	v Aust at Melbourne	1931-32
47	v Eng at Cape Town	1888-89
58	v England at Lord's	1912
72	v Eng at Johannesburg	1956-57
72	v Eng at Cape Town	1956-57

South Africa's lowest total since their return to Test cricket in 1991-92 is 84 against India at Johannesburg in 2006-07

Best match bowling

13-132	M Ntini	v W Indies at Port-of-Spain	2004-05
13-165	HJ Tayfield	v Australia at Melbourne	1952-53
13-192	HJ Tayfield	v England at Johannesburg	1956-57
12-127	SJ Snooke	v England at Johannesburg	1905-06
12-139	AA Donald	v India at Port Elizabeth	1992-93
12-181	AEE Vogler	v England at Johannesburg	1909-10
11-112	AE Hall	v England at Cape Town	1922-23
11-113	AA Donald	v Zimbabwe at Harare	1995-96
11-127	AA Donald	v England at Jo'burg	1999-2000
11-150	EP Nupen	v England at Jo'burg	1930-31

Hall was making his Test debut. His performance, and Vogler's, were at the old Wanderers ground in Johannesburg

Hat-tricks

GM Griffin	v England at Lord's	1960

Griffin achieved the feat in his second and final Test (he was no-balled for throwing in the same match).

GA Lohmann (for England at Port Elizabeth in 1895-96), TJ Matthews (twice in the same match for Australia at Manchester in 1912) and TWJ Goddard (for England at Johannesburg in 1938-39) have taken Test hat-tricks against South Africa

South Africa's Test match results

	Played	Won	Lost	Drawn	Tied	% win
v Australia	83	18	47	18	0	21.68
v Bangladesh	8	8	0	0	0	100.00
v England	138	29	56	53	0	21.01
v India	27	12	7	8	0	44.44
v New Zealand	35	20	4	11	0	57.14
v Pakistan	18	8	3	7	0	44.44
v Sri Lanka	17	8	4	5	0	47.05
v West Indies	25	16	3	6	0	64.00
v Zimbabwe	7	6	0	1	0	85.71
TOTAL	358	125	124	109	0	34.91

*Figures to 26.09.11. Updated records can be found at **www.cricinfo.com/ci/engine/records***

SOUTH AFRICA *One-day International Records*

Most appearances

309	JH Kallis	
294	SM Pollock	
287	MV Boucher	
248	HH Gibbs	
245	JN Rhodes	
188	WJ Cronje	
185	G Kirsten	
172	M Ntini	
171	L Klusener	
171	GC Smith	

Kallis, Pollock, Boucher, Ntini and Smith also appeared in official ODIs for composite teams

Most runs

		Avge
11198	JH Kallis	46.27
8094	HH Gibbs	36.13
6798	G Kirsten	40.95
6280	GC Smith	39.49
5935	JN Rhodes	35.11
5565	WJ Cronje	38.64
4501	MV Boucher	28.66
4373	AB de Villiers	46.52
3860	DJ Cullinan	32.99
3576	L Klusener	41.10

Kallis (29 runs), Smith (0), Boucher (163) and de Villiers (150) also appeared in official ODIs for composite teams

Most wickets

		Avge
387	SM Pollock	24.31
272	AA Donald	21.78
265	M Ntini	24.53
260	JH Kallis	31.82
192	L Klusener	29.95
114	WJ Cronje	34.78
106	A Nel	27.68
100	CK Langeveldt	29.62
95	N Boje	35.27
95	PS de Villiers	27.74
95	AJ Hall	26.47

Pollock, Ntini, Kallis and Boje also appeared in ODIs for composite teams

Highest scores

188*	G Kirsten	v UAE at Rawalpindi	1995-96
175	HH Gibbs	v Australia at Johannesburg	2005-06
169*	DJ Callaghan	v N Zealand at Verwoerdburg	1994-95
161	AC Hudson	v Netherlands at Rawalpindi	1995-96
153	HH Gibbs	v B'desh at Potchefstroom	2002-03
147*	MV Boucher	v Zimbabwe at Potchefstroom	2006-07
146	AB de Villiers	v West Indies at St George's	2006-07
143	HH Gibbs	v N Zealand at Johannesburg	2002-03
141	GC Smith	v England at Centurion	2009-10
140	HM Amla	v Bangladesh at Benoni	2008-09

Gibbs has scored 21 one-day hundreds, Kallis 17, Kirsten 13 and de Villiers 11

Best bowling figures

6-22	M Ntini	v Australia at Cape Town	2005-06
6-23	AA Donald	v Kenya at Nairobi	1996-97
6-35	SM Pollock	v W Indies at East London	1998-99
6-49	L Klusener	v Sri Lanka at Lahore	1997-98
5-18	AJ Hall	v England at Bridgetown	2006-07
5-20	SM Pollock	v Eng at Johannesburg	1999-2000
5-21	L Klusener	v Kenya at Amstelveen	1999
5-21	N Boje	v Australia at Cape Town	2001-02
5-21	M Ntini	v Pakistan at Mohali	2006-07
5-23	SM Pollock	v Pakistan at Johannesburg	2006-07

Klusener has taken five wickets in an ODI innings six times, Pollock five and Ntini four

Record wicket partnerships

1st	235	G Kirsten (115) and HH Gibbs (111)	v India at Kochi	1999-2000
2nd	209	G Kirsten (124) and ND McKenzie (131*)	v Kenya at Cape Town	2001-02
3rd	221	HM Amla (113) and AB de Villiers (134)	v Netherlands at Mohali	2010-11
4th	232	DJ Cullinan (124) and JN Rhodes (121)	v Pakistan at Nairobi	1996-97
5th	183*	JH Kallis (109*) and JN Rhodes (94*)	v Pakistan at Durban	1997-98
6th	137	WJ Cronje (70*) and SM Pollock (75)	v Zimbabwe at Johannesburg	1996-97
7th	114	MV Boucher (68) and L Klusener (75*)	v India at Nagpur	1999-2000
8th	138*	JM Kemp (100*) and AJ Hall (56*)	v India at Cape Town	2006-07
9th	65	WD Parnell (49) and DW Steyn (35)	v India at Jaipur	2009-10
10th	67*	JA Morkel (23*) and M Ntini (42*)	v New Zealand at Napier	2003-04

Figures to 26.09.11. Updated records can be found at **www.cricinfo.com/ci/engine/records**

One-day International Records **SOUTH AFRICA**

Most catches

Fielders

122	JH Kallis	
108	HH Gibbs	
105	JN Rhodes	
104	SM Pollock	
94	GC Smith	

Most dismissals

Wicketkeepers		*Ct/St*
412	MV Boucher	391/21
165	DJ Richardson	148/17
47	AB de Villiers	45/2
9	SJ Palframan	9/0
8	MN van Wyk	7/1

Highest team totals

438-9	v Australia at Johannesburg	2005-06
418-5	v Zimbabwe at Potchefstroom	2006-07
399-6	v Zimbabwe at Benoni	2010-11
392-6	v Pakistan at Centurion	2006-07
365-2	v India at Ahmedabad	2009-10
363-3	v Zimbabwe at Bulawayo	2001-02
358-4	v Bangladesh at Benoni	2008-09
356-4	v West Indies at St George's	2006-07
354-3	v Kenya at Cape Town	2001-02
354-6	v England at Cape Town	2009-10

438-9 was the highest total in all ODIs at the time, and came from 49.5 overs; all the others above were scored in 50 overs, apart from 353-3 (40)

Lowest team totals

Completed innings

69	v Australia at Sydney	1993-94
83	v England at Nottingham	2008
101*	v Pakistan at Sharjah	1999-2000
106	v Australia at Sydney	2001-02
107	v England at Lord's	2003
107	v England at Lord's	2003
108	v NZ at Mumbai	2006-07
119	v Eng at Port Elizabeth	2009-10
123	v Aust at Wellington	1994-95
129	v Eng at East London	1995-96

* One batsman retired hurt

Most sixes

130	JH Kallis
128	HH Gibbs
94	WJ Cronje
81	MV Boucher
76	L Klusener
72	AB de Villiers
55	SM Pollock
52	JM Kemp
47	JN Rhodes
38	GC Smith

Boucher (2), Pollock (3), Kemp (1) and de Villiers (4) also hit sixes for the Africa XI

Best strike rate

Runs per 100 balls		*Runs*
101.38	JA Morkel	657
92.76	HM Amla	2462
91.31	AB de Villiers	4373
89.91	L Klusener	3576
89.29	N Boje	1410
85.55	SM Pollock	3193
85.07	JP Duminy	2194
84.62	MV Boucher	4501
83.61	PL Symcox	694
83.26	HH Gibbs	8094

Qualification: 500 runs

Most economical bowlers

Runs per over		*Wkts*
3.57	PS de Villiers	95
3.65	SM Pollock	387
3.94	CR Matthews	79
4.15	AA Donald	272
4.15	PL Symcox	72
4.28	BM McMillan	70
4.44	WJ Cronje	114
4.50	RP Snell	44
4.51	N Boje	95
4.51	AJ Hall	95
4.51	M Ntini	265

Qualification: 2000 balls bowled

South Africa's one-day international results

	Played	Won	Lost	Tied	No result	% win
v Australia	77	35	39	3	0	47.40
v Bangladesh	14	13	1	0	0	92.85
v England	45	23	19	1	2	54.65
v India	66	40	24	0	2	62.50
v New Zealand	52	30	18	0	4	62.50
v Pakistan	57	38	18	0	1	67.85
v Sri Lanka	46	22	22	1	1	50.00
v West Indies	51	38	12	0	1	76.00
v Zimbabwe	32	29	2	0	1	93.54
v others (see below)	19	19	0	0	0	100.00
TOTAL	**459**	**287**	**155**	**5**	**12**	**64.76**

Other teams: Canada (P1, W1), Ireland (P3, W3), Kenya (P10, W10), Netherlands (P3, W3), Scotland (P1, W1), United Arab Emirates (P1, W1).

259

SRI LANKA
Test Match Records

Most appearances

132	M Muralitharan	
122	DPMD Jayawardene	
111	WPUJC Vaas	
110	ST Jayasuriya	
100	KC Sangakkara	
93	PA de Silva	
93	A Ranatunga	
90	MS Atapattu	
83	HP Tillekeratne	
71	TM Dilshan	

Ranatunga uniquely played in his country's first Test and their 100th

Most runs

		Avge
9852	DPMD Jayawardene	52.40
8651	KC Sangakkara	55.81
6973	ST Jayasuriya	40.07
6361	PA de Silva	42.97
5502	MS Atapattu	39.02
5105	A Ranatunga	35.69
4683	TT Samaraweera	52.61
4545	HP Tillekeratne	42.87
4382	TM Dilshan	42.96
3089	WPUJC Vaas	24.32

RS Mahanama (2576) and AP Gurusinha (2452) also reached 2000 runs

Most wickets

		Avge
795	M Muralitharan	22.67
355	WPUJC Vaas	29.58
101	SL Malinga	33.15
100	HMRKB Herath	34.87
98	ST Jayasuriya	34.34
94	CRD Fernando	36.97
85	GP Wickremasinghe	41.87
73	RJ Ratnayake	35.10
69	HDPK Dharmasena	42.31
64	DNT Zoysa	33.70

Muralitharan also took 5 wickets for the World XI

Highest scores

374	DPMD Jayawardene	v SA at Colombo	2006
340	ST Jayasuriya	v India at Colombo	1997-98
287	KC Sangakkara	v SA at Colombo	2006
275	DPMD Jayawardene	v Ind at Ahmedabad	2009-10
270	KC Sangakkara	v Zim at Bulawayo	2003-04
267	PA de Silva	v NZ at Wellington	1990-91
253	ST Jayasuriya	v Pak at Faisalabad	2004-05
249	MS Atapattu	v Zim at Bulawayo	2003-04
242	DPMD Jayawardene	v India at Colombo	1998-99
240	DPMD Jayawardene	v Pak at Karachi	2008-09

Jayawardene made 29 Test centuries, Sangakkara 25, de Silva 20, Atapattu 16 and Jayasuriya 14

Best innings bowling

9-51	M Muralitharan	v Zimbabwe at Kandy	2001-02
9-65	M Muralitharan	v England at The Oval	1998
8-46	M Muralitharan	v West Indies at Kandy	2005
8-70	M Muralitharan	v England at Nottingham	2006
8-83	JR Ratnayeke	v Pakistan at Sialkot	1985-86
8-87	M Muralitharan	v India at Colombo	2001-02
7-46	M Muralitharan	v England at Galle	2003-04
7-71	WPUJC Vaas	v West Indies at Colombo	2001-02
7-84	M Muralitharan	v South Africa at Galle	2000-01
7-94	M Muralitharan	v Zimbabwe at Kandy	1997-98

Muralitharan took five or more wickets in an innings a record 67 times

Record wicket partnerships

1st	335	MS Atapattu (207*) and ST Jayasuriya (188)	v Pakistan at Kandy	2000
2nd	576	ST Jayasuriya (340) and RS Mahanama (225)	v India at Colombo	1997-98
3rd	624	KC Sangakkara (287) and DPMD Jayawardene (374)	v South Africa at Colombo	2006
4th	437	DPMD Jayawardene (240) and TT Samaraweera (231)	v Pakistan at Karachi	2008-09
5th	280	TT Samaraweera (138) and TM Dilshan (168)	v Bangladesh at Colombo	2005-06
6th	351	DPMD Jayawardene (275) and HAPW Jayawardene (154*)	v India at Ahmedabad	2009-10
7th	223*	HAPW Jayawardene (120*) and WPUJC Vaas (100*)	v Bangladesh at Colombo	2007
8th	170	DPMD Jayawardene (237) and WPUJC Vaas (69)	v South Africa at Galle	2004-05
9th	118	TT Samaraweera (83) and BAW Mendis (78)	v India at Colombo	2010
10th	79	WPUJC Vaas (68*) and M Muralitharan (43)	v Australia at Kandy	2003-04

Figures to 26.09.11. Updated records can be found at **www.cricinfo.com/ci/engine/records**

Test Match Records

SRI LANKA

Most catches

Fielders

172	DPMD Jayawardene	
89	HP Tillekeratne	
78	ST Jayasuriya	
70	M Muralitharan	
64	TM Dilshan	

Most dismissals

Wicketkeepers   *Ct/St*

151	KC Sangakkara	131/20
119	RS Kaluwitharana	93/26
106	HAPW Jayawardene	80/26
35	HP Tillekeratne	33/2
34	SAR Silva	33/1

Highest team totals

952-6d	v India at Colombo	1997-98
760-7d	v India at Ahmedabad	2009-10
756-5d	v South Africa at Colombo	2006
713-3d	v Zimbabwe at Bulawayo	2003-04
644-7d	v Pakistan at Karachi	2008-09
642-4d	v India at Colombo	2010
628-8d	v England at Colombo	2003-04
627-9d	v West Indies at Colombo	2001-02
610-6d	v India at Colombo	2001-02
606	v Pakistan at Lahore	2008-09

952-6d is the highest total in all Tests. In all Sri Lanka have reached 500 on 27 occasions

Lowest team totals

Completed innings

71	v Pakistan at Kandy	1994-95
73*	v Pakistan at Kandy	2005-06
81	v England at Colombo	2000-01
82	v India at Chandigarh	1990-91
82	v England at Cardiff	2011
93	v NZ at Wellington	1982-83
95	v S Africa at Cape Town	2000-01
97	v N Zealand at Kandy	1983-84
97	v Australia at Darwin	2004
101	v Pakistan at Kandy	1985-86

* One batsman absent hurt

Best match bowling

16-220	M Muralitharan	v England at The Oval	1998
14-191	WPUJC Vaas	v West Indies at Colombo	2001-02
13-115	M Muralitharan	v Zimbabwe at Kandy	2001-02
13-171	M Muralitharan	v South Africa at Galle	2000
12-82	M Muralitharan	v Bangladesh at Kandy	2007
12-117	M Muralitharan	v Zimbabwe at Kandy	1997-98
12-225	M Muralitharan	v South Africa at Colombo	2006
11-93	M Muralitharan	v England at Galle	2003-04
11-110	M Muralitharan	v India at Colombo	2008
11-132	M Muralitharan	v England at Nottingham	2006

Muralitharan took ten or more wickets in a match a record 22 times; the only others to do it for Sri Lanka are Vaas (twice), UDU Chandana and BAW Mendis

Hat-tricks

DNT Zoysa	v Zimbabwe at Harare	1999-2000

He dismissed TR Gripper, MW Goodwin and NC Johnson with the first three balls of his first over, the second of the match.

Four hat-tricks have been taken against Sri Lanka in Tests, all of them for Pakistan: two by Wasim Akram (in successive Tests in the Asian Test Championship at Lahore and Dhaka in 1998-99), Abdul Razzaq (at Galle in 2000-01) and Mohammad Sami (at Lahore in 2001-02)

Sri Lanka's Test match results

	Played	Won	Lost	Drawn	Tied	% win
v Australia	23	1	14	8	0	4.34
v Bangladesh	12	12	0	0	0	100.00
v England	24	6	9	9	0	25.00
v India	35	6	14	15	0	17.14
v New Zealand	26	7	9	10	0	26.92
v Pakistan	37	9	15	13	0	24.32
v South Africa	17	4	8	5	0	23.52
v West Indies	15	6	3	6	0	40.00
v Zimbabwe	15	10	0	5	0	66.66
TOTAL	204	61	72	71	0	29.90

Figures to 26.09.11. Updated records can be found at **www.cricinfo.com/ci/engine/records**

SRI LANKA
One-day International Records

Most appearances

441	ST Jayasuriya
347	DPMD Jayawardene
343	M Muralitharan
321	WPUJC Vaas
308	PA de Silva
294	KC Sangakkara
269	A Ranatunga
268	MS Atapattu
214	TM Bilshan
213	RS Mahanama

HP Tillekeratne also played in 200 ODIs

Most runs

		Avge
13664	ST Jayasuriya	32.51
9644	DPMD Jayawardene	33.02
9284	PA de Silva	34.90
9281	KC Sangakkara	37.88
8529	MS Atapattu	37.57
7456	A Ranatunga	35.84
5616	TM Dilshan	35.10
5162	RS Mahanama	29.49
4054	WU Tharanga	35.87
3950	RP Arnold	35.26

Jayasuriya (66), Jayawardene (269) and Sangakkara (259) all scored additional runs in ODIs for composite teams

Most wickets

		Avge
523	M Muralitharan	23.07
399	WPUJC Vaas	27.45
320	ST Jayasuriya	36.67
176	CRD Fernando	30.26
151	UDU Chandana	31.72
149	SL Malinga	25.03
138	HDPK Dharmasena	36.21
121	MF Maharoof	25.89
109	GP Wickremasinghe	39.64
108	KMDN Kulasekara	31.82
108	DNT Zoysa	29.75

Murali (11), Vaas (1), Jayasuriya (3) and Fernando (4) took wkts for other teams

Highest scores

189	ST Jayasuriya	v India at Sharjah	2000-01
160	TM Dilshan	v India at Rajkot	2009-10
157	ST Jayasuriya	v Netherlands at Amstelveen	2006
152	ST Jayasuriya	v England at Leeds	2006
151*	ST Jayasuriya	v India at Mumbai	1996-97
145	PA de Silva	v Kenya at Kandy	1995-96
144	TM Dilshan	v Zimbabwe at Pallekele	2010-11
144	DPMD J'dene	v England at Leeds	2011
140	ST Jayasuriya	v N Zealand at Bloemfontein	1994-95
138*	KC Sangakkara	v India at Jaipur	2005-06

Jayasuriya has scored 28 centuries, Jayawardene 14, WU Tharanga 12, MS Atapattu, de Silva and Sangakkara 11, and Dilshan 10

Best bowling figures

8-19	WPUJC Vaas	v Zimbabwe at Colombo	2001-02
7-30	M Muralitharan	v India at Sharjah	2000-01
6-13	BAW Mendis	v India at Karachi	2008
6-14	MF Maharoof	v West Indies at Mumbai	2006-07
6-20	AD Mathews	v India at Colombo	2008-09
6-25	WPUJC Vaas	v B'desh at P'maritzburg	2002-03
6-27	CRD Fernando	v England at Colombo	2007-08
6-29	ST Jayasuriya	v England at Moratuwa	1992-93
6-29	BAW Mendis	v Zimbabwe at Harare	2008-09
6-38	SL Malinga	v Kenya at Colombo	2010-11

Vaas's 8-19 are the best bowling figures in all ODIs. In his 6-25 Vaas took a hat-trick with the first three balls of the match, and four wickets in all in the first over

Record wicket partnerships

1st	286	WU Tharanga (109) and ST Jayasuriya (152)	v England at Leeds	2006
2nd	170	S Wettimuny (74) and RL Dias (102)	v India at Delhi	1982-83
	170	ST Jayasuriya (120) and HP Tillekeratne (81*)	v New Zealand at Bloemfontein	2002-03
3rd	226	MS Atapattu (102*) and DPMD Jayawardene (128)	v India at Sharjah	2000-01
4th	171*	RS Mahanama (94*) and A Ranatunga (87*)	v West Indies at Lahore	1997-98
5th	166	ST Jayasuriya (189) and RP Arnold (52*)	v India at Sharjah	2000-01
6th	159	LPC Silva (67) and CK Kapugedera (95)	v West Indies at Port-of-Spain	2007-08
7th	126*	DPMD Jayawardene (94*) and UDU Chandana (44*)	v India at Dambulla	2005-06
8th	91	HDPK Dharmasena (51*) and DK Liyanage (43)	v West Indies at Port-of-Spain	1996-97
9th	132	AD Mathews (77*) and SL Malinga (56)	v Australia at Melbourne	2010-11
10th	51	RP Arnold (103) and KSC de Silva (2*)	v Zimbabwe at Bulawayo	1999-2000

Figures to 26.09.11. Updated records can be found at **www.cricinfo.com/ci/engine/records**

SRI LANKA

Most catches

Fielders

177	DPMD Jayawardene	
128	M Muralitharan	
123	ST Jayasuriya	
109	RS Mahanama	
95	PA de Silva	

Most dismissals

Wicketkeepers   *Ct/St*

344	KC Sangakkara	269/75
206	RS Kaluwitharana	131/75
45	HP Tillekeratne	39/6
34	DSBP Kuruppu	26/8

Highest team totals

443-9	v Netherlands at Amstelveen	2006
411-8	v India at Rajkot	2009-10
398-5	v Kenya at Kandy	1995-96
357-9	v Bangladesh at Lahore	2008
349-9	v Pakistan at Singapore	1995-96
343-5	v Australia at Sydney	2002-03
339-4	v Pakistan at Mohali	1996-97
332-7	v Canada at Hambantota	2010-11
332-8	v Bangladesh at Karachi	2008
329	v West Indies at Sharjah	1995-96

Sri Lanka scored 324-2 in 37.3 overs against England at Leeds in 2006

Lowest team totals

Completed innings

55	v W Indies at Sharjah	1986-87
78*	v Pakistan at Sharjah	2001-02
86	v W Indies at Manchester	1975
91	v Australia at Adelaide	1984-85
96	v India at Sharjah	1983-84
98	v S Africa at Colombo	1993-94
98	v India at Sharjah	1998-99
99	v England at Perth	1998-99
102	v W Indies at Brisbane	1995-96
105	v SA at Bloemfontein	1997-98

* One batsman absent hurt

Most sixes

268	ST Jayasuriya	
102	PA de Silva	
64	A Ranatunga	
52	DPMD Jayawardene	
44	KC Sangakkara	
42	AP Gurusinha	
35	TM Dilshan	
27	CK Kapugedera	
22	UDU Chandana	
22	MF Maharoof	
22	WPUJC Vaas	

Jayasuriya also hit 2 for the Asia XI

Best strike rate

Runs per 100 balls		*Runs*
91.27	ST Jayasuriya	13364
87.44	TM Dilshan	5616
86.80	RJ Ratnayake	612
85.19	MF Maharoof	984
83.39	AD Mathews	1065
81.13	PA de Silva	9284
77.91	A Ranatunga	7456
77.73	M Muralitharan	674
77.70	RS Kaluwitharana	3711
77.41	DPMD Jayawardene	9644

Qualification: 500 runs

Most economical bowlers

Runs per over		*Wkts*
3.92	M Muralitharan	523
4.18	WPUJC Vaas	399
4.18	SD Anurasiri	32
4.27	HDPK Dharmasena	138
4.29	VB John	34
4.29	BAW Mendis	95
4.29	CPH Ramanayake	68
4.50	DS de Silva	32
4.50	RS Kalpage	73
4.52	DNT Zoysa	108

Qualification: 2000 balls bowled

Sri Lanka's one-day international results

	Played	Won	Lost	Tied	No result	% win
v Australia	77	24	50	0	3	32.43
v Bangladesh	29	27	2	0	0	93.10
v England	50	24	26	0	0	48.00
v India	129	50	68	0	11	42.37
v New Zealand	74	34	35	1	4	49.28
v Pakistan	121	46	71	1	3	39.40
v South Africa	46	22	22	1	1	50.00
v West Indies	49	20	26	0	3	43.47
v Zimbabwe	47	39	7	0	1	84.78
v others (see below)	16	15	1	0	0	93.75
TOTAL	**638**	**301**	**308**	**3**	**26**	**49.42**

Other teams: Bermuda (P1, W1), Canada (P2, W2), Ireland (P1, W1), Kenya (P6, W5, L1), Netherlands (P3, W3), Scotland (P1, W1), United Arab Emirates (P2, W2).

WEST INDIES
Test Match Records

Most appearances

133	S Chanderpaul
132	CA Walsh
130	BC Lara
121	IVA Richards
116	DL Haynes
110	CH Lloyd
108	CG Greenidge
102	CL Hooper
98	CEL Ambrose
93	GS Sobers

Sobers played 85 successive Tests between 1954-55 and 1971-72

Most runs

		Avge
11912	BC Lara	53.17
9367	S Chanderpaul	49.04
8540	IVA Richards	50.23
8032	GS Sobers	57.78
7558	CG Greenidge	44.72
7515	CH Lloyd	46.67
7487	DL Haynes	42.29
6373	CH Gayle	41.65
6227	RB Kanhai	47.53
5949	RB Richardson	44.39

Greenidge and Haynes put on 6482 runs together, the Test record by any pair of opening batsmen

Most wickets

		Avge
519	CA Walsh	24.44
405	CEL Ambrose	20.99
376	MD Marshall	20.94
309	LR Gibbs	29.09
259	J Garner	20.97
249	MA Holding	23.68
235	GS Sobers	34.03
202	AME Roberts	25.61
192	WW Hall	26.38
161	IR Bishop	24.27

In all 18 West Indians have reached 100 Test wickets

Highest scores

400*	BC Lara	v England at St John's	2003-04
375	BC Lara	v England at St John's	1993-94
365*	GS Sobers	v Pakistan at Kingston	1957-58
333	CH Gayle	v Sri Lanka at Galle	2010-11
317	CH Gayle	v South Africa at St John's	2004-05
302	LG Rowe	v England at Bridgetown	1973-74
291	IVA Richards	v England at The Oval	1976
291	RR Sarwan	v England at Bridgetown	2008-09
277	BC Lara	v Australia at Sydney	1992-93
270*	GA Headley	v England at Kingston	1934-35

Lara scored 34 Test centuries, Sobers 26, Richards 24, S Chanderpaul 23, CG Greenidge and CH Lloyd 19

Best innings bowling

9-95	JM Noreiga	v India at Port-of-Spain	1970-71
8-29	CEH Croft	v Pakistan at Port-of-Spain	1976-77
8-38	LR Gibbs	v India at Bridgetown	1961-62
8-45	CEL Ambrose	v England at Bridgetown	1989-90
8-92	MA Holding	v England at The Oval	1976
8-104	AL Valentine	v England at Manchester	1950
7-22	MD Marshall	v England at Manchester	1988
7-25	CEL Ambrose	v Australia at Perth	1992-93
7-37	CA Walsh	v New Zealand at Wellington	1994-95
7-49	S Ramadhin	v England at Birmingham	1957

Valentine was playing in his first Test, Croft and Noreiga in their second

Record wicket partnerships

1st	298	CG Greenidge (149) and DL Haynes (167)	v England at St John's	1989-90
2nd	446	CC Hunte (260) and GS Sobers (365*)	v Pakistan at Kingston	1957-58
3rd	338	ED Weekes (206) and FMM Worrell (167)	v England at Port-of-Spain	1953-54
4th	399	GS Sobers (226) and FMM Worrell (197*)	v England at Bridgetown	1959-60
5th	322	BC Lara (213) and JC Adams (94)	v Australia at Kingston	1998-99
6th	282*	BC Lara (400*) and RD Jacobs (107*)	v England at St John's	2003-04
7th	347	DS Atkinson (219) and CC Depeiaza (122)	v Australia at Bridgetown	1954-55
8th	148	JC Adams (101*) and FA Rose (69)	v Zimbabwe at Kingston	1999-2000
9th	161	CH Lloyd (161*) and AME Roberts (68)	v India at Calcutta	1983-84
10th	106	CL Hooper (178*) and CA Walsh (30)	v Pakistan at St John's	1992-93

Figures to 26.09.11. Updated records can be found at **www.cricinfo.com/ci/engine/records**

Test Match Records

Most catches

Fielders

164	BC Lara
122	IVA Richards
115	CL Hooper
109	GS Sobers
96	CG Greenidge

Most dismissals

Wicketkeepers		Ct/St
270	PJL Dujon	265/5
219	RD Jacobs	207/12
189	DL Murray	181/8
122	D Ramdin	119/3
101	JR Murray	98/3

Highest team totals

790-3d	v Pakistan at Kingston	1957-58
751-5d	v England at St John's	2003-04
749-9d	v England at Bridgetown	2008-09
747	v South Africa at St John's	2004-05
692-8d	v England at The Oval	1995
687-8d	v England at The Oval	1976
681-8d	v England at Port-of-Spain	1953-54
660-5d	v New Zealand at Wellington	1994-95
652-8d	v England at Lord's	1973
644-8d	v India at Delhi	1958-59

West Indies have passed 600 in Tests on nine further occasions

Lowest team totals

Completed innings

47	v England at Kingston	2003-04
51	v Aust at Port-of-Spain	1998-99
53	v Pakistan at Faisalabad	1986-87
54	v England at Lord's	2000
61	v England at Leeds	2000
76	v Pakistan at Dacca	1958-59
77	v NZ at Auckland	1955-56
78	v Australia at Sydney	1951-52
82	v Australia at Brisbane	2000-01
86*	v England at The Oval	1957

*One batsman absent hurt

Best match bowling

14-149	MA Holding	v England at The Oval	1976
13-55	CA Walsh	v N Zealand at Wellington	1994-95
12-121	AME Roberts	v India at Madras	1974-75
11-84	CEL Ambrose	v England at Port-of-Spain	1993-94
11-89	MD Marshall	v India at Port-of-Spain	1988-89
11-107	MA Holding	v Australia at Melbourne	1981-82
11-120	MD Marshall	v N Zealand at Bridgetown	1984-85
11-126	WW Hall	v India at Kanpur	1958-59
11-134	CD Collymore	v Pakistan at Kingston	2004-05
11-147	KD Boyce	v England at The Oval	1973

Marshall took ten or more wickets in a Test four times, Ambrose and Walsh three

Hat-tricks

WW Hall	v Pakistan at Lahore	1958-59

The first Test hat-trick not for England or Australia.

LR Gibbs	v Australia at Adelaide	1960-61

Gibbs had taken three wickets in four balls in the previous Test, at Sydney.

CA Walsh	v Australia at Brisbane	1988-89

The first Test hat-trick to be split over two innings.

JJC Lawson	v Australia at Bridgetown	2002-03

Also split over two innings

West Indies' Test match results

	Played	Won	Lost	Drawn	Tied	% win
v Australia	108	32	52	23	1	29.62
v Bangladesh	6	3	2	1	0	50.00
v England	145	53	43	49	0	36.55
v India	85	30	12	43	0	35.29
v New Zealand	37	10	9	18	0	27.02
v Pakistan	46	15	16	15	0	32.60
v South Africa	25	3	16	6	0	12.00
v Sri Lanka	15	3	6	6	0	20.00
v Zimbabwe	6	4	0	2	0	66.66
TOTAL	**473**	**153**	**156**	**163**	**1**	**32.34**

WEST INDIES *One-day International Records*

Most appearances

295	BC Lara
268	S Chanderpaul
238	DL Haynes
227	CL Hooper
225	CH Gayle
224	RB Richardson
205	CA Walsh
187	IVA Richards
176	CEL Ambrose
173	RR Sarwan

25 West Indians have played more than 100 ODIs. Lara and Gayle also played for the World XI

Most runs

		Avge
10348	BC Lara	40.90
8778	S Chanderpaul	41.60
8648	DL Haynes	41.37
8032	CH Gayle	39.37
6721	IVA Richards	47.00
6248	RB Richardson	33.41
5761	CL Hooper	35.34
5644	RR Sarwan	43.41
5134	CG Greenidge	45.03
3675	PV Simmons	28.93

Gayle and Lara scored 19 100s, Haynes 17, Greenidge, Richards and Chanderpaul 11

Most wickets

		Avge
227	CA Walsh	30.47
225	CEL Ambrose	24.12
193	CL Hooper	36.05
157	MD Marshall	26.96
156	CH Gayle	34.71
146	J Garner	18.84
142	MA Holding	21.36
136	DJ Bravo	29.81
130	M Dillon	32.44
118	IR Bishop	26.50
118	IVA Richards	35.83

WKM Benjamin (100) and RA Harper (100) also reached 100 wickets

Highest scores

189*	IVA Richards	v England at Manchester	1984
181	IVA Richards	v Sri Lanka at Karachi	1987-88
169	BC Lara	v Sri Lanka at Sharjah	1995-96
157*	XM Marshall	v Canada at King City	2008-09
156	BC Lara	v Pakistan at Adelaide	2004-05
153*	IVA Richards	v Australia at Melbourne	1979-80
153*	CH Gayle	v Zimbabwe at Bulawayo	2003-04
153	BC Lara	v Pakistan at Sharjah	1993-94
152*	DL Haynes	v India at Georgetown	1988-89
152*	CH Gayle	v S Africa at Johannesburg	2003-04
152	CH Gayle	v Kenya at Nairobi	2001-02

S Chanderpaul scored 150 v SA at East London in 1998-99

Best bowling figures

7-51	WW Davis	v Australia at Leeds	1983
6-15	CEH Croft	v England at Kingstown	1980-81
6-22	FH Edwards	v Zimbabwe at Harare	2003-04
6-27	KAJ Roach	v Netherlands at Delhi	2010-11
6-29	BP Patterson	v India at Nagpur	1987-88
6-41	IVA Richards	v India at Delhi	1989-90
6-50	AH Gray	v Aust at Port-of-Spain	1990-91
5-1	CA Walsh	v Sri Lanka at Sharjah	1986-87
5-17	CEL Ambrose	v Australia at Melbourne	1988-89
5-22	AME Roberts	v England at Adelaide	1979-80
5-22	WKM Benjamin	v Sri Lanka at Bombay	1993-94

Edwards's feat was in his first ODI

Record wicket partnerships

1st	200*	SC Williams (78*) and S Chanderpaul (109*)	v India at Bridgetown	1996-97
2nd	221	CG Greenidge (115) and IVA Richards (149)	v India at Jamshedpur	1983-84
3rd	195*	CG Greenidge (105*) and HA Gomes (75*)	v Zimbabwe at Worcester	1983
4th	226	S Chanderpaul (150) and CL Hooper (108)	v South Africa at East London	1998-99
5th	154	CL Hooper (112*) and S Chanderpaul (67)	v Pakistan at Sharjah	2001-02
6th	154	RB Richardson (122) and PJL Dujon (53)	v Pakistan at Sharjah	1991-92
7th	115	PJL Dujon (57*) and MD Marshall (66)	v Pakistan at Gujranwala	1986-87
8th	84	RL Powell (76) and CD Collymore (3)	v India at Toronto	1999-2000
9th	77	RR Sarwan (65) and IDR Bradshaw (37)	v New Zealand at Christchurch	2005-06
10th	106*	IVA Richards (189*) and MA Holding (12*)	v England at Manchester	1984

Figures to 26.09.11. Updated records can be found at www.cricinfo.com/ci/engine/records

Most catches

Fielders

120	CL Hooper	
117	BC Lara	
100	IVA Richards	
98	CH Gayle	
75	RB Richardson	

Most dismissals

Wicketkeepers		*Ct/St*
204	PJL Dujon	183/21
189	RD Jacobs	160/29
114	D Ramdin	109/5
68	CO Browne	59/9
51	JR Murray	44/7

Highest team totals

360-4	v Sri Lanka at Karachi	1987-88
347-6	v Zimbabwe at Bulawayo	2003-04
339-4	v Pakistan at Adelaide	2004-05
333-6	v Zimbabwe at Georgetown	2005-06
333-7	v Sri Lanka at Sharjah	1995-96
333-8	v India at Jamshedpur	1983-84
330-8	v Netherlands at Delhi	2010-11
324-4	v India at Ahmedabad	2002-03
324-8	v India at Nagpur	2006-07
319	v India at Kingston	2009

All these totals came from 50 overs except the 333-8 (45)

Lowest team totals

Completed innings

54	v S Africa at Cape Town	2003-04
80	v Sri Lanka at Mumbai	2006-07
87	v Australia at Sydney	1992-93
91	v Zimbabwe at Sydney	2000-01
93	v Kenya at Pune	1995-96
103	v Pak at Melbourne	1996-97
110	v Australia at Manchester	1999
111	v Pak at Melbourne	1983-84
112	v Pakistan at Dhaka	2010-11
113	v Aust at Kuala Lumpur	2006-07

The 87 was in a match reduced to 30 overs: Australia made 101-9

Most sixes

168	CH Gayle	
133	BC Lara	
126	IVA Richards	
85	S Chanderpaul	
81	CG Greenidge	
75	RL Powell	
65	CL Hooper	
56	RR Sarwan	
54	RB Richardson	
53	DL Haynes	

XM Marshall holds the West Indian record for sixes in an innings (12)

Best strike rate

Runs per 100 balls		*Runs*
102.22	KA Pollard	826
97.26	DR Smith	925
96.66	RL Powell	2085
96.54	DJG Sammy	670
90.20	IVA Richards	6721
83.89	CH Gayle	8032
81.86	DJ Bravo	1910
81.22	CH Lloyd	1977
79.62	BC Lara	10348
77.70	D Ramdin	899

Qualification: 500 runs

Most economical bowlers

Runs per over		*Wkts*
3.09	J Garner	146
3.32	MA Holding	142
3.40	AME Roberts	87
3.48	CEL Ambrose	225
3.53	MD Marshall	157
3.83	CA Walsh	227
3.97	RA Harper	100
4.00	CE Cuffy	41
4.09	EAE Baptiste	36
4.15	WKM Benjamin	100

Qualification: 2000 balls bowled

West Indies' one-day international results

	Played	Won	Lost	Tied	No result	% win
v Australia	125	57	63	2	3	47.54
v Bangladesh	17	12	3	0	2	80.00
v England	83	41	38	0	4	51.89
v India	101	56	42	1	2	57.07
v New Zealand	51	24	20	0	7	54.54
v Pakistan	120	66	52	2	0	55.83
v South Africa	51	12	38	0	1	24.00
v Sri Lanka	49	26	20	0	3	56.52
v Zimbabwe	41	31	9	0	1	77.50
v others (see below)	19	17	1	0	1	89.47
TOTAL	657	342	286	5	24	54.42

Other teams: Bermuda (P1, W1), Canada (P4, W4), Ireland (P4, W3, NR1), Kenya (P6, W5, L1), Netherlands (P2, W2), Scotland (P2, W2).

ZIMBABWE
Test Match Records

Most appearances

67	GW Flower
65	HH Streak
63	A Flower
60	ADR Campbell
46	GJ Whittall
37	SV Carlisle
30	HK Olonga
29	DD Ebrahim
27	CB Wishart
26	BC Strang
26	T Taibu

Zimbabwe played no Test cricket between September 2005 and August 2011

Most runs

		Avge
4794	A Flower	51.54
3457	GW Flower	29.54
2858	ADR Campbell	27.21
2207	GJ Whittall	29.42
1990	HH Streak	22.35
1615	SV Carlisle	26.91
1464	DL Houghton	43.05
1414	MW Goodwin	42.84
1457	T Taibu	31.00
1225	DD Ebrahim	22.68

CB Wishart (1098) and GJ Rennie (1023) also reached 1000 runs

Most wickets

		Avge
216	HH Streak	28.14
70	PA Strang	36.02
69	RW Price	35.86
68	HK Olonga	38.52
56	BC Strang	39.33
53	AM Blignaut	37.05
51	GJ Whittall	40.94
32	M Mbangwa	31.43
30	DH Brain	30.50
26	EA Brandes	36.57

GW Flower, TJ Friend and AG Huckle all took 25 wickets

Highest scores

266	DL Houghton	v Sri Lanka at Bulawayo	1994-95
232*	A Flower	v India at Nagpur	2000-01
203*	GJ Whittall	v New Zealand at Bulawayo	1997-98
201*	GW Flower	v Pakistan at Harare	1994-95
199*	A Flower	v South Africa at Harare	2001-02
188*	GJ Whittall	v New Zealand at Harare	2000-01
183*	A Flower	v India at Delhi	2000-01
166*	MW Goodwin	v Pakistan at Bulawayo	1997-98
163*	TMK Mawoyo	v Pakistan at Bulawayo	2011
156*	GW Flower	v Pakistan at Bulawayo	1997-98
156	A Flower	v Pakistan at Harare	1994-95

Of Zimbabwe's 45 Test centuries, 18 came from the Flower family – 12 by Andy and six by Grant

Best innings bowling

8-109	PA Strang	v New Zealand at Bulawayo	2000-01
6-59	DT Hondo	v Bangladesh at Dhaka	2004-05
6-73	RW Price	v West Indies at Harare	2003-04
6-73	HH Streak	v India at Harare	2005-06
6-87	HH Streak	v England at Lord's	2000
6-90	HH Streak	v Pakistan at Harare	1994-95
6-109	AG Huckle	v New Zealand at Bulawayo	1997-98
6-121	RW Price	v Australia at Sydney	2003-04
5-27	HH Streak	v WI at Port-of-Spain	1999-2000
5-31	TJ Friend	v Bangladesh at Dhaka	2001-02

AJ Traicos took 5-86 in Zimbabwe's inaugural Test, against India in 1992-93: he was 45, and had played three Tests for South Africa 22 years previously

Record wicket partnerships

1st	164	DD Ebrahim (71) and ADR Campbell (103)	v West Indies at Bulawayo	2001
2nd	135	MH Dekker (68*) and ADR Campbell (75)	v Pakistan at Rawalpindi	1993-94
3rd	194	ADR Campbell (99) and DL Houghton (142)	v Sri Lanka at Harare	1994-95
4th	269	GW Flower (201*) and A Flower (156)	v Pakistan at Harare	1994-95
5th	277*	MW Goodwin (166*) and A Flower (100*)	v Pakistan at Bulawayo	1997-98
6th	165	DL Houghton (121) and A Flower (59)	v India at Harare	1992-93
7th	154	HH Streak (83*) and AM Blignaut (92)	v West Indies at Harare	2001
8th	168	HH Streak (127*) and AM Blignaut (91)	v West Indies at Harare	2003-04
9th	87	PA Strang (106*) and BC Strang (42)	v Pakistan at Sheikhupura	1996-97
10th	97*	A Flower (183*) and HK Olonga (11*)	v India at Delhi	2000-01

Figures to 26.09.11. Updated records can be found at **www.cricinfo.com/ci/engine/records**

Test Match Records ZIMBABWE

Most catches

Fielders

60	ADR Campbell	
43	GW Flower	
34	SV Carlisle	
19	GJ Whittall	
17	DL Houghton/HH Streak	

Most dismissals

Wicketkeepers — Ct/St

151	A Flower	151/9
57	T Taibu	53/4
16	WR James	16/0

Flower also took 9 catches when not keeping wicket

Highest team totals

563-9d	v West Indies at Harare	2001
544-4d	v Pakistan at Harare	1994-95
542-7d	v Bangladesh at Chittagong	2001-02
507-9d	v West Indies at Harare	2003-04
503-6	v India at Nagpur	2000-01
462-9d	v Sri Lanka at Bulawayo	1994-95
461	v New Zealand at Bulawayo	1997-98
457	v Bangladesh at Bulawayo	2000-01
456	v India at Harare	1992-93
441	v Bangladesh at Harare	2003-04

Zimbabwe's 456 in 1992-93 is the highest by any country in their first Test match

Lowest team totals

Completed innings

54	v SA at Cape Town	2004-05
59	v N Zealand at Harare	2005-06
63	v WI at Port-of-Spain	1999-2000
79	v Sri Lanka at Galle	2001-02
83	v England at Lord's	2000
94	v Eng at Chester-le-Street	2003
99	v N Zealand at Harare	2005-06
102	v S Africa at Harare	1999-2000
102	v WI at Kingston	1999-2000
102	v Sri Lanka at Harare	2003-04

Zimbabwe were bowled out twice in a day by New Zealand at Harare in 2005-06, only the second such instance in Test cricket

Best match bowling

11-255	AG Huckle	v N Zealand at Bulawayo	1997-98
10-158	PA Strang	v N Zealand at Bulawayo	2000-01
10-161	RW Price	v West Indies at Harare	2003-04
9-72	HH Streak	v WI at Port-of-Spain	1999-2000
9-105	HH Streak	v Pakistan at Harare	1994-95
9-235	RW Price	v W Indies at Bulawayo	2003-04
8-104	GW Flower	v Pakistan at Chittagong	2001-02
8-105	HH Streak	v Pakistan at Harare	1994-95
8-110	AM Blignaut	v Bangladesh at Bulawayo	2000-01
8-114	HH Streak	v Pakistan at Rawalpindi	1993-94

Blignaut was playing in his first Test, Huckle in his second

Hat-tricks

AM Blignaut	v Bangladesh at Harare	2003-04

Blignaut dismissed Hannan Sarkar, Mohammad Ashraful and Mushfiqur Rahman to reduce Bangladesh to 14-5.

The only Test hat-trick against Zimbabwe was taken by DNT Zoysa for Sri Lanka at Harare in 1999-2000, when he removed TR Gripper, MW Goodwin and NC Johnson with the first three balls he bowled, in the second over of the match

Zimbabwe's Test match results

	Played	Won	Lost	Drawn	Tied	% win
v Australia	3	0	3	0	0	0.00
v Bangladesh	9	9	1	3	0	55.55
v England	6	0	3	3	0	0.00
v India	11	2	7	2	0	18.18
v New Zealand	13	0	7	6	0	0.00
v Pakistan	15	2	9	4	0	13.33
v South Africa	7	0	6	1	0	0.00
v Sri Lanka	15	0	10	5	0	0.00
v West Indies	6	0	4	2	0	0.00
TOTAL	**85**	**9**	**50**	**26**	**0**	**10.58**

Figures to 26.09.11. Updated records can be found at **www.cricinfo.com/ci/engine/records**

ZIMBABWE
One-day International Records

Most appearances

221	GW Flower	
213	A Flower	
188	ADR Campbell	
187	HH Streak	
147	GJ Whittall	
143	T Taibu	
135	P Utseya	
133	E Chigumbura	
126	BRM Taylor	
111	SV Carlisle	

*H Masakadza (110) and
S Matsikenyeri (109) have also
played in more than 100 ODIs*

Most runs

		Avge
6786	A Flower	35.34
6571	GW Flower	33.52
5185	ADR Campbell	30.50
3675	BRM Taylor	32.23
3228	T Taibu	29.61
2938	H Masakadza	27.71
2901	HH Streak	28.44
2740	SV Carlisle	27.67
2705	GJ Whittall	22.54
2622	E Chigumbura	23.83

*S Matsikenyeri (2196) and V Sibanda
(2170) have also scored more than
2000 runs*

Most wickets

		Avge
237	HH Streak	29.81
106	P Utseya	46.14
104	GW Flower	40.62
97	RW Price	33.58
96	PA Strang	33.05
88	GJ Whittall	39.55
82	E Chigumbura	38.86
75	GB Brent	37.01
70	EA Brandes	32.37
67	CB Mpofu	36.89

*Brandes took Zimbabwe's only ODI
hat-trick, against England at Harare in
1996-97*

Highest scores

194*	CK Coventry	v Bangladesh at Bulawayo	2009
178*	H Masakadza	v Kenya at Harare	2009-10
172*	CB Wishart	v Namibia at Harare	2002-03
156	H Masakadza	v Kenya at Harare	2009-10
145*	BRM Taylor	v S Africa at Bloemfontein	2010-11
145	A Flower	v India at Colombo	2002-03
142*	GW Flower	v Bangladesh at Bulawayo	2000-01
142*	A Flower	v England at Harare	2001-02
142	DL Houghton	v New Zealand at Hyderabad	1987-88
140	GW Flower	v Kenya at Dhaka	1998-99

*ADR Campbell made seven ODI centuries for Zimbabwe, and
GW Flower six*

Best bowling figures

6-19	HK Olonga	v England at Cape Town	1999-2000
6-20	BC Strang	v Bangladesh at Nairobi	1997-98
6-28	HK Olonga	v Kenya at Bulawayo	2002-03
6-46	AG Cremer	v Kenya at Harare	2009-10
6-52	CB Mpofu	v Kenya at Nairobi	2008-09
5-20	BV Vitori	v Bangladesh at Harare	2011
5-21	PA Strang	v Kenya at Patna	1995-96
5-22	PA Strang	v Kenya at Dhaka	1998-99
5-28	EA Brandes	v England at Harare	1996-97
5-30	BV Vitori	v Bangladesh at Harare	2011

*Vitori took five wickets in each of his first two ODIs, a
unique feat*

Record wicket partnerships

1st	167	V Sibanda (96) and H Masakadza (80)	v West Indies at Bulawayo	2007-08
2nd	150	GW Flower (78) and GJ Rennie (76)	v Kenya at Nairobi	1997-98
3rd	181	T Taibu (98) and CR Ervine (85)	v Canada at Nagpur	2010-11
4th	202	SV Carlisle (109) and SM Ervine (100)	v India at Adelaide	2003-04
5th	186*	MW Goodwin (112*) and GW Flower (96*)	v West Indies at Chester-le-Street	2000
6th	188	T Taibu (103*) and S Matsikenyeri (86)	v South Africa at Benoni	2009-10
7th	130	A Flower (142*) and HH Streak (56)	v England at Harare	2001-02
8th	117	DL Houghton (142) and IP Butchart (54)	v New Zealand at Hyderabad	1987-88
9th	55	KM Curran (62) and PWE Rawson (19)	v West Indies at Birmingham	1983
10th	60	SW Masakadza (45*) and IA Nicolson (14)	v Ireland at Harare	2010-11

Figures to 26.09.11. Updated records can be found at **www.cricinfo.com/ci/engine/records**

ZIMBABWE

Most catches

Fielders

86	GW Flower	
74	ADR Campbell	
49	H Masakadza	
45	E Chigumbura	
45	HH Streak	

Most dismissals

Wicketkeepers		Ct/St
165	A Flower	133/32
143	T Taibu	111/32
59	BRM Taylor	41/18
31	DL Houghton	29/2
6	F Mutizwa	4/2

Highest team totals

351-7	v Kenya at Mombasa	2008-09
340-2	v Namibia at Harare	2002-03
338-7	v Bermuda at Port-of-Spain	2005-06
329-3	v Kenya at Harare	2009-10
325-6	v Kenya at Dhaka	1998-99
323-7	v Bangladesh at Bulawayo	2009
313-4	v Kenya at Harare	2009-10
312-4	v Sri Lanka at New Plymouth	1991-92
312-8	v Bangladesh at Bulawayo	2009
310-6	v Bangladesh at Dhaka	1998-99

Zimbabwe have made nine further totals of 300 or more

Lowest team totals

Completed innings

35	v Sri Lanka at Harare	2003-04
38	v Sri Lanka at Colombo	2001-02
44	v Bang at Chittagong	2009-10
65	v India at Harare	2005-06
67	v Sri Lanka at Harare	2008-09
69	v Kenya at Harare	2005-06
80	v Sri Lanka at Mirpur	2008-09
85	v WI at Ahmedabad	2006-07
92	v England at Bristol	2003
94	v Pakistan at Sharjah	1996-97

Zimbabwe have also been bowled out for 99 twice

Most sixes

77	E Chigumbura	
48	HH Streak	
45	BRM Taylor	
44	ADR Campbell	
38	H Masakadza	
37	GW Flower	
30	T Taibu	
28	SV Carlisle	
28	CK Coventry	
26	A Flower	
26	GJ Whittall	

Best strike rate

Runs per 100 balls		Runs
106.28	AM Blignaut	626
88.37	CK Coventry	821
85.54	SM Ervine	698
82.63	E Chigumbura	2622
75.94	CN Evans	764
75.69	TJ Friend	548
75.65	CR Ervine	581
74.59	A Flower	6786
73.94	H Masakadza	2938
73.61	HH Streak	2901

Qualification: 500 runs

Most economical bowlers

Runs per over*		Wkts
3.88	AJ Traicos	19
3.89	RW Price	97
4.13	BC Strang	46
4.23	P Utseya	106
4.37	PA Strang	96
4.37	AR Whittall	45
4.40	EC Rainsford	45
4.50	HH Streak	237
4.52	AH Shah	18
4.64	GW Flower	104
4.66	DH Brain	21

*Qualification: 1000 balls bowled

Zimbabwe's one-day international results

	Played	Won	Lost	Tied	No result	% win
v Australia	28	1	26	0	1	3.70
v Bangladesh	56	26	30	0	0	46.42
v England	30	8	21	0	1	27.58
v India	51	10	39	2	0	21.56
v New Zealand	29	7	20	1	1	26.78
v Pakistan	44	2	40	1	1	5.81
v South Africa	32	2	29	0	1	6.45
v Sri Lanka	47	7	39	0	1	15.21
v West Indies	41	9	31	0	1	22.50
v others (see below)	43	34	6	1	2	79.06
TOTAL	401	106	281	5	9	27.67

Other teams: Bermuda (P2, W2), Canada (P2, W2), Ireland (P5, W3, L1, T1), Kenya (P32, W25, L5, NR 2), Namibia (P1, W1), Netherlands (P1, W1).

INTERNATIONAL SCHEDULE 2011-12

	Tests	ODIs	T20Is
October 2011			
India v England	–	5	1
Bangladesh v West Indies	2	3	1
Zimbabwe v New Zealand	1	3	2
South Africa v Australia	2	3	2
Pakistan v Sri Lanka in UAE	3	5	1
November 2011			
India v West Indies	3*	5*	–
December 2011			
Australia v New Zealand	2	–	–
South Africa v Sri Lanka	3	5	–
Australia v India	4	–	2
Bangladesh v Pakistan	2*	3*	–
January 2012			
Pakistan v England in UAE	3	4	3
New Zealand v Zimbabwe	1	3	2
February 2012			
Australia v India v Sri Lanka	–	14/15	–
New Zealand v South Africa	3	3	3
March 2012			
Sri Lanka v England	2	–	–
West Indies v Australia	3*	5*	1*
India v Pakistan	3*	5*	–
Bangladesh v Sri lanka	–	5*	–
April 2012			
Pakistan v Bangladesh	2*	3*	–

	Tests	ODIs	T20Is
May 2012			
England v West Indies	3	3	1
Sri Lanka v Pakistan	3*	5*	2*
June 2012			
England v Australia	–	5	–
July 2012			
England v South Africa	3	5	3
Sri Lanka v India	3*	–	–
West Indies v New Zealand	3*	5*	2*
August 2012			
Under-19 World Cup in Australia	–	–	–
Pakistan v Australia in UAE	–	5*	1*
Zimbabwe v Bangladesh	2*	3*	2*
September 2012			
World Twenty20 in Sri Lanka	–	–	27*
October 2012			
India v New Zealand	3*	–	–
November 2012			
India v England	4*	–	–
Australia v South Africa	3	–	–
Sri Lanka v New Zealand	2*	5*	1*
Bangladesh v West Indies	2*	5*	1*
December 2012			
Australia v Sri Lanka	3	5	2
South Africa v New Zealand	2*	3*	2*
Zimbabwe v Pakistan	2*	3*	2*

Details subject to change. Some tours may continue into the month after the one shown above. An asterisk signifies that the number of matches is unconfirmed.